# INVISIBLE LIVES

*The Erasure of Transsexual and Transgendered People*

Viviane K. Namaste

D1595859

THE UNIVERSITY OF CHICAGO PRESS

CHICAGO AND LONDON

Viviane K. Namaste holds a doctorate in semiotics from the Université du
Québec à Montréal and is also trained as a sociologist. She is the coordina-
tor of a community-based transsexual health care project of CACTUS-
Montréal. Active in the field of HIV, she is involved with different advisory
committees and initiatives relating to prisons, transsexual health, prostitution, and harm reduction.

The University of Chicago Press, Chicago 60637
The University of Chicago Press, Ltd., London
© 2000 by The University of Chicago
All rights reserved. Published 2000
Printed in the United States of America

09   08   07   06   05   04   03   02   01   00   1   2   3   4   5
ISBN: 0-226-56809-1 (cloth)
ISBN: 0-226-56810-5 (paper)

Library of Congress Cataloging-in-Publication Data
Namaste, Viviane K.
  Invisible lives : the erasure of transsexual and transgendered people /
Viviane K. Namaste.
      p.   cm.
  Includes bibliographical references and index.
  ISBN 0-226-56809-1 (cloth: alk. paper) —0-226-56810-5 (pbk.: alk.
paper)
  1. Transsexuals—Canada.   2. Transvestites—Canada.   3. Female
impersonators—Canada.   4. Marginality, Social—Canada.   I. Title.
HQ77.95.C2 N35 2000
305.9′066—dc21 00-024155

For the transsexuals who have not survived.

# Intelectuales Apolíticos

Un día,
los intelectuales
apolíticos
de mi país
serán interrogados
por el hombre
sencillo
de nuestro pueblo.

Se les preguntará,
sobre lo que hicieron
cuando
la patria se apagaba
lentamente,
como una hoguera dulce,
pequeña y sola.

No serán interrogados
sobre sus trajes,
ni sobre sus largas
siestas
después de la merienda,
tampoco sobre sus estériles
combatas con la nada,
ni sobre su ontológica
manera
de llegar a las monedas.
No sé les interrogará
sobre la mitología griega,
ni sobre el asco
que sintieron de sí,
cuando alguien, en su fondo,
se disponía a morir cobardemente.
Nada se les preguntará
sobre sus justificaciones
absurdas,
crecidas a la sombra
de una mentira rotunda.

# Apolitical Intellectuals

One day
the apolitical
intellectuals
of my country
will be interrogated
by the simplest
of our people.

They will be asked
what they did
when their nation died out
slowly,
like a sweet fire,
small and alone.

No one will ask them
about their dress,
their long siestas
after lunch,
no one will want to know
about their sterile combats
with "the idea
of the nothing"
no one will care about
their higher financial learning.
They won't be questioned
on Greek mythology,
or regarding their self-disgust
when someone within them
begins to die
the coward's death.
They'll be asked nothing
about their absurd
justifications,
born in the shadow
of the total lie.

Ese día vendrán
los hombres sencillos.
Los que nunca cupieron
en los libros y versos
de los intelectuales apolíticos,
pero que llegaban todos los días
a dejarles la leche y el pan,
los hueovos y las tortillas,
los que les cosían la ropa,
los que les manejaban los carros,
les cuidaban sus perros y jardines,
y trabajaban para ellos,
          y preguntarán,
"¿Qué hicistéis cuando los pobres
sufrían, y se quemaba en ellos,
gravemente, la ternura, y la vida?"

Intelectuales apolíticos
de mi dulce país,
no podréis responder nada.

Os devorará un buitre de silencio
las entrañas.
Os roerá el alma
vuestra propria miseria
Y callaréis,
          avergonzados de vosotros.

On that day
the simple men will come.
Those who had no place
in the books and poems
of the apolitical intellectuals,
but daily delivered
their bread and milk,
their tortillas and eggs,
those who mended their clothes,
those who drove their cars,
who cared for their dogs and gardens
and worked for them,
          and they'll ask:
"What did you do when the poor
suffered, when tenderness
and life burned out in them?"

Apolitical intellectuals
of my sweet country,
you will not be able to answer.

A vulture of silence
will eat your gut.
Your own misery
will pick at your soul.
And you will be mute
          in your shame.

—Otto René Castillo,
   Let's Go! Vamonos patria a caminar, *trans. Margaret Randall*

# CONTENTS

ACKNOWLEDGMENTS

This book was written with the support and assistance of so many people. First and foremost, I would like to thank the transsexuals who agreed to speak with me about their experiences with violence, employment, health care, social services, civil status, and the law. These people trusted me enough to recount personal and intimate details about their lives, in the hopes that the situation could be improved for other individuals who change sex. It is my sincere wish that the results presented herein offer a contribution in this regard.

Many years ago, I began this work with words of encouragement and inspiration from two incredible transsexual women, Mirha-Soleil Ross and Xanthra Phillippa. They urged me to begin the very long and arduous process of collecting data on transsexual lives, even if I didn't always feel I had the political savvy, street smarts, or methodological expertise required to do the job. They have read and listened to countless versions of this material in various forms, offering critical feedback and insightful comments. From helping me to find interview participants, to long discussions about the different ways transsexuals live in Québec, English Canada, and the United States, to reading drafts of grant proposals, to writing letters of support, they have helped nourish this work and my own life.

Michael du Plessis has also read version after version of the chapters contained herein, offering critical feedback to help make the arguments more clear, concise, and politically relevant. I have further benefited from discussion and exchange with Max Wolf Valerio, Jayson Barsic, Jessica Rylan Piper, and Trish Salah. In particular, they have supported me in asking questions quite unpopular within American transgender theory and politics. And their sense of humor has helped me laugh and relax, and get on with the work that needs to be done.

Much of the theoretical and methodological work herein is indebted to conversations and exchanges with sociologists and community-based researchers. I would especially like to thank Lorna Weir, Eric Mykalovskiy, Carol-Anne O'Brien, Ann Scott, Henry Rubin, and Steven Seidman. Martha Sully has played a quiet but important role in the articulation of the ideas herein. Over many years now, she has encouraged me to elaborate the compatibility of my interest in poststructuralist inquiry with the ethical, moral, and practical demands of social theory. This book offers one possible articulation of this problematic. The chapter on nationalism benefited from comments and conversations with Sabina Sawhney, whom I thank deeply for friendship and intellectual stimulation.

Emerging out of community-based research initiatives, the empirical research herein was made possible through the support of committed individuals. For assistance in finding interview subjects, relevant documentation, and pertinent methodological comments, I thank Kara Gillis, Wayne Travers, Sonny Wong, Diane Gobeil, Mario Bilodeau, Rick Lines, Catherine Hankins, Benoît Vigneau, and Margaret Deirdre O'Hartigan.

My friends in Montréal have put up with me as I brought this manuscript to completion. They have had the keen ability to accept my need for solitude and quiet as I write, understanding when I declined invitations to socialize. And they have also recognized that sometimes I have just needed to get out and have fun, at a *soirée Joe Dassin,* an El Vez concert (or two), yet another church bazaar, or an excursion into buying still more vinyl. For their support and amitié, thanks especially to Karen Herland, Edie Cameron, Dominique Loubette, Stéphanie-Ann Brisson, and Lynne Trépanier.

My editor at Chicago, Doug Mitchell, has offered unfailing support for this project at all levels. From the perils of having the manuscript seized as it crossed the border into the United States (Derrida's postal principle is always in play) to allowing me the freedom to frame the questions herein in terms relevant to transsexual lives, his enthusiasm for this work has provided the necessary motivation for its completion. Thanks also to Matthew Howard for administrative support and a cheery voice. Two anonymous reviewers at the University of Chicago commented on preliminary versions of this book. Their reviews helped me to focus my arguments and to bring out its original insights.

During the process of researching and writing this book, I have had the unique experience of being a transsexual who presents myself to gender identity clinics and other health care institutions not to obtain services or undergo a psychiatric assessment, but to study how these institutions work and to identify potential gaps in the services. I am grateful to the health care professionals who allowed me to interview them. Although they may not agree with all of the interpretations of the data I offer here, I hope that they will nonetheless acknowledge the contribution of this research to an international social science body of literature. I also hope that these individuals understand that the research was conducted in the interests of improving access to health care, so that transsexuals can obtain the information and resources they require.

Excerpts of chapters 1 and 2 were originally published in "'Tragic Misreadings': Queer Theory's Erasure of Transgender Subjectivity," *Queer Studies: A Lesbian, Gay, Bisexual, Transgender Anthology,* ed. Brett Beemyn and Mickey Eliason (New York: New York University Press, 1996): 183–203.

Chapter 6 was originally published under the same title in *Environment and Planning D: Society and Space* 14 (1996): 221–40 (published by Pion, London).

Permission to reprint "Intelectuales Apolíticos/Apolitical Intellectuals" granted from Curbstone Press (Otto René Castillo, *Let's Go! Vamanos patria a caminar,* trans. Margaret Randall).

# INTRODUCTION

This book is centrally concerned with research on transgendered people. The word "transgender" is an umbrella term used to refer to all individuals who live outside of normative sex/gender relations—that is, individuals whose gendered self-presentation (evidenced through dress, mannerisms, and even physiology) does not correspond to the behaviors habitually associated with the members of their biological sex. A variety of different identities are included within the "transgender" label: cross-dressers, or individuals who wear the clothes associated with the "opposite" sex, often for erotic gratification; drag queens, or men who usually live and identify as gay men, but who perform as female impersonators in gay male bars and leisure spaces; and transsexuals, or individuals who take hormones and who may undergo surgery to align their biological sexes with their genders.[1]

In this book I attempt to take up the job of the sociologist: to collect some empirical data on the everyday lives of transsexual and transgendered people and to put forth some interpretations of what this data means.[2] Rather than programmatically outlining how TS/TG people ought to identify, live, and organize, I begin with the assumption that academics must first concentrate their energies on collecting information about how TS/TG individuals are located in the world. The reason for this is simple: to date, very few of the monographs, articles, and books written about us deal with the nitty-gritty realities of our lives, our bodies, and our experience of the everyday world.[3] Research and theory in psychiatry, the social sciences, and the humanities are preoccupied with issues of origin, etiology, cause, identity, performance, and gender norms. These questions are not unwarranted. But our lives and our bodies are made up of more than gender and identity, more than a theory that justifies our very existence, more than mere performance, more than the interesting remark that we expose how gender works. Our lives and our bodies are much more complicated, and much less glamorous, than all that. They are forged in details of everyday life, marked by matters not discussed by academics or clinical researchers. Our lives and our bodies are constituted in the mundane and uneventful: going to the pawn shop; finding a doctor; bad clients; electrolysis; looking for a job; losing a lover; perfecting the art of binding breasts; trying to get a date; fixing junk; watching films featuring psychotic transsexual characters; learning how to inject hormones; recovering from surgery; electrolysis;

Norvir, Crixivan, and Interferon; overdoses; visiting the hospital; trying to find a surgeon willing to perform sex reassignment surgery on a seropositive transsexual; attending funerals; and changing legal documents. As transsexual and transgendered people, these are the activities of our day-to-day, the fabric of how our bodies are located in, and move through, the world. Although banal, these events merit consideration: anything less produces a knowledge of little practical relevance to our lives, reinforcing a world that treats transsexual and transgendered people as inconsequential.

In addition to research, I am interested in considering how we come to understand transsexual and transgendered people. I examine the limitations of the existing frameworks—including queer theory, Anglo-American sociology, and Anglo-American transgendered activism—invoked to make sense of TS/TG people. My recognition of TS/TG people's everyday lives as well as their considerable diversity reveals the irrelevance of most of the existing scholarship and activism in this domain for many transsexuals: those who do not align themselves with American lesbian/gay politics; those who are poor (and who live in poverty as a function of their transsexualism); those who do not speak English (only); those who are prostitutes; and those who do not live in the United States. I then outline what kind of practical research is needed to improve everyday life for TS/TG people, through different case studies and applied research initiatives.

Many English-language studies on transsexuals are preoccupied with the production of transsexuality, emphasizing its social construction in and through medicine, psychiatry, and technology. My thesis throughout this book departs radically from this notion. I argue that transsexuals are continually and perpetually *erased* in the cultural and institutional world. The different chapters illustrate how this erasure functions.

In the first part of the book I review two prominent theoretical frameworks used to make sense of transsexual and transgendered people: queer theory and the social sciences. Chapter 1 demonstrates how queer theory's invocation of a transgendered figure neglects the everyday social world, while an American application of French poststructuralist theory to transgendered phenomena voids the possibility of transsexual and/or transgendered bodies. Chapter 2 turns to the English-language social science literature. While this scholarship sometimes engages the everyday world as lived and experienced by TS/TG individuals, in many instances the social sciences enact an objectivist research program. The questions scholars ask, as well as the interpretations they offer, reflect professional allegiances of university-based scholarship. Such an approach duplicates the problems of queer theory, to the extent that the production of knowledge remains disconnected from the transsexual and transgendered people positioned as an object of investigation. Chapter 3 attempts to draw on the theoretical and methodological approaches of both poststructuralism and the social sciences, while advancing an understanding of the social world that is pertinent to TS/TG individuals. Taking up a poststructuralist concern for the textual mediation of the social world, as well as a commitment to reflexive social inquiry and the project of social theory, I outline what a poststructuralist sociology could look like, and why it is useful. I discuss some of the theoretical and methodological questions central to the formulation and realization of a poststructuralist sociology, avoiding the limitations of both queer theory and objectivist social science. The remainder of the book illustrates this position through specific readings, case studies, and institutional analyses.

While part 1 concentrates on how transsexual and transgendered people are erased in different theoretical paradigms, part 2 analyzes how transsexuals disappear from view through discourse and rhetoric. In chapters 4 and 5 I examine how the linguistic, rhetorical, and discursive production of the social are realized at a micrological level. In chapter 4, a reading of discourse on punk, I show how the gendered production of statements on punk rock precludes the possibility of transsexual punks. And in chapter 5 I consider the use and function of rhetoric, notably how an invocation of transgendered figures in mass culture reduces transsexuality to the figural dimensions of discourse. Within such constraints, transsexuality is inscribed as *literally impossible.*

The final part of the book shifts the focus of analysis to research within a variety of different institutional settings. Chapter 6 considers the regulation of public space, addressing "queerbashing" and the complicated relations among gender and sexuality in the acts of aggression against sexual and gender minorities. Through a review of scholarly literature on this topic, I show the central role gender plays in motivating instances of assault. Furthermore, I offer a critical reading of antiviolence activism that cannot account for violence against transsexuals and prostitutes. Finally, a case study from Montréal explains how the exclusion of transsexuals from the institutional world is organized. Chapter 7 moves in a more empirical direction, drawing on interviews with transsexuals and transgendered people on the subject of health care and social services. This chapter demonstrates the kinds of discrimination and systemic obstacles confronted by these individuals in the health care and social service network. I also explore why many transsexuals—especially poor transsexuals, prostitutes, seropositive individuals, and ex-convicts—do not make use of services, and how social policy in this domain actually functions to exclude TS people from the institutional world. Chapter 8 takes up the contentious issues of gender identity clinics (GICs), based on interviews with both transsexuals and service providers. I document transsexuals' dissatisfaction with the GIC services and demonstrate the exclusion of prostitutes from GICs in Canada. This case offers another example of how transsexuals are erased in the daily work of administration. I then describe the tension between transsexuals and psychiatrists in terms of specific institutional relations of health care: how people define health, the process through which informed consent is achieved, and the ways in which access to health care is dependent on employment. These institutional relations foster transsexuals' distrust of psychiatric caregivers and explain why many individuals refuse to use their services. In Chapter 9 I concentrate on the issue of HIV and AIDS, exploring how the social marginalization of transsexual and transgendered people in Québec makes them vulnerable to the transmission of HIV. The conferral of civil status and legal identity are important questions in this domain, since the social integration of a transsexual individual requires the production of legal documents which confer their chosen name and sex. In this regard, the chapter explores the administrative processes through which name and sex are conferred in Québec, showing the arbitrary procedures and protocols for the institutional management of transsexuals. A focus on administration provides the appropriate context in which to understand this marginalization of TS/TG individuals. As a result, appropriate social policies can be formulated, including community-based health promotion and HIV prevention programs for transsexuals. Like the other chapters in part 3, chapter 9 shows that the erasure of transsexuals is coordinated through the institutional practices that deny these individuals appropriate legal identity, thereby excluding them from health care, education, and employment.

The argument I present is layered: I begin by outlining how TS/TG people are made invisible in the daily work of academic inquiry. The issue is to understand not only what the existing theoretical frameworks overlook regarding transsexual lives, but also what they actually preempt. From there, I try to articulate a theoretical and methodological program that recognizes, documents, and challenges such erasure. Such effacement is organized on a micrological level, whether in the discourse and rhetoric of mass culture, in the social policies of women's shelters and health agencies, or the administrative practices of civil status. This book demonstrates that erasure is a defining condition of how transsexuality is managed in culture

4

and institutions, a condition that ultimately inscribes transsexuality as impossible.

The development of appropriate solutions to the problems currently faced by transsexual and transgendered people must recognize how the erasure of TS/TG people is realized in and through the production of knowledge. This book offers a preliminary contribution in this regard.

# I

# THEORY

# "Tragic Misreadings"

## Queer Theory's Erasure of Transgender Subjectivity

The study of transgendered people brings with it important questions about theory and research methods. How do academics understand transgendered lives, bodies, and experiences; how is data gathered to further this understanding; and what are the implications of this research when it is applied to concrete social problems—to the daily life circumstances of transgendered people?

To focus on these relations between knowledge and action is to force a kind of academic inquiry that is theoretically sophisticated, politically engaged, and practically relevant. The need for such an analysis is especially compelling given the absolute neglect of everyday life for transgendered people within the recently emerged area of scholarship known as queer theory. In this chapter, I outline this field of study, including the kinds of questions it asks, how it answers them, its theoretical underpinnings, and its implicit strengths and limitations. In my view, queer theory as it is currently practiced needs to be rejected for both theoretical and political reasons.

### BODIES THAT MATTER?

In recent years, the field known as queer theory has witnessed a veritable explosion of essays, presentations, and books on the subject of drag, gender, performance, and transsexuality.[1] Yet these works have shown very little concern for the individuals who live, work, and identify themselves as drag queens, transsexuals, or transgenderists. Although the violation of compulsory sex/gender relations is one of the topics most frequently addressed within queer theory, this body of knowledge rarely considers the implications of an enforced sex/gender system for the people who have defied it, who live outside it, or who have been killed because of it. Critics in queer theory write page after page on the inherent liberation of transgressing normative sex/gender codes, but they have nothing to say about the precarious position of the transsexual woman who is battered and who is unable to access a woman's shelter because she was not born a biological woman.[2]

What are some of the prominent texts within queer theory, and how do they present (or, perhaps more appropriately, ignore) the bodies and lives of transgendered people? It is useful to begin this discussion with the work of Judith Butler, since the publication of her book *Gender Trouble* played a tremendous role in the development of queer theory. Butler argues that drag exposes the imaginary relations of compulsory heterosexuality. Drag queens do not mime "real" women but demonstrate the ways in which categories such as "women" can only be secured through a process of "metalepsis," where the effects of meaning are taken to be the cause of its articulation. In her words, *"drag implicitly reveals the imitative structure of gender itself—as well as its contingency."*[3] In this manner, Butler exposes the appeal to origin for the ideological myth that it is.

This proposition is surely an important one, and Butler's work has been instrumental in the advancement of queer theory and gender studies. But it fails to account for the context in which these gender performances occur. The drag queens Butler discusses perform in spaces created and defined by gay male culture. Although Butler locates these spaces in relation to heterosexual hegemony, she refuses to examine this territory's own complicated relations to gender and gender performance. Consider the paradox that drag queens live: while many gay male bars have drag queens on stage, some of them deny entry to women. In the late 1980s in Montréal, for example, the leather bar K.O.X. banned nontranssexual women, males in "women's" clothes, males in lipstick, and all transsexuals.[4] At the time, other gay bars in the Montréal area were almost exclusively segregated along sex/gender lines. As a result, "Ladies' Nights" became popular venues for men and women—"fag hags," lesbians, gay and bisexual men, bisexual women, transsexuals—who wished to socialize together. Here was the ultimate paradox: gay male bars would refuse nontranssexual women admittance but would then turn around and capitalize on this discrimination at a later time (only once a year, in the case of K.O.X.) by allowing them entry. Elements of femaleness and femininity are highly regulated within gay male consumer culture.

Even when nontranssexual women, transsexual women, and males in drag are allowed in gay male establishments, they remain peripheral to the activities at hand. Drag queens, for example, are tolerated as long as they remain in a space clearly designated for performance: the stage. According to Michelle de Ville, interviewed in the fanzine *Fuzzbox* (circa 1990), "The drag queen in the gay world is meant to be on stage or 'walking' the streets.

Don't get off the stage, baby! It's like the bird in the gilded cage." The *Fuzz-box* writer concurs: "K.O.X. says that on their 'Ladies' Night' they won't accept women wearing make-up, high heel shoes, dresses, loud clothing, etc. Yet they had a woman perform tarted up to the hilt, wearing all these things. Because she was on stage, they could handle her."

DeVille raises a crucial point: drag queens can move freely within gay male settings as long as they abide by the implicit rules of such circulation. What would happen if a drag queen was not on the stage but rather cruised one of the many dark corridors of K.O.X. in search of a sexual partner? That gay men can accommodate the presence of drag queens on stage does not mean that gender liberation has arrived. Indeed, relegating such gender performances to the stage implies that gay men do not "perform" their identities: they just *are*.[5] This containment of gender transgression can, in turn, work against transgendered people in a variety of ways. Drag queens are reduced to entertainment, coifed personalities whose only purpose is to titillate the gay male viewer. Framed as pure spectacle, this negates a variety of reasons why people might choose to cross-dress in a club: an exploration of one's gender identity, a gesture of political intervention, a creative solution to boredom, and/or a way to pay the rent.

A restriction of drag queens to the stage also suggests that drag is something you do; it is not someone you are. Eve Sedgwick disavows drag subject-positions in precisely this way when she establishes a relation "between drag performance and homoerotic identity formation and display."[6] Note the ways in which categories of sexuality and gender work against each other, even as they are syntagmatically aligned. Drag is about performance, while the homoerotic is about identity. Moreover, Sedgwick claims that the performance of drag secures a homoerotic identity. She does not stipulate why a *drag* performance cannot articulate a *drag* subject-position.

In Montréal, the organizers of the 1992 Lesbian and Gay Pride Parade attempted to ban drag queens from participating.[7] They believed that drag queens and people in leather exceeded "respectable" community standards. When challenged on their anti-drag attitudes, organizers pointed to the presence of L'Entrepeau (a drag queen bar) in the parade as evidence of their inclusive politics. The relegation of drag queens to the stage is a supplementary move that excludes transgendered people even as it includes us. Appropriate objects to look at, we are not subjects alongside whom one marches.

In 1993, a new Pride committee emerged in Montréal under the rubric of "Divers/Cité." As the name suggests, this organization seeks to be as inclusive as possible, and the banner at the front of the parade is subtitled

"La fierté gaie, lesbienne, bisexuelle, travestie, et transsexuelle" (lesbian, gay, bisexual, and transgender pride). Notwithstanding this comprehensive semantic field, parade organizers have yet to include any bisexual and/or transgendered activists among the political speakers at the event.[8] It goes without saying that drag queens continue to provide entertainment for the activities on the day of the march. Despite their rhetorical strategies, the organizers of Divers/Cité stage transgendered identities in exactly the same manner as the organizers of previous Pride parades in Montréal.

The relegation of drag queens to the stage has profound implications when it comes to the politics of HIV and AIDS. Sandra Laframboise, a former executive director of High Risk Project, a drop-in center for transgendered sex trade workers in Vancouver, points out the irony of the fact that few HIV/AIDS education materials address transgendered people:

> [HIV/AIDS is] a condition of living, and a teacher. And people have not learned yet. Because if I look around, there's nothing for transgendered people. All over again! Then I'm going, "Geesh! Guys, this is chicken shit!" You know? Like, fuck. We were in the forefront for gay community activists. We raised thousands of dollars for your projects, transvestites on the stages. And now we're here, and you're putting us aside again. . . . And that's the bottom line. What I've found [from predominantly gay-defined AIDS service organizations] is a lot of patronizing.[9]

If drag queens are forced to remain within a space clearly designated for performance, transsexuals experience a similar staging within lesbian and gay male communities. Recent events in Toronto's lesbian and gay arts organizations validate this claim. The program for the Third Annual Inside Out Lesbian and Gay Film and Video Festival (May 6–16, 1993) included a night titled "gender-bending":

> Bearded ladies, chicks with dicks and drag queens are among the queer sightings in Gender Bender, an evening of gender-bending film and video. Throwing open the question of sex and its relation to gender identification and sexual orientation, this programme explores cross-dressing, transsexualism, transvestism, androgyny, and other sexual anomalies [sic].

The classification of transsexuals, drag queens, and other transgendered people as "sexual anomalies" incensed many of Toronto's transgendered activists. From their perspective, this description represents one of the many ways in which lesbian and gay identities position others as "anomalies" in order to portray themselves as "natural." The publication of this program gave birth to a new activist group: Transsexual Activist Collective (TAC).

TAC produced a flyer that reprinted the above description while proclaiming, "NO TO THE GERALDO APPROACH! TRANSSEXUALS ARE NOT YOUR ENTERTAINMENT!!" This strategy interrogates the staging of transgendered subjects within a lesbian and gay setting.

TAC's intervention offers a useful starting point for thinking about how critics in queer theory represent transgendered people. Butler's presentation of drag queens, like the description of "gender-bending" in the Inside Out Film Festival program, ignores the specificity of the milieu in which drag practices are situated. Given the overwhelmingly gendered nature of such a setting, it is problematic to merely cite drag practices as an exposition of the constructed nature of all gender. While Butler reads drag as a means of exposing the contingent nature of gender and identity, I suggest that we point to the essential paradox of drag within gay male communities: at the precise moment that it underlines the constructed nature of gendered performances, drag is contained as a performance in itself.[10] Gay male identity, in contrast, establishes itself as something prior to performance.

Butler's more recent work continues this distortion of transgendered realities. In *Bodies That Matter,* Butler provides a reading of transsexual Venus Extravaganza from the film *Paris Is Burning.* Butler argues that Extravaganza enacts an imaginary relation to the category "woman" in order to escape the cruel realities of her class and ethnicity (Latina) in New York City. Gender is thus a vehicle that functions to displace the material and symbolic conditions of race and class. When Venus Extravaganza is murdered, presumably by one of her clients (she is a prostitute), Butler writes that her death represents "a tragic misreading of the social map of power."[11] For Butler, Extravaganza does not escape her situation; rather, she is treated as women are treated—especially women of color.

In this interpretation, Butler elides both Extravaganza's transsexual status and her work as a prostitute. Here is the point: Venus was killed because she was a transsexual prostitute. An acknowledgment of violence against transsexual prostitutes is explicit in *Paris Is Burning,* although Butler chooses to ignore it. After the death of Extravaganza, her best friend, Angie, insightfully comments, "But that's part of life. That's part of being a transsexual in New York City and surviving." Since Butler has reduced Extravaganza's transsexuality to allegory, she cannot conceptualize the specificity of violence with which transsexuals, especially transsexual prostitutes, are faced. This, to my mind, is the most tragic misreading of all. More than simply denying Extravaganza's transsexuality, Butler uses it in order to speak about race and class. While she makes a vague gesture toward the economic and social realities of Latinas in New York City, she only arrives at these "realities" through the tropological use of Extravaganza's gender.[12]

Clearly, as scholars and as activists, we need to challenge Butler's negation of transgendered identity. Moreover, we must account for the boundaries that are implicitly drawn by her research: drag queens expose compulsory sex/gender relations, while transsexuals can only offer "an uncritical miming of the hegemonic [sex/gender system]."[13] This framework is questionable for three overlapping reasons: (1) it can be deployed in a violently *anti-transsexual* manner; (2) it forces a separation of drag queens from transsexuals (a division that is already quite strong within transgendered communities); and (3) it prevents the elaboration of a broad-based transgendered politics. Moreover, by lauding drag practices over transsexual identities, Butler ignores political activism within transsexual communities, particularly efforts to repeal cross-dressing ordinances.[14] Once we acknowledge the energies transsexuals have invested in repealing legislation that enforces a compulsory sex/gender system, it is impossible to reduce transsexual identities to those that enact an "uncritical miming of the hegemonic."

While Butler ignores the context in which drag performances occur, critics such as Marjorie Garber undermine transgendered identities in a different manner. Garber contends that most academic analyses of the transvestite appropriate it to a binary framework, looking *through* the transvestite in order to understand the constructed nature of gender. Against the grain of this argument, Garber proposes that we look *at* the transvestite. From this stance, we can observe a destabilization of the categories "male" and "female." In Garber's words, "*transvestite is a space of possibly structuring and confounding culture:* the descriptive element that intervenes not just as a category crisis of male and female, but the crisis of category itself."[15] This formulation allows Garber to observe that transvestites locate a crisis that is often elsewhere—in relations of class or race, for example. Yet as interesting as Garber's claims may be, they remain politically suspect. While I share her concern with theorizing the transvestite, we part ways when it comes to methodology.

As a literary critic, Garber is interested in the representation of crossdressing. Her analysis spans a wide variety of cultural texts, from the Kabuki theater to the Renaissance stage to the performances of David Bowie. But what is missing from her research is a conceptualization of transvestite identity as a real, lived, viable experience. Naming the second section of her book "Transvestite Effects," Garber implies that the transvestite is an effect of performance and nothing else. Insofar as she reduces the transvestite to a mere tropological figure, a textual and rhetorical device that points to the crisis of category and the category of crisis, she has effectively undermined the possibility of "transvestite" as a viable identity in and of itself. In this light, I want to turn Garber back upon herself and suggest that the real "crisis of elsewhere" to which she refers is the very possibility of a transvestite identity. In other words, the "crisis of elsewhere" is always-already a crisis of *here*.

Like Butler, Garber engages in a superficial reading of transgendered culture that distorts the diversity within transgendered communities. She moves from a discussion of Hollywood films like *The Silence of the Lambs* to magazines produced by and for transgendered people, such as *Tapestries*. Garber never examines the social context of these representations, implying that academics can "look at" transvestites in these texts without accounting for their material, discursive, and institutional locations. Since she ignores the context of production for the images she examines, it is little wonder that she makes a rather dubious statement like "*The Silence of the Lambs* is, in one sense, determinedly politically correct—Buffalo Bill is *not* a transsexual, and both transsexuals and gender clinics are exonerated from even associative blame."[16] Although not a transsexual, it is clear that Buffalo Bill is gender dysphoric. To merely accept psychiatric categories of gender identity, as Garber does, is to unwittingly legitimate this institution's control in both regulating and defining transsexuality.

Garber's paradigm of "looking at" is limited insofar as it ignores the intertextual relations in which meaning is situated. This framework also enacts familiar oppositions between academics and "our" objects of inquiry. Transvestites are those figures "we" look at; they are not those people with whom "we" speak. And "they" are certainly not "us."

Queer theory scholar Carole-Anne Tyler adopts a methodology similar to that of Butler and Garber. Taking up the example of drag and gay male camp practices, Tyler attempts to account for their implicit racism and misogyny:

> If boys will be girls they had better be ladies. A real woman is a real lady; otherwise she is a female impersonator, a camp or mimic whose "unnaturally" bad taste—like that of the working-class, ethnic, or racially "other" woman—marks the impersonation as such. Miming the feminine means impersonating a white, middle-class impersonation of an "other" ideal of femininity.[17]

Tyler's intervention is remarkable for it contradictions. While some gay male camp and drag practices can be interpreted as misogynistic and racist, it is curious that Tyler overlooks African-American and working-class forms of drag, as for instance in the performances and representations of Joan Jett Blakk, Vaginal Creme Davis, and DeAundra Peek.[18] In this light, Tyler's argument is tautological: she looks at drag practices within white, middle-class gay male communities in order to claim that drag per se reflects white, middle-class, masculinist values.[19] Like Butler and Garber, Tyler offers very little analysis of the social context in which drag and camp practices are produced.

The writings of Butler and Garber have defined the terms of debate on transgendered people within American cultural studies of the 1990s: terms wherein transvestites and transsexuals function as rhetorical figures within cultural texts; terms wherein the voices, struggles, and joys of real transgendered people in the everyday social world are noticeably absent.

## QUEER THEORY, POSTSTRUCTURALIST THEORY

The presentation of transgendered issues within queer theory does not account for the quotidian living conditions of transgendered people. The political objections to this field are clear: queer theory begins its analysis with little thought of the individuals designated as the objects of study. At best, this perspective is an unfortunate and unacceptable oversight; at worst, it belies a kind of academic inquiry that is contemptuous and dismissive of the social world. While such political objections are not to be discounted—indeed, given the ubiquitous nature of queer theory in the U.S. academy and elsewhere, they must be reiterated continually—it might also be useful to reflect on the theoretical underpinnings of queer theory. An examination of the theoretical presuppositions that inform the practice of queer theory can illuminate why critics in queer theory choose particular facts for presentation. Queer theory's selection and interpretation of evidence is guided by its understanding of poststructuralist thought. In order to better understand queer theory, then, a discussion of poststructuralism is required.

Poststructuralism is associated with two French thinkers, Michel Foucault and Jacques Derrida.[20] Both Foucault and Derrida advocate what is known as an antifoundationalist perspective, characterized by a refusal to accept individual social agents as "masters" of their lives, identities, and worlds. Such a framework, amply illustrated in the works of French philosopher René Descartes, appeals to the voluntaristic will and ability of individual subjects.[21] Poststructuralism challenges this assumption and asks us to consider the ways in which subjects are constituted in and through social institutions and the language employed by these administrative bodies. Rather than searching for some essential origin or telos, poststructuralism seeks to examine the constitution of subjectivity in social life.

Foucault's work in *The History of Sexuality* illustrates this framework. He begins by considering the claim that sexuality has been repressed historically, that it has been silenced due to its controversial nature. Foucault labels this theory the "repressive hypothesis."[22] In contrast to this view, Foucault demonstrates the production of sexuality in a variety of administrative, juridical, and medical domains. The issue is not that speech about sexuality has been *prohibited,* but rather that it has been *prescribed.* By attending to the ways in which knowledge about sexuality is organized in law, medicine, and sexology, Foucault shows how specific sexual identities, such as that of the homosexual, have been manufactured in a variety of institutions. Foucault's empirical investigation allows him to advance a macrological theory about the productive nature of power. Having outlined both how the homosexual is produced and controlled (the conditions and effects of power), Foucault goes on to consider the sites of resistance opened up by the operations of such regimes. In the case of the homosexual, Foucault remarks on the contradictory possibilities engendered through the productive nature of power:

> There is no question that the appearance in nineteenth-century psychiatry, jurisprudence, and literature of a whole series of discourses on the species and subspecies of homosexuality, inversion, pederasty, and "psychic hermaphroditism" made possible a strong advance of social controls into this area of "perversity"; but it also made possible the formation of a "reverse" discourse: homosexuality began to speak in its own behalf, to demand that its legitimacy of "naturality" be acknowledged, often in the same vocabulary, using the same categories by which it was medically disqualified.[23]

In advancing this notion of a "reverse discourse," Foucault does not suggest that the productive nature of power preempts any and all resistance. In this manner, poststructuralist theory does not foreclose the possibility of political action; it merely asks some important questions about the terms through which such interventions are articulated.

Derrida raises questions similar to those of Foucault. He is interested in examining what he refers to as "binary oppositions"—that is, pairs of concepts whose terms are diametrically opposed, such as "man/woman" or "nature/culture." Derrida contemplates the extent to which such oppositions—which appear to be fixed, ahistorical, and "natural"—ultimately break down, since each term can only achieve its value in relation to its apparent "opposite."[24] Throughout Derrida's oeuvre, he introduces a variety of concepts that attempt to make sense of the relations between such opposites. In *De la grammatologie,* Derrida advances the notion of *supplementarity,*[25] while elsewhere he speaks of *dissémination,*[26] *invagination,*[27] *différance,*[28] and *iterability.*[29] In all instances, Derrida advances these concepts to investigate the relations between two terms that are juxtaposed, rather than focusing exclusively on each term in isolation.

In a critique of anthropologist Claude Lévi-Strauss,[30] for instance, Derrida takes issue with Levi-Strauss's juxtaposition of nature and culture.[31] In his discussion of the Nambikwara culture of South America, Lévi-Strauss states that writing did not exist within this culture and that its members communicated through speech. He further reflects on the impact of his own field research: when members of the Nambikwara culture witnessed Lévi-Strauss taking notes, he claims, they understood the significance (if not the actual meaning) of writing as a means of communication, thought, and knowledge. Lévi-Strauss uses the example of writing in order to illustrate the apparently "natural," primordial state in which the Nambikwara live. Derrida disputes this narrow conception of writing. He claims that the differentiation of members within Nambikwara societies through the use of proper names is a form of writing—that is, a manner of classification, arrangement, and meaning. Derrida shows that Nambikwara culture is marked by classificatory systems and that these systems are an integral part of social order and social relations. In this way, Derrida exposes the romanticist underpinnings of Lévi-Strauss's work by illustrating that the people within Nambikwara culture are not autonomous agents who live without the complication of cultural systems such as writing. They are ranked and classified through the use of proper names.

Furthermore, Derrida contends that Lévi-Strauss's argument depends on an unacknowledged opposition between nature and culture—an opposition that breaks down once we consider the role culture plays in distinguishing members of this society. Derrida's notion of supplementarity seeks to explain this play between nature and culture.

Derrida's work on the relations between *présence* and *absence,* illustrated through the concept of supplementarity, adopts an antifoundationalist position insofar as it examines how subjects are produced in writing. Like Foucault, Derrida scrutinizes the terms through which "resistance" is imagined. He does not suggest, however, that we cannot or should not select a particular term upon which to found our theoretical analysis and/or political strategy. Rather, Derrida makes the point that each time we invoke this term, its opposite will be similarly recalled within this process of enunciation.

Three common themes in the work of Foucault and Derrida exemplify their antifoundationalist stance: (1) they reject a voluntarist understanding of agency, in which individuals are responsible for their destiny; (2) they conceive of the productive nature of power; and (3) they demand reflection on the specific terms chosen (such as names, identities, or nations) as the basis for political action.

But how does queer theory engage poststructuralism? And how does this particular understanding of poststructuralism inform queer theory's selection of evidence for interpretation?

Queer theory takes up Derrida's notion of inside/out in order to explain the relations among heterosexuality and homosexuality. The field, which emerged in the early 1990s in American departments of literature, film, and cultural studies, offers interpretative, semiotic, and deconstructive readings of various texts.[32] Queer theory is especially interested in how these texts construct sexual objects and sexual relations. One of the central aims of queer theory is to demonstrate the textual production of sexual and gender identities. Queer theory applies Derrida's notion of supplementarity in order to reveal the reciprocal relations among heterosexuality and homosexuality.

In Diana Fuss's introduction to an edited collection of essays, for instance, she argues that heterosexuality typically defines itself only in relation to what it is not: homosexuality.[33] Having outlined these workings between heterosexuality and homosexuality, inside and out, Fuss expands on Foucault's notion of a reverse discourse. Summarizing Foucault, she contends that the production of the homosexual in medical, psychiatric, and juridical discourse at the same time produced a category through which one could claim specific rights and articulate resistance. Fuss continues by arguing that such resistance, based on a homosexual identity, is only possible given its absence—that is, the presence of homosexuals who are not "out" about their identities. For Fuss, the emergence of the homosexual brought with it the notion of the closet. The possibility of being "out" as homosexual depends on individuals who do not declare themselves to be homosexual. Fuss shows her readers how the production of an "outside" always brings with it a corresponding "inside."

These workings between inside and out are evident in the writings of Butler and Garber discussed earlier. When Butler makes the claim that drag exposes the constructed nature of gender, she illustrates that what is ostensibly "outside" of social norms—males dressed in women's clothes— is actually fully inside normative sex/gender relations, since these relations require that gender be secured through the repetition of particular acts and codes. Likewise, when Garber argues that transgendered figures in culture point to a "crisis of elsewhere," she shows her readers the relations between gender and race, and/or gender and class.[34] In this manner, Garber exposes that what is deemed to be outside culture is fully inside of it.

Butler and Garber, moreover, subscribe to a poststructuralist understanding of power as productive by showing the textual production of gender identities and gendered subject positions. Queer theory draws on poststructuralism to raise questions about the terms through which resistance is articulated. This interrogation of categories deemed useful for political action is most evident in Butler's writings, in which she asks her readers to consider the possibility and the import of suspending the name "lesbian" as a foundation for political activism.[35]

As a field that has only recently achieved currency in the university, queer theory contributes to an antifoundationalist agenda characteristic of poststructuralism. A rejection of individualist agency, a conception of the productive nature of power, and a questioning of the terms of political action constitute three of the central elements of this framework. In raising these theoretical issues, queer theory hopes to envision a different kind of sexual and gender politics.

Queer theory is clearly informed by poststructuralism. Reflection on the field, however, indicates that critics in queer theory endorse a certain conception of poststructuralist theory. Furthermore, this interpretation of poststructuralism determines the selection and presentation of evidence within the field. A consideration of the disciplinary and national locations of queer theory will clarify these issues.

Queer theory emerged within American departments of English, film studies, cultural studies, and the humanities.[36] Given these disciplinary locations, scholars in the field habitually choose a narrow scope of texts for analysis: novels, films, plays, drag performances, and other sites of cultural representation.[37] Although critics in queer theory appeal to the social location of the cultural texts they cite, they offer little analysis of how social relations are inscribed therein, and virtually no examination of the institutional mechanisms in which these texts are produced, nor those in which they emerge and circulate.[38] Both Foucault and Derrida ask questions about how discourse produces its own object: in the first volume of *L'Histoire de la sexualité,* Foucault inquires as to the production of the homosexual through juridical and medical discourse; while in *De la grammatologie,*

Derrida considers how members of Nambikwara culture are brought into being, ranked in the social order, through the use of proper names. In both instances, the inquiry concerns itself with the *social* institutions and taxonomic practices that produce subjects. For Foucault, the concern is with psychiatry, medicine, and the law—regimes interpreted through the notion of *discourse*. Derrida, in contrast, is concerned with the use of proper names in locating individuals within the collective hierarchy, a process he refers to as *writing*. Both Foucault and Derrida begin with particular social relations, such as psychiatric discourse or the hierarchy embedded in taxonomy and proper names, in order to make the general theoretical claim that knowledge creates its own objects and that a reflexive approach to knowledge production is thus required for critical inquiry.

Queer theory, of course, does not dispute these poststructuralist claims to the construction of knowledge. Despite a strong endorsement of a constructionist perspective, however, reflection on the objects chosen for study within queer theory reveals a limited frame of reference for the practice of poststructuralist theory. A further consideration of Butler's work will illustrate the particular brand of poststructuralist theory advanced within queer studies, as well as some of the theoretical weaknesses of this framework. Butler uses the example of drag queens in order to claim that all gender is socially constructed. Yet as we observed earlier, Butler's project is insufficient because she does not examine the institutional site in which the gendered performances of drag queens occur. In this manner, her citation of drag comes to stand in for sex/gender relations more broadly. Similarly, in her presentation of Venus Extravaganza from the film *Paris Is Burning,* Butler's nebulous reference to the economic and social realities of Latina women in New York City enables her to claim that Extravaganza is treated by the symbolic order in a manner similar ·to that of (nontranssexual) women of color.[39] Just as her earlier citation of drag queens stands in for sex/gender relations more broadly, this excerpt of Extravaganza's life serves as an explanation of race as a social relation. Both of these examples elucidate the theoretical difficulties in Butler's narrow conception of poststructuralism. Since she does not offer a sustained examination of the social practices and institutions in which gender and race are embedded, Butler requires that her readers extrapolate from particular objects—a drag performance in a gay bar or the death of a Hispanic transsexual prostitute—to the social relations that produce those objects and events. Whereas poststructuralism suggests that we need to cite the social and institutional operations that produce subjects, Butler advocates a type of inquiry that does not explain these relations between object and its discourse. Ironically, then, Butler proposes a representationalist conception of language: she demands that her citation of specific instances of gendered performance stand in for gendered relations; likewise, her discussion of Venus Extravaganza is used to speak about the complex relations among gender, race, and economics in contemporary America.[40] Such a representationalist conception of language is also evident in Garber's work, notably in her contention that transgendered figures conceal relations of race and class as well as gender. Like Butler, Garber's discussion of race and class compels the reader to extend from a transgendered figure to the social relations of race and ethnicity. What is noteworthy about these methods is that Butler and Garber enact a significant detour from the kind of poststructuralism practiced by Foucault and Derrida. Whereas Foucault and Derrida examine the social institutions that produce subjects (e.g., psychiatry; an ordering system through the use of proper names), Butler and Garber do not offer a similar analysis that is rooted in the everyday social world. Despite their insistence on the productive nature of power, they do not demonstrate how drag queens or transgendered people of color are produced in different institutional, social, economic, and historical settings. And because they do not offer this type of analysis, they ignore the role their own theories play in creating transgendered people as an object of academic discourse.

Although queer theory draws heavily on poststructuralism, its reading of poststructuralist theory is not engaged. Critics in queer theory habitually fail to consider that their selection of texts is a social process that embodies the production of knowledge and discourses on sexual and gendered objects. In this manner, queer theory is blind to its own institutional workings.[41] Moreover, these scholars merely apply their interpretative frameworks to specific texts, in an attempt to illustrate the workings between inside (heterosexuality) and outside (homosexuality). Insofar as queer theory limits itself to an application of poststructuralist ideas, the field provides descriptive—but not explanatory—evidence about the social relations of sexuality and gender.[42]

Queer theory's disciplinary location, as well as its somewhat formulaic application of poststructuralist thought, determines the selection and interpretation of evidence for the field. By privileging literary and cultural objects, and by ignoring the social and institutional relations in which these objects are located and embedded, queer theory enacts a restricted use of the notion of "text"—a narrow conception of writing and inscription that is incongruent with a poststructuralist project. Such a limited understanding of text precludes a developed social analysis.

22

My objections to queer theory outlined previously in this chapter focus on political arguments: that queer theory as it is currently practiced must be challenged because it exhibits a remarkable insensitivity to the substantive issues of transgendered people's everyday lives. Given this utter disregard for how transgendered people live, a rejection of queer theory based on such a political argument is both worthy and warranted. Yet queer theory ought also to be interrogated from a theoretical perspective. Its restricted conception of text determines the selection and interpretation of evidence, facts, and objects—in other words, what counts as knowledge. While queer theory clearly needs to be repudiated due to the political effects of the field, a sophisticated intellectual response should also understand that queer theory's designation of an object is a function of its theoretical presuppositions. It is because queer theory considers only certain cultural and literary objects appropriate for examination, and because it is merely interested in an application of poststructuralist ideas to these objects, that the lives, bodies, and experiences of transgendered people are eclipsed. Queer theory's epistemological and methodological presuppositions authorize a political agenda that robs transgendered people of dignity and integrity.

As the following chapter will demonstrate, the English-language social science literature approaches the study of transsexual/transgendered people in a manner markedly different than that of queer theory. Drawing on interviews, media images, field research, and historical inquiry, social science sometimes succeeds in examining the lives of transsexual and transgendered people without reducing them to objects of curiosity or fascination, or useful cases to illustrate a particular position. In many instances, however, social scientists create knowledge that is of questionable import to transsexual and transgendered people, and that objectifies them in precisely the same way as queer theory.

## ◅ 2 ▻

# THEORY TROUBLE

*Social Scientific Research and Transgendered People*

Research in the social sciences offers a different approach to the study of transgendered people than that of queer theory. Some of the social science research asks different questions than critics in queer theory. Yet much of this research presents its own theoretical, methodological, and political problems. While some difficulties are unique to social science inquiry, others repeat the erasure and contempt for transsexual people evidenced in queer theory.

The most obvious place to begin a discussion of sociological research on transsexuals is with Harold Garfinkel's ethnomethodology.[1] Ethnomethodology is the name given to the sociological framework that helps uncover the unwritten rules by which all social actors guide their lives. Garfinkel studied the case of Agnes, a male-to-female (MTF) transsexual who presented herself to the gender identity clinic in Los Angeles in 1958. Agnes had already been living as a woman for years. What Garfinkel found interesting about this case is how Agnes's behavior revealed the unspoken rules of gender that we all follow. For instance, Agnes spoke in a soft voice, waited to hear the opinions of others (especially men) before voicing her own, and worked in the kitchen. According to Garfinkel, Agnes's example demonstrates how gender is managed on a daily basis.

Other ethnomethodologists have continued the project initiated by Garfinkel. Suzanne Kessler and Wendy McKenna, for instance, examined how gender is coded in Western cultures.[2] They presented undergraduate students with a variety of visual images and asked them to identify the gender of each picture's subject. Some pictures depicted an individual with long hair, breasts, and a vagina, while others presented a person with a vagina, short hair, and no visible breasts. Kessler and McKenna discovered that when a penis was visible, the picture would be classified as "male" approximately 95 percent of the time. In contrast, an image with a vagina required at least two other secondary sex characteristics indicating femininity in order to be classified as "female" with a similar frequency. Kessler and McKenna concluded that the cultural interpretation of gender is overwhelmingly skewed in favor of masculine referents.

More recently, Kessler's research has focused on intersexed infants, those individuals with "ambiguous" genitalia at birth.[3] That these individuals are surgically altered to have a sex that can be "recognized" illustrates the priority this culture places upon genitals in the attribution of gender identity. Kessler also notes that the criterion of chromosomes is less relevant in determining an intersexed child's gender than the length and appearance of the phallus. Like Garfinkel, Kessler exposes some of the underlying assumptions that govern our most taken-for-granted conceptions of gender. Sexed bodies (male or female) are not the basis of gender identities (men or women); rather, our binary conception of gender produces these sexed bodies.

Research in the discipline of anthropology raises some important methodological questions with respect to studying transgendered people and cultures. In Esther Newton's examination of drag queens, she gives an ethnographic account of the work environments, identities, and lives of female impersonators.[4] She notes that within this subculture, people can adopt a variety of drag identities, such as the "street fairy," who flaunts femininity in public; the "glamour queen," who adopts an air of sophistication and aristocracy; and the impressionist, who mimics Hollywood stars such as Mae West and Bette Davis.[5] Newton also examines the different kinds of shows that can be created by female impersonators. Drag queens stripping in front of a predominantly heterosexual audience, she claims, must always remove their bras to reveal their flat chests. The same performers in front of a gay crowd, in contrast, do not remove their bras.[6] While heterosexual patrons need the biological status of the female impersonator confirmed (through the removal of the bra), gay patrons do not.

This attention to social context proves particularly useful for thinking about the politics of gender. Newton's research reveals that gender is highly regulated even within the world of female impersonators. For example, while all female impersonators wear "women's" clothes for their performances, within the communities studied by Newton those individuals who wore "women's" clothes in their everyday lives were viewed with disdain: "'[T]ransy drag' is either some item of feminine apparel which is not related to the necessities of performance, or feminine clothing which is worn in everyday circumstances. . . . transy drag is wrong [within the subculture of female impersonators] because it violates the glamour standard."[7] Newton's scholarship certainly reveals that gender is socially constructed. Yet it is especially valuable because it illustrates that this construction varies in different social, historical, political, and regional locations. Throughout her work, Newton remains faithful to the project of ethnography: she presents the ways in which female impersonators perceive their social world, rather than how she as a researcher sees it.[8] Moreover, Newton explains the meanings of particular cultural symbols and signs (such as clothing that could be classified as "transy drag") in terms of the worldview of female impersonators.

Anne Bolin's study of transgendered people in the United States reflects a similar commitment to anthropological inquiry.[9] She interrogates the uniform nature of psychiatric categories of transsexualism and transvestism. In particular, Bolin examines the ways in which psychiatric discourses assume that all transsexuals are heterosexually identified, an assumption that was not validated by her field research.[10] She also remarks on the diversity of gender identities among transvestites and transsexuals, noting that a fluid articulation of gender identity has been marked at the semantic level: "*Transgenderist* is a community term denoting kinship among those with gender-variant identities. It supplants the dichotomy of transsexual and transvestite with a concept of continuity. Additionally, it highlights a growing acceptance of nonsurgical options for physical males who wish to live as women."[11] By attending to the particular ways in which transgenderists conceive their gender identities, Bolin exposes the regulatory functions of psychiatric practices.[12] This perspective also acknowledges the manner in which transgenderists expand gender identities, rather than reify a binary gender system.[13] Bolin is careful to situate the practices she cites within their proper historical contexts. For instance, she maintains that a specifically *transgender* identity is a relatively recent phenomenon, which can be understood with reference to three factors: "(1) the closing of university-affiliated gender clinics [in the United States], (2) the grass-roots organizational adoption of a political agenda and (3) social alternatives to embodiments of femininity as somatic frailty."[14] Bolin does more than state that we are presently witnessing a variety of transgendered identities. She situates the fluidity of these positions with regard to broader social processes, such as the decreased regulation of transgender and transsexual identities with the closing of university-based gender clinics. In this context of an emerging transgendered identity and politics, seemingly contradictory subject-positions, such as MTF transsexual bodybuilders, are possible.[15]

Recent scholarship in the social sciences examines transgendered issues in a manner that is relevant to transgendered communities. Vern Bullough and Bonnie Bullough, for instance, document individuals who cross-dressed throughout history, and discuss cross-dressing in different cultures.[16] The strength of their work is a historical, contextualized interpretation of what cross-dressing means and how these meanings can change across time and cultures. In addition to providing historical data, Bullough and Bullough investigate the development of a medical model of transvestism and transsexualism. Tracing the emergence of these categories through the writings of nineteenth-century sexologists, they demonstrate a collapse of gender and sexuality in the definition of transvestism, such that effeminacy was equated with homosexuality.[17] The authors subsequently explore how gender and sexuality can be juxtaposed, as they were in the writings of Magnus Hirschfeld,[18] in an explicit rejection of this collapse. This *historical* approach encourages critical reflection on the *contemporary* definitions of transvestism and transsexualism.

## PRESUPPOSITIONS AND LIMITATIONS OF SOCIAL SCIENCE RESEARCH

The social scientific research discussed here shares a common orientation, namely to understand how society works. Of course, different disciplines, fields, and substantive areas may develop distinct aspects of this research problematic. In the case of transgendered people, for instance, scholars with an interest in history may examine the emergence of transsexuality in the twentieth century, and/or how the social recognition or acceptance of transgendered people has changed over time.[19] An anthropologist, in contrast, could examine the meanings of gender roles in different cultural settings.[20] And an ethnomethodologist could offer a detailed, micrological analysis of conversations with respect to gender in an attempt to better understand the relations among gender and speech patterns.[21] What unites these diverse methodological approaches is a commitment to social scientific inquiry, to research that investigates the thoroughly social nature of historical transformations, cultural meanings, or conversation patterns.

An approach that focuses on the social aspect of gendered identities, meanings, and relations allows scholars and activists to articulate a nuanced understanding of gender as a social construct. This perspective has obvious advantages over that of queer theory, since it begins its investigation in the everyday world and its findings can be practically applied therein.

Despite an investment in social inquiry, however, prevailing paradigms within the social sciences risk objectifying the issues, populations, and people they study. Within such a framework, a research problematic is defined by and for sociologists instead of the people who live in the milieu being studied. Such an objectivist approach is limited on a variety of levels: the questions it identifies as important for study, the methods chosen to gather data, the relevance of the information gathered for the research population, the attention to difference within the community under investigation, and the subsequent implications of this knowledge for social policy.

The theoretical, methodological, and political difficulties of such an objectivist framework belie fundamental questions about the nature, function, and practice of sociological theory and research. Scholars interested in the development of theory that is pertinent to the members of a given population are faced with an enormous challenge. First, their work needs to adequately describe how the individuals under investigation are situated in the world, as well as how they make sense of this location. Second, such theory needs to move beyond a mere description of a particular population, to a critical examination of how the life experiences of these people are shaped and ordered through specific social, cultural, economic, and historical relations. Third, theory needs to be explicitly linked to social practice. This requirement of social theory ensures that its production will emerge from the everyday social world, and therefore that the elements of a theory that focus on the transformation of social relations are constituted in and through the world as it is actually organized, rather than offering a programmatic or utopian vision of how things should be, or could be, arranged. In his book *Social Theory and Political Practice,* Brian Fay outlines five basic requirements of a *critical* social theory:

1. reflexivity—that subjects can understand their dissatisfactions and contradictions in the social world;
2. an ideology-critique—that the illusory nature of our beliefs and thoughts, and how this supports the status quo, be exposed;
3. that the theory analyze the specific changes in a society;
4. that these changes be examined in relation to the real needs of the people implicated in them;
5. the transformation of a critical social theory into social practice, involving the active participation of social actors.[22]

For Fay, theory that accepts these tenets plays an active role in the process of social change. The production of knowledge both describes and legitimates the world. As such, the articulation of a theory can play a fundamental role in a broader process of improving everyday life for people:

> According to the critical model of social science, a social theory does not simply offer a picture of the way that a social order works; instead, a social theory is itself a catalytic agent of change, within the complex of social life which it analyzes.[23]

Not all social scientists produce theory that endorses these relations between knowledge and action, however. Steven Seidman offers a useful distinction between *sociological theory* and *social theory*. In his view, sociological theory is preoccupied with advancing a general, totalizing explanation of society. This fixation on the universalizing elements of sociological theory has created a situation in which "theory" is produced by and for sociologists:

> Sociological theory has gone astray. It has lost most of its social and intellectual importance; it is disengaged from the conflicts and public debates that have nourished it in the past; it has turned inward and is largely self-referential.[24]

Social theory, in contrast, emerges out of public debates, moral concerns, and social conflicts. It aims to describe and explain particular social, cultural, or historical issues, and to influence them. Whereas sociological theory takes for granted an audience of academic sociologists, social theory invokes a much broader field of reference, including academics, policy makers, activists, legislators, and the individuals who make up a given constituency under review.

Much of the current English-language social science research on transsexual and transgendered (TS/TG) people reflects the objectivist, self-referential nature of sociological theory. Two recent studies of transgendered people illustrate the theoretical, methodological, and political shortcomings of such a framework. Leon Pettiway's *Honey, Honey, Miss Thang: Being Black, Gay, and on the Streets* is an ethnographic account of five African-American MTF TS/TG prostitutes living and working in American inner-city communities.[25] Their narratives describe verbal and physical abuse, social isolation and familial rejection, drug use, poverty, and police harassment. In terms of substantive inquiry, Pettiway's research offers a wealth of information and rich descriptive data. Yet ultimately this ethnography offers only a touristic view of the lives of poor, urban TS/TG prostitutes. Although Pettiway maintains that his voice is absent from the study in order to give priority to his interview subjects,[26] his introduction undermines this claim. In one telling phrase, Pettiway states that his subjects "are addicted to drugs and commit sex work."[27] This choice of terminology is significant, for it aligns the author with the prevalent American moralistic discourse against drugs and prostitution. A more neutral wording of these issues— for instance, the statement that the interview subjects "use drugs and work as prostitutes"—would have different political effects.[28] Despite his desire to allow these transgendered people to speak for themselves, Pettiway's use

29

of language legitimates the criminalization and state repression of both drugs and prostitution.[29]

Pettiway's overall presentation of the research further contradicts his claims of neutrality. Consider his introductory description of the interviewees:

> They came to the interviews dressed as women, but to varying degrees they still appeared masculine. Some had thick hands, wide shoulders, and large feet, and no matter how they attempted to disguise their voices, their large adam's apples vibrated to produce sounds that hinted at a masculine voice. After several hours of listening, however, it became apparent that one was not talking to a man at all. They were women. In their hearts and minds they were truly women, and it became natural to refer to them as women.[30]

While this passage attempts to persuade the reader that the MTF TS/TG people interviewed were "truly women," its function in the book's introduction serves to define the research agenda on nontranssexual terms. The gender identities of interviewees is subject to intense scrutiny and analysis, while the genders of Pettiway as a researcher and the assumed nontransgendered readers[31] are, quite simply, unremarkable. This introductory passage, then, tells us more about Pettiway and his imagined readers than it does about the interviewees.

Within the actual text, Pettiway's transgendered interviewees do tell their stories. Yet because the interview questions are excluded, the reader has very little knowledge about the dynamic or rapport between Pettiway and his subjects. Furthermore, we are given no information about how the questions were developed—were transgendered people consulted in this matter? A consideration of the research process would provide further insight into the subjects addressed by interviewees. For instance, although we learn that the participants take hormones, we are not told how they access them.[32] And whereas Pettiway states that the interviewees work as prostitutes to pay for their drugs, he does not address the absolute lack of social services for transgendered people who wish to stop using drugs and/or working as prostitutes.[33] An ethnographic research study that does not account for these kinds of systemic difficulties is insufficient, because it does not situate transgendered prostitutes within the social and administrative contexts that, in part, manage their lives.

Pettiway offers a book that allows young, urban, MTF TS/TG prostitutes to convey some crucial information about their lives. But he does not provide the proper frame for readers to understand adequately the social conditions in which they live. And because Pettiway does not fully succeed in documenting how his interviewees situate themselves in the world, particularly the institutional world, he does not fulfill the terms of social theory as outlined by Brian Fay. As such, he cannot discuss the changes they would propose to improve their current situations. Since the real needs of his interviewees are not addressed, his theory cannot involve TS/TG people in a broader process of social change. Nor can it offer any significant direction to legislators or social policy specialists in housing, employment, and drug use.

Richard Ekins's recent book, *Male Femaling: A Grounded Theory Approach to Cross-Dressing and Sex-Changing,* offers a sociological approach to transgendered people in the British context, through an application of the methods of grounded theory.[34] Ekins's research spans seventeen years, so he cannot be criticized for capitalizing on this subject matter due to a timely academic interest in transgendered phenomena. And the data that is generated and interpreted clearly emerges from the everyday social world of his research participants. His work raises questions, however, about the diversity of his sample population, as well as the definition of the research agenda.

In his chapter called "Fantasying Male Femaling," for instance, Ekins discusses fantasy phone lines that cater to a transvestite/transsexual/transgendered clientele.[35] Although Ekins examines transvestite gender in great depth within this context, he offers no consideration of these phone lines from the perspective of the women—be they transgendered or not—who work them. His analysis focuses only on the gender play and gendered fantasies of transvestites. The function of gender in terms of work, specifically for the women who make their livings on these phone lines, is not a topic of consideration.

Ekins claims that the information gathered in his study has implications for the substantive area of the sociology of gender.[36] He appeals to a tradition of grounded theory in order to assert that the process of male femaling described and interpreted in his book can illuminate gender meanings and gender relations more broadly defined. His claim is certainly not unfounded. However, we ought to consider who gets to determine this research agenda and how, in most academic analyses of transgendered people, what merits attention is the fact that some individuals have transgressed a sex/gender binary. Transgendered activist Jeanne B. persuasively argues that this type of inquiry satisfies the curiosity of nontransgendered men and women:

One interesting thing, a lot of people ask me: "What do you do to pass as a woman? To look, walk, and talk like a woman?" But nobody asks me: "How did you manage to live and pass as a man for so many years?"[37]

This intervention is remarkable because it illustrates how the questions posed with respect to transgendered people do not reflect our daily life circumstances or how we see ourselves.[38] A preoccupation with what people do to live and pass as a member of a chosen gender ultimately seeks to explain or justify the presence of transgendered people in this culture. Furthermore, such an inquiry takes for granted that the management of one's assigned gender is "natural." Such an assumption is especially questionable in a critical examination of how gender is achieved and ascribed.

Ekins's research methods can be questioned, moreover, on the terms of grounded theory that he claims informs his study. His fixation on the chosen genders of transgendered people illustrates a theoretical and methodological framework that considers the management of gendered meanings for individuals who transgress normative sex/gender relations, and that further asserts the relevance of this inquiry for a broad analysis of the social construction and management of gender. Yet as Jeanne B. points out, this approach does not examine how transgendered people also manage their genders before they change the physical and social appearances of their bodies. In this manner, Ekins's research does not enact the type of comparative inquiry advocated within grounded theory. As Barney Glaser and Anselm Strauss contend, grounded theory requires that one's explanatory conceptual categories be generated from the everyday social world.[39] These categories are valid because they have been created from a process of data collection, and because they reflect the experiences of the subjects in the population under investigation. While Ekins's work is valuable because it illustrates how transgendered people successfully manage a chosen gender, it is limited insofar as it does not also consider how transgendered people manage an assigned gender. Because his study lacks such a comparative analysis, its application of grounded theory methods is incomplete.

Recent sociological studies of transgendered people, such as those offered by Pettiway and Ekins, enact an objectivist framework in which the definition of a research problematic does not consider the everyday life of the subjects, but rather reflects the institutional and administrative questions identified as important by sociologists. Such a framework is insufficient on a variety of levels. The diversity of the sample population may be overlooked, as illustrated by Ekins's exclusion of the people (including transvestites and transsexuals) who staff phone sex lines. In the studies offered by both Pettiway and Ekins, the research agenda has been defined by the sociologists rather than by members of the sample population. This bias is most evident in their discussions of the genders of their subjects: Ekins's analysis of post-transition genders and Pettiway's somewhat liberal insistence that the MTF transgendered people he interviewed were "truly women" despite the physical appearance of their bodies.[40] Moreover, the relevance of this information to the transgendered people in the sample population is not specified. Finally, neither Ekins nor Pettiway clarify the implications of their research for social policy. This is especially remarkable in Pettiway's work, which provides the reader with some quite significant empirical data on the lives of transgendered prostitutes who use drugs while ignoring the kinds of social relations and social policies that shape and order these experiences. The reader is given no direction or reflection on significant policy issues for transgendered people such as access to hormones, the regulation of prostitution, or the criminalization of drug use. Pettiway's research illustrates a type of inquiry produced primarily for university-based academics. It is a form of sociological research that does not require intervention in the world it studies. In this regard, Pettiway's work reflects a commitment to sociological theory as outlined by Seidman. The more transformative project of social theory, in which theory functions as an agent of change in the everyday world, remains outside the scope of his project.

## BEYOND MEDICINE AND PSYCHIATRY?

The limits of objectivist sociology are well illustrated in the writings of certain social scientists concerning the medical and psychiatric production of transsexuals. In *The Transsexual Empire: The Making of the She-Male,* Janice Raymond argues that transsexuals are created through medicine.[41] In her view, psychiatric evaluation as well as the availability of surgery function to produce transsexuals. Raymond claims that transsexuality embodies the sexist stereotypes and relations of medicine. This position is also advocated by sociologists Dwight Billings and Thomas Urban, who contend that the case of transsexuality provides insight into the social construction of illness. Like Raymond, they argue that "transsexualism is a socially constructed reality which *only* exists in and through medical practice."[42] Billings and Urban extend Raymond's position with the claim that transsexuality is also marked by, and is an effect of, capitalism and consumerism. Referring to sex reassignment surgery as "genital amputation,"[43] they maintain that the capitalist industry of medicine created transsexualism:

Human experiences such as sexual fulfillment and gender-role comfort were thus transformed into luxury commodities available at high prices from U.S. physicians; victims [sic] of aberrant gender role conditioning and other sexual deviants [sic] were induced to seek gratification in a commodified world of "artificial vaginas" and fleshy, man-made penises.[44]

Social scientists such as Raymond, Billings, and Urban study transsexuals in order to make broader claims about medicine and psychiatry. Yet significantly, all three are also fundamentally invested in advancing political arguments about the nature and existence of transsexuals. Their remarks and judgments of transsexuals are evident in their language—for instance, their repeated designations of MTF transsexuals with the pronoun "he,"[45] or the arrogant labeling of sex reassignment surgery as a form of "genital amputation."[46] Furthermore, all too often research on the medical and psychiatric production of transsexuals degenerates into an attack against self-identified transsexuals. In many instances, this anti-transsexual agenda is masked under the guise of theory or research, as demonstrated by Bernice Hausman's preface to *Changing Sex:*

> [w]hile in the end I am critical of the phenomenon of transsexualism, I hope it is clear that I do not (cannot) condemn transsexuals themselves.[47]

Toward the conclusion of her book, however, Hausman is much less cautious, declaring that because transsexuals seek to align biological sex and social gender, they are highly conservative individuals who reinforce normative sex/gender relations. For Hausman, this investment in surgery and body change explains how "transsexuals are the dupes of gender."[48] Although she contends that she is not interested in condemning individual transsexuals, she nonetheless chooses language that situates transsexuals in the realm of illusion, duplicity, and deception.

Transsexuals in this type of scholarship can only exist in medical practice, so individuals who live and identify as transsexuals are best understood as victims of sexist and capitalist ideology. Taken to its logical conclusion, this position argues that transsexuality as a social phenomenon, and therefore transsexuals as individuals, should not exist. Such a contempt for transsexuals is most apparent in Raymond's programmatic statement that "the problem of transsexualism would best be served by morally mandating it out of existence."[49] Thus, although Raymond, Hausman, Billings, and Urban would situate their work as part of a broader project of the sociology of medicine, they engage in this analysis in order to advance political claims about the nature and function of transsexuality: whether or not transsexuals do, or should, exist. Although all these writers would maintain that they advocate a type of radical inquiry—Billings and Urban conclude their essay with a brief discussion on its implications for critical theory—their political claims as to the nature and function of transsexuality are informed by deeply conservative social theories. This preoccupation with the very actuality of transsexuality establishes a crucial role for the theories they advocate: if scholars can explain what causes transsexuality, then it can also be prevented. In sociological terms, this reflects a positivist approach, in which the scientist seeks to explain, predict, and control a particular social phenomenon.[50] From the perspective of a radical social theory, positivist inquiry should be rejected because it presupposes value-neutral knowledge, and because the framework emerged with, and reinforces, industrial capitalism.[51] While Raymond, Hausman, Billings, and Urban claim a critical position because of the *content* of their theories, their *methods* of producing theory are far from radical.

The writings of Raymond, Billings, and Urban represent a significant current of scholarship on transsexualism in the social sciences. This field is preoccupied with the medical management of transsexuality. Indeed, Billings and Urban go so far as to locate transsexuality exclusively in relation to medical practice. Sociological inquiry with respect to transsexuals is clearly flawed. While the questions asked by the Ekins are not in line with how transsexuals live and experience the everyday world, the questions identified as important by researchers such as Raymond, Billings, and Urban limit their consideration of transsexuality to medical and psychiatric institutions. This narrow focus distorts the complexity of transsexual lives and bodies. In reasoning that transsexuals exemplify the commodified relations of medicine, as well as commodified images of femininity, Billings and Urban conclude that "many patients are themselves transformed into commodities, resorting to prostitution to pay their medical bills."[52] This perspective neglects the complicated situation of MTF transsexuals who need money to pay for health care and who may not be able to find stable employment outside of prostitution. It categorically ignores employment discrimination against transsexuals, overlooks the lack of government funding for transsexual and transgendered health care needs, and disregards the social integration of individuals who have changed sex.[53] A restricted consideration of transsexuality distorts the complexity of the social world as it is lived and experienced by transsexual and transgendered people. While many MTF transsexuals may work as prostitutes to pay for their health care, many may also work as prostitutes because it is the only form of work available to them.

35

Furthermore, the argument collapses the institutional relations of capitalist medicine and the individuals who are located therein. Patients who pay for heart surgeries are not similarly indicted for being victims of capitalist medical technologies, men and women who are not real because they live in bodies altered through surgery. Such viciousness is reserved for transsexuals within the sociology of medicine.[54]

In his outline of a critical social theory, Brian Fay offers a case study of women's liberation. In order to examine the dissatisfaction of women in the Western world, he argues, a scholar would need to consider a variety of macrological and micrological social relations: transformations in the production and distribution of goods and services in industrial society; redefinitions of both wage and domestic labor; educational opportunities; and how women come to define themselves.[55] This example illustrates the very complex analysis that is required in order to make sense of how particular actors situate themselves in the world, as well as the historical, cultural, economic, and social relations that in part determine this situation. Yet in much of the academic English-language scholarship on transsexuals, a similarly complex, multifaceted analysis is not offered. Scholars focus exclusively on the act of sex reassignment surgery, claiming that it exemplifies the false consciousness of individuals who call themselves transsexuals. Issues of employment, identity papers, and social integration are completely obscured within such an analysis. This restricted emphasis on sex reassignment surgery is questionable for two other reasons. First, as Henry Rubin points out, this perspective takes for granted MTF transsexual bodies.[56] Since female-to-male (FTM) transsexuals are ignored within this framework, the theory belies an unacknowledged gendered bias—surely a flagrant contradiction for scholarship that labels itself feminist. Second, the fact that these scholars limit their analyses to the act of sex reassignment surgery—regularly excluding the social context in which transsexuals live—legitimates and consolidates a cultural equation between genitals and gender. Paradoxically, while transsexuals are condemned for seeking to align their genitals and their genders, academic sociologists who confine their investigation of (MTF transsexual) gender to the presence, status, function, or modification of an individual's genitals are not subject to similar reproaches. Indeed, one could charge that in their silence concerning the substantive issues of MTF transsexual lives, feminists and sociologists are guilty of precisely the slippage between gender and genitals of which they accuse MTF transsexuals.

The kind of objectivist sociological inquiry evidenced in the work of Pettiway, Raymond, and Billings and Urban can be rejected for a number of reasons, particularly because such studies are of little practical relevance for individuals who call themselves transsexual. Such writings ought to be questioned in terms of their potential contribution—and damage—to the everyday lives of transsexuals. Yet they must also be interrogated insofar as they advocate a kind of sociological theory and practice that remains disconnected from the world as it is lived and experienced by members of a research population. These scholars clearly advance an ideology critique (albeit one that is flawed), but fail to involve transsexuals themselves in a broader process of social change. At best, such work can only offer an inquiry along the lines of sociological theory, as outlined by Seidman. The more radical—and more transformative—project of social theory remains outside the scope of such an analysis.

## CONCLUSION

English-language social science literature on transsexual and transgendered people approaches the subject in a markedly different way than critics in queer theory. Drawing on interviews, ethnographic field research, and historical inquiry, researchers investigate gender as a social relation, cultural meanings, and historical transformation. While this specifically social focus on the lives of transsexual and transgendered people should be welcomed and encouraged, many scholars limit their studies to the medical and psychiatric production of transsexuals, neglecting other important features of everyday life. Significantly, this inquiry advocates a type of sociological theory and practice that is created primarily for academics, not for members of the research population, nor even for legislators, jurists, social policy experts, or the administrative personnel of community-based organizations that work with the individuals under investigation. The studies of Pettiway, Raymond, Hausman, and Billings and Urban clearly illustrate the arrogance that underlines so much academic sociology. Most of this scholarship assumes that transsexuals would not change their sex once they have read enough Marxist or feminist theory: a hypothesis that cannot account for the realities of individuals who change sex *after* exposure to Marxist, socialist, or feminist theories and politics.

While social scientists may appeal to different kinds of texts in their analysis of transsexuality than critics in queer theory (i.e., relying on interviews and field research), the evidence that they present is not necessarily pertinent to the daily lives and issues of transsexual and transgendered people. Indeed, much social science establishes an opposition between liberated academics who understand the constructed nature of gender and the poor duped transsexuals who are victims of false consciousness. An exclusive focus on the medical and psychiatric production of transsexuality subverts a nuanced understanding of everyday life as it is lived and experienced by transsexual and transgendered people in a variety of social spheres, such as employment, housing, health care, social services, and civil status.

A sociological study of transsexuality relevant to transsexual and transgendered people—as well as staff of health care and social service agencies, legislators, and policy makers—must expand its scope of inquiry far beyond the current research in the field. Drawing from the strengths and limitations of both queer theory and mainstream social science, the following chapter provides a theoretical framework that seeks to realize such a project.

# BEYOND TEXTUALIST
# AND OBJECTIVIST THEORY

*Toward a Reflexive Poststructuralist Sociology*

The analyses of transgendered people offered by both queer theory and mainstream sociology are each limited with respect to their theoretical contributions and their practical applications. Queer theory draws on poststructuralism in an attempt to examine the productive nature of power and to ask important questions about articulating resistance. Its exclusive reliance on literary and cultural texts and its representationalist conception of language, however, offer an underdeveloped account of the relations between discourse and society. This lack of attention to the social and institutional locations in which texts circulate erases the everyday experiences, bodies, and lives of transgendered people. Queer theory is limited theoretically insofar as it only offers an application of poststructuralist thought, in addition to its restricted conception of text. The field's neglect of the social and economic conditions in which transgendered people live makes it of questionable political import. Social scientific investigations of these issues, in contrast, offer some valuable insight into the everyday social world of transgendered people. Yet objectivist sociological approaches do not necessarily resolve the theoretical and political dilemmas present in queer theory. In the ethnographic study of MTF transgendered prostitutes conducted by Pettiway, for instance, a narrow framework determines the selection and interpretation of evidence. Such a paradigm frames the research questions according to the dictates of the criminologist-as-investigator rather than the lives of the transgendered prostitutes interviewed. Like queer theory, this theoretical approach needs to be interrogated politically, since the relevance of this study for the research population is never made clear.

Despite the theoretical and political limitations of mainstream sociology and the kind of poststructuralism practiced within queer theory, each area of inquiry offers some unique contributions concerning the analysis of transgendered people. Why is it useful to consider these fields, and how might they be rearticulated to offer a research program that is both theoretically engaged and practically relevant? What could a poststructuralist sociology offer to the study of transgendered people? How could it avoid the constricted poststructuralism of queer theory and the rigid empiricism of mainstream sociology? Which aspects of poststructuralism and social inquiry should be emphasized, and why? What would a poststructuralist sociological research program look like, how would it be enacted, and why would it be useful?

Poststructuralism's emphasis on the productive nature of power makes an important contribution to sociological practice, because it conceives of macrological power relations in terms of their micrological realizations.[1] Similarly, its antifoundationalist focus extends a long sociological tradition that cautions against a simplistic conception of agency in theories about a structure/agency nexus.[2] And its insistence on thinking through the categories of resistance is valuable for sociological theory and practice. These three aspects of poststructuralism, then, ought to be considered in the development of a critical research program. Yet as we have observed, the interpretation and practice of poststructuralism in an Anglo-American context, such as that of queer theory, is not interested in a specifically *social* inquiry. In this light, reflection on the theories, methods, and research strategies of the social sciences is required. The discussion of sociological research outlined earlier uncovers two central components of a critical sociological research program: (1) a framework that explains social relations; and (2) a practice that is reflexive rather than objectivist. This notion of social relations recognizes that meanings and texts are embedded in particular forms of social organization, whether that organization comprises members of a given culture or the administrative or organizational bodies of this culture.[3] The challenge for a critical sociological program is to comprehend individual actors, meanings, and organizations in terms of their macrological social relations as well as their micrological instantiations. Building on the concept of social relations, the requirement that social theory and practice be reflexive demands that the researcher be located in the everyday social world, and furthermore, that the explanatory framework offered account for how that world is perceived, lived, and experienced by members of the research population.[4] It is in fostering this type of inquiry that sociological research can inform the development of appropriate political and policy interventions in the social world. Whereas an objectivist sociology is content with a description of the world—one wherein the experiences of the research subjects may or may not be present—a reflexive sociology demands that researchers account for the role that sociological theory and methods play in producing their objects of investigation.

In this view, knowledge legitimates—not merely describes—particular understandings of the social world.

While queer theory and objectivist sociology both provide frameworks that are limited in terms of theory, politics, and social policy, they also offer potentially innovative ways of understanding how transgendered people are situated in the social world. The challenge now is to forge a kind of inquiry that draws on the positive, engaging aspects of poststructuralism as well as those of a reflexive sociology. How could such an investigation be organized, what could it contribute to transgendered people, and why is it worth pursuing? A consideration of specific examples will help answer these questions and illustrate the theoretical and political contributions of a poststructuralist sociological research program for transsexual and transgendered people.

## THE TEXTUAL PRODUCTION OF SEX AND GENDER

A conversation between Diane Gobeil and Mirha-Soleil Ross, two MTF transsexual activists, offers a useful point of departure for this inquiry. Gobeil and Ross reflect on the lack of HIV/AIDS services for transsexuals within Canadian and Québécois contexts:

> [Ross]: Why do you think AIDS organizations and AIDS prevention groups have neglected the transsexual community to such an extreme extent? How come they never thought about us? I've always had that question.
>
> [Gobeil]: Try to take a census of the AIDS cases in Canada that are transsexual. It's hard because many [MTF] transsexuals have male papers and are classified as male.
>
> [Ross]: Yeah, I know. They classify us [MTFs] as male if we are pre-/nonoperative and as women if we're post-operative. And there's no way to keep track because there's no mention of transsexuality.[5]

Gobeil and Ross frame their questions in the everyday world, asking about the neglect of transsexual and transgendered people within AIDS service organizations (ASOs). They move beyond a mere lack of services, however, to an appreciation of how gendered knowledge about HIV and AIDS excludes transgendered people, an exclusion that is both reflected and reinforced in the daily work of administrative bodies and AIDS organizations. Just as Foucault rejects a repressive hypothesis with regard to sexuality,

Gobeil and Ross repudiate the thesis that a lack of services for transsexuals is exclusively a result of discrimination against or discomfort in treating the transgendered. Rather, they contemplate how transsexuality is effaced through the sexed classification of seropositive bodies, illustrating how particular categories of knowledge shape the administrative practices of AIDS organizations. Transsexuals are excluded in these practices.

This example is especially insightful in a consideration of the value of a poststructuralist sociology. Gobeil and Ross emphasize the productive nature of power by demonstrating that bipolar notions of sex and gender preclude the possibility of transsexual and transgendered bodies. At the same time, they offer an analysis that is thoroughly social, examining the actual workings of institutions such as ASOs. Finally, they advocate a reflexive inquiry, recognizing that the effacement of transsexual and transgendered people is directly related to the sexed categories of knowledge that are generated within a particular culture. Although neither Gobeil nor Ross would situate their conversation as part of a poststructuralist sociology, they nonetheless illustrate some of the fundamental tenets of such an inquiry. Their intervention successfully avoids the theoretical and political difficulties inherent in a formulaic application of poststructuralism, as well as the limitations of an objectivist sociology.

The issues raised by Gobeil and Ross, however, are not magically resolved with the invocation of a category designed to include transgendered people. Research on the practices of intravenous drug users in Montréal provides a concrete illustration of such difficulties.[6] In an attempt to account for transgendered people among the clients of a community-based needle exchange, an administrative form employed three different categories with respect to gender: men, women, and other, the last to include transvestites, transsexuals, and transgendered people. Notwithstanding a well-meaning interest in gathering data on a transsexual and/or transgendered population, the category "other" presents a host of methodological difficulties. First, certain clients of the needle exchange could check the "other" box without being transgendered themselves.[7] Second, the broadness of this category ignores the differences within transsexual and transgendered communities. There is no distinction among transsexuals and transvestites, despite the fact that such a distinction could be potentially significant in a consideration of injection practices, including hormones and steroids, that extend beyond those of "illicit drugs."[8] Moreover, this category does not distinguish between MTF and FTM transgendered people. Finally, this classification does not respect how transgendered people perceive themselves; many MTF transsexuals, for instance, refer to themselves as "women," not as "other," "transgendered," "transsexual," or (in a francophone context) "*les hormonées*" or "*les travelos*." Thus, the third category does not necessarily include the experiences of the agency's transsexual and transgendered clients, since they may have identified themselves as "women" or "men" on their intake forms.[9]

"Other" is clearly insufficient as an interpretative classification that seeks to comprehend the unique experiences of transvestites, transsexuals, and transgenderists. It forecloses a consideration of the diversity of identities, bodies, and experiences among transgendered people, and it does not begin by inquiring how transsexuals locate themselves in the social and institutional world. An appeal to the umbrella category of "transgender" is marked by similar methodological difficulties, as evidenced by the results of a community-based study on violence against lesbians and gay men. The sample population of 368 individuals comprised 181 females, 171 males, and 16 people who did not indicate a sex. The research asked respondents to situate themselves in terms of sex/gender relations: 9 transgendered people identified themselves as female, and 8 referred to themselves as male.[10] While the transgendered respondents can identify themselves both in terms of sex and (trans)gender identity, the relations among these categories are not considered. If we accept the notion that "sex" refers to one's biology (chromosomes, morphology, genitals) and "gender" indicates one's social role (how one interacts and lives in the world), then by extension the transgendered people who are associated with a "female" sex must be individuals who were born and raised as females but have decided to live and identify as men; in other words, FTM transsexuals and transgendered people. It is not clear, however, that FTM transsexuals would identify their sex as "female"; after all, they claim a masculine identity and social role and may have male genitals. Likewise, there is no discussion of the 16 individuals whose sex is "unknown": perhaps the refusal to indicate a sex is one strategy adopted by transgendered people when they fill out administrative forms that require that they sex themselves. Despite an appeal to the term "transgender," this employment of descriptive taxonomy does not consider how these categories are perceived and managed by members of the research population. Given a lack of attention to these issues, the differences within and among transsexual, transvestite, and transgendered identities are ignored. Thus, we do not know if the people who identified themselves as transgendered take hormones and have had genital surgery, if they presently live in their assigned gender with the hope of living in a chosen gender, or if their relation to the category "transgender" in no way involves hormonal or surgical options. Since these issues are significant in terms of

how transgendered people live in the world, as well as how they are perceived and treated therein, they remain relevant for a study on violence
against sexual (and gender) minorities.

From a poststructuralist perspective, what is important to understand
about these categories is how they produce their own objects. In the case
discussed by Gobeil and Ross, the absence of transgendered people within
seropositive statistics prevents the recognition of transgendered people's
specific needs, because the available ways of knowing about HIV/AIDS a
priori exclude transsexual and transgendered bodies. An "other" gender
category, in contrast, allows for a transgendered identification but also denies a simultaneous identification with the gender of "man" or "woman"
while collapsing the different ways of identifying as transgendered and living one's life. A statistical invocation of a "transgender" category does not
resolve these methodological difficulties, since it does not necessarily adequately conceptualize the relations between sex and gender and can in fact
obscure the diverse array of experiences among transgendered people.
From the perspective of a reflexive sociology, all such categories are insufficient because they do not reflect the world as experienced by transgendered people and thus can only offer a limited analysis of the social relations
of gender.

Gobeil and Ross ask some crucial questions about how classification
processes inform a certain account of the social world. Their discussion
points to the legitimation of social relations through knowledge and its designated categories. They continue this analysis in a scathing critique of how
the current clinical, psychological, and sociological studies of transgendered people are preoccupied with gender, to the extent that this paradigm
does not respond to the actual needs of transsexuals.[11] Despite a marked
interest in transgendered phenomena, there remains a dearth of research on
transsexual and transgendered health care, economic conditions, or employment.[12] Gobeil and Ross contend that a preoccupation with gender
identity and gender role remain part of an objectivist framework. They refer
to the issue of HIV/AIDS prevention:

> [Gobeil]: It's hard for existing services to go and do [HIV/AIDS] preven-
> tion, communicate with transsexuals. As I said earlier, it's easier for them
> to ignore people they don't know. . . . For them, we're almost always some
> sort of an attraction. They want to *understand why*. But me, when I go to
> meet a transsexual, I'm not there to understand why she is a transsexual. I
> couldn't care less 'cause I know why she's a transsexual—I am one. Right
> off the top, that eliminates 3/4 of the stupid questions. [*both laugh*] The

*Why?, Since when?, Have you always known?* and *How did your family take it?* We're sick of them and we don't want to be asked those questions anymore. [*both laugh again*]

[Ross]: People have been babbling the same questions for over 20 years. They should know the answers by heart now. Oh and what about: *Are you going to get the operation?*

[Gobeil]: Or *Are you sure you're going to be able to have orgasms like a real woman?* [*both laugh hersterically* (sic)]

[Ross]: Or *Promise me you'll let me see it!* or *I want to be the first one to lick it.* [both are laughing breathlessly]

[Gobeil]: We are so tired of answering those stupid questions.[13]

As Gobeil points out, a preoccupation with gender identity prevents effective communication among transsexuals and social service providers. Within such a context, transsexuals do not receive the same services as men and women. Rather, they are required to justify their choices, describe their genitals, provide an autobiography upon demand, and educate their service providers. This framework locates transgendered people within a social relation that neither accepts nor understands the validity of transsexual bodies.

These political questions about the study of TS/TG people are also of a theoretical order. Gobeil and Ross raise questions about the selection and interpretation of evidence, suggesting that an exclusive focus on gender identity and the aesthetic or physical functions of transsexual genitals are two of the primary ways to make sense of transsexual bodies. A preoccupation with gender identity and the results of surgery, in other words, produces transsexual and transgendered people as an object of inquiry. What is significant about this intervention, from a theoretical perspective, is the recognition that transsexuals and transgendered people are produced not merely through the relations of psychiatry or the medical establishment, but are constructed in the practice of social work.

Gobeil and Ross advocate a reflexive inquiry that is in keeping with a poststructuralist understanding of power. They offer a sophisticated reading of how transsexual and transgendered people are managed in the frameworks of knowledge deployed to study them, and illustrate how the choice of certain theoretical and methodological frameworks determines the selection and interpretation of evidence. In this manner, they elaborate a developed conception of "text" that accounts for how transgendered people are

inscribed in culture. Just as Derrida demonstrates the inscription of subjects in Nambikwara society through the use of the proper name, Gobeil
and Ross cite the location of transgendered and transsexual people through
the deployment of theoretical categories preoccupied with gender. They
show how transsexuals are produced in the social and institutional relations of knowledge. This intervention is in keeping with a poststructuralist
inquiry, since it examines the production of different subject-positions
through the discourse of social work practice.

## Institutional Ethnography

While a poststructuralist emphasis on the textual production of sex and
gender offers useful insights into the social relations of gender, a reflexive
sociological inquiry is still faced with the challenge of understanding how
transsexual and transgendered people situate themselves in the everyday
world. Moreover, a critical sociology must create knowledge that can be
used to improve this world in ways identified as important by transsexuals
and transgendered people themselves. In this regard, a reflexive sociology
needs to consider how to go about collecting, interpreting, and validating
data in a manner that respects the members of the sample population. This
is especially important within the context of studying transsexuality, given
the outright disrespect and contempt of transsexuals within the studies
that limit themselves to the medical and psychiatric production of transsexuality.

English Canadian sociologist Dorothy Smith offers a useful contribution
in this regard.[14] Smith is concerned with both epistemological and methodological questions—questions of how we know the things we know, and
how we research social issues. She argues that traditional sociological methods treat women as objects of study, if they are recognized at all. In contrast,
Smith proposes that we develop ways of knowing and ways of doing research that begin from the perspective of the lived experience of the people
under investigation. In such a framework, women and other marginalized
groups are the *subjects* rather than the objects of knowledge.

One of the concrete strategies Smith proposes for enacting such a research program is what she refers to as an "institutional ethnography." Institutional ethnography draws on standard qualitative research methods,
such as interviews and participant observation, although it need not limit
itself to these techniques of data collection.[15] The goal of this research
strategy is to allow particular subjects to speak about how they understand
their situation. It is the task of the researcher to move from the standpoint

of the subjects under investigation to a conceptual problematic that accounts for how people are related to their everyday worlds, through institutions and relations of ruling. This framework is concerned with the social relations that organize how people live and experience their everyday social worlds.

In her analysis of education, for instance, Smith focuses on the organization of a particular classroom to explain how the experiences of the students and teachers within it are managed through the current educational administration. In this manner, she illustrates the institutional ordering of experience:

> The classroom is embedded in a hierarchy of administrative and political processes. The teacher works within certain definite resource conditions under definite forms of scrutiny from the school administration. . . . The teacher works within budgetary constraints determining the number of children she has in her class, the materials and space available, the specialized skills she can draw on, the time she has for preparation. . . . Such decisions as dividing a reading class into three groups are rule-of-thumb solutions to practical experience of what will best combine the multiple pressures, limitations, standards, supervisory practices of the principal, and classroom resources. In these ways the general policies and budgetary constraints of the administrative hierarchy of the educating state are directly implicated in the classroom work organization.[16]

Smith's work has been particularly influential in English Canadian sociology. Carol-Anne O'Brien, for example, applied institutional ethnography to her interviews of lesbian and gay youth in Toronto, examining their experiences in group and foster homes. She discovered that because many staff members of these institutions regard homosexuality as deviant and pathological, the lesbian and gay youth within them are often isolated and alienated. Furthermore, O'Brien observed an important gender difference with respect to these agencies: while the treatment of lesbians was dominated by an official discourse of silence, the experiences of gay men were shaped through official tolerance of verbal and physical abuse by residents and staff.[17] O'Brien's work thus demonstrates the social relations that underlie how foster and group homes are experienced by lesbian and gay youth. In a different English-Canadian study, Roxana Ng analyzed the documents within a state-funded community-based organization dedicated to promoting employment for immigrant women. Through her textual analysis, Ng shows how the category of immigrant women was actually "produced as a labour market category."[18] While counselors at this agency may have been primarily interested in helping immigrant women procure decent working conditions, the agency depended on the successful placement of women into jobs—any job—to secure its ongoing and future funding. Within this limitation, a comprehensive approach to employment for the individual client often became a secondary priority. Ng explains the circular logic of this situation, which devalues the immigrant women for whom the agency was created:

> The requirements of the employers . . . became integral constituents of the counselling process which the counsellors carried out as a matter of course. In this way, the counsellors' work became part of the coordinated activities of the state in organizing and mediating labour market demands.[19]

Like Smith and O'Brien, Ng's study focuses on the institutional relations that order the experiences of her subjects.

The framework of institutional ethnography has tremendous import in the work of social change. Since this perspective uncovers hidden social relations of everyday life, it has immediate relevance for social policy. Such pertinence is perhaps best illustrated in the work of George Smith. In an investigation of AIDS in Ontario in the late 1980s, Smith discovered that the Ontario Ministry of Health had no treatment infrastructure to serve the needs of seropositive people. Rather, the government's response to the epidemic regarding positive people focused on the delivery of palliative care. An investigation of the social relations that organize health care—the palliative care model—helped direct the energies of AIDS activists:

> First, it [a research program informed by Dorothy Smith's institutional ethnography] identified a major source of the problem of access to new treatments. Second, it raised the question of what other social relations were involved in the management of the epidemic. These discoveries had the effect of focusing the politics of AIDS Action Now! very concretely on the delivery of treatment.[20]

Dorothy Smith's framework is further valuable because it avoids an objectivist sociology, in which people living with AIDS are transformed into a mere object of study within a project on the sociology of health. In contrast, George Smith begins with the everyday experiences of seropositive people and goes on to outline how these experiences are not addressed within the Ontario government's management of the AIDS epidemic. This is a *reflexive* approach to sociology, wherein the experiences, perceptions, and needs of the community under investigation occupy a central component of the research.

Institutional ethnography, then, provides a useful framework for understanding how transsexual and transgendered people situate themselves in the everyday social world. This type of inquiry has much to offer in the development of a reflexive sociology.

Readers familiar with both poststructuralism and institutional ethnography may be curious about an apparent contradiction inherent in my proposed combination of these theoretical approaches. While poststructuralism clearly rejects an appeal to the experience of social agents as a basis for knowledge, institutional ethnography would seem to place a priority upon experience as a foundation for knowledge. Can these different foci be reconciled, or does their combination imply a theoretical and political bankruptcy of my project? A careful explanation of my reading of Dorothy Smith's work will clarify my approach.

Smith's work is often associated with a tradition known as "standpoint feminism," in which the researcher or theorist appeals to the experiences of women as a means to establish the legitimacy and validity of knowledge.[21] Poststructuralists reject this appeal to identity, claiming that categories such as "women" are merely social constructions and do not mean anything in and of themselves.[22] Indeed, some poststructuralists argue that standpoint feminism inevitably retreats into unstated assumptions about who "women" are, and that these definitions reflect the biases of middle-class and white feminists.[23] Within this perspective, a social constructionist approach is best suited to theorizing the differences among women.

Yet we need not necessarily accept the proposition that Smith's work makes an appeal to "experience" associated with standpoint feminism. Her framework of institutional ethnography is interested in uncovering how everyday institutional and administrative practices shape the experiences of women. To be sure, the words and interpretations women give to these experiences are central in terms of making sense of how the world works. But Smith does not propose that we accept uncritically what women say about their worlds as the ultimate truth of their lives. Rather, she wants us to acknowledge the world as women live it, and to offer an explanation about the social and institutional relations that determine this experience. In this light, Smith's framework is not in opposition to a constructionist approach: she begins with the experiences of women as a point of entry into more macrological social relations. This approach is consonant with a poststructuralist emphasis on the productive nature of power. It is also in keeping with the terms of a critical social science, which involves both an ideology critique and the explanation of social changes in view of the real needs of the individuals involved in those changes.[24]

Consider again the analysis of transsexual activists Gobeil and Ross that transsexuals are erased from the work of ASOs through the use of sexed identity categories—"men" and "women"—that exclude pre-operative, non-operative, and post-operative transsexuals. This example illustrates a post-structuralist concern with the textual production of sex and gender. By focusing on the specific classifications and categories of sex, a scholar can observe how both sex and gender are produced. Smith's model of institutional ethnography would arrive at a similar conclusion, though perhaps in a different way. Beginning with the experiences of the transsexuals cited, an institutional ethnography would commence its investigation with the recognition that transsexuals feel themselves to be erased in the institutional world. To explain how this erasure is organized on an administrative level, this research would subsequently turn to the categories that the agencies use to record the genders of their clients. In this way, it would be discovered that ASOs invoke "men" and "women" in the daily work that they do, thus effectively excluding transsexual and transgendered people from their activities. In this manner, institutional ethnography begins its inquiry with a recognition of how members of a research population situate themselves in the world, and it seeks to explain some of the administrative and institutional practices that shape this experience. This approach is not a naive appeal to an untheorized or unproblematized category of "experience." It is, rather, a recognition that theory needs to emerge from the everyday social world and that it must be practically relevant to the people about whom it speaks. As Marie Campbell and Ann Manicom write, this is necessarily a sociological endeavor:

> To begin in the everyday is not to claim the character of "experience" as "real," but rather to trace how everyday life is oriented to relevances beyond the particular setting. . . .

> This commitment to beginning in experience outside regimes of ruling is not the same as the recommendation being made by some feminists to "begin in women's experiences," that treats experience as unmediated and women's somehow more real, more complete than other people's. The intent is *not* to understand "experience" in a way that celebrates "subjectivity" (or claims to get at meanings and intentions of individuals), but rather to understand everyday experience, as George Smith puts it, reflexively. His point is that we need to see how experience is (or is shaped up to be) inextricably bound to regimes of ruling.[25]

50

A reliance on Dorothy Smith's framework of institutional ethnography does not represent a naive reification of individual subjectivity. Instead, this perspective offers a useful way to understand how subjectivity is constituted in the invisible work of institutions. Moreover, this method holds tremendous import regarding social policy and political action, since it helps clarify how and why social actors experience the world as they do.

## THEORIZING ERASURE

*Transexuelle veut donc dire: inapte à l'emploi, inapte à la surveillance de l'usure des camionnettes et du rendement des mandats, inapte à m'asseoir derrière un bureau. . . .*

*Je l'ai cherché mais j'enrage quand même. Je me gargarise de cette rage. L'intelligence et la compétence ont un sexe dans ce pays. . . . Je vais foutre ma vie en l'air. J'abandonne. Fac, famille, soi-disant carrière, cochon, couvée, feuille de paie. Ils me jettent à la rue, j'y resterai. Ils me condamnent à l'inexistence.*
—Maud Marin et Marie-Thérèse Cuny, *Le saut de l'ange*

As I argue in chapters 1 and 2, English-language scholarship on transsexual and transgendered people is severely limited to the extent that it does not account for how these individuals situate themselves in the everyday social world. Critics within queer theory write about the figural representation of transsexuals only to deny their literal referents, while objectivist sociologists focus exclusively on the medical and psychiatric production of transsexuality while ignoring how transsexuality is managed in a wide variety of social institutions. Both queer theory and objectivist sociology share a narrow understanding of how transsexuals live in the world. Importantly, both perspectives share another limitation: by focusing exclusively on the *production* of transsexuality (whether through an examination of culture or the medical establishment), queer theory and mainstream sociology are blind to the *erasure* of transsexuality and transgenderism.

A focus on the cultural and institutional erasure of transsexual and transgendered people constitutes the substance of this book. Whereas both queer theory and objectivist sociology are content to describe the production of transsexuals, it is essential that we understand how transsexual and transgendered people are erased in discourse and institutions. I use the term "erasure" in this book to refer to three mutually supportive social functions.

First, erasure designates a social context in which transsexual and transgendered people are reduced to the merely figural: rhetorical tropes and discursive levers invoked to talk about social relations of gender, nation, or class that preempt the very possibility of transsexual bodies, identities, and lives. This focus on the rhetorical representation of transgendered figures is especially important now, given the explosion of images of MTF transsexual and transgendered people in the media. Reduced to the figural dimensions of discourse, transsexuality as an embodied identity becomes *literally unthinkable*.

I also use "erasure" to explain how transsexual and transgendered people are made invisible. The third part of this book, which focuses on empirical research, provides the strongest evidence in support of this argument. For instance, in chapter 7 I examine how the discriminatory policies of shelters for youth, the homeless, and women do not serve the needs of a street transsexual/transgendered population. Forced to make their own arrangements for housing and shelter, transsexual and transgendered people are located outside an established social service network, made invisible through the existing policies (or lack of policy) with respect to a TS/TG clientele. Furthermore, the cycle repeats itself: because transsexuals do not go to shelters, the staff of these agencies have no familiarity with TS/TG issues and do not recognize the inadequacy of their training concerning the particular needs of this population. In this sense, social policy "erases" TS/TG people from the institutional world.

Finally, and most powerfully, "erasure" can refer specifically to the very act of nullifying transsexuality—a process wherein transsexuality is rendered impossible. As Ross and Gobeil elucidate, the use of "men" and "women" undermines the very possibility of a TS/TG position. Within this site, transsexuals cannot exist at all.

These three meanings of erasure support and sustain one another: the reduction of transsexuals to the figural dimensions of discourse preempts the possibility of transsexuality subjectivity; the exclusion of transsexuals from the institutional world reinforces a conception of that world that presupposes the existence of only nontranssexual men and nontranssexual women; and the act of invalidating the very possibility of transsexuality bolsters rhetorical operations that exclude literal transsexual bodies while reinforcing institutional practices that do not consider the needs of transsexual and transgendered people. In this manner, a reduction of transsexuals to rhetorical figures, institutional procedures that make transsexuals disappear, and the literal annulment of transsexual bodies all constitute a general social relation in which TS/TG people are situated.

This book suggests that erasure is a defining condition of transsexual and transgendered people. Challenging critics in queer theory and objectivist sociology, I believe that academics need to shift their focus radically, investigating some of the unremarkable aspects of transsexual lives in a variety of cultural and institutional sites. Whereas previous scholars contend that medical and psychiatric discourses produce transsexuals, I suggest that transsexual and transgendered people are produced through erasure, and that this erasure is organized at a micrological level, in the invisible functions of discourse and rhetoric, the taken for granted practices of institutions, and the unforeseen consequences of social policy.

The claim that transsexuals are produced through erasure can be substantiated by both theoretical and methodological explanations concerning how this erasure functions. To advance such a theory, a developed conception of "text" is required. In chapter 1, I argue that a limited conception of "text" within queer theory determines the selection and interpretation of evidence for the field, thus undermining the identities and substantive issues of everyday life for transsexuals. Chapter 2, in contrast, shows how social scientists rely on different kinds of texts than critics in queer theory: interviews, field research, and participant observation. Within this area of study, however, an exclusive focus on the textual production of transsexuality in medicine and psychiatry neglects important aspects of everyday life for transsexuals. As in chapter 1, I contend in chapter 2 that a narrow definition of "text" has expansive repercussions regarding the selection and interpretation of evidence.

In chapters 1 and 2 I also ascribe some of the most pressing political problems with the available research on transsexual and transgendered people to theoretical presuppositions of the research paradigms. If queer theory should be rejected because it precludes transsexual and transgendered subjectivity, the appropriate alternative is not an easy appeal to the inherently radical nature of social science inquiry—as if the fact that a social scientist interviews transsexuals necessarily implies that the knowledge produced will be relevant to members of the research population. Rather, scholars are faced with the challenge of explaining how social relations are realized in different texts, as well as justifying which texts to choose for analysis. This focus on the realization of social relations in text is at once poststructuralist and sociological.

In chapter 1, I review Derrida's expanded definition of text, arguing that a poststructuralist concern for the textual production of subject-positions must consider how this construction is organized. By relying on an elaborate definition of "text," Derrida allows for social inquiry that moves beyond an examination of written discourse (indeed, that situates this appeal to writing in terms of its cultural bias). It is important to understand the very complex conception of "text" with which Derrida operates in order to appreciate the subtlety of his philosophical exercise and refrain from a predictable Anglo-American social scientific rejection of the scholarship because of its appeal to discourse.[26] Indeed, this expanded definition of "text" is also present within a sociological tradition, notably within ethnomethodology. Dorothy Smith, for instance, situates texts as crucial sites wherein power is practiced. It is in and through texts that the social relations of gender, of race, and of class are organized:

> The relations of ruling in our kind of society are mediated by texts, by words, numbers, and images on paper, in computers, or on TV and movie screens. Texts are the primary medium (though not the substance) of power. The work of administration, of management, of government is a communicative work. Organizational and political processes are forms of action coordinated textually and getting done in words.[27]

Smith's words recall those of Derrida, whose discussion of taxonomy and the proper name in Nambikwara culture explain the textual coordination of power. In this regard, a poststructuralist interest in the textual organization of society is not incompatible with social inquiry.

A recognition that texts play a central role in the activities of daily life demands careful reflection on how to theorize the relations between text and society. The limitations of both queer theory and objectivist sociology provide valuable warnings of certain dangers involved in this theoretical work. An exclusive focus on the production of subjects through discourse can evacuate the possibility of agency.[28] This raises the immediate question of the relevance of the theoretical framework to members of the research population, and therefore its potential contribution to intervening in the everyday world. At the same time, inadequate attention to how the world is mediated through text and discourse can reify the apparently unmitigated "experience" of social agents, thereby missing a crucial opportunity for making sense of how the world is organized. This book represents one attempt to work through this tension, focusing on the textual organization of cultural and institutional life for transsexual and transgendered people. I show how the erasure of transsexuals and transgendered people functions at a micrological level, through a consideration of different cultural representations, institutional practices, and social policies. Since this book is centrally concerned with text, it is necessary at this point to delineate the kinds of texts I consider in my analysis, as well as some of the theoretical, methodological, and political justifications for my selection of these documents.

## SELECTION OF TEXTS FOR ANALYSIS

Chapters 1 and 2 trace some of the principal limitations of English-language scholarship on transsexual and transgendered people. As a response to research obsessed with identity, I emphasize the quotidian experiences of TS/TG people. This theoretical and methodological move situates my project within a sociology of knowledge, which places priority on investigating the unremarkable aspects of everyday life.[29] While the existing English-language scholarship on transsexuals inevitably returns to questions of identity, I seek to understand how the world is organized for and experienced by transgendered people. This commitment begins with the mundane assumption that TS/TG people exist, that we live—and die—in the world. And it suggests that we merit consideration not because we have decided to live in a gender other than the one to which we were assigned at birth, but simply because we live in the world. To that end, I am not concerned with how transsexual or transgendered people come to identify ourselves as a member of the "opposite" sex, the strategies we adopt to manage a chosen gender, or the aesthetic or physical functions of our genitals. I take it for granted that transsexual and transgendered people exist, and that we shall continue to do so even as the theoretical frameworks that explain our etiology, celebrate our transgression of a sex/gender binary, or condemn us to psychosis go in and out of style.

This political commitment to accepting the existence of transgendered people determines the kinds of research topics I consider worthy of investigation, as well as the substantive issues that are deliberately excluded from this study. If academics accept that transsexual and transgendered people exist, and if scholars do not consider transsexual genitals or gender identities to be incredible, what kinds of questions can be asked? This book offers one attempt to enact this kind of scholarly agenda: a recognition that transsexual and transgendered people are already in the world—not a polemical argument (masked under the guise of theory or research) that debates whether or not transsexual and transgendered people should exist. For these reasons, I am not interested in issues of identity,[30] nor am I concerned with tracing the historical emergence of transgendered people through medicine and psychiatry.[31] As Gobeil and Ross make clear, a preoccupation with how transgendered people come to identify themselves as a member of the "opposite" sex rarely deals with the nitty-gritty realities of transsexual and transgendered people. Similarly, scholarship that examines how transsexuals and transgendered people have been produced in medical and psychiatric discourse does not approach these issues from the perspective of transgendered people. I do not mean to suggest that critical work on identity, or the historical production of transsexuality through medicine and psychiatry, has no intellectual or political value. Rather, I wish to underline how my political commitment to accepting transsexual and transgendered people as ordinary people helps to focus my research program. Thus, rather than asking *what* or *why* questions about transsexuality, I am interested in learning more about how transsexual and transgendered people live in the social, institutional, and cultural world. And, since I remain somewhat of an idealist (a necessary precondition for social change, in my opinion), I hope that this knowledge of transgendered people can be practically applied to make things a little bit easier for us, as we try to negotiate a world that denies us employment, refuses us access to health care, and undermines our self-respect and dignity.

There remains a great danger, of course, in writing a scholarly book on transsexual and transgendered people that does not provide a historical overview of the production of transsexuality within medicine and that deliberately refuses to discuss how transsexual and transgendered people define themselves. Nevertheless, theoretical as well as political reasons justify such a choice. First, insofar as poststructuralism in general and a Derridean approach in particular forces scholars to examine the differences not only between center and margin, but also the differences within these terms, a poststructuralist sociology cannot limit itself to a mere interrogation of how transsexuality is produced, and how transgendered people define and organize themselves in response to this production. A poststructuralist sociology, in other words, must also examine the splits and fissures within networks of transgendered people. The empirical data I provide throughout the book offers such a perspective, illustrating that MTF transsexual prostitutes who transition in their teenage years organize their identities and lives in very different ways from middle-class professional MTF and FTM transsexuals who transition in their thirties and forties. As an intervention, then, this project hopes to raise some important questions about the lack of empirical data on a diversity of transsexual and transgendered people, particularly street transgendered people. The absence of data on a diversity of TS/TG people forces a reconsideration of the existing theoretical frameworks that outline how TS/TG people are produced and that sometimes programmatically delineate an appropriate strategy of resistance.

A second theoretical justification for excluding questions of identity and a genealogy regarding TS/TG people relates to the current interpretation of poststructuralism within the Anglo-American academy. As I discussed earlier, an American reading of poststructuralism frequently limits itself to a mere application of a particular thinker or thinkers. Moreover, Foucault's work in *L'Histoire de la sexualité* figures prominently within American interpretations of poststructuralism, perhaps even more so within the field of queer theory. In this work, Foucault shows both the production of the homosexual and the "reverse discourse" engendered therein. The parallels between transgendered people and lesbians/gays seem obvious: both identities have been generated in medical, psychiatric, and juridical institutions, and these productions simultaneously create the possibility for terms of resistance (e.g., the identities "homosexual," or "transsexual").[32] Yet the theoretical framework of *L'Histoire de la sexualité* may not be the most appropriate one for studying transgendered people. The conversation between Diane Gobeil and Mirha-Soleil Ross forces us to consider these issues more carefully. Recall Gobeil's statement that the classification of seropositive bodies according to sex—male or female—erases the very possibility of transsexual (and transgendered) bodies. Theoretically, Gobeil demonstrates that transsexuality is culturally impossible given sexed knowledge categories and the institutional effacement of transsexual and transgendered people. The development of appropriate political responses to this problem—ways of recognizing and accounting for transsexual bodies—is only possible once we understand how sexed knowledge erases transsexuals from the social and institutional text. This preoccupation with an *erasure* of transsexuality is of a different theoretical order than a concern with its *production*. If institutions manage bodies in a way that precludes the possibility of transsexual and transgendered people, then we need a theoretical framework that makes sense of this erasure. A theory that limits itself to how transsexual and transgendered people are produced is insufficient in this regard, since it can only study the production of transsexuality in sites where transsexuals have a priori been designated as the object of discourse (medicine and psychiatry the two most obvious sites herein). For this reason, we must reject a mere application of Foucault's work in *L'Histoire de la sexualité* to the study of transgendered people.[33] Such a program is politically inappropriate and intellectually underdeveloped, because it cannot account for the actual obliteration of transsexual and transgendered people in the social world. It is important to understand this issue, since it underlines the fact that the study of transgendered people demands its own theoretical and methodological approaches. Simply put, we cannot apply the theoretical models of Anglo-American lesbian and gay scholarship to an investigation of transgendered people and still claim the political relevance of this knowledge for the research population.[34]

Although an application of the ideas outlined in the first volume of Foucault's *L'Histoire de la sexualité* is clearly insufficient to a critical investigation of transgendered people, other elements of Foucault's corpus could prove themselves to be indispensable in the realization of such a project. More specifically, Foucault's work in *L'Archéologie du savoir* offers a theoretical framework that understands the production of subjects without reducing its scope to those same objects.[35] In this text, Foucault contends that we need to make an important distinction between discourse as a practice—an active function in its own right—and the object produced by that practice. In the case of transgendered people, such an approach would examine the workings of discourse practices that inscribe, efface, and order transgendered lives, bodies, and experiences. This offers a different point of departure than a theoretical program that begins with transgendered people as an object of discourse.[36] This is precisely the kind of analysis advanced by Gobeil and Ross: rather than limiting themselves to studying transgendered people as a self-contained unit of analysis, they propose a reflexive inquiry that appreciates the erasure of transsexual people in sexed discourse.

Different chapters of this book represent related attempts to theorize how the everyday world is organized for transsexual and transgendered people. In part 2, which focuses on culture (chapters 4 and 5), I examine how gender is realized at a micrological, linguistic level, seriously considering a poststructuralist concern with the textual production of the social. This demands sophisticated methodological frameworks for theorizing the relations between language and society. To that end, chapter 4 introduces the notion of "discourse" as elaborated in Foucault's *L'Archéologie du savoir,* while chapter 5 advances a specifically sociological theory of metaphor and rhetoric. If queer theory offers a perspective that does not adequately theorize the relations between language and society, an appropriate intellectual response would address this problematic directly. Thus, rather than claiming the importance of sociology over discourse analysis, or the value of empirical data over that of theory, part 2 focuses on how social relations are encoded in culture, as well as the relevance of specific interpretative methods that conceive and explain the relations between society and discourse. Such reflection constitutes an integral aspect of a poststructuralist sociology, demanding that a poststructuralist concern with language and discourse be connected to the social world. Chapters 4 and 5 offer different methodological approaches to theorizing precisely how such a connection functions. This focus on discourse and rhetoric investigates how different sexed and gendered subject-positions are constituted in the cultural world. Discourse and rhetoric form meanings that social actors can subsequently inhabit or reject.[37] The linguistic and rhetorical dimensions of language offer interpretative ways for subjects to situate themselves in the world. By examining the presentation and coding of different sexed and gendered meanings in discourse and rhetoric, we can understand how transsexual and transgendered people are erased in culture.

Part 2 concentrates on the *representation* of transsexual and transgendered people in culture, rather than offering an analysis explicitly concerned with TS/TG individuals as social agents. This focus on representation is in keeping with poststructuralist theory, which appreciates the social construction of the world through language. Yet this inscription of TS/TG figures is closely linked to the actual lives and bodies of people who call themselves transsexual and transgendered. In chapter 4, I illustrate how gendered discourse of punk preempts the possibility of transsexual punk rockers. Chapter 5, in contrast, explores how the negative stereotypes of transsexuals are realized and reinforced through the use of rhetoric in mass culture. The social relations of gender are realized in discourse and rhetoric, and these aspects of language undermine transsexual bodies and lives. Thus, while the cultural focus of part 2 is interested in theorizing the representation of gender, I seek to connect this representation to the very possibility of transsexual and/or transgendered identity. Building on my thesis that transsexuals are produced through erasure, I examine how transsexuality is inscribed as impossible through the use of discourse and rhetoric.

While part 2 investigates the textual production of the social world through a micrological analysis of discourse and rhetoric, part 3 theorizes how the world is organized through case studies of different texts and textual practices. The texts examined for analysis vary, including briefs presented to a government commission, interviews with transsexual and transgendered people, interviews with social service and administrative personnel, and social policies specific to transsexual and transgendered people. Through an appeal to these different texts, as well as a consideration of the settings in which these texts circulate, I examine how transsexual and transgendered people are located in the institutional world. Interviews with TS/TG people offer insight into the daily experiences of this world, while a detailed consideration of social policy (or its lack) explains how this world is ordered. The textual data from interviews, government briefs, and social policy illustrate how transsexual and transgendered people are erased from the institutional world, as well as how they situate themselves outside this world subsequent to this obliteration.

## NATION, LANGUAGE, POLITICS: BEYOND ENGLISH-SPEAKING LESBIAN AND GAY COMMUNITIES IN THE UNITED STATES

This project is clearly interested in asking different questions about transsexual and transgendered people than those posed by most English-speaking academics. One of the ways I propose to do so is by appealing to various texts for analysis. In chapter 1, however, I contend that the choice of text within queer theory should be understood as a function of both the disciplinary and national contexts of the field; that is, that the theory and practice of cultural studies in the United States determines the choice of text for analysis, such that scholars limit their inquiry to media representations of transgendered figures, as well as the odd drag performance in a gay bar. Given this restricted scope, the critical scholar must imagine a different kind of cultural studies, a move that requires an engagement with the cultural studies literature outside of Anglo-American humanities-based disciplines. In a parallel manner, if scholars want to ask different questions about how to study TS/TG people, a sustained reflection on transsexual individuals and communities outside the English-speaking United States is warranted. Such a methodological shift raises several important questions: the unstated presuppositions of English-speaking transgendered discourse in the United States, the relations between transsexual/transgendered identities and communities to those of lesbians and gay men, the organization of these identities that reflect different national contexts, and the constitution of transsexual and transgendered identities and communities through language.

Questions about the selection and interpretation of evidence in a specific national and linguistic context are especially important given the currency—and ambiguity—of the term "transgender" within Anglo-American academic and activist contexts. One of the potential strengths of the term "transgender" is its ability to include a wide variety of individuals who live outside normative sex/gender relations. At the same time, such a catch-all category fails to recognize the differences between transsexuals, cross-dressers, drag queens, FTM transsexuals, and gender atypical lesbians.

While the term "transgender" has entered into public discourse within certain Anglo-American academic and activist contexts, its use is challenged by transsexuals.[38] What does it mean to group the very different identities of FTM transsexuals and heterosexual male cross-dressers? How does this term function to define a specifically *transgendered* social movement? What kinds of issues are overlooked within such a perspective? What important differences within this category are being excluded? Are some bodies rendered invisible within this debate? What are the political implications of using the word "transgender" if, as Teresa de Lauretis argues, the term functions exclusively as a trope of language, unable to designate any referent whatsoever?[39]

In a critical examination of the use of "transgender," Margaret Deirdre O'Hartigan cites *The Advocate*'s Gabriel Rotello:

> I increasingly believe that I am transgendered. What's more, I believe that if you are lesbian or gay or bisexual, you are too. And I believe that an emerging definition of all gay people as transgendered is the wave of the future.[40]

O'Hartigan objects that Rotello effaces the specificity of transsexual difference, notably by making a virtual equation between lesbian, gay, bisexual, and transsexual identities. As O'Hartigan underlines, this position assumes that transsexuals and lesbians, gays, and bisexuals are natural allies, that the advancement of rights and improved social integration for transsexuals will be improved through an alignment with a lesbian and gay political agenda:

> Rotello's absorption of gay and lesbian identity in service to the transgender Borg promises the illusion of allies in a common struggle while in fact inflicting the same fate already suffered by transsexuals: the dominant, heterosexual culture dismisses our individual uniqueness—we become just another part of *them*.[41]

O'Hartigan argues that this discourse actually functions to erase the specificity of transsexual experience. Since this Anglo-American celebration of "transgender" identity functions to make transsexuals disappear, it reinforces a more general social relation in which transsexuality is both unthinkable and impossible.

FTM transsexual writer Max Valerio makes a similar point in an insightful critique of Leslie Feinberg, who argues that transgendered and lesbian/gay communities overlap, and that the interests of both transgendered people and lesbians and gays (as well as people who claim more than one of these identities) would best be served through a coalition of these identities and communities. Valerio protests the exclusively negative representation of FTM transsexuality by pointing out that Feinberg's fictional *Stone Butch Blues* situates the "transgendered" narrator firmly within lesbian-feminist communities. Feinberg's novel leaves little space for the possibility of an affirmative FTM identity: one character who used to live as a stone butch commits suicide after beginning to take hormones. The narrator, who also decided to take hormones and undergo a mastectomy, remains unhappy and eventually rejoins a lesbian community. As Valerio cogently argues, this work speaks more to lesbians than it does to FTM transsexuals:

> With its reliance on many of the stereotypes and cliches which people use in their arguments against transsexual men it undermines the very radical idea of changing sex. . . . Her tale is finally a comforting panacea to all those lesbians who are losing their friends or lovers to the ever growing specter of FTM sex change. . . . [B]ecause of its reliance on these shallow and negative cliches *Stone Butch Blues* is actually a revisionist lesbian feminist fairy tale about sex change. A comfort to those who don't want us to do this, and a highly pitched cautionary tale for all those who might attempt it.[42]

Valerio argues that the information Feinberg presents to her readers has been selected and interpreted according to a lesbian/gay framework. Mirha Soleil-Ross echoes this sentiment in a compelling review of Feinberg's nonfictional *Transgender Warriors*.[43] Ross asserts that Feinberg minimizes the conflicts between MTF transsexuals and lesbian-feminists. Ross finds Feinberg's lack of references to Janice Raymond's *The Transsexual Empire* significant, particularly considering that Feinberg's publisher, Beacon Press, published Raymond's book in 1979.

The interventions of O'Hartigan, Valerio, and Ross are crucial in a critical examination of "transgender" lives, identities, bodies, and politics. They all point out the implicitly lesbian/gay framework of transgender political activity within Anglo-American contexts. Moreover, these writers ask important questions about the use and definition of the term "transgender," inquiring about the extent to which it erases transsexual specificity. It is especially important to cite transsexuals (and transsexuals who refuse to call themselves "transgendered") given that the objections they raise rarely circulate within established lesbian and gay communities. Indeed, within Anglo-American debates on "transgendered" people, it is nearly impossible to hear the voices of individuals who claim *transsexual* rather than transgendered identities. The experiences of transsexuals who are heterosexual are equally absent. What does it mean if the current discussion of transgender identities and sexualities in Anglo-American contexts does not listen to the voices and experiences of FTM transsexuals who love women and MTF queens who are unapologetically heterosexual? What does it mean if we only hear the voices of people who call themselves "transgendered" while ignoring individuals who have changed sex and who call themselves "men" or "women"? Can an emerging Anglo-American transgender politics make sense of these identities on their own terms? Must theory and action on transgender issues always revert back to lesbian-and-gay business as usual? As O'Hartigan, Valerio, and Ross clearly demonstrate, the presentation of transsexual realities within terms intelligible to lesbians and gay men thwarts the complexity of our lives, bodies, and struggles as transsexuals. *In Anglo-America, access to the public sphere for transsexuals is facilitated to the extent that we express ourselves in the language of Anglo-American lesbian and gay theory and politics.*[44]

If critical social science examines the process of how data is collected and interpreted, then an analytic inquiry of transgendered people's everyday lives must consider the presence or absence of particular transgendered people in a sample population. The interventions of O'Hartigan, Valerio, and Ross should caution social scientists to be careful about how information has been gathered as well as the implicit biases in its presentation.

These questions of research methods are particularly pertinent given the increasing institutionalization of queer and transgender studies in American universities. As I argue in chapters 1 and 2, both queer theory and objectivist sociology select certain aspects of transgendered lives for presentation and analysis. Henry Rubin contends that much of the current Anglo-American scholarship only endorses transgendered people who define themselves as queer or align themselves with queer politics.[45] Rubin points out that this bias effectively excludes a diversity of transgendered and transsexual people:

> Queer appropriations and the new movement among some transgenders to resignify themselves in a queer register carry an implicit critique of transsexuals who choose not to queer their identities. These more traditional transsexuals (is that an oxymoron?) choose to "play it straight"—to pass, to assimilate. They refuse the confessional strategy of coming out. Like most of the FTMs in my research, these transsexuals do not conceive of their life projects as gender fucking.[46]

Rubin relates this valorization of queer-identified transsexuals to a process of the institutionalization of knowledge. Since many of his FTM interviewees do not define themselves as queer, he questions the pertinence of transgender studies that embrace lesbian and gay identities and politics:

These transsexuals are made to suffer from another kind of false consciousness within the queer paradigm, where essentialist narratives are assumed to recapitulate gender normativity. As trans scholarship enters the doors of the academy via queer theory, a rift is developing between members of the trans community and this emerging scholarship.[47]

Rubin's intervention signals two methodological and ethical issues: the generation of knowledge that emerges from the life experiences and interpretations of members of a research population, and the relevance of the knowledge created by academics to the individuals studied.

As Rubin, Ross, Valerio, and O'Hartigan demonstrate, the selection and interpretation of evidence are central to the knowledge created about a particular phenomenon. Currently in Anglo-America, transgendered identities are conceived as a function of a lesbian/gay identity politics. This framework does not respect the diverse ways transsexual and transgendered people make sense of themselves. In a recent article, for instance, Judith Halberstam contends that FTM transgendered people need to be queer.[48] Halberstam boldly concludes that "alternative masculinities, ultimately, will fail to change existing gender hierarchies to the extent that they fail to be feminist, antiracist, anti-elitist, and queer."[49] This position illustrates well the problematic described by Henry Rubin, in which scholarship can only endorse queer-identified transsexuals, condemning heterosexual transsexuals to a state of political conservatism. As Rubin eloquently argues, this programmatic position does not respect the identities and lives of heterosexual FTMs, assuming that one cannot be politically progressive and heterosexual, and that transsexuals need lesbian and gay communities to advance their collective situation. Given that Halberstam's argument is centrally concerned with an intersection of "transgender" and "queer" identities, her project reinforces a specifically Anglo-American model of sexual politics, since both "queer" and "transgender" identities are specific to Anglo-American locations. As such, her framework is irrelevant to linguistic and cultural contexts in which the terms "transgender" and "queer" have little or no currency—francophone Québec, for example. Halberstam demands that all FTM transsexuals speak English; a position that bolsters the English-only social policies advocated by the racist right in the United States, and that is linked to a more extensive social relation of U.S. nationalism and imperialism. In the final analysis, Halberstam's vision of "alternative masculinities" is not as alternative as she claims.

Theoretical reflection on transgendered identity is frequently extended into a more general issue of collective action and social movements. As

Halberstam demonstrates, Anglo-American discussions about transsexual and transgendered people habitually assume that we should be politically aligned with lesbian and gay communities, that we should organize ourselves according to their model. This position ignores the "community" work in which transsexuals are already engaged: collecting money to be used for posting bail when transsexual and transvestite prostitutes are arrested; reclaiming the bodies of transsexuals from the city morgue; sharing information about hormones, doctors, and surgeons; showing one another their scars and their bodies; educating one another about police entrapment of prostitutes; providing shelter for transsexuals rejected by friends, family, and social services; offering tips on preparing for surgery; and cleaning and cooking for a friend recovering from an operation.[50] These are among the invisible actions performed by transsexuals to support and sustain one another. Just as Rubin argues that we need to understand transsexual *identities* on their own terms, I suggest that we examine transsexual and transgendered *networks* as they are lived and socially organized. This methodological starting point avoids the somewhat arrogant assumption that transsexuals should model themselves after American lesbian and gay communities. Transsexuals and transgendered people have their own ways of organizing; critical research needs to understand and respect this organization on its own terms.

One severe limitation of current discussions of transgendered people in Anglo-America is the restriction of its sources: the works of Kate Bornstein, Riki Ann Wilchins, and Leslie Feinberg have received prominent distribution within established lesbian/gay activist and especially academic networks; their names are cited again and again in journal articles, conference presentations, workshops, and course reading lists.[51] Moreover, all three writers endorse a political affiliation with transgendered and lesbian/gay communities. From the perspective of a critical social science, the issue at hand is the selection of sources: we ought to be cautious in making claims about transgendered identity and/or a transgendered social movement based on the writings of three individuals.[52] As Henry Rubin points out in his critique of an institutionalization of transgender studies via queer theory in the American university, the knowledge generated within this field is circular, focusing exclusively on queer-identified transgendered people, ignoring all transsexuals outside a lesbian/gay discourse. The fact that most of Rubin's FTM interviewees do not interpret their identities according to a queer framework presents a flagrant disjuncture between identity as it is lived and experienced by members of a research population and identity as it is theorized by academics. The appropriate response to this dilemma is of a social science nature: to question the selection and interpretation of evidence on transgendered people.

A critical reflection of the language in which scholarship is produced can reveal its implicit biases concerning transsexual and transgendered issues. For instance, English-language scholarship for the most part ignores the presence and realities of MTF transsexual prostitutes, preferring instead to focus on questions of identity.[53] Francophone studies on transsexuals and transvestites, in contrast, routinely acknowledge the presence of MTF prostitutes and examine prostitution as it relates to the social integration of transsexuals and transvestites.[54] Research that does not consider studies on transsexuals and transvestites written in languages other than English misses important theoretical and methodological insight concerning the everyday social world for TS/TG people. Attention to different national contexts proves equally useful in a critical examination of contemporary transsexual and transgendered people. Canadian activist Mirha-Soleil Ross articulates an important distinction between Canadian and American transsexual and transgendered people:

> One thing that's interesting about Canada as opposed to the U.S. is that the activism that's very visible and thriving and alive and strong here [in Canada] revolves a lot around access to social services. . . . [A] lot of the organizations and the programmes that are out there right now, and that are very visible, are started by people who come from the street and that's a very big difference from the U.S. . . . [P]ersonally I feel it's resistance to the hegemony of the transgender American discourse. . . . so that's interesting in Canada, it's something to be happy about.[55]

Ross raises crucial questions about national differences in transsexual/transgendered organizing, drawing on examples in both Canadian and U.S. contexts. She does not claim that America lacks programs for transsexuals that focus on access to health care and social services. But she does raise questions about the invisibility of such programs, of the community organizers who work in them, and of the street transsexuals and transgendered people they serve. American transsexuals and transgendered activists who are visible (especially in lesbian/gay and academic contexts) do not focus their energies on the needs of street transsexuals. If the everyday lives of street transsexuals are not mentioned (let alone examined), the visions of community elaborated by American transsexual activists will reflect professional and middle-class biases. The critical social scientist studying TS/TG people must rely on a variety of sources for information. Extensive reflection on national contexts other than the United States offers a useful antidote in this regard, because such inquiry does not take for granted the kinds of questions asked (or not asked) by American transsexual activists and American transgender theorists.[56]

The case of Windi Earthworm illustrates the creation of knowledge and its political applications, particularly with respect to language, nation, and the relations between transsexual and lesbian/gay communities. In Montréal in the late 1970s, Earthworm, a MTF transsexual, applied for a job at a local hospital. Because she believed she was refused employment because of her transsexual status, Earthworm sought to prepare a case with Québec's Human Rights Commission. She asked for a letter of support from the local lesbian, gay, and feminist bookstore collective, Androgyne.[57] Before meeting to consider her request, members of the Androgyne collective were invited to read the French translation of Janice Raymond's *Transsexual Empire: The Making of the She-Male*.[58] At the meeting, the collective contended that MTF transsexuals enact sexual stereotypes of men and women, and that a nonsexist bookstore could not in good conscience write the requested letter of support (although two members of the collective stated their intention to write letters of support as individuals). Androgyne's decision exemplifies the exclusion of MTF transsexuals within organized lesbian and gay communities in a particular time and place (late 1970s Montréal). Perhaps more significantly, it also demonstrates the importance and impact of the knowledge that is created about transsexuals. The appeal to Raymond's work had immediate consequences for the decisions of the collective members and demonstrates the reciprocal relation between knowledge and action: what we know about a particular issue informs how we approach it and act upon it.

It would be possible, of course, to cite Earthworm's case as a demonstration of the hostility of lesbians and gays toward MTF transsexuals. Yet if we consider different contexts and different people, we may not arrive at a similar conclusion. In Guy Simoneau's 1980 documentary film on prostitution in Montréal, *Plusieurs tombent en amour,* a MTF transsexual prostitute is asked if she is accepted by the nontranssexual prostitutes with whom she works.[59] She comments directly that "C'est toute la même chose" [It's all the same thing]. Given the presence of lesbians within Montréal's prostitute communities,[60] this anecdote indicates that not all lesbians are hostile to MTF transsexuals. These different experiences of MTF transsexuals at the same time and place raise crucial questions as to how evidence is selected and interpreted and, in turn, how the discussion of transgendered people is framed and articulated.

The varied relations between MTF transsexuals and lesbians continues in the 1990s, according to which communities of "lesbians" and "MTF transsexuals" one considers. A needs assessment of prostitute women in Montréal conducted in the early 1990s provides evidence that lesbian and nontranssexual women prostitutes accept MTF transsexuals as women. The study reported that MTF transsexuals should be included within any programs and services developed for prostitute women in Montréal, because that was the desire of the prostitutes—transsexual or not—involved in the participatory research.[61] Like the example from *Plusieurs tombent en amour*, this study demonstrates that for many women, the "inclusion" of MTF transsexuals is not a contentious issue: MTF transsexuals are already integrated as women into women's work and social environments.

And yet attention to other networks of nontranssexual women and lesbians yields a different conclusion. Within Anglo-American debates on transgendered people, one of the most frequently discussed issues is the inclusion of MTF transsexuals within lesbian-feminist events. The presence of MTF transsexuals at the Michigan Women's Music Festival (MWMF), for instance, raises fundamental questions regarding who women are, how they are defined, and who is invested with the power and authority to confer the status of womanhood.[62] Increasingly, the example of the MWMF represents a more general inclusion of MTF transsexuals within lesbian and feminist communities.[63]

These examples tell us a great deal about how some self-defined lesbians and feminists accept—or reject—MTF transsexuals. But the discussion surrounding these matters remains incomplete to the extent that it recognizes only certain organized communities of lesbians and feminists. Indeed, while contemporary Anglo-American debates focus on the inclusion of MTF transsexuals within events like the MWMF, they rarely acknowledge the lives and work of MTF transsexual prostitutes, much less begin their inquiry with prostitution as a point of departure. The consequences of this neglect are important. By focusing on an inclusion of MTF transsexuals within lesbian-feminist events like the MWMF, the lives and social spaces of nontranssexual women who do not associate with such events are, de facto, considered to be neither "lesbian" or "feminist." Thus, researchers, theorists, and activists could base their conclusions on incomplete information. Consider the programmatic call for including MTF transsexuals within lesbian and feminist communities. Such a position presupposes that the only communities that count as lesbian and feminist are those that designate themselves as such. Although Anglo-American feminist academics and activists have discussed the issue of prostitution for quite some time, and although many feminists now readily admit that prostitution is not anathema to feminism,[64] this position has yet to be fully integrated into the research and political agendas of self-defined feminists.

If the job of the sociologist is to uncover the workings of the everyday world, then scholars ought to begin their inquiries with a focus on collecting information about how transsexual and transgendered people live. Only after such data has been gathered and interpreted will it be possible to develop a more general perspective on a transgendered social movement. By examining texts relating to transsexual and transgendered people in different national and linguistic locations, we can expose and avoid some of the limitations of Anglo-American theory, research, and politics on transsexual and transgendered people.

## CONCLUSION

Chapters 1 and 2 outline the principal problems in the treatment of transsexual and transgendered people within queer theory and objectivist social science. This chapter suggests an alternative theoretical framework to make adequate sense of everyday life for TS/TG individuals. Drawing on a poststructuralist emphasis on the production of the social, this work seeks to understand how it is that transsexual and transgendered people are produced in the cultural and institutional world. Dorothy Smith's framework of institutional ethnography is invoked as a means to appreciate how transsexual and transgendered people make sense of this world, as well as to explain some of the invisible administrative and institutional functions that shape such experience. Relying on these theoretical influences, it is hoped that the resulting research will shed light on how transsexual and transgendered people are managed in the cultural and social world, as well as some of the concrete strategies that could intervene in these current forms of social organization. While most academic analyses direct their attention to the medical and psychiatric production of transsexuals, I contend that we need to appeal to a much broader range of cultural and institutional texts. To that end, I consider transsexual and transgendered issues in the mass media, in antiviolence activism, in health care and social services, and in the realm of the law, civil status, and jurisprudence. I also consider texts created, disseminated, and interpreted outside the English-speaking United States. This shift in linguistic and national context reveals the implicit biases and assumptions of Anglo-American transgendered theory and politics. The empirical focus of this work allows me to make the theoretical claim that transsexuals are produced through erasure.

The first step in a critical appreciation of how transsexual and trans-gendered people are erased in the cultural and institutional world is a documentation of everyday life. This project represents one attempt at pro-viding such evidence, through a consideration of how this erasure func-tions in culture, institutional practices, and social policy. A commitment to documentation seeks to offer a knowledge of practical relevance to trans-sexual and transgendered people. This documentation challenges and in-tervenes within a general effacement of TS/TG people in the production of knowledge.

# II

## CULTURE

## ↠ 4 ↞

## "A GANG OF TRANNIES"

### Gendered Discourse and Punk Culture

*But inscribing ourselves in culture, making ourselves historical, means more than recovering or acknowledging the previously hidden. It has meant and will continue to mean resisting the notion that oversight or obliteration can be easily corrected—individually, at the level of personal experience. It demands that we rework those traditions, not of our own making, traditions into which we have blundered or stolen.*—Kathleen Perrie Adams

A poststructuralist sociology is concerned with the textual production of the social world. How is this production organized in specific cultural sites, and what kinds of theoretical and methodological frameworks are required to explain these relations?

Taking up Michel Foucault's notion of discourse as elaborated in *L'Archéologie du savoir,* this chapter examines how gender is organized at a micrological, textual level. Focusing on historical and contemporary media representations of punk culture, I show how discourse about punk is thoroughly masculinist and describe the conditions in which this conception of punk culture emerged. This gendered portrayal of punk thus authorizes a social world in which punk excludes transsexual and transgendered people. Statements about punk offer different meanings for social actors to take up or reject: in poststructuralist terms, discourse creates the conditions of possibility for subjectivity. Thus, while my analysis in this chapter concentrates on the discourses of punk rather than on punk rockers as individuals, this emphasis on the semiotic, linguistic, and discursive production of subjectivity has profound implications for the names social actors call themselves, as well as the ways in which they can situate themselves in the everyday world.

I choose punk as an "object" of analysis precisely because of the unlikely associations between MTF transsexual and punk identities. Yet I remain uninterested in a type of historical inquiry that would establish the presence of MTF transsexuals in punk culture. Rather, I examine how the "punk" object emerges in and through discourse and, more specifically, how its conditions of production are gendered as masculinist.

73

## POSTSTRUCTURALIST THEORY AND HISTORY

Contemporary debates in the field of history address methodological questions about how history gets written and interpreted. Current work in anglophone feminist history represents one significant body of thought within this debate.[1] This research has turned to French poststructuralist theory in an effort to understand the historical emergence of the category "woman." A traditional approach to women's history would begin with women as the basis for all empirical and theoretical investigation. Historians working within such a framework, for instance, could inquire as to the position of women within revolutionary France or within the anarchist collectives of Spain in the early twentieth century. A poststructuralist approach to history, however, would challenge this reliance upon "women" as an object upon which to found one's investigation. Since poststructuralism seeks to make sense of the emergence of various "objects" within particular social relations, a feminist poststructuralist history would examine how the category "woman" is produced in different sites—for instance, the media, religious institutions, or psychiatry. Methodologically, the historian can no longer rely uncritically on historical documents such as court records or birth registrations, but must rather explore how the discipline of history itself creates gendered knowledge. According to historian Joan Scott, "Feminist history then becomes not just an attempt to correct or supplement an incomplete record of the past but a way of critically understanding how history operates as a site of the production of gender knowledge."[2] Scott also observes that a poststructuralist approach "demands that the historian question the terms in which any document presents itself and thus how it contributes to constructing the 'reality' of the past."[3]

To state that scholars must examine the language and presentation of their documents is an interesting intervention in the field of historical studies. Yet how, methodologically speaking, does one go about such work? Feminist poststructuralist historians turn to the work of Michel Foucault for inspiration in this regard. In *L'Archéologie du savoir*, Foucault outlines a detailed program for analyzing the emergence of historical, social, and cultural objects. For Foucault, a statement associated with a particular object belongs to a specific discourse, which is in turn a product of a discursive formation—which is to say, the social process that organizes the emergence of statements. An understanding of these three central concepts for Foucault—statement, discourse, and discursive formation—is useful in relating the question of punk culture to gender and sexuality.

In a Foucauldian perspective, a statement makes up an elementary unit of discourse. It is not just a sign (something that represents something else), nor a single unit in and of itself. Rather, a statement is a function that groups together diverse units and illustrates their common properties. These common properties form the "materiality" of the statement:

> [materiality] . . . is constitutive of the statement itself: a statement must have a substance, a support, a place, and a date. And when these requisites change, it too changes identity.[4]

The material aspect of a statement is subject to change according to the conditions of its appearance. This means that a statement does not exist in isolation, for time immemorial. Its materiality gives it life, but at the same time outlines its limits as well as its possibility of reinscription:

> Instead of being something once and for all . . . the statement, as it emerges in its materiality, appears with a status, enters various networks and fields of use, is subjected to transferences or modifications, is integrated into operations and strategies in which its identity is maintained or effaced.[5]

These reflections on the statement lead us to Foucault's concept of discourse. For Foucault, a discourse is a collection of statements, and thus of a higher order than any one statement in itself. Discourse actively organizes the social world, yet it is itself governed by the notion of discursive formation. The idea of a discursive formation, for Foucault, refers to the ordering and dissemination of statements. The methodological challenge for an archaeological analysis is an examination of specific statements in terms of the rules of their appearance and circulation. To summarize, then, Foucault proposes that we consider statements with regard to how they are grouped into specific discourses, as well as the principles of regulation that determine their existence and circulation (a discursive formation). In Foucault's words, the challenge is

> [t]o define these *objects* without reference to the ground, the *foundation of things,* but by relating them to the body of rules that enable them to form as objects of a discourse and thus constitute the conditions of their historical appearance. To write a history of discursive objects that does not plunge them into the common depth of a primal soil, but deploys the nexus of regularities that govern their dispersion.[6]

Rather than a historical approach that does not question the essence of its objects, the scholar considers the linguistic, institutional, and social production of the statements in which these objects emerge. One studies the grouping of specific statements into a discourse, as well as the discursive formation that orders this discourse. This perspective illustrates how discursive formations are realized in particular statements. In this manner, Foucault's archaeological project offers a methodological framework that works at the conjuncture of micrological and macrological social processes.[7]

*L'Archéologie du savoir* also offers a useful framework for making sense of different media representations of punk. Rather than beginning one's historical analysis with an object of study, Foucault suggests that we turn our attention to the emergence of this object, that we make sense of the discursive formation that orders the discourse and groups the statements associated with this object. To state this in less theoretical terms: we want to examine how the identity "punk" gets defined, rather than taking for granted what this term already means.

Consider the representation of punk within the mainstream media of the early 1990s. A community meeting between young punks and neighborhood residents in one small Québec town, for instance, refers repeatedly to violence. An exposé in the tabloid newspaper *Photo Police* presents the meeting with the titles "Violence à Val d'Or" [Violence in Val d'Or], "Punks et skins envahissent les rues" [Punks and skins invade the streets], and "Police vs. punks."[8] In these instances, the theme of violence is immediately associated with punk identity and culture. To invoke Foucault's theoretical framework set out in *L'Archéologie du savoir,* we can observe here the common properties associated with a statement on punk identity. Such statements are marked by particular places (small town Québec), dates (early 1990s), genders (men), and age (youth). Taken together, these elements make up the repeatable materiality of statements on punk identity.

These elements of statements on punk are those most commonly found in the mainstream media. In certain instances, however, media reports present punks in a favorable light, even remarking that the individuals involved in this culture are not aggressive. One Montréal community newspaper describes a cleanup of a local park involving punks and senior citizens as "une rencontre originelle" (a unique meeting).[9] The nonaggressive nature of these punks came as a surprise to some individuals involved, a fact worth reporting:

> L'une des residents avouait à la fin de la journée, que ces jeunes n'étaient pas finalement dangereux et s'était rendue compte qu'ils étaient agréables. [One of the residents admitted at the end of the day that these youths were not really dangerous and realized that they were pleasant.] [10]

While most media representation of punks link them with criminality, racism, and violence, this example suggests that nonviolent punks are atypical examples of the culture. Violence, in other words, defines the repeatable materiality of statements on punk rockers. It is not necessarily that punks are aggressive, it is that the mainstream media presents them in such a manner and thereby defines the terms within which the identity is interpreted. This presentation is what Foucault calls a "discursive formation . . . the principle of dispersion and redistribution . . . of statements."[11] The repeatability of statements on punk identity—achieved in and through an invocation of violence—groups contradictory conceptions of punks into the same location. In the examples above, a discussion of friendly punks who help to clean up a park is situated alongside more "normative" depictions of punks as racist, aggressive, and antisocial. Both of these statements make up a discourse, in the sense outlined by Foucault: "the term discourse can be defined as the group of statements that belong to a single system of formation."[12] It is therefore important to examine the portrayal of nonviolent punk rockers not in terms of an innovative conception of punk identity, but rather as a way in which knowledge is organized in relation to a particular "body of rules" that "form . . . objects of a discourse and thus constitute the conditions of their historical appearance."[13] The issue is not who punk rockers are, but how they are represented.

Foucault's archaeological method contends that when the elements of a statement change, the statement is also modified. The representations of punk culture cited above were marked by particular places, historical periods, genders, and ages. A consideration of statements on punk culture situated in other historical periods and places yields different conclusions regarding punk identity and culture. A close reading of representations of punk within Anglo-American cultural studies literature, as well as the mainstream music press, depicts punk in radically unique ways. Foucault's methodological framework offers a valuable interpretative lens to make sense of these disparate accounts.

## REPRESENTATIONS OF PUNK IN CULTURAL STUDIES

An association between punks and violence in the mainstream media engenders the subculture as masculinist. Relying on this depiction of punk, cultural studies scholars habitually begin their analyses by either limiting their subcultural studies to males,[14] or by articulating the radical interventions of women as well as sexual and gender minorities active in punk communities.[15] In an article on "queer punk," for instance, Matias Viegener contends that the very novelty of queer punk in the 1990s is marked by its appeal to sexual and gender minorities:

Although the original punk movement seemed to have little tolerance for gays and lesbians, its edginess proved ready-made for a new generation of queers. . . . Contemporary gay [American] punk, in distinction to seventies British punk, tends to consider issues of sexual orientation and gender identity—marked especially by its affiliation to drag.[16]

A footnote makes clear the unstated presupposition that punk culture is blatantly intolerant of all differences: "Punk is infamously linked with homophobic, misogynist, and racist associations."[17] If we accept this interpretation of punk, it becomes impossible for us to imagine the existence of MTF transsexual punks. Viegener's claim as to the radical, interventionist nature of contemporary queer punk, specifically because of its connection with gender transgression, assumes that punk culture enforces rigid sex/gender relations.

Clearly, Viegener sets up a historical opposition between queers and punks.[18] Yet this portrayal of punk as misogynist and homophobic is but one take on the culture. Is this how punk is generally understood? What about the experiences of punks who are women, prostitutes, and/or transgendered? Have these questions been addressed within cultural studies of punk? Indeed, how do academics make sense of punk culture? A close reading of this body of literature reveals that cultural studies interpret punk's relation to gender and sexuality in a variety of contradictory ways. The literature indicates three conflicting perspectives on this issue: punk as asexual; punk as sexually fluid; and punk as heterosexist, homophobic, and misogynist. Because all three viewpoints are frequently expressed at different points within a single study, it is useful to examine these divergent characterizations.

In order to interpret punk as an asexual genre, many theorists situate its engagement with signs of sexuality to be an exposure of the excess of pleasure. Larry Grossberg, for instance, contends that in punk

. . . pleasure had become passé. The crescendo of rock and roll rhythms was replaced by the continuous noise, pulses, and droning of punk, suggesting something other than sexual satisfaction . . . the body appears only to be another artificial site on which style is enacted. Punk questioned the naive celebration of pleasure and its significance as a moment of resistance or transcendence.[19]

Jon Savage agrees with this view, claiming "the [punk] body was not something to be celebrated but . . . objectified through fear. Indeed Punk Rock's attitude to the sex act itself was not libertarian but puritan."[20] While Savage quotes Sex Pistols member Sid Vicious to support his argument—"I personally look on myself as one of the most sexless monsters ever"[21]—Jacques Attali cites other famous punks:

> Punks denied that their sexuality had any significance at all—"My love lies limp," boasted Mark Perry of Alternative TV; "What is sex anyway?" asked Johnny Rotten. "Just thirty seconds of squelching noises."[22]

Julie Burchill and Tony Parsons support this argument:

> None of these clothes were either designed or worn to make the customer look alluring; on the contrary, the flagrant fashion in which these clothes used sex as an offensive weapon required a certain asexuality on the part of the wearer. They used sex not to entice but to horrify . . .[23]

If, as these critics declare, punks decorate their bodies with the signs of sex in order to negate sexuality, then punk as a cultural identity necessarily precludes a developed sexual politics. In other words, if we accept this understanding of punk, we cannot imagine the possibility of punks who identified and lived as prostitutes, transsexuals, or sexual minorities.

On a more positive note, subcultural research frequently locates the fluidity of sexualities and genders within punk. Dick Hebdige characterizes sexual kinkiness as a punk signifier and maintains that it represents "a desire not only to erode racial and gender boundaries but also to confuse chronological sequence by mixing up details from different periods":

> overt displays of heterosexual interest were generally regarded with contempt and suspicion . . . and conventional courtship patterns found no place on the floor in dances like the pogo . . . the "couple" were generally of the same sex . . . admittedly there was always a good deal of masculine jostling in front of the stage.[24]

In a similar vein, Mike Brake writes of punk's "ambisexuality uncovering desires we hide even from ourselves."[25] Burchill and Parsons situate punk's confrontational aesthetic as "alluding to anything that would induce immediate outrage in the eye of the beholder—sore points like sadomasochism, fascism, and gender confusion."[26] Greil Marcus, establishing punk as a movement concerned with "taking chances," goes on to note its play with gender: "Males could abjure macho posing or push it to ridiculous extremes; females could ignore the few roles reserved for women in rock—they could ignore roles altogether."[27] Some critics assert that this fluidity of sexual and gender identities in punk allowed women to play visible roles in rock music.[28]

In direct contrast to this open outlook on punk, the literature in cultural studies also habitually faults punk for its fixed gender and sexual stereotypes. In reference to another band, for instance, Burchill and Parsons charge that "[t]he only thing The Stranglers are anti- is women":

> While their contempt for femininity is pushed as merely another facet of their massive masculinity, Wilhelm Reich might analyze it as a pubescent smut/old maid's distaste for the healthy animalism of humanity. A nightmare of reality in which sex, dirt, and vermin are interchangeable.[29]

Marcus, contradicting his earlier declaration that punk endorses gender confusion, asserts that "[t]he shock of punk is no longer in its thuggery, misogyny, racism, homophobia."[30] Through an invocation of a heterosexist metaphor, Marcus calls punk a "breeding ground for fascism."[31] Mike Brake extends this argument in noting the absence of sexual minorities within punk cultures:

> Subcultural studies of youth never mention homosexuals, and this is hardly surprising given the masculinist emphasis of practically all youthful subcultures. Young gay people are swamped by the heterosexist emphasis they find in peer groups and subcultures.[32]

Whereas the previous descriptions portray the punk culture as completely asexual or radically fluid and open, this conception of punk proclaims it to be deeply xenophobic. Within such a discourse, it is not possible to be both a punk and a prostitute, a transsexual, or a member of a sexual minority.

Scholars in cultural studies, then, refer to different places and people in their characterizations of punk. While some academics contend that punk is centrally about gender transgression and non-normative sexualities, others argue that punk epitomizes a deeply conservative culture. These divergent representations constitute distinct statements of the genre. As Foucault elucidates, statements are marked by a substance, a place, and a date. Cultural studies of punk written in the late 1980s and early 1990s are distinguished by statements that appeal to punk as asexual, punk as sexually conservative, and punk as a radical intervention into normative sexualities and sex/gender relations.

## GLAM ROCK

In order to better understand the emergence of punk, it is useful to consider the kinds of mass culture musical genres that preceded it, as well as their relations with gender and sexuality. For example, the phenomenon known as glam rock—popularized by David Bowie, Marc Bolan, and the New York Dolls—endorsed sexual and gender transgressions. A discussion of particular groups and song lyrics will support this claim.

The New York Dolls are one of the bands most associated with glam rock. Julie Burchill and Tony Parsons describe them as "a dead-on-arrival disaster-area outfit . . . who by 1975 had achieved the popularity of acne-blitzed transvestite hookers addicted to heroin." [33] The liner notes on a re-release of their popular songs on the album *Lipstick Killers* confirms this stereotype: "The myth about the New York Dolls was that they were soulless drugged transvestites who couldn't even play their instruments." [34] The lyrics of their songs, however, indicate a continual shifting between polarities of gender and sexuality. In "Personality Crisis," for instance, they sing about the extremes of masculinity and femininity:

> *Personality crisis . . .*
> *Frustration, heartache is what you've got . . .*
> *You're a prima ballerina on a spring afternoon*
> *Changed into the wolfman, you're howling at the moon. . . .*
> *Personality crisis*
> *That's all you've got.* [35]

In a similar manner, Marc Bolan of the group T. Rex shuttles between masculine and feminine identifications in the song "Rip-Off":

> *Rocking in the nude*
> *I'm feeling such a dude*
> *It's a rip-off.*
> *Dancing in the dark*
> *With the tramps in the park*
> *It's a rip-off. . . .*
> *I'm the King of the Highway*
> *I'm the Queen of the Hop*
> *You should see me at the Governor's Ball*
> *Doing the rip-off bop.* [36]

While some performers exploited gender transgressions by underlining the extremes of masculinity and femininity, other glam rock artists exploited gender confusion. The Sweet's song "Blockbuster," which reached number one on the British popular music charts in 1973, contains lyrics that emphasize such ambiguity: "You look in his eyes / Don't be surprised /

If you don't know what's going on behind his disguise."[37] And in T. Rex's song "Solid Gold Easy Action," Marc Bolan makes a transgendered street prostitute the object of his desire:

> I can't get no satisfaction
> All I want is easy action.
> I know it's true
> That she's a dude
> But all I want is easy action . . .
> Stroll on.[38]

As a musical genre, glam rock encouraged the transgression of normative sexual and gender relations. Through the self-presentation of performers (males who wore glitter), as well as the lyrical content of their songs, glam rock was a cultural phenomenon in which transsexuals, prostitutes, and bisexuals would play central roles.[39]

Transgression of rigid sexual and gender positions was an integral aspect of early punk culture. Some subcultural theorists argue that punk's play with gender develops from glam rock.[40] A consideration of the names of punk bands reveals an explicit concern with sexuality: the Sex Pistols, the Buzzcocks, the Vibrators, and Sham 69 are only a few examples of names that denote and connote sexual activities such as masturbation and oral sex. These same sexual connotations are evident in the lyrics, presentations, and subject matter of many early punk performers. Patti Smith, well known for her public appearances in "men's" clothing, sang about a lesbian suicide in "Redondo Beach," as well as the rape of a boy in "Land."[41] The Ramones, in their song "53rd and Third," recount the daily experiences of a New York City male hustler.[42] Siouxie Sioux addresses the song "Christine" to a woman lover.[43] Elsewhere in a cover version of a Beatles song, she comes out of the closet and asks her friend to join her: "Dear Prudence, won't you come out to play?"[44]

Frequently, the lyrics of punk songs do not specify the genders of their protagonists. This is the case in the Buzzcocks' hit single "Orgasm Addict":

> Well you tried it just for once
> Found it all right for kicks
> But now you found out
> That it's a habit that sticks
> And you're an orgasm addict
> Orgasm addict.[45]

A refusal to denote the genders of people referred to in punk songs is further evidenced in the Vibrators' songs "Wrecked on You" and "I Need a Slave Tonight."[46] As Bruce LaBruce and G. B. Jones contend, this play with gender was deliberate within the early days of punk: "Nervous Gender, Catholic Discipline, and the Dicks consciously played out gender-fuck."[47] Members of the Dicks acknowledge in an interview that they do drag to subvert dominant conventions of sexuality and gender. They also perform various types of drag in order to question its containment as a performance:

> Once, word went around that Gary was gonna dress up in drag. So the three of us came out in drag, and Gary came out as a construction worker. He said the rest of the band got killed in a car accident and he got this all-girl band to back him up.[48]

The experiences of Jayne County, a male-to-female transgendered person active in New York's early punk scene, provide further evidence that punk communities of this epoch were accepting of sexual and gender difference.[49] During one of her shows, she was heckled by a member of the audience, who called her a "queer." When County responded with insults of her own, the man approached the stage with the apparent intention to assault her. She subsequently hit him over the head with her microphone stand and proceeded to attack him with her fists. County was thrown in jail, and upon her release, the club where this incident took place, Max's Kansas City (one of the most infamous venues for New York punk), organized a benefit to cover her legal costs. In her telling of the events, the support for County is clear. She cites the involvement of some of the most prominent members of New York's punk scene at the time:

> Meanwhile, Max's organised a benefit to cover my legal costs. A hall was hired uptown, and we got some great bands to perform: Blondie, Robert Gordon, the Ramones . . . Divine, Jackie Curtis, Holly Woodlawn, the New York Dolls, Mink de Ville, Talking Heads and Richard Hell. . . . We had an auction: we sold an outfit that had belonged to Iggy Pop, a pair of David Bowie's platform boots from the Marquee special, a signed poster from Lou Reed, some stuff from Andy Warhol. It went on for hours. For the finale, I came out to thank everyone wearing a black-and-white striped convict's outfit, and I sang "Jailhouse Rock" and "The Last Time."[50]

A disregard of gender norms and sexual conservatism in early punk was not reserved to punk performers. Some empirical research and interviews, especially those recounted by Jon Savage in *England's Dreaming,* illustrate that punk emerged from the communities of the sexually disenfranchised:

> "People think that the early days of Punk were all banging along at The Sex Pistols gigs," says Debbie Wilson. "But for me it was camping it up down Park Lane with a gang of trannies. All my friends, John, Blanche, Tracey, Berlin, were on the game. Linda of course was on the whipping sessions. It was all in Park Lane: it was the most outrageous place in the world. All these queens going around in Punk gear and black leather, going 'Ooooooh!' They actually became quite famous down there: it got to the stage where prostitution wasn't that bad a thing to do. It became part of the new London."[51]

Clearly prostitutes and transgendered people were active members of early punk communities. The social spaces of prostitutes, transsexuals, and sexual minorities played an equally important role in offering a place for punks to gather. Consider how Siouxie Sioux of Siouxie and the Banshees describes Louise's, the London bar that she introduced to many punks (including the Sex Pistols) in 1976:

> "Before it got a label it was a club for misfits . . . [w]aifs, male gays, female gays, bisexuals, non-sexuals, everything. No one was criticized for their sexual preferences. The only thing that was looked down on was suburbia."[52]

New York's punk world, like that of London, had spaces defined and inhabited by sexual and gender minorities—transsexuals, drag queens, bisexuals, gay men, and lesbians. For instance, the Club 82, a drag queen/transsexual bar, was one of the few public spaces in 1973 and 1974 where punks could present their shows.[53] According to rock photographer Bob Gruen,

> Since the Club 82 had had this outcast image for so long, the punks and the early glitter kids were treated very openly by the management. They didn't think they were weird and didn't try to cash in on 'em—they'd been dealing with weirdos for forty years! So when bands started going there they brought the young rock & roll crowd.[54]

But the Club 82 was not the only public space to welcome punks in 1970s New York City. In 1975, punk groups also played at Mother's, a gay bar situated on Twenty-third Avenue.[55]

Punk communities outside urban centers like London, England, and

New York City also included MTF transsexuals. Margaret Deirdre O'Hartigan reports that in the midwestern United States, for example, the performer Skafish sang "Am I a girl, am I a boy?" This person, male at birth, had visible breasts, sang in a masculine voice, wore dresses and tube tops, and sported either masculine or feminine hairstyles.[56] Her participation in the 1970s punk milieu testifies to the presence and implication of MTF transsexuals in punk.

Non-normative sexualities and genders constituted an integral aspect of punk style and culture during their initial formation. If early punk culture encouraged the transgression of normative sexualities and sex/gender relations, if prostitutes and transsexuals were integral parts of punk networks, why do researchers in cultural studies refer to punk as a violent, masculinist world? If punk emerged in part from the communities of the sexually disenfranchised, as the data presented here suggests, why is that identity associated with violence and hypermasculinity today? When was this correlation between punk culture and violence established? In more theoretical terms, how are statements on punk identity produced, and how do they circulate?

## The Sex Pistols, Masculinity, and the Media

Throughout 1976 and 1977, the punk movement was the subject of numerous articles in the mainstream media. Yet this reportage did not speak about prostitutes, sexual minorities, or any "gang of trannies" to which Debbie Wilson refers. Media coverage of punk culture, rather, focused on the Sex Pistols. The British band's creator and manager, Malcolm McLaren, played a crucial role in helping to make the Sex Pistols synonymous with punk rock.[57] As the manager of the clothing shop "Sex" around which the London punk scene developed, McLaren was influential in defining the punk aesthetic.[58]

The Sex Pistols were formed in the summer of 1975 and first performed publicly in November of that year. In February 1976, they received their first review in *New Musical Express*, after playing at the Marquee Club— from which they were subsequently banned. Fear of violence, calls for censorship, and more media reports followed the Sex Pistols everywhere they went. In April 1976, they were barred from the Nashville; in July, from the Rock Garden Club and the French punk rock festival. In December, their appearance on Bill Grundy's *Today* show sparked off a well-organized anti-punk backlash. On the program, Sex Pistol member Steve Jones and the host had the following interchange:

Steve: You dirty sod. You dirty old man.

Grundy: Well keep going chief, keep going. Go on, you've got another ten seconds. Say something outrageous.

Steve: You dirty bastard.

Grundy: Go on, again.

Steve: You dirty fucker!

Grundy: *What* a clever boy!

Steve: You fucking rotter.[59]

In the days, weeks, and months that followed this interview, the Sex Pistols were the bad boys of rock and roll. Although they signed record contracts with EMI (January 1977) as well as A&M (March 1977), both companies broke the agreements in exchange for financial compensation. By August 1978, newspaper articles documenting violence at punk shows were widespread, and the Sex Pistols toured England under the pseudonym SPOTS [Sex Pistols On Tour]. As Steve Jones remarks, everything changed after the *Today* show interview: "Before then, it was just music; the next day, it was the media."[60]

Transgression of normative sexualities and sex/gender relations were integral aspects of punk culture in its early days, during 1974 and 1975. As early as 1977, however, the media focused on violence: at punk shows as well as in the streets. In *The Rolling Stone,* for instance, there are fifty-three references to punk culture (features, reviews, and opinion letters) between October 1974 and October 1980. Eighteen of these (or 34 percent) concern the Sex Pistols. Excluding record reviews, 51 percent of the articles on punk deal with the career of the Sex Pistols. The mainstream media ignored the experiences and contributions of women, transsexuals, and prostitutes within punk cultures. Violence became the lens through which all representations of punk were filtered.

After 1977, most self-identified punks accepted the presentation of the culture within the mainstream media. Punk became a homophobic, masculinist, and sexist culture.[61] This reification of punk is evidenced at the level of semantics: toward the end of the 1970s, the term "punk" was replaced with the word "hardcore." In December 1977, for instance, the Dead Boys use the word "hardcore" to signal their masculine position:

The nuns turn you into a wimp, totally dominated by your mother or your wife. Or you can become so hardcore that you can survive like us.[62]

This use of the term "hardcore" suggests that a man can only resist being dominated by a woman by adopting a tough, hypermasculine stance.

As punk moved into the early 1980s, its aesthetic changed. Downplaying any sexualized signs, punk rockers began to dress in a more "basic" look of jeans, a band T-shirt, and army boots.[63] Concurrently, punk music evolved into what is now known as "hardcore"—a music characterized by an aggressive, fast beat with often indiscernible lyrics.[64] Dance styles changed, too. No longer doing the pogo—dancing up and down in one spot—hardcore punks slam dance by colliding violently with one another.

The adoption of a masculinist position within punk created a culture in which women and MTF transgendered people were no longer welcome. On the dance floor as well as on the stage, men defined the meanings of punk style and music. As G. B. Jones and Bruce LaBruce argue, this emphasis on masculinity excluded women and nonmasculine males:

> In this highly masculinized world, the focus is doubly male, the boys on stage controlling the "meaning" of the event (the style of music, the political message, etc.) and the boys in the pit determining the extent of the exchange between audience and performer. And where does this leave the rest? "Wimpy" boys, with glasses, maybe, who can't compete, or girls who aren't exactly encouraged to participate? Their only option is to become a mere adjunct to the "scene." Unless, of course, they're willing to take a stand against "all that macho crap."[65]

The experiences of women and nonmasculine males in punk testify that slam dancing may be a covert way for macho punks to beat up on others perceived to be less strong. Such a gendered conception of punk can make it extremely difficult for women and/or male-to-female transgendered people to identify with this culture. Jeremy, the editor of the fanzine *High School Fag*, recounts being threatened by physical violence for wearing "women's" clothes within a punk scene:

> Last March I went to my third Fugazi show wearing fishnets under my shorts and almost got murdered by about half the crowd. Which really sucked. I still go to hardcore shows, I guess I'm addicted or something, but I'm growing increasingly alienated from it all.[66]

Since punk and hardcore cultures are gendered as masculine, women and nonmasculine males who circulate within these social spaces need to consider the extent to which they are not part of this community, at least insofar as it is conventionally understood.

## THE TRANSFORMATION OF DISCOURSE

The representations of punk cited here embody radically different conceptions of the genre. Individuals who lived and identified as punks in the mid-
1970s maintain that punk emerged, in part, from the communities of the
sexually marginalized. Statements about punk identity prior to 1976 are
marked by a "substance"[67] of nonheterosexuality in which transsexuals,
transgendered people, and prostitutes figure prominently. Together, these
statements constitute a discourse that emphasizes punk's sexual and gender
ambiguities—for example, Hebdige's comment that the symbols of punk
signify "sexual kinkiness"[68] or Mike Brake's remark that punk advocates an
"ambisexuality uncovering desires we hide even from ourselves."[69] These
common themes of gender confusion or fluid sexualities are grouped together within a specific body of knowledge that we can characterize as the
cultural studies literature.[70] At the same time, a significant conception of
punk associates it with violence and masculinity, as evidenced by 1990s
Québécois media and cultural studies accounts of punk. Within these depictions, punk is a culture created by and for masculinist, heterosexual
young men.

Many explanations of punk culture are contradictory. Critics such as
Viegener maintain that punk has always been misogynist and masculinist,[71]
while theorists such as Dick Hebdige contend that punk is open to sexual
and gender dissidence.[72] Still other researchers offer conflicting interpretations of the genre, claiming within the same study that punk is asexual and
sexually conservative.[73] These discrepant explanations of punk's relation to
gender and sexuality are further complicated by empirical data. The experience of Jayne County illustrates well such a paradox: although County
was verbally and physically assaulted due to her perceived gender difference, a large community of punk musicians organized to help in her
defense.

Accounts of punk differ according to the specific time period discussed.
To be more specific: the emergence of punk in the mid-1970s drew on a
tradition of glam rock, with its transgression of normative sexualities and
sex/gender relations. Following the controversy surrounding the Sex Pistols
in 1977, however, representations of punk in the mainstream media ignore
the participation of women and MTF transgendered people within the culture, and associate punk with both masculinity and violence. This gendered
conception of punk was subsequently taken up by punk rockers themselves, such that the early 1980s witnessed a further consolidation of masculinist positions within punk communities. The mainstream media of the

1990s habitually relies upon, and reinforces, this gendered portrayal of punk rock culture.

Poststructuralist theory is valuable here, because it offers a methodological framework to discern inconsistent representations of punk identity and culture. An archaeological investigation of this problematic would offer more than a mere citation of different statements on the genre. The critical theorist needs to situate the place, content, and date of statements on punk with respect to gender and sexuality. Theoretically, an attention to the production of a punk object is necessary so that we can better appreciate the function of discourse and its role in maintaining and reproducing social relations.

The mainstream media's representation of the Sex Pistols offers perhaps the most clear illustration of the theoretical and methodological issues discussed here. By limiting discussions of punk to the Sex Pistols and focusing on the violence perpetrated by young men at punk concerts, the mainstream media established violence and masculinity as crucial elements of statements on punk. Indeed, the relative absence of any statement on female, transgendered, or prostitute punks after 1977 demonstrates that gender regulates punk discourse, that it is in and through masculinist gender that a punk "object" is produced. Ironically, the discursive production of this object was ignored by many male punks after 1977. They eagerly adopted the masculinist conceptions of punk identity and culture and repeated the discourse on punk so prevalent in the mainstream media following the Sex Pistols—that punk was a movement of tough rebel boys.[74]

These events elucidate Foucault's articulation of the statement, describing it as endowed with a "repeatable materiality" and marked by "a substance, a support, a place, and a date." The transformation witnessed in punk discourse after 1977 provides ample evidence that when the elements that constitute a statement's materiality change, the statement is itself altered. The mainstream media's designation of gendered punk objects, for instance, grouped particular statements about punk identity into the same discourse. This function radically transformed the available statements on punk, such that the object "punks" could no longer designate women, transsexuals, or prostitutes. The identity of statements on punk was thus redefined and brought inside new "networks and fields of use."[75] Within such discourse processes, it is no longer possible to even imagine the "gang of trannies" discussed by Debbie Wilson in her characterization of early punk spaces.

Foucault's methodological framework is valuable in making sense of dissimilar representations of punk. By locating the grouping of statements into a discourse, as well as the principles that determine when and where such a discourse is to appear, Foucault's model offers a way to understand how and why different conceptions of punk emerge in distinct institutional sites (e.g., academic cultural studies, the mainstream media). Moreover, Foucault's archaeological method provides a means to appreciate the process of historical transformation as it is realized in discourse. The coding of punk as masculinist, achieved through an appeal to the representation of the Sex Pistols in the mainstream and the music media, defined punk culture and style as a thoroughly masculinist genre. In this manner, the theoretical issue at hand requires that the scholar do more than mention different characterizations of the punk genre. Critical inquiry demands a framework to make sense of how different conceptions of punk emerge and circulate. While a discussion of the presence of MTF transsexuals and prostitutes in punk is valuable, a more complex analysis would examine how the representations of punk altered to exclude these individuals from the terms of punk identity and culture. The topic for investigation is neither a notation of different ideas about punk nor even a claim that different historical periods had distinct understandings of the culture. The problematic to be explored centers around how these specific representations of punk changed historically, as well as how this change was realized at a micrological level of discourse. By contemplating the gendering of punk in the mainstream media, this chapter illustrates the central role played by discourse in the work of historical transformation.

## CONCLUSION

The analysis I have offered here seeks to uncover the emergence of statements on punk identity, and to further elucidate the discursive regulations that govern their appearance and circulation. This perspective offers some useful insights regarding theory, method, and politics: how people make sense of meanings in the social world, how subjects may internalize them, and the kinds of interventionist strategies that may be developed.[76]

While Viegener would situate the transgendered people currently involved in 1990s punk as representing a definitive break from punk's masculinist history, an archival analysis does not offer such an easy narrative of origin and progress. Poststructuralist theory requires that we examine how specific objects come into being, rather than limiting ourselves to merely citing their existence. It is a gendered discursive formation of punk that enables some individuals to disrupt its normative sexualities and genders. What is required, then, is not the bold statement that contemporary queer-punks are more hip than the old-school punk boys. Nor is it sufficient to make the political argument that transgendered people were present in punk communities all along. What is necessary, from the perspective of a poststructuralist sociology, is an archival investigation of how punk identity secures its value in discourse.

Foucault's notion of discursive formation is especially useful because it examines how evidence is both collected and interpreted. As outlined in this chapter, contemporary cultural studies of punk invariably read it through the mainstream and/or music press. Indeed, one wonders if punk would have received so much attention within cultural studies were it not for the controversy surrounding the Sex Pistols. Yet if we accept the analysis offered in this chapter, then we admit that the very object "punk" has emerged within a gendered discourse and that it is governed by gendered rules of its circulation and dispersion. If this thesis on the emergence of the object "punk" is valid, then a cultural studies analysis that does not account for the function of this discourse process becomes part of the same gendered discursive formation that produces the object "punk" and that delineates the fields in which it shall appear. Theoretically, this insight suggests that we need to develop a kind of cultural studies that is part of the broader project of social theory. We require an intellectual practice, in other words, that is reflexive enough to acknowledge the role that "theory" can play in constituting its object of study and that goes further to rearticulate the relations between knowledge and its designated object. Methodologically, if we appreciate that punk emerged within a gendered discourse, and that statements on punk identity are governed through gendered discursive formations, we must question our methods of data collection concerning this phenomenon. Such information is perhaps only accessible through empirical research that understands and attempts to critically distance itself from the enunciative function of discourse on punk. What this means practically is that in order to understand how punks conceived their relations to gender and subculture in the 1970s, a researcher cannot rely on the mainstream music press. Since most punk culture has not been preserved in government or community archives, such an undertaking is a formidable endeavor that requires methodological approaches such as oral history.

Foucault underlines that subjects are brought into being through discursive formations, themselves realized in discourse. This insight allows us to appreciate the value of discourse analysis in critical work on identity and agency. Poststructuralism maintains that scholars must not take the meanings of specific identities for granted, but rather need to analyze the macrological social relations that determine their value, order their circulation, and authorize their repetition. In this way, sociologists can draw on poststructuralist theory for insight into how different identities have emerged; information that may not be readily apparent in collecting data with members of a research population who claim a particular identity. The notion of discursive formation is useful *theoretically* because it forces a consideration of how "theory" constructs its object. The concept is also useful in *empirical investigation,* because it can illustrate the contribution of particular research methods—e.g., interviews or oral history—in gathering information and creating knowledge with respect to a research problematic.

Foucault's ideas in *L'Archéologie du savoir* provide a concrete framework for understanding how discourse comes to life and how history is written. Foucault's framework is useful because it allows us to understand precisely how statements on punk identity are grouped into a gendered discourse, and therefore how transgendered people are written out of culture. An appreciation of how discourse is gendered is more politically useful than a mere appeal to the presence of transsexual and transgendered people in the early days of punk. While certainly politically engaging, a claim that transsexual and transgendered people were present in early punk does not explain how this history was not merely forgotten but was fundamentally rewritten.

The erasure of transsexual and transgendered people in culture needs to be understood as a function of discourse processes. The regulation, distribution, and circulation of statements on punk identity determine the appearance and repetition of meanings related to the genre. The provision and coding of these meanings in turn provide the possibility for different subject-positions to be taken up. As such, an inscription of the masculinist nature of punk culture voids an MTF transsexual punk identity. It is in and through the micrological work of discourse that transsexuality is rendered impossible. To the extent that Foucault's archaeological method provides a framework to explain how these discourse processes function, it offers a valuable contribution to a poststructuralist sociology. A considered reflection on the invisible workings of discourse yields an engaging investigation of the erasure of transsexuals in the everyday cultural world.

# 5

## GENDERED NATIONALISMS

## AND NATIONALIZED GENDERS

### *The Use of Metaphor in Mass Culture and U.S. Transsexual Activism*

*This world of nations has certainly been made by men, and its guise must therefore be found within the modifications of our own human mind. And history cannot be more certain that when he who creates the things also describes them.*—Giambattista Vico

A poststructuralist sociology concerned with both the production and erasure of different subject-positions must consider how this construction functions at a textual level. Chapter 4 introduced the concept of discourse as a methodological tool to make sense of how transsexual and transgendered people are erased in culture, demonstrating how the invisible workings of masculinist discourse on punk precludes the possibility of MTF transsexual punks. In this manner, the theoretical notion of discourse explains how the obliteration of TS/TG people is textually organized. The concept of rhetoric—the study of how meanings are figuratively extended, transformed, and modified—brings to light different ways in which transsexuality is undermined in culture. While chapter 4 examined the effacement of transsexuals in gendered discourse, this chapter investigates how the figural representation of transgendered people prevents the actualization of TS/TG bodies. Given the explosion of images of MTF transsexuals in the media in recent years, a focus on this contradiction is valuable. Rhetoric illustrates how transsexuals are textually inscribed as *purely figural*—that is, *literally impossible*.

This chapter limits itself to the rhetorical concept of metaphor. As Mariana Valverde argues, rhetorical studies can offer some useful insights into the production of subjects and social relations.[1] She maintains that social scientists can learn a great deal from scholarship in the humanities:

> Discourse that aims at persuading an audience and generating social action is often structured not so much through formal logic but through tropes, most notably metaphors but including the whole range of techniques taught by the ancients. The literary critic Patricia Parker has argued that

classical rhetoric in fact organizes social relations of class and gender power through the apparently innocuous organization of tropes. This insight is very relevant to political sociologists and observers of social movements, who often ignore the rhetorical techniques used by their "subjects" while in hot pursuit of the material base underneath the discourse.[2]

As Valverde points out, however, most rhetorical studies limit themselves to literary texts, thereby presenting a methodological challenge for the social scientist interested in the rhetorical organization of social life.[3]

Many sociologists maintain that the metaphors we use do more than merely describe the social world; they actively create it. For instance, Lakoff and Johnson claim that metaphors of war employed with respect to verbal arguments and discussions frame our understandings of these processes.[4] Thus, if a man who presented a paper at a conference states that he was "attacked" by a member of the audience, the war metaphor both describes and constructs the event in question: wherein the public presentation of one's ideas requires a *defense* from an anticipated *assault*. Further, the use of metaphor provides a means to understand social and political issues. In Weber's work on governments and bureaucracy, for instance, he establishes a metaphorical connection between government and machines based on the common ground shared by productive industry and bureaucratic forms of administration.[5] As Grant Jordan summarizes, this particular metaphor organizes sociological inquiry in the field of government administration:

> In the machine version, organisations exist to implement goals established by political or other leaders. The organisation is the means to attain specific goals. The fact that the comparison between organisations and machines has some appropriateness (they both seek to operate with reliability, responding to controls, etc.) has encouraged other comparisons that might be less legitimate (organisations can therefore be consciously redesigned, they can be made more efficient by planned change, etc.).[6]

These examples provide a thoroughly social understanding of metaphor, one that appreciates how the everyday world and social relations are constituted through rhetoric.[7] Within such a perspective, metaphor cannot be reduced to a figure of speech; it is a figure of thought.

This chapter theorizes the metaphorical connections established between transgendered people and nation. As numerous scholars have pointed out, however, the study of rhetoric should not limit itself to the function of metaphor; it is but one trope within a very large field of inquiry. Indeed, classical rhetoric advocates the examination of a diverse range of functions:

*elocutio* (the choice of words in a phrase, stylistic figures), *inventio* (arguments, subjects, themes), *dispositio* (syntagmatic organization of the language), *pronuntiato* (narration, discussion), and *memoria* (memorization).[8] Although rhetorical studies in recent years have often limited themselves to the field of *elocutio* (figures of style), with metaphor occupying a central place therein,[9] my decision to consider the metaphorical connections between transgendered people and nation does not imply that metaphor ought to be privileged by sociologists in the rhetorical studies they offer. It merely delineates the terms of reference of this chapter.

If, as Valverde suggests, sociologists and historians can offer new fields of application and analysis for rhetorical studies, we can also learn from the methods of established rhetorical analysis. While we need not accept the premise that rhetoric is limited to the domain of literary studies, we ought to reflect carefully on how this inquiry is actually practiced. Otherwise we run the risk of claiming that we engage in rhetorical analysis simply by referring to particular key words such as "rhetoric," "metaphor," "tropes," and "figures," without adequately understanding either the specificity of each term or how to articulate a theory of these concepts. The point is not merely to claim that social relations are constituted through rhetorical operations, although this is a useful starting point. An engaged academic inquiry must demonstrate how these rhetorical operations are textually organized, a challenge that requires an examination of different methods of rhetorical analysis.

## METAPHOR: SUBSTITUTION, COMPARISON, INTERACTION

Given the central place occupied by the trope of metaphor within the field of rhetorical studies, there is a vast literature on different theories and applications of metaphor. For the purposes of this chapter, however, I will limit my analysis to the framework advanced by the philosopher Max Black.[10] Black argues that there are essentially three perspectives on the nature and function of metaphor: that it involves a substitution of one subject for another, that it compares two subjects, or that it engages interactive relations between two subjects.

In the substitution view of metaphor, a metaphor is used as a substitute for a literal expression:

> This account treats the metaphorical expression (let us call it "*M*") as a
> substitute for some other literal expression ("*L*," say) which would have
> expressed the same meaning, had it been used instead. On this view, the

metaphorical meaning of *M,* in its metaphorical occurrence, is just the *literal* meaning of *L.*[11]

While a substitution view of metaphor implies a literal substitution of one term for another, a comparison view holds that metaphor transforms the literal meaning of a term. This transformation suggests an analogy or a similarity between two terms.[12] Within such a perspective, one term cannot be substituted for another; the comparison between the terms allows for a connection between two subjects based on analogy or similarity, but it does not admit the equation of the literal meanings designated by these subjects. The statement that "Government departments run as quickly and as smoothly as molasses in January," for instance, implies a comparison between "governments" and "molasses in January," in which an underlying analogy is established wherein both subjects are congealed, constricted, and ineffective. Through this analogy, readers grasp the intended meaning of the statement: that government departments function slowly and are highly inefficient. A comparison view of metaphor posits that the phrase "molasses in January" cannot be substituted for the collocation "government department." It is the analogy established between these terms that allows for their comparison.

Black rejects both the substitution and comparison views of metaphor. With regard to a theory of substitution, he remarks on the inadequacy of a theory of rhetoric that is premised upon literal meanings: "Metaphor plugs the gaps in the literal vocabulary (or, at least, supplies the want of convenient abbreviations)."[13] The notion of catachresis, which involves the deliberate misuse of a term for which no literal referent exists, illustrates the limitations of the substitution theory of metaphor.[14] Examples of catachresis used in everyday language include the leg of a table, a head of cabbage, or the wings of an airplane. In these three instances, a term is deliberately used to designate some other object: tables do not really have legs, nor do airplanes have wings, nor do cabbages grow in heads. These terms, however, are used to designate these objects as a form of shorthand: they offer a way to make sense of them. Black points out that catachresis (1) invests old words with new meanings and (2) is most successful as a rhetorical operation when it disappears. If we accept the presence of catachresis in language (it would be difficult to deny), then we must reconsider a theory of metaphor based on substitution. It is insufficient because it presupposes a referential conception of language use, that language designates literal meanings and referents.

Black rejects a comparison view of metaphor because of its vagueness:

We are supposed to be puzzled as to how some expression (*M*), used meta-phorically, can function in place of some literal expression (*L*) that is held to be an approximate synonym; and the answer is that what *M* stands for (in its literal use) is *similar* to what *L* stands for. But how informative is this? There is some temptation to think of similarities as "objectively given," so that a question of the form "Is *A* like *B* in respect of *P*?" has a definite and predetermined answer. If this were so, similes might be governed by rules as strict as those controlling the statements of physics. But likeness always admits of degrees, so that a truly "objective" question would need to take some such form as "Is *A* more like *B* than *C* on such and such a scale of degrees of *P*?" Yet, in proportion as we approach such forms, metaphorical statements lose their effectiveness and their point.[15]

Black questions the "objective" nature of a given analogy or similarity between two terms: metaphor establishes such a similarity, but this similarity may not exist prior to the use and function of metaphor itself. If we reconsider the statement that "Government departments run as quickly and as smoothly as molasses in January," we must admit that there is no logical, a priori connection between "government departments" and "molasses in January," but that such a connection is one of the effects of metaphor. In this light, metaphor does not compare two realities that exist independently of each other; it associates these realities through its own rhetorical operations:

Metaphorical statement is not a substitute for a formal comparison or any other kind of literal statement, but has its own distinctive capacities and achievements. . . . It would be more illuminating in some of these cases [of metaphorical comparison] to say that the metaphor creates the similarity than to say that it formulates some similarity antecedently existing.[16]

Black proposes an interactionist view of metaphor as a solution to the problems inherent in both the substitution and comparison theories. The interactionist perspective understands that metaphor connects two subjects, one principal and one subsidiary, through what Black labels a "system of associated commonplaces."[17] This phrase refers to all associations invoked by a particular term, regardless of whether they are true. Black maintains that a principal subject is constituted through the metaphorical function of a subsidiary subject and its corresponding field of reference. He offers the example of the statement "Man is a wolf," contending that a reader can only interpret the meaning of this statement, and the designation of the principal subject "man," through an appeal to the associations evoked by the subsidiary subject "wolf." As Black demonstrates, the field of reference associated with "wolf" is subsequently extended to "man" in order to decipher the statement's meaning:

> If the man is a wolf, he preys upon other animals, is fierce, hungry, engaged in constant struggle, a scavenger, and so on. Each of these implied assertions has now to be made to fit the principal subject (the man) either in normal or in abnormal senses.[18]

The reader relies on the commonplaces associated with the term "wolf," thereby abandoning the implications associated with literal uses of the term "man." According to Black, this appeal to the field of reference associated with the subsidiary subject highlights and orders how the principal subject is conceived:

> Any human traits that can without undue strain be talked about in "wolf-language" will be rendered prominent, and any that cannot will be pushed into the background. The wolf-metaphor suppresses some details, emphasizes others—in short, *organizes* our view of man.[19]

The function of metaphor, then, demands an interaction between two subjects that cannot be reduced to their mere comparison.

Black's interactionist view of metaphor is particularly suited to a sociological investigation, since it highlights how metaphor organizes our knowledge of the social world and thereby influences how we act within it. By attending to the metaphors used in social life, sociologists can offer insight into how the world is created through rhetoric. For instance, if we think of governments as machines, what kinds of subjects are addressed? What topics are left unexamined?

An application of Black's interactionist theory of metaphor provides an occasion to illustrate how transsexual and transgendered people are rhetorically inscribed in the articulation of specifically nationalist political programs. This process reduces TS people to the purely figural, thereby erasing the literal transsexual body. Moreover, prominent American transsexual activism advocates the possibility of transsexual bodies through an implicit appeal to the terms of U.S. nationalism, a move that further reinforces the interactive relations between transgendered people and nationhood. The use of rhetoric inscribes a *gendered nationalism,* in which the imagined nation can only be comprised of masculine men and feminine women; as well as a *nationalized gender,* in which MTF transsexuals and transgendered people can never be citizens of the nation, but must instead only represent its identity crises.

## GENDER AND NATION IN MASS CULTURE

### The Adventures of Priscilla, Queen of the Desert

*Priscilla* presents the story of three MTF transgendered people—two drag queens (Felicia and Mitzi) and one MTF transsexual (Bernadette). All three live in Sydney and work as show girls within club culture.[20] The narrative of the film revolves around their trip to Alice Springs, where they have a performance contract. The trio buy a bus to make the journey to Alice Springs, located in the middle of the Australian desert.

The humor in *Priscilla,* as potential viewers can anticipate, will result from the actual journey across the desert rather than their arrival in Alice Springs. Indeed, this was the premise upon which the film was marketed. The videocassette's promotional copy, for instance, declares: "Their act might fly in Sydney, but the outrageous costumes, disco music and dancing is getting some pretty interesting feedback at every stop along the way." In this way, the film offers a contrast of transgendered people from the city with everyday life in the Australian desert. A metaphorical connection is established between MTF transgendered people and the urban metropolis, with a corresponding opposition posited between transgendered people and the Australian outback.

Several narrative events confirm this association of MTF transgendered people with urban social spaces. While discussing the possibility of the journey, Felicia tells Bernadette that ever since she was little, she had a dream to "travel to the center of Australia, [and] climb King's Canyon in a full-length Gaultier sequin [dress], heels, and a tiara." Bernadette's reply is terse: "Great. That's just what this country needs—a cock in a frock on a rock." The nation of Australia is positioned as the principal subject of this sequence, both through Felicia's anecdote (the use of synecdoche wherein the "center of Australia" stands in for its entirety) as well as Bernadette's reply, which explicitly names the notion of "country." The literal meanings of Australia invoke the rugged outback, in Felicia's use of the term "canyon" and Bernadette's designation of "rock." In this manner, a metaphorical connection is established between gendered space and the Australian nation: the terms "canyon" and "rock" designate hard, jagged surfaces not easily mastered by man. They function as subsidiary subjects that invoke a system of associated commonplaces such as hard surfaces, expansive space, and majestic power. These meanings are subsequently applied to the nation of Australia, portraying it as a country that is also hard, powerful, expansive, and sturdy. Through the meanings invoked by the subsidiary subjects of "canyon" and "rock," the principal subject of Australia is gendered as masculine, contrasting sharply with the presence of transgendered people. In Felicia's story, transgendered people such as herself enjoy wearing sequin gowns, heels, and tiaras—that is, MTF transgendered people enjoy feminizing themselves. Bernadette confirms this image: "cock" indicates a man (again, through the rhetorical device of synecdoche), and "frock" designates the feminine clothes and identity attributed to this man. The meanings associated with MTF transgendered people, then, involve signs of hyperfemininity: gowns, sequins, dresses, heels, jewelry, and cosmetics.

The humor in the film's narrative results from the contrast between an Australia that is thoroughly gendered as masculine and the presence of MTF transgendered people within it. This humor is further reinforced by Felicia's dreams of traveling to the center of Australia, a site that is clearly gendered as masculine. Were she to proclaim that she always wanted to grow up and become a transsexual sex trade worker in Sydney's King's Cross, for instance, her wish would not appear to be outrageous, impossible, or even anti-Australian: King's Cross, after all, is the urban area where transsexual prostitutes work. Thus, the system of associated commonplaces invoked by "country" is specific to the Australian outback and does not include the urban metropolis of Sydney. Sydney, the area from which emerge the three MTF transgendered protagonists of this film, is one of the few places where MTF transsexuals and drag queens can "survive." The presentation of both Australia and Sydney relies on a conjuncture between gender and geography through the rhetorical device of metaphor. In this way, the film offers a vision of gendered nationalism (which does not include the city of Sydney) as well as nationalized gender, in which MTF transgendered people cannot possess either the appropriate gender or national identity; they can only designate confusion and ambiguity with regard to both.

This contrast between Sydney and the Australian outback, between MTF transgendered people and "normal" gendered subjects, is pervasive throughout the film. The desert is continually represented as a space of reactionary politics, conservatism, and backwardness. When the bus breaks down, the trio encounter an Aboriginal Australian who takes them to his campsite. Upon entry, they hear everyone singing slow, mellow campfire songs. The atmosphere is calm and subdued. Within a matter of minutes, however, the showgirls unpack some bags, set out the tape player, and prepare to present a variety of numbers to their Aboriginal audience. The audience seems warm and appreciative, if somewhat confused and overwhelmed with all the glamour. One of the Aboriginal men even dons a dress himself to take part in the show. This scenario confirms the opposition between the desert and the city, but this time through recourse to culture and leisure activities. It offers a metaphorical connection between urban cities and transgendered people, wherein the leisure activities of MTF trans-gendered people (lip-synching, makeup, disco music, glamour) inform the notion of the city (Sydney in particular). In a parallel manner, the field of reference implied by Aboriginal leisure (campfires, mellow songs, subdued conversation, simplicity) organizes the rural space of the Australian desert. Just as the humor of Felicia's anecdote is derived from the juxtaposition of opposing realms (a MTF transgendered person climbing a canyon), the humor in this narrative sequence is also generated from an opposition, contrasting the leisure activities of urban and rural Australia. This contrast is most notable when the Aboriginal man dons a dress and dances energetically to disco music and ABBA.

A representation of the regressive, masculinist, and heterosexist social space of the desert is further evidenced when the trio meet Bob the mechanic, who assists them in repairing their bus. Bob is married to Cynthia. It is clear that the marriage has been arranged and that Cynthia is a Thai prostitute. When Bob convinces the three protagonists to perform at the local hotel, Cynthia protests that she wants to perform as well. She tells the trio, "Me like to sing, too. Me perform for you. Me dance too." Bob refuses to allow her to perform, without stating clearly why. When Bernadette, Felicia, and Mitzi begin their act, they are soon upstaged by Cynthia, who dances on stage as a stripper, shooting Ping-Pong balls across the room from her vagina. While the film's presentation of Aboriginal peoples situates them in a rural environment through an appeal to their leisure activities, its location of Thai prostitutes within rural Australia calls upon the arena of sexuality and performance. Cynthia's male audience is enthusiastic about her performance, in sharp contrast to their disinterest in the show offered by Sydney's female impersonators. In this way, a subsidiary subject of a Thai prostitute is used to further define the social space of the Australian desert. The commonplaces associated with this Thai woman—prostitution, performance, titillation, service—are extended and applied to the Australian outback. Through this metaphorical connection, the narrative offers a conjuncture of blatant heterosexuality and neocolonialism, one dependent on the market services of Asian women (individuals who seem only too happy to oblige the masculine, heterosexual men of the Australian desert). The three MTF transgendered protagonists clearly do not belong in the desert since they challenge the heterosexist definition of this space.

The juxtaposition between the desert and the city is most notable when

Felicia decides to take some drugs, dress up in drag, and go out alone on the (very small) town. She stumbles into a beer party, a men-only gathering. When they discover that Felicia is in drag, the men chase and assault her. They almost castrate Felicia, save for Bernadette's intervention. Afterward, Bernadette comforts a visibly shaken Felicia:

> It's funny. We sit around mindlessly slacking off that vile, stinkhole of a city. But in some strange way it takes care of us. I don't know if that ugly wall of suburbia has been put there to stop them getting in, or us getting out.

These events illustrate the metaphorical connections established between gender and space. The desert is associated with masculinity, through a diverse field of reference including men-only gatherings, small towns, everyday clothes, and the consumption of beer. The city, in contrast, is correlated to MTF transgendered people through signs such as makeup, glamorous clothing, and recreational drugs. Furthermore, Bernadette's comment situates MTF transgendered people firmly within an urban environment: they do not belong within the Australian desert because they are males who are not masculine. The film's vision of Australian national identity excludes places like Sydney, offering us a nationalized gender constituted through masculine men in the rugged outback.

After completing their contract, the three prepare to leave for the comfort, sanctity, and liberalism of Sydney. Just prior to departure, however, Bernadette announces that she has decided to remain in Alice Springs. When Mitzi asks whether Bernadette is sure about her decision, Bernadette replies, "No, I'm not sure. Although I'll never know unless I give it a shot." Bernadette's decision seems peculiar and ill-informed, especially considering the ways in which spatial metaphors are mobilized to construct the masculinist, racist, and xenophobic nature of the outback. The decision appears all the more bizarre considering that Bernadette does not seem convinced that this is the right choice for her.

At the end of the film, Felicia and Mitzi are back in Sydney performing in a club. The crowd is both appreciative and enthusiastic. Mitzi proclaims with a smile, "It's good to be home!" In case there was any doubt in the viewer's mind, this closing sequence confirms the freedom and liberty experienced by drag queens in the city. This proposition is secured through an invocation of the spatial metaphor of the city, which stands in sharp contrast to the Australian desert and the people within it.

This subplot with Bernadette complicates the previous representation of Sydney. The city is now construed as a site that is comfortable for drag queens but not necessarily for MTF transsexuals. Indeed, Bernadette has a flirtatious affair with Bob, the older, "simpler" mechanic the trio met in their wanderings across the desert. Her decision to remain in Alice Springs is interpreted in light of this romantic interest, serving to align heterosexuality with the desert once more. This representation relies on a discourse of transsexual women as heterosexual, politically conservative, and perpetually confused. Such a "tragic" characterization of MTF transsexuals suggests that we deserve nothing more than the geopolitical site of the Australian desert; indeed, that we actively choose it.

### Le sexe des étoiles

The use of metaphor to locate MTF transgendered people in the city occurs in other mass culture representations. Québec author Monique Proulx's novel, Le sexe des étoiles, as well as Paule Baillargeon's film adaptation of it, offer further examples of this use and function of metaphor.[21]

In Le sexe des étoiles, a MTF transsexual named Marie-Pierre Deslauriers has just returned to Montréal from New York, seeking to renew her relationship with her daughter Camille. Like Priscilla, Le sexe des étoiles presents a narrative concerned with nationalism. The gendered inscription of Marie-Pierre and Camille figures centrally in this discourse.

The film and novel narratives inscribe Marie-Pierre as an emasculated man: "Tétons seulement. Kaput les couilles" ("Tits only. The balls are history").[22] This statement serves as a frame to make sense of MTF transsexuals. It refers to a physiological process in which MTF transsexuals take estrogen and/or anti-androgens to produce female secondary sex characteristics, hormones that override or block the production of testosterone in the testicles. Yet this statement is then extended to the social status of men and women in Québec society. Since a MTF transsexual taking estrogen no longer has the strength or physical appearance of a man, she has been emasculated and is powerless. Thus, to utter "kaput les couilles" in reference to MTF transsexuals is to invoke the system of associated commonplaces with respect to the reproductive system (ingestion of estrogen and/or an anti-androgen in the genetic male, constriction of the testicles, decreased capacity for physical strength, reproduction) in order to situate the position of MTF transsexuals in society (emasculated, lack of power, inability to function).

Despite a lack of male hormones, privilege, or status, however, the narrative contends that Marie-Pierre can only be configured as an imitation of a woman—something else entirely:

On regardait Marie Pierre Deslauriers et on se surprenait à penser que, oui, cette . . . chose, femme ou extra-terrestre, était belle. [Looking at Marie-Pierre Deslauriers, one was surprised to find oneself thinking that, yes, this . . . thing, woman or alien, was beautiful.] [23]

This sequence locates Marie-Pierre outside of, and apart from, the very status of personhood. Although she may have the appearance of a woman, she is immediately reinscribed as a thing ("chose") or an alien ("extra-terrestre"), words invoking associations that are subsequently applied to Marie-Pierre and transsexuals in general. In the case of the word "thing" (*chose*), the field of reference delineates an object, something that may be aesthetically beautiful but that nonetheless has no real purpose, utility, or function. Transsexuals are thus devoid of human attributes. This dehuman-ization is extended through the use of the term "alien" (*extraterrestre*), which can mean unknown creatures from another planet, which live but are clearly other than human, and often present a threat both to humans and earth. These associations inscribe transsexuals outside of a human sphere. A metaphorical connection between aliens and MTF transsexuals occurs repeatedly throughout the novel. Marie-Pierre admits that she has "le sentiment d'être un échec vivant, un mensonge d'être égarée parmi des extra-terrestres" ("the feeling of being a living failure, a lie lost among the aliens").[24] This sentence extends the previous connotations to include the dimension of being lost. Uttered by a transsexual, the statement situates men and women as aliens. Ironically, it is in fact Marie-Pierre who is foreign to humans because of her transsexuality. The alien nature of transsexuality is further reinforced through the notions of "failure" and "lie." These terms provide additional associations to understand transsexuality: that trans-sexuals are failures as both men and women, and that transsexuality is a lie, since MTF transsexuals are not women. In this complex way, *Le sexe des étoiles* presents a conjunctural system of meanings that are extended to make sense of transsexuality: lies, deceit, failure, disorientation, aliena-tion. The collective force of these meanings situate transsexuals outside of humanity.[25]

The impossibility of Marie-Pierre's transsexual identity is inscribed alongside the neutered sexuality of her daughter Camille. In the begin-ning of the novel, Camille is described as a young girl

à la jupe ni *preppy*, ni *mod*, ni rien, une souris effarouchée, sans mascara et sans poitrine, à qui l'on avait honte d'avoir accordé de l'importance [with a skirt, neither preppy, nor mod, nor anything, a frightened little mouse, without mascara or breasts, a person someone would be ashamed of noticing].[26]

Camille is an adolescent girl who has not gone through puberty, a female who is not yet a woman. Metaphor functions to connect the principal subject of Camille through subsidiary subjects of makeup and breasts. Their lack is thus extended to Camille's identity such that her sexuality and gender are neutered. She has no style and is utterly unremarkable as a woman.

The genders of both Camille and Marie-Pierre are described and achieved through metaphor. The presentation and realization of gender identity through this rhetorical operation is reinforced through the deployment of particular spatial metaphors in the narratives of both the novel and the film. Spatial metaphors rely on a contrast between the city, a site of poverty, debauchery, and criminal activities; and the suburbs, a locale associated with peace, serenity, and middle-class comfort.

This city-suburb opposition functions through a comparison of Marie-Pierre and her ex-wife, Michèle. As a man, Marie-Pierre lived with Michèle and Camille in a grand house in the suburbs. Michèle still lives in the house with Camille. Marie-Pierre's home in New York is never depicted: her decision to live as a woman thus entailed a loss of heterosexual male privilege in the realm of housing. The opening sequence of the film presents Marie-Pierre in a cheap motel room, looking down at the bus terminal. Her status as an entity in transit is confirmed throughout the film, notably while she lives in downtown Montréal in a tourist room. These spatial metaphors provide background information necessary to understand and situate Marie-Pierre's gender. Metaphor functions to extend the associations of motels and bus terminals (poverty, motion, instability, perpetual movement, transit) to transsexuals. As such, transsexuals are inscribed as constantly in flux and unstable. The novel also presents the clearly erratic nature of transsexual identity. Marie-Pierre, for instance, is described as the "sujet de cette folle, de ce transsex-transit, au sujet de cette hormonée, bref" ("the subject of this crazy bitch, this transsexed-in-transit, this hormoned thing, in brief").[27] In this example, an association of transsexuality with transit is manifest at the syntactic level through the use of the hyphen ("transsex-transit"). The semantic connotations of the term "transit" indicate a process of interminable motion, a constant crossing. "Transit" also stands in close relation both to "transition" and to "transportation," processes of change and of movement that are also applied to transsexuality. Furthermore, one of the meanings associated with the term "transit" in French refers to passengers who have a stopover at a particular location. *Le Petit Robert,* for instance, provides the following definition:

> Situation de voyageurs à une escale (aérienne, maritime, . . . ) lorsqu'ils ne franchissent pas les contrôles de police, de douane. [Situation of travelers at a stopover (airport or sea) when they do not cross border, customs, or police inspection].[28]

The emphasis here is on individuals who do not cross through official border patrols. Transsexuals can thus be positioned as individuals who temporarily cross genders without going through the appropriate inspections and controls. Transsexuality is a constant process, an identity that can never be realized or properly verified. The instability and impermanence of transit is bolstered with the invocation of madness ("folle"), such that a conjunctural field of reference of transit and madness is applied to MTF transsexual identity. In this way, transsexuals are inscribed to be not only in perpetual motion, but perpetually mad. In both the film and the novel, transportation and transit metaphors situate MTF transsexuals as mentally ill.

Spatial metaphors recur throughout the narrative, connecting the city of Montréal with danger. In one sequence, Marie-Pierre and Camille are walking at night when Camille senses danger.[29] Marie-Pierre soothes her by pointing out that two people in a car are having sex and are too occupied with themselves to notice other people. Marie-Pierre explains to her daughter about the transaction under way, one that involves an adult and a young prostitute. As the sequence closes, we discover that the prostitute is actually Lucky, a friend of Camille's from school. This information forces us to reconsider how Lucky presents himself: he always carries a great deal of money, as well as drugs, and claims that he receives this money from his father. We now know, however, that his father is absent and that Lucky earns his money through prostitution. The activities witnessed by Marie-Pierre and Camille invoke several notions: the corruption of youth, sexual exploitation, prostitution. These notions are subsequently applied to make sense of the city of Montréal, such that the urban environment is considered unsafe for youth. Interestingly, this entire sequence is preceded by a description of the serenity of the city on the night of Marie-Pierre and Camille's walk: "Accalmie et beauté. La ville devenue métaphore . . ." ("Calm and beautiful, the city as metaphor . . . ").[30] The statement makes explicit the role that metaphor occupies in the novel. Through the events involving Lucky and his client, the space of the city is metaphorically connected to corruption, depravity, and the lost innocence of youth, a sharp contrast to the declaration that the city is calm and beautiful.

An association between the city and perversion is most notable in the description of a transsexual/ transvestite bar named Nefertiti:

> L'endroit était semblable aux autres du sud-est de la ville dans lesquels elle [Marie-Pierre] s'était quelquefois fourvoyée. . . . il abritait des transsexuels de tout acabit, faux et vrais, achevés et en devenir. Femmes pour la plupart — ou du moins s'affichant comme telles — mais femmes exacerbées, au maquillage et aux atours de caranaval, fauve théâtrale semblant sortir tout droit d'une ancienne oeuvre de Michel Tremblay. [The place was like the others of the south-east of the city where she {Marie-Pierre} had sometimes been led astray. . . . it housed transsexuals of all sorts, true and false, complete and in transition. Women mostly — or at least presenting themselves as such — but exaggerated women, in makeup and carnival finery, theatrical beasts seemingly straight out of an old Michel Tremblay piece.] [31]

Here, a metaphorical connection is posited between a principal subject of transsexuals and a subsidiary subject of carnivals. Makeup, appearance, disguise, and the realm of the theater (the invocation of Québec -playwright Michel Tremblay, whose works often represent MTF transgendered people) function to undermine the legitimacy of transsexual identity. The realm of the theater and the carnival inscribes the impossible, imitative nature of transsexuals. Proulx further situates transsexuals with respect to Montréal's city space, locating them in the southeast section of the city. This predominantly francophone and working-class neighborhood is characterized by homelessness, poverty, prostitution, and intravenous drug use. [32] In this manner, Proulx establishes a metaphorical connection between MTF transsexuals and unstable, impoverished daily conditions. This connection solidifies the impossible, transitive, and pathetic nature of MTF transsexual identity.

The metaphorical association between the city and degeneracy is all the more interesting upon reflection of Montréal's actual nightlife and bar culture. In fact, *Café Cléopâtra,* a bar catering to a transsexual/transvestite clientele is located on Boulevard Saint-Laurent close to Sainte-Catherine, not far from the southeast section of the city. The realm of Egyptian princesses metonymically links this bar to Proulx's fictional counterpart, *Nefertiti.* Furthermore, *Café Cléopâtra* is in the middle of Montréal's red-light district. [33] (Prostitution in Montréal is not limited to this area, but it is highly visible therein.) To situate a transsexual bar within such a neighborhood, then, is to locate transsexuals within the system of associated commonplaces of prostitution: corruption, drug use, sexual exploitation, vileness.

The conclusions of both the novel and the film confirm the central role occupied by Camille in *Le sexe des étoiles*. In the film version, Camille is presented as the protagonist. Marie-Pierre is a central character, but the focus of events is in and through the eyes of Camille. At the end of the film, Camille puts on some mascara. This gesture metaphorically associates makeup with femininity and demonstrates that Camille has finally achieved an "appropriate" feminine gender. In the last scene of the movie, Camille and Lucky ride out of Montréal on a motorbike. Pure heterosexual youth are thus represented as those individuals who leave the city at breakneck speed. In this manner, the film configures reproductive heterosexuality outside of the metropolis. The virgin womanhood of Camille must not remain in the city, given its association with prostitution and sexual corruption. The novel ends in a parallel manner, with Camille getting her period and her mother Michèle commenting that "décidément la métropole devenait bien insalubre" [the city had definitely become unhealthy].[34] Disease and debauchery are associated with the urban metropolis and its inhabitants, while the suburbs represent pure, uncomplicated heterosexuality.[35]

Thus, although one could argue that *Le Sexe des étoiles* makes use of a transsexual character to illustrate the current turmoil of the nation of Québec, it more pointedly suggests that Québec can establish its own identity, much as Lucky and Camille—who are both without fathers—articulate their sense of themselves. Filmmaker Paule Baillargeon comments on her work:

J'en suis venue à la conclusion qu'il faut parler de demain ou d'hier si l'on veut faire un film sur quoi que ce soit au Québec. Le présent est si plate qu'on dirait presque qu'il n'existe pas. Si j'étais première ministre du Québec, je m'interrogerais sur le monde que ça va laisser à notre jeunesse. Nos jeunes se tuent, se suicident, ne font plus de projets et ne pensent pas à l'avenir. Il n'y a plus de parents à la maison, il n'y a plus de temps pour les enfants, et ce ne sont pas les parents qui sont coupables—parce que c'est bien plus grave que ça. Et tant qu'on n'aura pas trouvé la réponse, on va continuer sur le chemin de l'extinction. [I've come to the conclusion that we need to speak of tomorrow or yesterday if we want to do a film on anything in Québec. The present is so boring we could almost say that it doesn't exist. If I were prime minister of Québec, I would ask myself what kind of world this is going to leave our youth. Our youth kill each other, kill themselves, aren't involved in any projects and don't think about the future. There are no longer any parents in the house, they don't have any more time for the kids, and it's not the parents who are responsible—because it's much more serious than that. And as long as we have not found the solution, we will continue on the road to extinction.] [36]

That this Québécois film opened the Festival des Films du Monde (World Film Festival) in 1993, forcing the recognition of Québec as a nation in its own right, indicates the central role it occupies in a Québécois nationalist cultural project.

Yet as we have observed, the film enacts metaphorical associations between transgendered people and the city of Montréal. Metaphor functions not merely as a rhetorical means to reinforce stereotypes and misconceptions about MTF transsexuals; it also connects the subsidiary subject of MTF transsexuals to the city of Montréal. To that end, the film is not just an indiscriminate trashing of MTF transsexuals. Through the use of metaphor, it suggests that the city of Montréal is, like MTF transsexuals, impoverished, corrupt, debauched, and cheap. This use of metaphor raises the important question about the extent to which the nation of Québec can embrace the metropolis of Montréal. Such a question is particularly relevant since Montréal is the geographic site in Québec most populated by anglophones and allophones, the city with the most visible population of people of color. It is, in a sense, the place in Québec most unlike Québec. In this way, the metaphors used in *Le sexe des étoiles* are not merely damaging to MTF transsexuals; they are also deployed against the entire city of Montréal, perhaps especially against members of its ethnocultural communities given their almost exclusive representation within the transsexual bar.[37] By implying that MTF transsexuals are impoverished, mad, and ridiculous, and by metaphorically associating the city of Montréal with these people, *Le sexe des étoiles* suggests that the project of Québec nationalism can advance through an explicit rejection of Montréal's plural cultures, languages, and populations. In a manner parallel to *Priscilla,* transsexuality functions as a metaphor in order to claim the importance of a normatively gendered national identity. The novel and film enact a vision of nationalized gender that demand complementary heterosexual identities gendered as masculine and feminine. The figural representation of the transsexual Marie-Pierre underscores this crisis of Québécois national identity.

### *Hosanna*

Both *Priscilla* and *Le sexe des étoiles* rely on the rhetorical device of metaphor to advance specifically gendered national identities of Australia and Québec by linking transgendered people with the urban metropolis. An appeal to a subsidiary subject of transgendered people offers a frame of reference for situating a principal subject of the nation. This metaphorical connection between gender and nation, between MTF transgendered people and the urban metropolis, is also evident in Québec playwright Michel Tremblay's *Hosanna*.[38] The play focuses on two characters, Cuirette and Hosanna, who have just returned to their apartment from a Halloween ball held at one of the bars on Montréal's Saint-Laurent Boulevard. The bar sponsored a drag contest with the theme "great women of history." Tremblay inscribes Hosanna and Cuirette within a gay drag subculture. Both characters know almost everyone in the bar, including the organizers of the contest. Hosanna spent a great deal of time and money in preparing her outfit for the evening, Elizabeth Taylor playing Cleopatra. Despite these efforts, she still looks somewhat pathetic. The stage directions in the English translation of the play describe Hosanna as "a cheap transvestite, touching and sad, exasperating in her self-exaltation."[39]

The events of the evening did not meet Hosanna's expectations. When Hosanna arrived at the club, she discovered that all of the other drag queens were dressed as Elizabeth Taylor in Cleopatra garb, and all were more beautiful than Hosanna. They mock and taunt her as she enters the costume contest. Hosanna realizes that her lover Cuirette has helped them orchestrate this event and runs from the club back to her apartment.

The play is centrally concerned with Québécois nationalism. In 1973, when *Hosanna* was written and produced for the first time, tensions regarding the status of Québec as an independent nation were high. Only three years previously, the militant Front de libération du Québec (FLQ) had kidnapped and murdered key government officials. The Canadian government responded to this situation by invoking the War Measures Act— legislation allowing the police to arrest and detain anyone without explanation. In 1973, many nationalist francophones felt that Québec was a country unto itself, but there remained the political problem of how to bring that sovereign state into being.[40]

These political events were the backdrop against which *Hosanna* was interpreted. The nation of Québec was figured in and through the character of Hosanna. Tremblay himself makes this metaphorical connection explicit. In a 1981 interview, he conjoined transvestism and nation in the most obvious manner:

> je me suis toujours servi du monde homosexuel pour dire autre chose, soit l'état de travestissement d'un pays voulant donner l'illusion d'être différent

de ce qu'il est. [I've always relied on the gay world to say something else, for instance a country which dresses itself up/betrays itself in order to give the illusion that it is something other than what it is.] [41]

Tremblay's comments indicate the central role of metaphor in his project. He relies on the practice and identity of transvestism in order to illuminate the political circumstances of Québec. His understanding of transvestism, however, invokes a complex system of associated commonplaces. It is first assumed that transvestites present an illusion of something or someone other than their essential identities: that transvestites are males who dress up and present themselves as women. Tremblay also presupposes that the self-presentation of transvestites involves a betrayal, a deliberate treason of identity. In this way, transvestism is not limited to the act of dressing up, but includes a process of deceiving oneself and others as to one's true identity. (These commonplaces are most evident in Tremblay's comments when read and interpreted in the original French, in which the term "travestissement" signifies both dressing up and duplicity.) Notions of illusion, betrayal, and deception, associated with a subsidiary subject of transvestites, are subsequently extended to a principal subject of Québec. Through metaphor, Tremblay thus raises questions about the political project of Québec sovereignty, asking to what extent the nation of Québec may be an illusion, deceiving itself through its self-presentation.

Tremblay's 1981 sentiments were repeated in the program notes of a 1991 production of the play:

> I began to think of the crisis of identity that was wracking Québec, and to search for a character through whom I could speak about it and what it was like to not know who you were, or to try and resemble someone else because you didn't have your own identity. [42]

These comments reiterate the system of associated commonplaces of transvestites: that transvestites dress up because they do not know themselves, that they attempt to pass themselves off as something other than their "true" natures, and that they lack their own identities. As Tremblay himself spells out, he relies on these associations with transvestites in order to raise questions about the state of Québec. The field of reference invoked by the subsidiary subject, transvestites, is thus extended to the principal subject, the Québec nation. Tremblay situates MTF transgendered people within the rhetorical mode of metaphor only to deny their very possibility. In such a version of nationalized gender, MTF transgendered people can represent the crisis of Québec, but they cannot be its citizens.

Robert Schwartzwald argues that Tremblay's *Hosanna* relies on an intersection of sexuality and nation.[43] For Schwartzwald, the character of Hosanna is connected to, and ultimately represents, Québec. Hosanna realizes at the end of the play that she is not Elizabeth Taylor, Cleopatra, or even Hosanna. She is, however, Claude. In the conclusion, Claude exclaims to his lover, "Look, Raymond, I'm a man!" ["R'garde Raymond, chus t'un homme!"][44] Schwartzwald interprets this as Claude's "coming out" scene, in which he finally accepts himself for who he is, and in which homosexuality is inscribed as a legitimate social identity.[45] Metaphorically, Québec needs to accept its own identity in order to be recognized as a nation unto itself in the world.

In the more recent version of *Hosanna* staged in 1991, Claude/Hosanna's declaration "I'm a man!" is framed with a question mark. This syntactical difference recasts the terms of the discourse, in which the final line "resembles less an affirmation than an interrogation charged with ambivalence."[46] Given that the province of Québec remained within the Canadian nation-state in 1991—almost twenty years after *Hosanna*'s original production—a questioning of Québécois nationalist strategies would not appear to be unusual. In this shift, Schwartzwald contends, the play no longer relies on a metaphor of sexual authenticity ("coming out"). Rather, it turns around a sexual ambivalence. Schwartzwald concludes that despite the interpretive richness of Tremblay's *Hosanna*, this move from authenticity to ambivalence may function to undermine the representation of homosexuality in Québec culture.[47]

Schwartzwald's interpretation is significant. Yet it depends upon positioning the character of Hosanna as a gay or homosexual man. This identity is not fully supported by the textual evidence of the play. Although Hosanna and Cuirette are clearly lovers, and although they are both integrated into a certain gay bar culture, Tremblay nonetheless relies centrally upon a discourse of gender dysphoria to describe Hosanna. It is necessary to examine the inscription of Hosanna in order to understand the associations made between transgendered people and deceit, as well as the kind of collapse between gender and sexuality enacted by Schwartzwald.

Hosanna tells Cuirette of her initial realization that a queer sexuality is much more than an act; it is fundamental to one's sense of self:

> When I saw that to be queer doesn't just mean that you act like a girl, but can also mean that you really want to be a girl, a real girl, and that you can manage to become one. . . . Chriss, you can actually manage to become a real girl.[48]

Instead of sexual minority, Hosanna endorses a position of gender inversion. Through a discourse of "becoming a real girl," she inscribes herself as transgendered.[49] Interestingly, the ontological status of transsexuality ("to be a girl") is contrasted with the performative nature of homosexuality ("doesn't just mean that you act like a girl").

The transsexual/transgendered status of Hosanna is marked early in the narrative. Offering Hosanna assistance in removing her dress, Raymond says: "Okay, butterfly, you can climb out of your cocoon now. . . . Come on, spread your wings, the night air awaits you."[50] The allegory of the butterfly is overdetermined as one appropriate for transsexual people—individuals who are involved in a process of transition and metamorphosis through which they will emerge as beautiful and liberated creatures.[51] This idea of a butterfly invokes a system of associated commonplaces of transition, metamorphosis, and beauty that is subsequently applied to MTF transgendered people such as Hosanna. The discourse of gender dysphoria is most evident after Hosanna has removed her dress:

> When I'm dressed like a man, I'm ridiculous. When I'm dressed like a woman, I'm ridiculous. But I'm really ridiculous when I'm stuck between the two, like I am right now, with my woman's face, my woman's underwear, and my own body.[52]

In this passage, Tremblay locates the utter impossibility of MTF transgendered identities: individuals who are ridiculous as men, as women, and as transgendered. Hosanna's in-between state is the source of her tragic nature.

The inscription of Hosanna as transgendered—perhaps transsexual, perhaps transvestite, decidedly in-between—is necessary for the conclusion of the play to have its impact. Hosanna comes to realize her "true" nature:

> I'm a man, Raymond. If I ran out of there like that, tumbling down the stairs almost breaking my bloody neck, if I ran out, Raymond, it's because . . . I'm not a woman.[53]

Once Hosanna has renounced her transgendered status, once she declares her masculine gender, Claude and Raymond embrace. The gendered conclusion of the play resolves its transgendered narrative.

Attention to the textual inscription of the character of Hosanna within the play is necessary for its interpretation. Unfortunately, Schwartzwald's analysis ignores the central role occupied by a discourse of gender inversion. Although Claude is clearly homosexual at the conclusion, the entire narrative revolves around "his" intermediary gendered state. For this reason, it is problematic to make the theoretical claim that Tremblay compares homosexual men with the nation of Québec in this play.[54] As Tremblay's own comments indicate, he relies on a figure of the transvestite. He does, however, establish a metonymic link among transvestites and gay men: Tremblay assumes that transvestites circulate in gay male communities, and that their elaborate dress masks their true gay selves. Given this association, engaged criticism ought to reflect on the specificity of transvestite locations.

Tremblay places transvestism alongside homosexuality, at least until the conclusion of the play. By resolving Hosanna's identity crisis through a reclamation of a stabilized gender position, however, Tremblay allows for gender (transvestism) to work against sexuality (gay maleness). Schwartzwald's interpretation of the play makes such a juxtaposition of gender and sexuality explicit:

> I know very well that an important aspect of that coming out as represented by Tremblay was its message that being gay didn't mean you had to be effeminate or a drag queen. That message reassured me then in a way that embarrasses me today, when my respect for the courage of a drag queen is bound up with a much greater awareness of the manner in which all gendered behavior is performative.[55]

Notwithstanding Schwartzwald's liberal declaration of his "respect for the courage of a drag queen," he remains incapable of theorizing the particular location occupied by transgendered figures within Hosanna. This oversight is further ironic given his careful critique of Québécois intellectuals who have expressed concern over the prevalence of homosexuality within Québec film and literature.[56] Schwartzwald notes that for some cultural critics, homosexuality represents an arrested state of development. Yet if homosexuality is conceived as an immature, underdeveloped state, one akin to the not-yet-nation of Québec, does this mean, following the logic of such critics, that a fully sovereign Québec would be devoid of homosexuals? In Schwartzwald's words,

> If the representation of homosexuality is merely the symptom of an identitary impasse, are we to conclude that it will "disappear" once the nationally inflected problem of the relation to the Other is "resolved"?[57]

The question is pointed, yet crucial. In uncovering the workings of a metaphorical comparison between homosexuality and nation, Schwartzwald asks his readers to also consider the referent of homosexuals upon which this metaphor depends. In so doing, he illustrates a current of intellectual thought in Québec that is openly and decidedly homophobic. Schwartz-wald illustrates the connections between a subsidiary subject of homosexuals and a principal subject of Québec. Furthermore, his thesis advances an interactionist theory of metaphor by demonstrating that the political stakes involved in this connection cannot be reduced to a mere substitution of homosexuals for Québec, nor their simple comparison. Rather, Schwartz-wald reveals how this particular metaphorical connection organizes our understanding of the social world and ultimately legitimates a nation devoid of homosexual citizens.

While his interpretation of a homophobic nationalist discourse forces a consideration of the relations between "real" homosexuals and their figural representation, Schwartzwald does not extend this analysis to his discussion of transvestites. Indeed, were he to do so, he might have to challenge the profoundly anti-transgendered nature of Tremblay's discourse. Tremblay depends upon a system of associated commonplaces invoked by transvestites to raise questions about the nation of Québec. The field of reference attributed to transvestites claims that these individuals dress up in search of an elusive identity, that they do not or cannot know themselves, and that they present themselves to the world in a false form. A reliance upon these ideas of illusion, deception, and betrayal presupposes that we as transgendered people do not know who we are. It assumes that we want to be somebody else—that the non-transgendered body is more real, more authentic, and more credible than the bodies of transvestites, transsexuals, and transgenderists. And this discourse speculates that, given the chance, we who are transgendered would always choose to be non-transgendered; that there is no joy or power in our bodies and our lives. It is through such a violently anti-transgendered discourse that Tremblay enables gay male subject-positions. Schwartzwald's neglect of the metaphorical connections between MTF transvestites and the nation of Québec maintains and fosters this violence. In this way, Schwartzwald perpetuates the erasure of transsexual and transgendered people in culture.

The impossible and tragic state of transvestism, for Tremblay, provides the theoretical backing for a comparison among transvestites and Québec. Although he establishes a metonymic connection among transvestites and gay men, an invocation of the discourse of gender dysphoria advances Tremblay's argument and narrative. For this reason, Schwartzwald's interpretation of the play is insufficient: he pays scant attention to this discourse within the play, or to the "real" transgendered people upon whom it apparently draws. Ironically, although he laments cultural criticism that elides the possibility and reality of homosexual citizens in Québec, Schwartzwald does not remark on an analogous slippage in Tremblay's *Hosanna:* transvestites function to represent the national identity crisis of Québec, but they cannot be its citizens. This thesis exemplifies the erasure of MTF transvestites and transsexuals in culture, in which these individuals can only exist as rhetorical figures, never as literal referents.

The impossibility of literal transsexual bodies is well evidenced in the comments of Québécois actor and writer André Montmorency. Montmorency has often portrayed the various protagonists of Tremblay's theater.[58] In his autobiography, he reflects on the Québécois film *Il était une fois dans l'est,* a collaborative project between Tremblay and filmmaker André Brassard. Based on Tremblay's oeuvre, the film includes the scene from *Hosanna* when Hosanna enters the club dressed as Cleopatra only to discover that everyone else is wearing similar costumes. Montmorency recounts the production process of the film, in which the filmmaker Brassard considered casting in the lead role a MTF transgendered person (Belinda Lee) who frequented one of Montréal's main transvestite/transsexual bars. Montmorency's comments depend upon, and reinforce, a system of associated commonplaces in which MTF transgendered people are cheap imitations of women, betraying themselves through illusion. His words are explicit, revealing the strength of his convictions:

> Le monde des travestis et des transsexuels est impitoyable de méchanceté et de frustration. Plusieurs souvenirs de ce tournage me reviennent en mémoire. Le traitement hormonal que suivent ceux qui aspirent à changer de sexe donne des seins magnifiques mais le pénis rétrécit, disparaissant presque. [The world of transvestites and transsexuals is a pathetic one marked by bitchiness and frustration. Several memories come to my mind during the shoot. The hormone therapy undertaken by those who want to change sex gives magnificent breasts, but the penis retracts, almost disappearing.][59]

As in Proulx's *Le sexe des étoiles,* this reference to the penis of MTF transsexuals invokes a metaphorical connection between chemical castration and the loss of masculinist status and privilege. Discussing the suicide of a transsexual hired for the film, Montmorency suggests that all MTF transsexuals end up killing themselves:

> Nous sommes consternés, Tamara était arrivée à cette échéance qui attend presque toutes ces désemparées de la vie. [We were all upset, Tamara had just achieved the failure for which almost all these lost souls of life were destined.][60]

Montmorency's comments are insightful to the extent that they evidence stereotypes about MTF transsexuals—stereotypes that are reinforced in Tremblay's work.

These clichés about MTF transvestites and transsexuals underlie Tremblay's metaphorical connection between transgendered people and the nation of Québec. This connection is reinforced through specifically spatial metaphors, in a manner similar to both *Priscilla* and *Le sexe des étoiles*. The play takes place in Hosanna and Cuirette's bachelor apartment, located near Métro Beaubien. The apartment is dark, cramped, and filled with cheap, tacky objects. The neon sign of a nearby pharmacy blinks continuously into the space throughout the play, enhancing the surreal, seedy, and thoroughly urban nature of the setting. Finally, the neighborhood is a traditionally working-class francophone district, located in the east of the city.

The apartment is contrasted with the bar, located on Saint-Laurent. As Schwartzwald remarks, the street of Saint-Laurent, colloquially known as "The Main," represents a site of liberty and transgression for Tremblay.[61] It marks the dividing line between the east and west sides of the city, between the poor francophones and the more affluent anglophones. Saint-Laurent is also the street on which many immigrants have settled and established small businesses; perhaps the emblematic street for allophones in the city, those who are neither francophone nor anglophone. Finally, the lower part of Saint-Laurent is also the city's sex worker district. Historically, prostitution, nightclubs, and burlesque theaters have been located along this strip.[62]

In *Hosanna*, Saint-Laurent is represented as a seedy, tacky street: that region of the city where transvestites go (presumably in search of themselves). Tremblay's location of the transvestite/transsexual bar on Saint-Laurent provides a further system of associated commonplaces that are subsequently applied to transvestites. The street of Saint-Laurent is inscribed as a dividing line between the east and the west, between the poor and the rich, between the French and the English, a line along which only immigrants and prostitutes actually make their livings. Thus, Tremblay suggests that transvestites are transient, caught in the middle—entities that mark borders.

The play also compares the city of Montréal with the smaller towns and villages located in Québec. Hosanna recounts her experience living as an effeminate boy in Sainte-Eustache. The city of Montréal offers an escape from the masculine gendered position required of all males in small-town Québec:

> But the day I turned sixteen I was on my way to Montréal with the first
> trick that I could lay my hands on. And then . . . step by step . . . little by

little . . . I became Hosanna. . . . Hosanna, the biker's girlfriend! Hosanna, the stud's favourite hairdresser! Hosanna, the motorcycle queen![63]

The emergence of Hosanna occurs in and through the city of Montréal, notably through Boulevard Saint-Laurent. In this manner, Tremblay relies on a conjuncture of geographic space and gender. If Québec is gendered as masculine, the city of Montréal is associated with transvestism. In a manner similar to Proulx's *Le sexe des étoiles,* Tremblay's *Hosanna* presents a bleak picture of the city of Montréal within the nation of Québec. It remains the city in search of itself, perpetually doomed to misrecognition.

Contemporary mass culture thus links gender and nation through the rhetorical device of metaphor. This connection is significant, because it relies on stereotypes about the impossibility of MTF transgendered identity: that we are ridiculous, suicidal, cheap imitations, mad, poor, aliens, emasculated, pathetic. One of the immediate effects of the use of metaphor within these texts, then, is a legitimation of a social world in which MTF transgendered people are inscribed in a discourse of impossible tragedy. *Priscilla, Queen of the Desert; Le sexe des étoiles;* and *Hosanna* all rely on the system of associated commonplaces attached to a subsidiary subject of MTF transgendered people in order to make a political statement about a principal subject of national identity. Such a rhetorical inscription erases the possibility of the literal transsexual or transvestite body.

As Black's interactive theory of metaphor makes clear, metaphorical associations offer a way to make sense of a particular subject, emphasizing certain aspects of the connection and suppressing others. A similar function occurs in the texts discussed here: an appeal to MTF transgendered people orders and organizes the conceptions of national identity advanced by the narratives. Furthermore, Black's theory contends that metaphor cannot be reduced to the mere comparison of two subjects; it functions to organize our understandings of the social world, and thus our actions within it. This emphasis on the interactive nature of metaphor is particularly relevant to representations such as *Priscilla, Le sexe des étoiles,* and *Hosanna,* which clearly rely upon and enact negative stereotypes about MTF transgendered people. Politically, it is important to both understand and challenge these myths and misconceptions about MTF transgendered people in order to assert the viability of our bodies and our lives. Yet if we are to draw on theories of metaphor in order to understand the negative representation of MTF transgendered people in mass culture, we ought also to reflect on the subjects with which these individuals are metaphorically connected. In *Priscilla, Le sexe des étoiles,* and *Hosanna,* metaphor links MTF transgendered people with the urban metropolis. This connection posits a gendered, masculinist national identity in contradistinction to the cities within these nations, the geographic areas inhabited by (among others) MTF transgendered people. Thus, while the use of metaphor within these texts clearly enacts negative stereotypes about MTF transgendered people, it also posits a vision of normatively gendered national identity that ignores the plural cultures, regions, and inhabitants of the nation's cities.

## THE NATIONALIST METAPHORS OF U.S. TRANSSEXUAL ACTIVISM

Cultural representations such as *Priscilla, Le sexe des étoiles,* and *Hosanna* offer a metaphorical connection between transgendered people and the urban metropolis to advance a specifically gendered national identity. As we have observed, these cultural products appeal to a referential frame in which transgendered people are confused and pitiful. Attention to the use of metaphor can enable activist strategies wherein transsexual and transgendered people can denounce the discourse of tragedy in which they are inevitably inscribed. Remarkably, a metaphorical association among transgendered people and the city is also made within the sphere of U.S. transsexual activism. The type of activism endorsed by some American transsexuals is authorized through their use of rhetoric. Reflection on the use and function of rhetoric, then, can help us to identify the strengths and limitations of proposed activist strategies.

### San Francisco's Transsexual Renaissance?

In her article on the San Francisco Bay Area's transsexual arts scene in 1994, Susan Stryker offers one example of transgendered activism that associates transsexuality and nation.[64] Stryker begins with an overview of the numerous art events and activities involving Bay Area transsexuals: poetry readings, plays, photography exhibitions, and more. Stryker then goes on to offer an analogy between the creation of transsexual culture in San Francisco in the 1990s and the production of African-American culture in the early twentieth century in New York City—the Harlem Renaissance:

> Having spent way too many years in grad school studying American history, I start to salivate at the slightest suggestion of a long-term, multicausal explanation for anything, and have learned to draw pointed analogies between any two seemingly unrelated cultural phenomena.[65]

Stryker goes on to explain that the Harlem Renaissance was an effect of particular historical relations, in which blacks from the U.S. South migrated north in search of employment and a better life. The settlement of southern blacks in American cities like New York created a fertile environment for literary and cultural production, perhaps most notable in the thriving jazz scene of New York City. In case the analogy with transsexuality is not explicit, Stryker ruminates:

> I have to wonder: will there be a transsexual equivalent of jazz? Can we see its dim outlines today in the streets of San Francisco? Are we feeling the birth pangs of a Transsexual Renaissance?[66]

Stryker's invocation of the Harlem Renaissance functions as a subsidiary subject in order to make sense of a principal subject: transsexuals. This metaphorical connection is established through a diverse system of associated commonplaces, notably an urban environment (New York, San Francisco), and the production of art (music, poetry, visual art in the Harlem Renaissance; music, poetry, photography, video in the "Transsexual Renaissance"). Furthermore, Stryker links African-Americans in New York's Harlem Renaissance with transsexuals in today's Bay Area through the thematic expression of individual and collective pain, struggle, and emancipation. She writes that African-American music, literature, and culture addressed "the multi-faceted experiences of racial discrimination," while transsexual culture explores the uniqueness of sex and gender change, as well as the concomitant marginalization that may accompany this process.[67]

Stryker expands her argument through a discussion of the classic slave narrative in African-American literature, in which people are located in relation to three phases: "African freedom," a transitional period of enslavement, and "a new kind of freedom after slavery."[68] According to Stryker, such a tripartite form is shared by transsexual narratives. Transsexual autobiographies, she claims, begin with one's life before transition, present the process and effects of transforming one's body, and conclude with "post-transition life experiences in a new gender."[69] For Stryker, such autobiographies are crucial elements in the articulation of transgender subjectivity and politics. She suggests that like the anguish of slavery depicted in slave narratives, transsexual autobiographies focus on the pain and struggle of the transition process. Moreover, her argument proposes that just as African-American slave narratives culminate in "a new kind of freedom after slavery," transsexual narratives conclude with a new kind of freedom after surgery. Stryker relies on common elements within the narrative structure of African-American slave narratives and transsexual autobiographies in order to establish a metaphorical connection between these two subjects.

Stryker's intervention is overtly political. She associates African-Americans and transsexuals in order to raise questions about the individual and collective emancipation of transsexuals:

> Perhaps, like Africans americanized through slavery, we must define ourselves partly by claiming the full content of our historical experience, and partly by opposing the narrative that has been imposed upon our flesh. The tale of gender dysphoria and its cure is the medical/ psychiatric narrative of transsexuality. Must it also be our own?[70]

This question is surely provocative. Yet careful reflection upon her argument indicates that a parallel between African-Americans and transsexuals does not hold and is not the most appropriate analogy. Consider, for instance, the metaphorical connection between African-American slave narratives and transsexual autobiographies. Stryker states that slave narratives, beginning with "African freedom," focus on a transitional process of enslavement to finally conclude in a post-slavery freedom. Transsexual autobiographies follow a similar narrative structure: an introductory section on pre-transitional life and experiences, an in-depth presentation of transition, and a post-transition conclusion. A metaphorical comparison between African-American and transsexual narratives based upon a tripartite structure is simplistic. Stryker's argument rests on a link between African-American and transsexual narratives based on both form (tripartite structure) and content (freedom, enslavement, freedom). Although Stryker clearly outlines the thematic links among the final two sections (enslavement/transition; freedom after emancipation/freedom after surgery), she does not comment on the substantive connection to be established among the first sections of such works ("African freedom"/pre-transition life). Indeed, to push Stryker's metaphor to the extreme would require that transsexuals situate their pre-transition lives in terms of "freedom." Yet she clearly argues that transsexuals only achieve freedom post-surgically.

Consider, as well, Stryker's presentation of the migration of southern blacks to northern cities. Historical data certainly indicates that the possibility of employment motivated many people to move and settle in cities like New York and Chicago.[71] Yet the mere presence of black people in these cities does not suffice to explain the birth of a Harlem Renaissance. As American historians have amply demonstrated, families and residential neighborhoods facilitated the adjustment process of new arrivals to the city.[72] Moreover, the poverty in which many African-Americans lived in early twentieth-century Harlem forced individuals to develop creative solutions to economic uncertainty. Some individuals would host a party and charge fees for food and beverages in order to earn enough money to pay the rent. It was in these "rent parties" that many musical, artistic, and cultural productions were generated. The explosion of African-American culture must be interpreted, then, with regard to more than a demographic shift in population across regional locations, as Stryker implies. Questions of economic uncertainty and kinship were central in the formation of the Harlem Renaissance.

Stryker's neglect of economic and kinship relations with regard to African-Americans in Harlem is paralleled in her presentation of Bay Area transsexual communities in the 1990s. Rather than offering a historical and economic analysis of transsexual migration to the Bay Area (albeit a formidable challenge), she merely cites the presence of transsexual artists in and around San Francisco, and provides no discussion of kinship within transsexual communities. Do Bay Area transsexuals open their homes to transgendered people from elsewhere, for instance, in order to help them adjust upon arrival to the new city? Do Bay Area transsexuals hold rent parties or similar events to help them live in a world ruled by capital? Similarly, Stryker advances no analysis concerning access to the art world, as if all transsexuals living in and around San Francisco have the economic and cultural capital to gain entry into a world of galleries, exhibitions, and playhouses. This is not to discredit the efforts and struggles of transgendered people who have made such inroads. But gaining such access may be directly related to one's cultural capital.[73]

Stryker's discussion of the classic transsexual narrative is also oblivious to economic issues. She fails to consider the absence of sex work within such narratives, for instance, despite the fact that many MTF transsexuals obtain the funds required to modify their bodies through prostitution.[74] Finally, Stryker positions psychiatry in the role of slave master, suggesting that we transsexuals need only unleash ourselves from the psychiatric institution in order to be free:

> Almost every one of us has had to sit down with a psychological evaluation questionnaire and seriously address some version of the question, "How did you develop your sense of gender identity? Please give a brief personal statement." The very fact of our medical colonization incidentally produces a composite record of our lives.[75]

Stryker's concern with the power of psychiatry over the lives and bodies of transgendered people is engaging. Yet in the political context of the United States, in which health care is offered as a commodity to be bought,[76] it is more than problematic to assume that all transgendered people have made appointments with psychiatrists in order to address their gender identity issues. The reality of health care for U.S. transsexuals is quite a different story: one where poor transsexuals obtain hormones through an underground market economy; wherein a psychiatric assessment of gender dysphoria is a luxury available only to transsexuals with money.[77]

Stryker's metaphorical connection between African-Americans of New York's Harlem Renaissance and transsexuals of the Bay Area in the 1990s invokes a broad system of associated commonplaces: an urban milieu, the production of culture, the thematic content of this culture, and the narrative structures of literature. Careful reflection on her argument, however, reveals that Stryker does not present crucial information on the field of reference of both African-American communities during the Harlem Renaissance as well as Bay Area transsexual communities of the 1990s.

Because Stryker does not provide an economic, political, or social analysis of 1990s transgendered communities in the Bay Area, her discussion of a "Transsexual Renaissance" is strictly idealist. An appeal to the geographic site of San Francisco and its environs is supported by a belief in America as the land of freedom. A realization of transsexual subjectivity, for Stryker, can be achieved in and through the Bay Area arts community, with its strong transsexual presence. This argument implies that, just as African-Americans moved to northern U.S. cities to achieve social, economic, and artistic freedom in the early twentieth century, transsexuals of the 1990s can be emancipated by moving to San Francisco. Despite Stryker's claims, she does not succeed in making a logical argument or a cogent analogy; there is no discussion of how or why transsexuals would fare better in San Francisco than elsewhere, nor of the specific economic or kinship relations that (white) transsexuals in the 1990s share with African-Americans at the turn of the century.[78]

Stryker's argument rests upon the assumption that freedom—for the (white) transsexual as for the African-American—can be found in the urban centers of the U.S., an assumption questionable for African-Americans, transsexuals, and African-American transsexuals alike. Given this appeal to a nationalist origin, Stryker's characterization of "the medical colonization" of transsexual health seems especially ironic. If psychiatry has *colonized* transsexual bodies, as Stryker maintains, her response only reconfirms a world in which the United States is central, and in which all transgendered people ought to either model themselves after their American counterparts or move to San Francisco. Such a position is itself deeply imbricated in the ideological and material relations of (neo)colonialism.

The previous section focuses on how the use of metaphor enacts both a nationalized gender, in which MTFs can only represent the crises of the nation, as well as a gendered nationalism, which depends on a nation composed of masculine men and feminine women, usually outside of a large metropolis. Stryker's discourse repeats these arguments, although in a slightly different form. While she allows for the possibility of transsexual identity, she only does so through an appeal to American nationalism. Her use of metaphor situates transsexuals as American and further claims the cities of the United States as integral to its national identity. In this way, Stryker reiterates visions of both nationalized gender (transsexuals are American) and gendered nationalism (liberal U.S. cities can accommodate transsexuals).

## The Apartheid of Sex

The nationalist underpinnings of U.S. transsexual activism are further evidenced in the writings of Martine Rothblatt, notably in her book titled *The Apartheid of Sex*. Rothblatt's focus is on the legal definition of humans into two sexes. She makes explicit the parallel with race:

> Genitals are as irrelevant to one's role in society as skin tone. Hence, the legal division of people into males and females is as wrong as the legal division of people into black and white races. It is to the abolition of this legal apartheid of sex that this book is addressed.[79]

Rothblatt links an apartheid sex system and an apartheid system of race by referring to the realm of physiology. Within an apartheid race system, one's skin tone determines one's social status. Rothblatt takes this example of racial segregation based on the physiology of the body and extends it to make sense of men, women, and transgendered people by claiming that within an apartheid sex system, one's genitals determine one's social status. In other words, the meanings linked to the concept of racial apartheid are metaphorically connected to the social definitions and divisions of sex.

Rothblatt's argument, like Stryker's, is premised on an ethnic/racial identity model of transsexuality. Transsexuals are considered to be a distinct category of people who deserve fair and equal treatment under the law. This position is a common one in the context of the United States. Critics in U.S. lesbian and gay studies, for instance, have demonstrated the ways in which contemporary lesbian and gay political organizing depend on a notion of gay men and lesbians as an ethnic group.[80] This framework is flawed in that it presupposes that lesbians and gay men are white; lesbians and gay men of color are inconceivable in such a discourse. Moreover, as bisexual activists have pointed out, an ethnic identity model of sexuality appeals to a "natural" state of sexuality in which people are *purely* lesbian/ gay. This perspective cannot account for the contradictions of sexual identities and behaviors, thus actively excluding bisexuals from its parameters.[81] The writings of Rothblatt and Stryker repeat the problems with a lesbian/ gay ethnic identity model of politics: a comparison of transsexuals and African-Americans implicitly assumes that all transsexuals are white.

An American frame of reference is pervasive throughout Rothblatt's book. In making an argument for the legal reform of sex categories, she invokes the example of "illegitimate" children:

> Up through the nineteenth century "illegitimate" children could be disavowed of almost all legal rights. It took Supreme Court decisions to finally ban discrimination based on the marital status of a person's parents. Since the marital status of one's parents is wholly irrelevant to a person's humanity, we would be shocked today if people's life paths were sharply limited by when or whether their parents stood before a judge and exchanged vows. But at one time, even in America, that's how it was.[82]

Rothblatt's use of the modifier "even" reinforces the nationalist myth of "America" as a land of freedom and justice for all. The title of her book— *The Apartheid of Sex*—reconfirms America as a land of freedom, by juxtaposing the apartheid regime of South Africa with the ostensibly liberal and tolerant United States. Moreover, Rothblatt's use of metaphor functions to elide the actual presence of African-Americans, since race only stands in to represent gender. Schwartzwald argues that while homosexuality is represented symbolically to address Québec's identity crisis, it can only exist in a rhetorical mode, which effectively creates a nation of Québec devoid of homosexual citizens.[83] A similar logic operates in both Rothblatt and Stryker's metaphorical associations between African-Americans and transsexuals: race can only be a metaphor for gender, such that nonwhite citizens are invoked exclusively to represent white transsexuals. This rhetorical argument erases the actuality of the lives of nonwhite individuals and communities in the United States.

Perhaps one of the most interesting aspects of Rothblatt's book is how she parallels the work of U.S. transgendered activists in the 1990s with civil rights activists in the 1960s: "in every society there are the free spirits, the stubborn, and the insistent. In the 1960s they fought for civil rights. In the 1990s they fight for gender rights."[84] This statement somewhat naively assumes that all the battles fought during the U.S. civil rights movement of the 1960s have been won, and that we now need to put our collective energies into the fight against gender oppression. A consideration of the current economic and political realities for African-Americans, Hispanics, Asian-Americans, indigenous Hawaiians, and Native Americans living in the United States would dispute this assumption.

Both Stryker and Rothblatt enact metaphorical comparisons between blacks and transsexuals. This association, however, is even more specific: they are not comparing the situation of transsexuals in America with black people in Québec or the Antilles. Rather, both Stryker and Rothblatt depend on an implicit American frame of reference to make their point. In this manner, while on the surface they compare race and transsexuals, they can only link these two entities through an invocation of American citizenship and civil rights. An unacknowledged and pervasive nationalism functions as the driving force of their arguments. In a manner similar to the cultural representations discussed previously, prominent U.S. transsexual activists employ metaphorical strategies that rely on specific places and spaces; in the cases of Stryker and Rothblatt, the never-stated yet pervasive nation of the United States.

Black's interactive theory of metaphor advocates that the connection established between a subsidiary and a principal subject cannot be reduced to the substitution of one term for another, nor to their simple comparison. The preceding section on mass culture illustrated the value of such a developed theory of metaphor: the links established between MTF transgendered people and national identity within mass culture have important consequences for both subjects. Metaphor enacts myths and stereotypes of MTF transgendered people and also advances normatively gendered visions of national identity. The writings of Stryker and Rothblatt offer additional evidence as to the interactions between gender and nation within rhetoric. The metaphorical associations they establish between African-Americans and transsexuals provide a clear rejection of the misconceptions commonly associated with MTF transgendered people. As such, their work affirms transsexual identity. Yet this affirmation is only possible given the system of associated commonplaces linked to their subsidiary subjects of African-Americans and the U.S. nation: freedom, liberty, civil rights, and justice. In this regard, Stryker and Rothblatt assert transsexual and transgendered identities through an appeal to the terms of American nationalism. Although a validation of transsexuality is a worthwhile endeavor, their use of metaphor simultaneously legitimates a world in which the United States is central, and in which American paradigms of political citizenship and social movements (civil rights) are the only models considered. Indeed, it is striking that both Stryker and Rothblatt appeal to nation; one wonders whether it is possible to imagine an affirmation of transsexual identity that is not premised upon American nationalism. If, as critics in the sociology of metaphor contend, the rhetorical device of metaphor creates (not merely describes) a particular social world, there are certain consequences of using metaphors that presuppose and reinforce American identities and models of political activism. The kind of transsexual health care activism advocated by Rothblatt and Stryker exemplifies these consequences.

In an appendix to her book, Rothblatt includes "The International Bill of Gender Rights." This bill was approved and adopted by the Second International Conference on Transgender Law and Employment Policy (ICTLEP) in Houston, Texas, in August 1993. Rothblatt has been an active member of ICTLEP, serving as the chair of the Health Law Project. This bill may be appended to her book not only due to its relevance for the realm of gender law, but also given Rothblatt's contribution to its formulation.

The bill covers a wide range of legal, medical, and social areas, including an individual's right to self-definition, the right to change one's body, the right to medical care, the right to freedom from psychiatric treatment, and parental rights. A consideration of the sections of the international bill relating to health reveals the implicitly American bias of this so-called international activism:

*The Right to Competent*
*Medical and*
*Professional Care*

Given the individual right to define one's gender identity, and the right to change one's own body as a means of expressing a self-defined gender identity, no individual should be denied access to competent medical or other professional care on the basis of chromosomal sex, genitalia, assigned birth sex, or initial gender role.

*The Right to Freedom*
*from Psychiatric*
*Diagnosis or Treatment*

Given the right to define one's own gender identity, individuals should not be subject to psychiatric diagnosis or treatment solely on the basis of their gender identity or role.[85]

Both of these sections of the international bill may appear to be well-conceived, reflective pieces to help transgendered people define and live their bodies on their own terms. But a closer examination reveals a specifically U.S. understanding of "health." In the prescriptive piece on the right to competent and professional medical care, for instance, the bill appeals to an individual's right to determine her/his gender. It is noteworthy that although this bill is clearly relevant for some imagined community of transgendered people, it is less specific when it comes to the diversity of that community. The authors of this bill claim that no one should be denied access to health care due to their sex, genitalia, or gender, but they do not include a variety of other factors that prevent people from accessing primary medical care. Why does this bill not demand health care for transgendered people of all economic levels? Is competent health care something that is only relevant for transgendered people with insurance and financial resources? Aside from the question of economics, this bill ignores a variety of reasons why some transsexual and transgendered people in America (even in America) do not receive health care: individuals who are prostitutes, those who are in prison, those who are seropositive, those who are homeless, those who are not "naturalized" as U.S. citizens. Thus, although this international bill would have transgendered people with money receive health care, it does not challenge how health care is organized and managed in the United States—an administration that benefits the hospital and insurance industries and that transforms physical, mental and social well-being into a commodity.[86] The section of the bill addressing psychiatry is equally inattentive to the political economy of health care for transgendered people in an international perspective. A right to define one's gender identity and enact the desired bodily modifications without the approval of psychiatrists is, to say the least, a proposal worth considering. Yet in countries where sex reassignment surgery is covered through federal, provincial, or state health ministries, these procedures are insurable precisely because psychiatrists recommend individuals for surgery. Therefore, it seems politically insufficient to propose a situation in which transgendered people can change their bodies without consulting psychiatrists. This perspective does not adequately consider the situation of transsexuals who live in Canada, Australia, or England—to name but three nations other than the United States. (To say that activists must consider the relations of transsexuals with psychiatrists in Commonwealth countries is not an endorsement of how health care is currently organized for transgendered people with respect to psychiatry, in these countries or in the United States. It is merely an acknowledgment that the administration of health care varies in different national locations.) Nor does this kind of activism address economic access to transsexual health care for poor transsexuals in the United States, as certain U.S. transsexual activists have pointed out.[87]

In a review of the Health Law Project of ICTLEP, Stryker addresses the question of a psychiatric diagnosis and the insurance of transsexual health care.[88] Like Rothblatt, she advocates a situation in which transsexuals can obtain access to health care without a diagnosis of "gender dysphoria." Insurance coverage should be made available for transsexual health care based on the unique needs of transsexuals, and not on a psychiatric diagnosis:

> The focus of activism should be to insure [sic] that we have access to health care based on our unique needs as transsexual people, and not because we have some illness requiring treatment.[89]

Although this position is engaging, it does not acknowledge the actual workings of insurance agencies, which require a diagnosis of gender dysphoria in order to cover transsexual health care costs and which refuse to reimburse surgery or hormone treatments classified as cosmetic. This limitation becomes more evident in Stryker's conclusion, in which she endorses a model of consumer activism in health care as a means for transsexuals to obtain the services they desire:

> Transsexuals approaching doctors directly and working with them to get the kinds of services we want is part of a pattern of consumer activism that has been emerging in the transgender community for several years. It is as consumers of medical services that we exercise real power over how these services are provided. No one forces us to change sex; doctors can't make their money off us without our compliance.[90]

This discourse of consumer activism in health care, of course, assumes that it is appropriate to understand health as a commodity to be bought and sold. This position legitimates an administrative and political context in which health care is the individual responsibility of consumers, rather than the responsibility of the state. Furthermore, it figures the collective power of transsexuals in exclusive relation to their purchasing potential: social movements as shopping.

Stryker and Rothblatt both advocate a situation in which transgendered people are "free" from medical and psychiatric control over their bodies.[91] This notion of "freedom" is elaborated through the concept of the sovereignty of the body, as when Rothblatt writes of "the right to change one's body"[92] or that "the progressive track of transgender health law is to guard against government withdrawal of freedom of choice over one's body."[93] Stryker echoes this discourse in arguing that "[w]e need to find the courage to stand up for our rights."[94] Neither author appreciates that the very concepts of "individuals" and "rights" are highly specific to the United States.[95] Although their interventions complement the U.S. legal context, in which the rights of an "individual" are secured through the constitution, they do not necessarily apply to other nationalities. Within a francophone context, for instance, the body is legally inscribed as a matter of public order.[96] To that end, it is inappropriate for transsexual health activism that calls itself "international" to base its political positions on concepts that are specific to the United States juridical context (individuality, sovereignty of the body).

Although Stryker and Rothblatt clearly affirm transsexual identities in their work, they simultaneously create a vision of the world that limits itself to the United States, and that therefore perpetuates a rather dangerous and solipsistic nationalism. The metaphorical associations between African-Americans and transsexuals made by Stryker and Rothblatt have expansive repercussions, both in terms of gender (transsexuals) and in terms of nationalism (the myth that America is a land of freedom, the assumption that American consumer models of health care activism are the most appropriate ones for international work in this area).

## CONCLUSION

Black's interactive theory of metaphor provides an excellent framework for understanding the metaphorical connections established between gender and nation. In mass cultural representations such as *Priscilla, Le sexe des étoiles,* and *Hosanna,* for instance, metaphorical associations between MTF transgendered people and the urban metropolis achieve two related functions: an enactment of negative stereotypes about MTF transgendered people, and a normatively gendered vision of national identity. As Black explains, these two functions interact, each one providing the frame and means to interpret the other. The use of metaphor within these texts posits a nationalized gender (MTFs are not citizens of the nation, but can only represent its crises), as well as a gendered nationalism (the nation is comprised of masculine, heterosexual men complemented by feminine, heterosexual women). Within U.S. transsexual activism, a similar interaction between gender and nation occurs. Through the metaphors they use, writers like Stryker and Rothblatt situate MTF transgendered people within the nation of America. They too offer an analysis and political manifesto that decrees both a nationalized gender (transsexuals are American) as well as a gendered nationalism (the urban centers of the United States are cosmopolitan sites of "freedom" that can accommodate transsexuals). Both mainstream mass culture and prominent U.S. transgendered activism realize and reinforce interactive relations between gender and nation.

Within mass cultural representations such as *Priscilla, Le sexe des étoiles,* and *Hosanna,* the figure of the MTF transvestite, drag queen, and/or transsexual is invoked as a means to articulate a position centrally concerned with nationalism. The use of rhetoric reduces transsexual and transgendered people to the merely figural, while reinforcing negative stereotypes that associate MTF transgendered people with illusion, deception, madness, suicide, and tragedy. This exclusively figural representation of transsexuality inscribes the identity as literally impossible. Prominent transsexual activism in the English-speaking United States, in contrast, affirms the possibility of transsexual and transgendered identities through an implicit appeal to American nationalism. An assertion of transsexual identity via American models of consumer health activism has the lamentable consequence of obliterating transsexuals living outside the United States, as well as neglecting poor transsexuals within it. In the case of mass culture as well as U.S. transsexual activism, this effacement of transsexual and transgendered people is textually organized through the use of rhetoric. For this reason, reflection on the micrological realization and function of rhetoric is an integral component of understanding how transsexual and transgendered people are erased in the everyday cultural world.

# III

## RESEARCH

# 6

## GENDERBASHING

*Sexuality, Gender, and the Regulation of Public Space*

In chapters 4 and 5, I examined the effacement of transsexual and transgendered people through the micrological work of discourse and rhetoric. Chapter 4 illustrated how gendered discourse undermines transsexual
identities, while chapter 5 explored the concept of erasure in terms of the
reduction of TS/TG people to the merely figural, a reduction that makes
transsexuality literally impossible. This chapter provides a different lens
through which to consider the obliteration of transsexual and transgendered people, taking up the question of violence against sexual and gender
minorities.[1]

The chapter has two aims. (1) a critical reflection of the conceptual
relations between gender and sexuality within the realm of violence against
sexual and gender minorities, and (2) an analysis of how the documents
produced by activists, the police, and policy makers are used in specific
institutional sites to frame particular understandings of violence. A case
study of antiviolence activism in Montréal exposes the effacement of transsexual and transgendered people in lesbian/gay community-based discussions of violence. The stated goals of this chapter, of course, are related.
Reflection on how violence is conceptualized can raise important questions
about the oversights within the institutional policies and practices designed
to respond to violence against sexual and gender minorities.

In North America, violence against lesbians, gay men, and bisexuals is
escalating at an alarming rate. A survey conducted in 1986–87 by the
Philadelphia Lesbian and Gay Task Force reports that violence against lesbians and gay men in that city had doubled since 1983–84.[2] The United
States National Gay and Lesbian Task Force (NGLTF) documents that incidents of violence against sexual minorities increased 127 percent from
1988 to 1993.[3]

Though scholars[4] and community activists[5] have increasingly addressed the issue of violence against lesbians and gay men, there remains
very little reflection on the function of gender within these acts of aggression. In this chapter, I argue that a perceived transgression of normative

sex/gender relations motivates much of the violence against sexual minorities, and that an assault on these "transgressive" bodies is fundamentally concerned with policing gender presentation through public and private space. I also consider the implications of this research for transsexual and transgendered people. Given that the perception of gender dissidence informs acts of queerbashing, we can deduce that those individuals who live outside normative sex/gender relations will be most at risk for assault. Finally, I examine some of the ways in which educational strategies on violence separate gender and sexuality, and thus prevent a political response that accounts for the function of gender in queerbashing. Specific examples are taken from briefs presented in November 1993 to the Québec Human Rights Commission's public hearings in Montréal on violence and discrimination against lesbians and gay men.[6] I demonstrate the ways in which gender and sexuality are separated, and thus how the issue of gender is foreclosed by certain gay male community activists.

These briefs occupy central roles in defining the issue of violence against sexual minorities within a Québécois context. They coordinate how violence is understood, and therefore the kinds of strategies, interventions, and programs needed to adequately respond to the situation. Although antiviolence activists in Québec had claimed that the issue of violence against sexual minorities was by no means new, the public consultations held in 1993 were the first official recognition of this phenomenon by the state. Because agencies such as the Québec Human Rights Commission make use of these texts to organize their activities, these briefs are much more than political position papers: they function to order our understandings, and actions, of violence against sexual and gender minorities. As Canadian sociologist Dorothy Smith claims, such texts are central to the ongoing, practical work of governments:

> The relations of ruling in our kind of society are mediated by texts, by words, numbers, and images on paper, in computers, or on TV and movie screens. Texts are the primary medium (though not the substance) of power. The work of administration, of management, of government is a communicative work. Organizational and political processes are forms of action coordinated textually and getting done in words. It is an ideologically structured mode of action—images, vocabularies, concepts, abstract terms of knowledge are integral to the practice of power, to getting things done.[7]

If, as Smith argues, texts are central to the coordinating activities of government, a critical examination of some of the texts presented to the Québec

Human Rights Commission provides an opportunity to examine the social relations of gender in one institutional site. My analysis is particularly concerned with how transsexual and transgendered people are rendered invisible by key texts that ignore violence against transsexual and transgendered people. In this regard, the circulation of these briefs in the institutional world represents one of the ways in which the erasure of transsexual and transgendered people is textually coordinated. I use the term "erasure" to designate a conceptualization of gender that excludes the bodies and experiences of transsexual and transgendered people, and that informs the taken-for-granted work of institutions. "Erasure" refers to the conceptual and institutional relations through which transsexual and transgendered individuals disappear from view.

## GENDER AND SEXUALITY

The relations between gender and sexuality figure centrally in this chapter, and it is necessary to clarify how they can at once intersect and diverge. The theoretical work of Gayle Rubin is useful for this purpose.[8] In 1975, Rubin wrote a by-now famous anthropological essay on women and kinship. Taking up Claude Lévi-Strauss's notion of exchange,[9] in which one's social status is achieved in part through the exchange of gifts, she remarks that it was always women who were exchanged by men. Rubin argues that this defines women in terms of their reproductive capabilities, thereby making biology a social phenomenon and consolidating a heterosexual contract. In 1984, however, Rubin revised her statement, at least in terms of its application within Western societies. She notes that her earlier work had confused gender and sexuality:

> In contrast to my perspective in "The Traffic in Women," I am now arguing that it is essential to separate gender and sexuality analytically to more accurately reflect their separate social existence.[10]

Because gender and sexuality are not the same thing, Rubin suggests, scholars interested in theorizing sexuality should not assume that feminist theory is the perspective best able to account for the social organization of erotic life:

> I want to challenge the assumption that feminism is or should be the privileged site of a theory of sexuality. Feminism is the theory of gender oppression. To automatically assume that this makes it the theory of sexual oppression is to fail to distinguish between gender, on the one hand, and erotic desire, on the other.[11]

In 1992, Rubin offered a further clarification of the relations between gender and sexuality: while it is certainly true that gender and sexuality are not the same thing, it is also true that they intersect in quite significant ways. Rubin considers the question of FTM transsexuality, remarking that there is a great deal of common ground between butch lesbians and FTMs. Despite these similarities, lesbian communities are often openly hostile to transsexuals: "A woman who has been respected, admired, and loved as a butch may suddenly be despised, rejected, and hounded when she starts a sex change." [12] In Rubin's analysis, lesbian communities should not instantly reject an FTM transsexual, because this individual elaborates a unique vision of gender. Rubin reminds her readers that sexual and gender outlaws share a common history: "Lesbian communities were built by sex and gender refugees; the lesbian world should not create new rationales for sex and gender persecution." [13]

The development of Rubin's thinking on the relations between gender and sexuality provides an occasion to reflect on the difficulties involved in theorizing this question. In certain social, cultural, and historical contexts, a separation of gender and sexuality seems impossible. In other locations, however, they appear markedly distinct. One of Rubin's most important contributions in this area is the acknowledgment that these issues change over time. In her discussion of lesbian communities, for instance, she observes that bars that catered to lesbians were also havens for transsexuals. Ruben even notes that many "butch" women who are embraced as important figures in lesbian history could also, and in some instances more accurately, be labeled transsexual. [14] To appreciate the ways in which gender and sexuality intersect historically, as Rubin does, is to demand a critical examination of more contemporary relations between these issues. While Rubin discusses the expulsion of transsexuals from lesbian communities, she highlights the ways in which lesbian sexuality is defined in exclusive relation to a "naturalized" gender category rooted in biology. Lesbian identity is secured through the invocation of a sexual category, not a label of gender. Rubin observes how contemporary lesbian identity forces a separation of gender and sexuality, despite the fact that they were entwined historically.

Throughout this chapter I will explore the insights of Rubin in an attempt to develop an effective response to violence against sexual and gender minorities. What role does gender play in attacks against lesbians and gay men? Is violence against transsexuals common, and is it of a different order than that against sexual minorities? Does the response to violence offered by gay male communities actually prevent activists and educators from addressing the needs of women and transgendered people? How are gender and sexuality linked, or juxtaposed, within a problematic of "queer-bashing"? This chapter hopes to shed light on several issues: how violence affects TS/TG individuals; how the notion of gender is frequently eclipsed within discussions on violence against gays and lesbians; how we can develop appropriate responses to this problematic; and how we can go about gathering and interpreting data on the relations between gender and violence.

The chapter is primarily a theoretical one: I do not present the results of comprehensive empirical research on violence against TS/TG people. Nevertheless, it is my hope that the chapter will clearly illustrate the value of careful theoretical reflection on the issue of violence in the development of appropriate solutions to this problem. Drawing on the kind of poststructuralist sociology I propose in chapter 3, I am interested in examining several related issues with respect to violence: the everyday social world; the production and/or effacement of transgendered people within that world; the development of appropriate interventionist political strategies; and a reflexive sociological practice, which understands how different theories construct, legitimate, and/or obliterate their objects. But this chapter is only a beginning: although I try to illustrate how transgendered people are erased within select community discourses on violence, and although I use this insight to consider more appropriate ways for scholars and activists to collect and analyze data, I do not offer an empirical study herein. The present chapter, then, ought to be interpreted in light of these strengths and limitations.

I use the term "violence" to refer to a variety of acts, mannerisms, and attitudes. It can range from verbal insults (e.g., calling someone a "fag"), to an invasion of personal space (e.g., throwing a bottle at a lesbian as she walks by), to intimidation and the threat of physical assault. "Violence" also includes the act of attacking someone's body—whether through sexual assault (rape), beating, or with weapons like baseball bats, knives, or guns. The question of violence is obviously linked to that of discrimination: in the case of queerbashing, the denial of same-sex insurance benefits, for example, privileges heterosexual relationships over homosexual ones, and thus fosters an atmosphere of intolerance of sexual minorities. The NGLTF reports a marked rise in violence against sexual minorities in Colorado immediately following the passage of Amendment 2, a state ordinance prohibiting antidiscrimination legislation on the basis of sexual preference.[15] While violence and discrimination support each other, this chapter focuses on the notion of violence as defined above.

## LIMITS OF TOLERANCE: GENDER NORMS
## AND GENDER TRANSGRESSIONS

"Gender" refers to the roles and meanings assigned to men and women based on their presumed biological sex.[16] It is a social function, neither timeless nor historical. For example, we generally associate the color pink with girls and femininity and the color blue with boys and masculinity. There is nothing inherent in either of these colors that links them to a particular gender: pink, or turquoise, could just as easily designate masculinity. Gender is also about what men and women are supposed to do in the world—men wear pants, have short hair, can grow beards, and are considered more physically aggressive than women. Women can wear skirts, have longer hair, wear makeup, and are judged to be emotional. In Western societies, it is thought that there are only two genders—men and women.[17]

"Sexuality," in contrast, refers to the ways in which individuals organize their erotic and sexual lives. This is generally categorized into three separate areas: heterosexuals—individuals who have sexual relations with members of the opposite sex; homosexuals—those who have sexual relations with members of the same sex; and bisexuals—people who relate erotically to both men and women.[18]

In Western societies, gender and sexuality get confused. For example, when a fifteen-year-old boy is assaulted and called a "faggot," he is so labeled because he has mannerisms that are considered "effeminate." He may or may not be gay, but he is called a "queer" because he does not fulfill his expected gender role. A young girl can be a tomboy until the age of eleven or so, but she must then live as a more "dainty," "feminine" person. If she does not, she may be called a "dyke"—again, regardless of how she actually defines her sexual identity. In both examples, the presentation of gender determines how these youths are received by their peers. When people shout "faggot" at a fifteen-year-old boy, they really mean that he is not a "masculine" man. Gender and sexuality are collapsed. As Rubin points out, the merging of gender and sexuality enables some feminist theorists to write about erotic desire.[19]

The fusion of gender and sexuality has distinct implications for the problematic of violence. The connotations of the pejorative names used against individuals who are assaulted—names like "sissy," "faggot," "dyke," "man-hater," "queer," and "pervert"—suggest that an attack is justified not in reaction to one's sexual identity, but to one's gender presentation. Indeed, bashers do not characteristically inquire as to the sexual identity of their potential victims, but rather make this assumption on their own. On what basis do "queerbashers" determine who is gay, lesbian, or bisexual?

Joseph Harry's research suggests that gender be considered an important variable in queerbashing incidents.[20] Harry found that groups of assailants involved in these crimes relied on gender cues to ascertain sexual identity. If they judged a potential victim to be "effeminate," for example, he was subject to attack. A related study confirms this hypothesis: 39 percent of men surveyed who behaved in a "feminine" manner had been physically assaulted, compared with 22 percent of men who were "masculine" and only 17 percent of men who conducted themselves in a "very masculine" fashion.[21] According to this survey, males who are classified as "effeminate" are more than twice as likely to experience physical violence than males whose gender presentation corresponds to social norms. A study of anti-lesbian abuse in San Francisco indicates that 12 percent of lesbians surveyed had been punched, kicked, or otherwise physically assaulted.[22] Significantly, the only justification offered relates to gender:

> [F]ourteen of the women said that the only explanation for incidents they had experienced was the fact that they had short hair and were wearing trousers and in most cases were in the company of another woman.[23]

Women and men who transgress acceptable limits of self-presentation, then, are among those most at risk for assault. Assaults against men judged to be "effeminate" or women deemed "masculine" reveal the ways in which gender and sexuality are intertwined. Gender is used as a cue to locate lesbians and gay men. Though the perceived transgression of gender norms motivates bashing, this affects men and women differently. The gendered construction of space—both public and private—figures centrally in these acts of aggression.

## GENDERED SPACE AND THE PUBLIC/PRIVATE DICHOTOMY

One of the remarkable things about the study of violence against sexual minorities is the way in which such aggression can be linked to common-sense assumptions of what constitutes "public" space, who has the right to occupy it, and how people should interact therein. The gendered dimension of the public space has been examined by many feminist scholars.[24] Shirley Ardener remarks that the presence of men is used to define a particular place as "public."[25] This means that women are confined to the private sphere. A public/private, masculine/feminine opposition has deep historical roots. In *Prostitution and Victorian Society,* Judith Walkowitz notes that society sanctioned the presence of men in the streets as well as public establishments such as taverns and gambling houses. Women who were found in these same sites, however, had violated middle-class notions of what "decent" women did and did not do, and the places they frequented. Walkowitz provides an elaborate analysis of the ways in which prostitutes came to be labeled "public" women.[26]

In this light, attacks against lesbians and gay men can be interpreted in terms of a defense of the "public" as that domain that belongs to men—heterosexual men, to be more precise. Entrance into the public sphere is secured through the enactment of a sanctioned gender identity, preferably within the context of a heterosexual dyad. Couples who violate this prescription, and perhaps especially transgendered people who walk alone, pose a fundamental challenge to public space and how it is defined and secured through gender.

Empirical data support such statements. Social scientists like Comstock and Valentine have recently explored the gender and geographic differences in cases of anti-lesbian abuse and anti-gay assault. It is argued that while both lesbians and gay men are attacked, lesbians are assaulted in "ordinary" public spaces. Gay men, in contrast, are habitually beaten in areas known to be gay—ghettoes, parking lots of gay bars, or public parks where men have sex with other men. For instance, in Comstock's study, 45 percent of lesbians were queerbashed in public lesbian/gay spaces, 42 percent in non-lesbian/gay areas, 30 percent in the home, and 17 percent in the school. In contrast, 66 percent of gay men were attacked in gay areas, only 29 percent in "ordinary" public space, 26 percent in the home, and 24 percent in the school. Thus, men "experience more violence in lesbian/gay areas and in secondary school settings," while women "experience more violence in straight-identified, domestic, and higher-education settings."[27] The presence of women in public who are not accompanied by men is a threat to the implicit masculine dimension of public space. It is for this reason that lesbians, and other females perceived to be a threat to normative heterosexuality, are assaulted in the streets. The issues become even more complex when variables of race are examined: in Comstock's empirical study, 20 percent of people of color surveyed were assaulted in lesbian/gay space, compared with only 9 percent of white lesbians and gay men.[28] This data suggests that geographic areas known to be gay villages and/or cruising grounds are most dangerous for men of color. Conversely, women (especially those who are perceived to be lesbians or "masculine") are most at risk in everyday locations that assume the "naturalness" of heterosexuality.[29]

Comstock demonstrates that gay men are usually attacked when alone (66 percent of survey respondents), while lesbians are often attacked in pairs (44 percent of respondents).[30] It is noteworthy, however, that these numbers are drastically reduced when men and women walk together: only 8 percent of women respondents were physically assaulted when they were with a man. The figure drops to 1 percent for men accompanied by women. The safety secured through an opposite-sex partner seems to hold regardless of the public space that one occupies (i.e., lesbian/gay or "ordinary" space).

This research underlines the importance of gender as a variable in the issue of violence. Gay men can avoid assault within a space designated as gay by having a woman with them, while lesbians can escape physical harm in the "everyday" (i.e., heterosexual) world by having a man with them. Both of these strategies rely on implicit assumptions about who men and women are and how they should interact in public. As G. Valentine expresses it,

> Heterosexuality is ideologically linked to the notion of gender identities (masculinity and femininity) because the notion of opposite-sex relationships presumes a binary distinction between what it means to be a man or a woman.[31]

Valentine articulates a position similar to that of Rubin: gender and sexuality are intertwined, such that "masculinity" and "femininity" appear to be the "natural," complementary extremes of heterosexuality. Homosexuality, then, is associated with gender inversion. Furthermore, heterosexual men and women can walk together safely in the streets; gay men and lesbians, in contrast, must negotiate the threat of violence each time they enter the public realm—particularly if they walk with a same-sex partner.

The gendered nature of both public and private space upholds a binary opposition between men and women and thus bolsters the ideological workings of heterosexual hegemony. Individuals who are perceived to be— or who declare themselves as—lesbian, bisexual, or gay are among those most likely to be attacked, given a cultural conflation between gender and sexuality. Yet the issue is much deeper than perpetrators using gender cues to identify potential victims. A more profound question centers around the ways in which men and women should interact in public. The demarcation of public space is intimately related to the articulation of culturally sanctioned gender identities.[32]

## Transsexual and Transgendered People and Violence

The perceived violation of gender norms at the root of many instances of assault, harassment, and discrimination affects all males and females—not just those whose sexual identity is located outside of heterosexuality. By emphasizing the function of gender in queerbashing, research can help develop education and activist programs that are relevant to people of all sexual and gender identities. A stress on the intersection of gender and violence demonstrates that the issue of queerbashing profoundly affects heterosexuals, insofar as the threat of violence polices one's gender presentation and behavior.

Although this research is desperately needed and must be strongly encouraged, it should be supplemented with an investigation of the everyday experiences of people who live outside normative sex/gender relations. An attention to people who call themselves transsexual and/or transgendered can provide more insight into the relations between gender and violence.

Despite the variety of gender identities available in transgender networks, and despite the prevalence of transgendered people in other cultures, most people in Western societies assume that there are only two sexes (males and females) and two genders (men and women).[33] For transsexual and/or transgendered people, this poses a significant problem: a person must choose the gender to which he/she belongs and behave accordingly. Because most people believe that there are only "men" and "women," transgendered people need to live as one or the other in order to avoid verbal and physical harassment. In transgendered communities, this is known as the need to pass. Passing is about presenting yourself as a "real" woman or a "real" man—that is, as an individual whose "original" sex is never suspected.[34] Passing means hiding the fact that you are transsexual and/or transgendered. Most people go to extraordinary lengths to live undetected as transsexuals. Electrolysis, voice therapy, the binding of breasts, mastectomy, and plastic surgery are some of the more common means employed to ensure that people pass successfully.

The necessity of passing is directly related to the cultural coding of gender. In their ethnomethodological study of the implicit ways in which gender operates, Suzanne Kessler and Wendy McKenna demonstrate that social meanings are grafted onto bodies in order to give them one of two binary sexes. The researchers presented 960 students with representations of many different bodies. For example, they showed a picture of a body with long hair, breasts, and wide hips, and asked the participants in the study to tell them if the person was a "man" or a "woman." Kessler and McKenna found that the interpretation of sexed bodies was overwhelmingly skewed in favor of masculine referents. If a penis was present, a "male" gender attribution was made 96 percent of the time. Yet in order for a figure to be considered "female" more than 95 percent of the time, it needed to have a vagina *and* two other cues indicating femininity (e.g., long hair, breasts).[35]

This research has profound implications for the study of violence and gender. If gender ambiguity is habitually resolved within a masculinist frame of reference, then genetic males who live as women will be among those most at risk for assault. Simply put, within Western societies, it is easier for females to pass as men than for males to pass as women. Ethnographic research on gender confirms this hypothesis: in Holly Devor's study of "gender-blending" females, she notes that several of the women she interviewed felt free enough to walk down dimly lit streets late at night, given that they were perceived to be men.[36] Furthermore, many genetic females can live full-time as men without plastic surgery and/or male hormones. Conversely, many genetic males need to take female hormones in order to pass successfully as women.

Although nonpassing transsexuals would seem to be foremost among those at risk, other individuals experience similar harassment, such as non-transsexual people with seemingly transsexual characteristics. Tall women with broad shoulders and men with wide hips and little facial hair are among those most likely to be mistaken for transsexuals.

Given the cultural coding of gender into a binary framework, a high incidence of violence directed against TS/TG people is not surprising. Although there is very little data available on transgendered people as victims of violence, a 1992 study showed that 52 percent of MTF transsexuals and 43 percent of FTM transsexuals surveyed in London, England, had been physically assaulted.[37] Contrast these numbers with data from a 1989 American telephone poll, which revealed that 7 percent of lesbians and gay men were victims of assault in the previous year.[38] Although these samples represent two different countries, the statistical difference of violent incidents against gay/lesbian and transgender individuals is remarkable and certainly suggests that gender plays a crucial role in the attacks generally referred to as "gaybashing."

Although gender plays a central role in incidents of queerbashing, a collapse of gender and sexuality precludes a consideration of how this violence specifically affects transgendered people. Dorian Corey notes that contemporary gay antiviolence activists do not recognize the different ways aggression is, and has historically been, directed against transgendered people and gays:

> When the closet doors were shut [for gays, in the past], drag queens, of course, were out there anyways. We never had a closet. Let's face it, when you put on a dress and hit the world, you're declaring what you are. . . . These children that are supposedly straight looking, they're the ones getting bashed, so now [in the 1990s] they're protesting. The girls were always getting their asses kicked. It's just a thing of who you are and what you are.[39]

Transsexual activists have suggested that one of the ways we can respond to the function of gender in violence is by naming it directly. As an activist button proclaims, "transsexuals get queerbashed too." Activists also insist that we need to speak of *genderbashing*, not gaybashing. This discourse separates gender and sexuality, since their collapse prevents an appreciation of the specificity of violence against transsexual and transgendered people.

## TRANSSEXUAL/TRANSGENDERED PEOPLE AND PUBLIC SPACE

If lesbians and gay men are attacked differently according to the public space they occupy, how can we think about the relations between space and gender for transgendered people? Despite the lack of empirical research on this phenomenon, we can stipulate that transsexual and transgendered people are at risk in known lesbian/gay areas, as well as in "ordinary" public spaces. An MTF transsexual in a gay village, for example, may be perceived as a gender outlaw by a homophobic assailant and attacked as a "faggot."[40] Analogously, an FTM transsexual walking on an "ordinary" street may be perceived as a threat to masculine, heterosexual public space, especially if he does not completely pass as a genetic male. The issue of passing is especially complex in the case of many FTMs, who are often perceived to be young, slightly effeminate boys.[41] To pass as a man, in such an instance, can involve the dangers associated with a public gay identity. Yet the issues become even more complex if it is discovered that the person being attacked is transgendered, not (or not only) lesbian, gay, or bisexual. When FTMs are assaulted, for instance, rape is a routine part of the violence they endure.[42] This suggests that gender functions not merely as a cue to identify potential victims. FTMs who are raped are told, through the act of sexual assault, that they are "really" women, and they will be treated as such.

Biology is destiny. The rape of an FTM declares that "women" have no right to be out in public—especially when unaccompanied by a man—and that these individuals have no right to act "as if" they are men. This instance of violence is more than a mere attack on someone perceived to be a gay man; it is fundamentally about policing one's gender presentation in public sites. The act of rape functions as an aggressive reinscription of the FTM individual's biological sex and social gender.

The division of public and private spaces, which relies upon and reinforces a binary gender system, has profound implications for people who live outside normative sex/gender relations. Transgendered people are in jeopardy in both "ordinary" public spaces and in those designated as lesbian/gay. While one must address the workings of gender in these sites, an investigation of violence against TS/TG people would also account for the emergence of TS/TG public space.

## SEX WORK AND TRANSSEXUAL/TRANSGENDERED PUBLIC SPACE

"Transsexual and transgendered public space" refers to urban areas known for their transsexuals and transvestites, such as the Meat District on the border of New York's Greenwich Village, Santa Monica Boulevard in Los Angeles, or the Tenderloin in San Francisco. While gay male public space is defined through the presence of gay businesses and bars, transsexual public space reflects the areas of the city frequented by transsexual and transvestite sex workers.

Since gender and sexuality are not the same, it is not surprising that most cities have separate geographic areas known for transgendered people and lesbians/gays. Pat Califia articulates the differences between gay ghettoes and sex worker areas:

> Gay ghettos operate differently than other types of sex zones. They are more likely to be residential districts for gay men as well as places where they can find entertainment. Although johns still enter gay ghettos in quest of pleasurable activities not available within the nuclear family, they have better luck scoring if they camouflage themselves as residents of the area.[43]

Because transgender areas are not tied to a notion of a resident (as in the case of gay ghettos), the ways in which the space can be defined varies. Although certain sections of the city are known for their transsexuals and transvestites, these people are usually only visible at night. New York's Meat Market District is so named because of its many meat-packaging warehouses. When these businesses close at the end of the day, transgendered sex workers come out to earn their livelihoods, and thus transform the meaning of the term "meat" into one with explicit sexual connotations. Time of day and geographic space converge to establish a public transgender identity. For example, a Toronto sex worker interviewed in David Adkin's film *Out: Stories of Lesbian and Gay Youth* refers to the area where transgender prostitutes solicit clients as "trannie town."[44]

As Califia demonstrates, the recent emergence of gay ghettos has separated sexual minorities from transsexual prostitutes. Although bars catering to transgendered people are extremely rare, they are usually located in sex worker districts rather than in gay villages. In Montréal, for example, the transsexual/transvestite bar Café Cléopâtra is situated near the corner of Sainte-Catherine and Saint-Laurent streets, in the heart of the red-light district.[45] The bar is widely known for its prostitutes—it is a space not only where transgendered people can socialize, but where they can also earn their livings. Montréal police observe the establishment regularly. While recent years have not witnessed any official raids on the bar, it is common for officers to walk in, "do the rounds," and inspect bar patrons, sex workers, and their prospective clients.[46]

This police harassment of transgendered people relates to the laws against prostitution. In Canada, prostitution is entirely legal, but soliciting clients is not.[47] Individual officers have enormous scrutiny in the interpretation of what constitutes "solicitation": it may be a verbal agreement about sexual acts in exchange for financial compensation, or it may be a smile or glance directed at an undercover officer. While the latter instance would probably not be considered "solicitation" in a court of law, officers still have the power to charge individuals with the crime and place them in custody for a night. The crime of "soliciting" sex, of course, is fundamentally concerned with the regulation of public space, and it implicitly assumes that independent women have no right to be on the street at night.[48] It is the communication of sexual desire that is criminalized in Canada, not sexual desire or its enactment per se. Not surprisingly, this legislation does not affect all sex workers equally. Cathy, the operator of an escort service, remarks that street prostitutes—those most visible in the public eye—are most affected by this law: "escort services . . . have enjoyed . . . tolerance as we go tiptoeing around in the night, not bothering communities because we're not standing in people's front yards."[49] Research indicates that police use the soliciting law to harass prostitutes, following them down the street in a patrol car or stopping to talk with them during their work.[50]

## LIMITS OF ANTIVIOLENCE ACTIVISM:
## OPPOSING GENDER AND SEXUALITY

The preceding discussion has emphasized some of the ways in which gender is fundamental to a conceptual organization of violence, most especially
violence in public space: that males judged to be "effeminate" are subject to
verbal abuse and physical attack; that lesbians are subject to a lesser degree
of aggression in public when they are with a male partner as opposed to a
female; and that more than half of MTF transsexual respondents in one
survey reported being victims of a physical attack. The final section of this
chapter considers the conjuncture of gender, violence, and public space,
with a particular concern for how community-based responses to violence
against sexual and gender minorities can actually eclipse the realities of
violence against transsexual and transgendered prostitutes.

Much of the activist response to violence against sexual and gender minorities has centered on the gay village of a particular city.[51] As most gay
men are assaulted in areas demarcated as "gay," this focus is useful. Yet such
a strategy forecloses an investigation of gender and ignores the different
experiences of lesbians, bisexual women, and transgendered people with
respect to public space and violence. By emphasizing sexual identity, this
discourse establishes an antiviolence agenda that is, at best, only somewhat
useful. Consider the text of an educational poster produced by Montréal's
police department (Service de police de la communauté urbaine de Montréal, or SPCUM): "Being lesbian, gay, or bisexual is not a crime. Bashing
is." The slogan—which also appears on buttons produced by antiviolence
activists in Toronto—addresses the perpetrators of violence directly, and in
that, it is to be commended. Despite this direct address, however, the poster
does not engage the cognitive processes at work that perpetrators use to
determine who is gay, lesbian, or bisexual. In this discourse, identity is
mobilized as the ground upon which acts of violence are established.
People are bashed because they are gay, lesbian, or bisexual. But we have
already seen that bashing occurs due to the perception of potential victims,
and that compulsory sex/gender relations figure centrally in these acts of
interpretation. In this light, educational materials that address the perpetrators of violence should focus on the interpretive processes these people use
to locate queerbashing victims. Because gender is the primary mechanism
through which this takes place, there is a desperate need for posters,
pamphlets, and presentations that outline the ways in which a binary gender system is upheld, as well as the power relations concealed within it.

Through a stress on being, rather than on the perception of doing, the SPCUM poster reifies sexual identity and prevents a proper investigation of gender in the problematic of violence.

Implicitly, gender and sexuality are juxtaposed. This opposition can be witnessed in the brief presented by the SPCUM to the Québec Human Rights Commission in association with its public hearings on violence and discrimination against lesbians and gay men (November 1993). The relationship between sexual minorities and the police figured centrally in the public consultation. Only three years earlier, the SPCUM had publicly *assaulted* lesbians, bisexuals, and gay men during a raid on Sex Garage, an underground warehouse party raided by the MUC police. Activists also expressed ongoing concern about the possibility of a serial murderer in Montréal who targeted gay male victims. In addition to these issues, activists charged that the SPCUM had little knowledge of, or interest in, the increased violence against sexual minorities—particularly the assaults that occurred in the gay village.[52]

In their brief to the commission, the SPCUM presented data on the prevalence of crime in District 33—the geographic area that includes (but is not limited to) the gay village. The borders of the village (René-Lévesque and Ontario, Amherst and Papineau) were compared to a similar section of the city—that demarcated by the streets René-Lévesque and Ontario (north/south axis) and Amherst and Saint-Laurent (east/west). The SPCUM was interested in comparing these two sections of District 33 in order to evaluate the frequency of violent incidents (thefts, sexual assault, harassment). The areas are proportional in size, each comprising about 20 percent of the district. Moreover, they share certain similarities in terms of the businesses, bars, and people present:

> Tous deux sont dans l'axe de la rue Ste-Catherine, rue très fréquentée de jour comme de nuit et où l'on retrouve divers commerces, restaurants, bars et salles d'amusement. On y retrouve également des activités reliées à la vente et la consommation de stupéfiants, à la prostitution masculine et féminine contrôlée, en partie, par deux groupes de motards criminels. [Both include Sainte-Catherine street, which is busy both day and night, and where one can find a variety of businesses, restaurants, bars, and amusement halls. One can also find activities related to the sale and consumption of drugs, as well as male and female prostitution, which is controlled, in part, by two groups of criminal bikers.][53]

The SPCUM data indicates that between November 1991 and October 1993, a total of 1,454 crimes were recorded for the gay village—approximately 18 percent of the total number of reported crimes in District 33.[54] Given that the gay village comprises 20 percent of the district, the study implies that incidents of violence and crime correspond proportionately to geography. (However, the brief does not address the population of the gay village in relation to that of the entire district, thus associating violence with city space rather than demographics.)

The SPCUM offers comparative data to legitimate this figure. The section of District 33 to which the gay village is compared indicates 2,774 incidents of violence over the same time period, a statistic that amounts to 34 percent of the violence in the total district.[55] Since the comparison territory is relatively equal in size to that of the gay village, it is suggested that violence and crime occur more frequently in this area than in the section of the city known to be populated by gay men. By demonstrating the ways in which crime in the gay village is statistically *below* the proportional incidents of violence in District 33, the SPCUM attempts to dismiss activists who point to increased instances of bashing in Montréal's gay village. (The results of the SPCUM study are presented in figure 1.)

There are, of course, tremendous differences in the data on violence collected by police departments and that collected by lesbian and gay community groups.[56] What is perhaps even more remarkable about the research presented by the SPCUM, however, is the way in which it forces a separation between sexuality and gender in terms of public space. The comparative section of District 33—that area bordered by Saint-Laurent, Amherst, Ontario, and René-Lévesque—is well-known as the city's sex worker district. The city's only transsexual/transvestite bar is located here, and streets in this region are also frequented by TS/TG prostitutes. Although the SPCUM maintains that both the gay village and this comparative section are homes to prostitution, they do not account for the gendered breakdown of this activity. Field research conducted in the summer of 1993 indicates that most male prostitutes work in the gay village, toward Papineau; directly on its borders (Parc Lafontaine, located just above Amherst and Ontario); or in an adult cinema at the corner of Sainte-Catherine and Amherst. In contrast, most female prostitutes work on the corner of Saint-Laurent and Sainte-Catherine, on Saint-Denis, or on side streets in the vicinity. Transgendered prostitutes can also be found in this area. (The geographic location of sex workers in District 33 is depicted in figure 2.)

Regarding incidents of violence, most TS/TG prostitutes work in an area with a much higher frequency of criminal acts than the gay village (34 percent versus 18 percent). Although these statistics do not necessarily indicate that more transgendered people (proportionally) are victims of

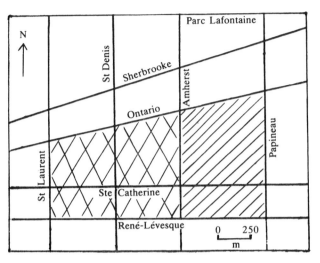

**Figure 1.** Incidents of violent crimes in two sections of Police District 33, Montréal, November 1991–October 1993 (source: SPCUM 1993, 10–11).

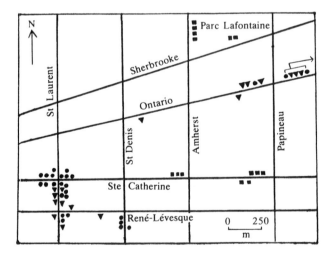

**Figure 2.** Sex-worker presence according to gender in Police District 33, Montréal, November 1991–October 1993 (source: field research). Note: more sex workers can be found further east on Ontario.

violence than gay men, it is certainly fair to stipulate that they work in an area known for criminal activities. To present this region as a comparative sample against the gay village is, then, to juxtapose gender and sexuality. While the SPCUM attempts to dispel fears about the high incidence of violence in gay space, it offers no examination of the role gender plays either in this site or its comparative territory. Because gender is not signaled as a factor in the discussion of District 33—along with other variables including poverty and homelessness—the SPCUM assumes that crime does not vary according to the gendered dimension of public space. The focus accorded to sexuality and the gay ghetto makes it impossible to address the violence that is directed against TS/TG people—whether they are in the gay village, a sex worker zone, or elsewhere.

It is important to understand the ways in which gender and sexuality can work against each other in the issue of violence. Because many of Montréal's gay male activists decried an increase in anti-gay violence within the city's gay village, the police department responded by documenting violent crimes committed in this area and contrasting the results with a comparison territory in the same district. Gay activists fused sexuality and geography, and did not account for the ways in which gender functions in queerbashing. The SPCUM, in turn, responded to the discourse established by gay male activists (violence against gay men in the village) and used comparative data to refute the proposed frequency of these instances. Both strategies relied on a separation of gender and sexuality, and thus prevented a political coalition among gay men, women, lesbians, and transsexuals.[57]

The brief presented by the SPCUM is significant precisely because of its refusal to address the gendered nature of violence. It serves to define the problematic of violence against sexual minorities (against gay men, more specifically), but it eclipses questions of gender and therefore cannot address the realities of women and transsexuals. The SPCUM document, as a response to an activist position on violence against men in the gay village, exemplifies the erasure of TS/TG people in the institutional world. The conceptualization of violence and public space offered by certain gay male activists relies upon a gendered understanding of public space and forecloses an adequate appreciation of violence directed against TS/TG individuals. The SPCUM brief subsequently takes up this conjuncture between gender and public space in order to refute the claims of the significant number of aggressive incidents against men in the gay village of Montréal. In this manner, transsexual and transgendered people are obscured both within a gay male activist discourse and within the police response to this position. A conceptual association among gender and geography makes transsexuals disappear from public space. This conceptual problematic is taken up in the administration of the everyday world. This effacement marks one instance of an institutional erasure of transsexual and transgendered people.

A separation of gender and sexuality becomes more complicated when we consider the ways in which gender, sexuality, and prostitution overlap in specific public spaces. While most TS/TG prostitutes in Montréal are visible in the vicinity of Saint-Laurent and Sainte-Catherine, many of these people also frequent Ontario *est*—a street that falls within the border of the gay village. Despite its location in a gay area, sections of Ontario *est* (between Panet and Dufresne) are known for transgendered prostitution—particularly at night. In the summer of 1993, residents of this sector (Centre-Sud) protested the presence of prostitutes and intravenous drug users. Groups of citizens harassed and assaulted sex workers in the area, intimidated their clients, and vandalized an apartment known to be a *piquerie,* or shooting gallery.[58] A community group was established to continue this pressure, although it officially distanced itself from the violent tactics employed. At one meeting I attended, residents discussed various strategies that could be employed to evict sex workers from the area. One man stood up and spoke out about his plan to take a baseball bat and assault two Haitian transgendered prostitutes, known to work on the corner of Ontario and Panet Streets. Like many perpetrators of queerbashing who target black gay men as easy victims,[59] this attacker viewed black transgendered women as those least likely to retaliate and most worthy of assault. Notwithstanding the fact that such violence occurs within the gay village, it cannot be explained as an instance of homophobia. Rather, this proposed assault emphasizes the importance of accounting for gender, race, class, and public space in an analysis of violence. An investigation of gender and space cannot merely accept an area known as a gay ghetto to be monolithic, but must examine the ways in which subsections of this region can be claimed, or contested, as transgendered locations.[60] These differences can be subtle, changing from one block to the next and varying with the hour of the day (or night) and the passage of time more generally. Once the definition of TS/TG public space is acknowledged, we can examine the complexity of the violence that occurs within these sites, accounting for the specificity of violence against TS/TG individuals. That people of color are singled out for attack in TS/TG public spaces parallels the increased violence they face within gay villages.[61]

## CONCLUSION

Taking up the kind of poststructuralist sociology proposed in chapter 3, this chapter reflects on the issue of gender and violence. The erasure of transgendered people from the social text is amply illustrated by the anti-violence discourse proposed by gay male activists in Montréal and subsequently adopted by the Montréal police. One of the political arguments to be made from this insight is not that transgendered people experience more violence than lesbians and gay men (although that may be a valid observation). Rather, I consider how a gendered knowledge on violence—one that presupposes men's bodies—ignores and excludes the bodies and experiences of transsexual and transgendered people. Since such an exclusion is made possible by a collapse between gender and sexuality, a careful theoretical reflection on the relations between these terms is warranted. This theoretical reflection can in turn inform both how we gather data on the issue, as well as the political responses we develop. Such a reflexive sociology appreciates how an object of inquiry is constructed in and through a process of research.

The theoretical issues presented here, especially the relations between gender and sexuality, raise additional questions as to the collection and interpretation of evidence on gendered violence. What implications does the presence of TS/TG people in public space hold in terms of violence? Do bashers drive into these areas, looking to assault a transsexual woman or a transvestite prostitute, as they often drive into gay villages in search of queerbashing victims?[62] Are transgendered people of color assaulted more frequently than those who are white? What happens when transgender prostitutes enter areas demarcated as "gay"? Are these people subject to assault because of an association between prostitution and AIDS, and if so, how does this relate to increased violence against those perceived to be HIV-positive?[63] Since much of the data on queerbashing indicates that it is often perpetrated by young males, usually in groups,[64] are transgendered youth most at risk for assault? What are the specific methodological difficulties involved in collecting data on violence against transgendered people? Will these people be reluctant to report the assaults they experience to the police, as are many lesbians, gay men, and bisexuals? Given that transsexuals are incarcerated according to their "original," biological sex (e.g., an MTF person is placed in an all-male jail), can we expect transsexuals to consider police and law enforcement officials in a favorable light?[65] Do transgendered people even inform gaybashing hotlines when they are assaulted, or do they not consider themselves part of these communities? How can we record incidents of genderbashing for the collection of hate crime statistics? [66] These are only a few of the questions that a more detailed, empirical study of violence against transgendered people would address.

In recent years, the issue of violence has received increased attention in the communities of the sexually marginalized, as well as within the academy. Although some of the research emphasizes the role of gender in violence,[67] it has yet to explore the implications of this issue for transgendered individuals and communities. The definition of public space is intimately linked to culturally sanctioned gender identities. This has profound implications for people who live outside normative sex/gender relations: "ordinary" public space as well as regions known as gay ghettoes are sites where the potential of being verbally abused, and/or physically assaulted, is remarkably high. Furthermore, although gender and sexuality are conventionally confused, such that "effeminate" men and "masculine" women are "gaybashed" irrespective of their sexual identities, the variables of gender and sexuality can also be juxtaposed. Such an opposition can be quite explicit, as when middle-class gay men struggled to evict transgendered prostitutes from Vancouver's West End.[68] A separation of gender and sexuality can also be more subtle, as in the discourse on violence proposed by many gay male activists that privileges sexuality over gender, and hence develops a political response that is only valid for urban, middle-class gay men.

Taking up the issue of violence against sexual and gender minorities, this chapter has attempted to illustrate how some of the responses to violence preclude an adequate conceptualization of gendered aggression. Through a literature review on gender and violence, as well as a preliminary analysis on the geographic location of Montréal prostitutes in 1993, I have argued that the discourse of violence against sexual minorities excludes transsexual women. Furthermore, the briefs presented to the Québec Human Rights Commission offer an engaging case study of how the social relations of gender are textually coordinated in one institution, such that transsexuals are beyond consideration.

If TS and TG individuals are rendered invisible through the daily work of institutions, the generation of knowledge that makes sense of this effacement is crucial. While this chapter outlines some theoretical reflections concerning this problematic, the following chapters broaden this inquiry by engaging in a process of empirical research.

# ≪ 7 ≫

## ACCESS DENIED

### The Experiences of Transsexuals and Transgendered People
### with Health Care and Social Services in Toronto

In chapter 6, I offered a theoretical reflection on the collapse of gender and sexuality, as well as the implications of this collapse in considering the issue of violence against sexual and gender minorities. Taking up the briefs prepared for the Québec Human Rights Commission, I examined both how the work of institutions is textually coordinated, and how this administration preempts a developed understanding of gendered violence against sexual and gender minorities. Much of the knowledge generated on violence precludes the possibility of transsexual and transgendered bodies, effectively erasing TS/TG people from the social text.

The issues raised in chapter 6 adhere to the kind of poststructuralist sociology outlined in chapter 3. If the institutions of the social world function to exclude TS/TG people, there is a need for critical research that makes sense of how that erasure works, as well as research that provides an occasion for TS/TG people to make themselves visible. Although the type of conceptual analysis offered in chapter 6 is worthwhile, and while it is both useful and necessary in the development of appropriate interventionist strategies, it must be supplemented with a research agenda that verifies and validates the findings with members of a sample population. Through interviews with TS/TG individuals about their experiences with health care and social services, this chapter attempts to enact this type of reflexive sociological program.

There is no shortage of studies on transgendered people, whether these are conducted by psychiatrists, clinical researchers, psychologists, or sociologists. A comprehensive annotated bibliography on the subject of gender dysphoria, for instance, spans more than 600 pages.[1] Despite this marked interest in researching transgendered people and bodies, few investigations examine the politics of health care and social services as they are experienced by transsexuals and transgenderists. Such an absence in the literature is particularly noteworthy given the difficulties TS/TG people have with regard to health care: too often we face systemic obstacles and institution-alized discrimination that impede and sometimes prevent us from living our bodies as we choose.

In addition to documenting the refusal of health care and social services to members of the TS/TG population, this chapter also explores the development of a research methodology that demands an engaged, reflexive stance: one in which the researcher begins with the experiences of the people in question and goes further to locate the social relations that order this experience. Drawing on the work of English Canadian sociologist Dorothy Smith,[2] I offer an overview of how health care and social services are experienced by TS/TG individuals.

The data for this chapter were originally gathered as part of a research project known as Project Affirmation. Funded by Health Canada, Project Affirmation conducted a needs assessment of health care and social services for sexual minorities (lesbians, gay men, bisexuals, and transgendered people) in the province of Ontario. This chapter offers an expansion and revision of the final report I produced for Project Affirmation on the situation of health care and social services for transgendered people in Ontario.[3]

The total sample population comprised thirty-three TS/TG individuals. The population was quite diverse, with ages ranging from twenty to sixty. Of the thirty-three people interviewed, nineteen were enrolled in the Gender Identity Clinic at the Clarke Institute of Psychiatry. There were seven people of color (black, native, and métis; Asian-Canadian transsexuals are a significant absence in the sample). Four of the individuals had a mother tongue other than English (French in three cases, Spanish in one instance). A variety of sexualities were represented in the sample: of the thirty-three people I interviewed, fourteen identified themselves as something other than heterosexual, including bisexual, lesbian, queer, polysexual, and asexual. Six of the MTF transsexuals interviewed were post-operative. Twelve people, representing 36 percent of the sample population, were sex trade workers: some on the streets, some over the telephone from their homes, and some both on the street and over the phone. Two individuals were FTM transsexuals. Although the sample population is predominantly MTF transsexuals and transgenderists, I try to outline some of the specific needs and concerns of FTMs with regard to health care and social services throughout this chapter. Further research on FTM issues is, however, necessary. Due to limited resources, almost all of the people contacted were from the metropolitan Toronto region. The findings contained herein thus reflect the geographic location of this study. Yet Toronto is the largest city in Ontario, and the fact that transgendered people have many problems accessing health care and social services in this city suggests that these difficulties can only be exacerbated in smaller cities and especially in rural regions of the province.[4]

Given a dearth of academic studies on TS/TG health care, my focus is on recording how TS/TG people experience the institutional world. A more in-depth analysis of health care and social services would interview service providers and agency administrators in order to understand their perspective on the organization of this institutional site. The section on shelters for homeless women and homeless youth draws on a small number of interviews with service providers, as one means to understand the rationale and justifications for specific institutional policies and procedures.

Following the presentation of some raw data on how TS/TG people experience health care, I examine some of the common themes and conceptual problematics that explain the institutional management of transsexual and transgendered people. Emerging from the sociological tradition known as grounded theory (see chapter 2), this approach seeks to move inductively from the everyday world as described by members of a research population to the conceptual categories that order and reproduce that world.[5] The themes common to how TS/TG people perceive health care explain how these individuals are excluded from the institutional world through specific administrative policies, procedures, and practices. Demonstrating the thesis of this book that transsexuals are erased in the everyday social world, the concept of erasure here designates the exclusion of TS/TG people from the institutional site of health care. This exclusion refers to the denial of services to TS/TG people, as well as to the decision by many TS/TG individuals not to rely on the existing services within the health care and social service network.

The data in this chapter are grouped according to specific topics within the realm of health care and social services, following the structure of the interviews: hormones and primary health care; relations with the police; shelters (for women, youth, and the homeless); and alcohol and drug rehabilitation programs.[6]

## Primary Health Care and Hormones

Hormones are an integral part of the daily lives of transsexuals and transgenderists. They change one's physical appearance and aid in an individual's level of comfort with one's body. In the case of FTM transsexuals and transgenderists, the administration of testosterone has dramatic effects: the voice lowers, facial and body hair grow, muscles develop, and menstruation ceases. In the case of MTF transsexuals and transgenderists, the ingestion of estrogen redistributes fat tissue throughout the body, softens the skin, promotes breast development, and arrests male pattern baldness.

Hormones can also have serious side effects, including nausea, vomiting, headaches, mood swings, blood clots, liver damage, heart and lung complications, and problems with blood circulation and veins (phlebitis).[7] For these reasons, it is important that individuals who take hormones be monitored regularly by a physician. Ideally, an individual should have a complete physical examination before taking hormones. Blood tests ranging from liver and kidney levels to blood sugar and cholesterol should be taken and recorded.[8] As an individual undergoes transition, these levels can be monitored accordingly.

This is an admittedly brief summary of hormones, their effects on the body, and the importance of working with medical professionals to maintain one's health as a transsexual and/or transgenderist. My research indicates that despite the central role hormones play in their lives, and despite the value of being monitored for the effects of hormones, TS/TG people encounter serious difficulties in obtaining safe access to hormones. Furthermore, they are generally more knowledgeable than their doctors about how hormones will affect their bodies. And finally, many of the subjects I interviewed reported that they often obtained their hormones from doctors without undergoing regular physical examinations and blood work.

## Access

The people I interviewed noted that it was extremely difficult to obtain hormones. As a rule, transsexuals and transgenderists obtained their hormones through three means: illegally; through a doctor; or through the Gender Identity Clinic of the Clarke Institute of Psychiatry.

Hormones acquired surreptitiously were obtained in one of two ways: either from a family member (often unknowingly) or through an underground market. In the first instance, MTF transsexuals told me that they would take the medications prescribed for their wives and mothers:

> Well, first of all I stole some, from my mother-in-law, actually. She had had a hysterectomy and I would go and take some of her pills every now and again.

> My wife has a health problem, where she had to have her ovaries removed. So she's on Premarin [a form of estrogen]. So I took hers [hormones] for about six months.

Other people I interviewed stated that they persuaded female friends to get a prescription for birth control pills, which the transsexual would then take regularly.

More commonly, however, TS/TG individuals said they bought their hormones on the street. Some obtain multiple prescriptions and then sell hormones to any individuals interested—friends or strangers. Sources for hormones can be contacted through bars known for their TS/TG clientele, as well as through the TS/TG community.

> She [my transsexual friend] told me that whenever I would want hor-
> mones, she could get some for me. So what she did is when I decided to
> get hormones, I called her and asked for some. I paid for it, she got it from
> her own prescription.

> I get them from my family doctor and sell them to the girls.

Transsexuals obtain their hormones on the street for several reasons. First, it is extremely difficult to find a doctor who is willing to prescribe hormones. This creates a situation in which transsexuals buy their hormones on the street even when they would like to secure them through a doctor and have their health monitored:

> I bought hormones off the street for a year and a half before I attempted to
> go to my family practice. . . . I went to him [my doctor] and told him that
> if he doesn't give them [hormones] to me, I'm going to continue buying
> them off the street. So he took it in his own hands to monitor me, and put
> me on them legally. . . . He believed in me.

One interviewee maintained that many doctors are reluctant to prescribe hormones to transsexuals due to a fear of malpractice suits:

> I haven't had any luck [obtaining a prescription for hormones] from my
> doctor. He refused—point blank. . . .

> Q: Did he give a reason?

> A: He said he didn't want to be engaged in a lawsuit. As if I'd sue him!
> [laughter] . . . He said he'd only do it on the recommendation of the
> Clarke [Gender Identity Clinic].

For some transsexuals and transgenderists, obtaining their hormones from a doctor is not an option. The quotation below is from a conversation with four transgender sex trade workers (two of whom were on hormones, one of whom took hormones sporadically). When one transsexual reported that she obtained her hormones through an underground market, another transsexual joked, "You'd have to [buy your hormones illegally] or they'd ship your little ass back [to your country of origin]!" Transsexuals who do not have access to health care in Canada—those who are "illegal" refugees—are forced to buy their hormones on the street.

Hormones can be bought on the street in both pill and injection forms. Research in the field of HIV/AIDS education has suggested that in the context of American inner-city transsexual communities, transsexuals may share needles with their lovers and friends in order to inject their hormones.[9] This practice puts transsexuals at increased risk of contracting HIV, as well as other health complications (e.g., hepatitis). The transsexuals I interviewed indicated that pills were most commonly sold on the underground market. Although some admitted that they also bought injection hormones, they maintained that they did not share needles with others.

Some of the individuals in the survey received hormones from doctors with "questionable" reputations: "I got them from a little doctor who's famous for prescribing yellow jackets, and who'd been reprimanded in court . . ." One individual obtained hormones for the first time when she was sixteen years old:

> [I first got my hormones] through a back-street doctor, a pill pusher. . . . I ran away from home, to find myself, became a prostitute, and I met transsexuals and I wanted to know how I could get on hormones. I was living as a girl, I was dressing and everything, hooking as a girl, dressing. And they told me about this doctor . . . and he was like a pill pusher, and he would give anybody hormones. So I went in there and he just gave me them. . . .
>
> Q: You just walked in and said you wanted hormones?
>
> A: Yeah.
>
> Q: You were 18, 17?
>
> A: 16. You know. I went in fully dressed and everything, and I told him I'd been living this way for about six months. And he examined me a bit and just gave me a prescription. . . . I got them off him for about a year.

These individuals did not expect any follow-up monitoring of their general health, nor did they necessarily believe that these doctors would prescribe their hormones indefinitely.

Many other individuals recounted stories of being flatly refused hormones by their general practitioners. People reported that their doctors knew little or nothing about transsexuality, and furthermore expressed little interest in pursuing the topic. Their doctors feared legal repercussions if they initiated hormonal treatment. Doctors would either refer their transsexual patients to the Clarke Gender Identity Clinic or flatly refuse to prescribe hormones at all. In some instances, doctors would prescribe hormones if they had a letter of recommendation from a psychiatrist, presumably to protect them from any possible legal action in the future. This creates a situation in which transsexuals must consult other doctors and specialists before beginning hormonal treatment:

> I just went to see a psychiatrist. . . . I was dressed up [as a woman] and I said I was a transsexual and I wanted to get hormones. So he said, "No problem." I sat down with him, he said, "How long have you been like that? How long have you been a transsexual?" I said, "Since I was born." And then he said, "Well I can see you're a sane person, blah, blah, blah." So he writes me a letter right away without any examination. And he wrote a letter saying . . . "I have subjected [this candidate] to a total psychological evaluation and I found her to be a sane person and a fit candidate for sex change procedures."
>
> Q: And you'd spoken for how long?
>
> A: About four or five minutes, maximum.

The transsexuals in this survey expressed their need to "prove" themselves as "really" transsexual in the eyes of their psychiatrists and doctors. Even when they found doctors who would prescribe hormones willingly, most transsexuals were expected to provide letters and supporting documentation from a psychiatrist.

While some doctors insisted that their transsexual patients undergo a psychiatric evaluation, others decided for themselves whether or not a particular patient was "really" transsexual. One MTF transsexual I spoke with recounted a rather humorous story that illustrates how much doctors rely on the visual presentation of transsexuals to determine gender identity.

> And another time, I got them [hormones] from a female doctor. . . . she wouldn't give them to me the first time [I went to see her, because I was dressed as a male]. But my [friends were] going there, and I knew they were getting them [hormones], so I, I just went back, and this time I did all my kohl [makeup], inside and outside my eyes, my little fake fur jacket and my tight black pants. And she said, "You've come a long way since I

163

saw you first. And now I'm convinced that you're transsexual." It was like
three weeks later! [At the original visit,] she said, "No [I won't prescribe
hormones]. I'm not sure that you're transsexual. I don't believe that you
are." So a little makeup, a little fun fur, and she's eating out of the palm of
my hand! [laughter] I thought, "Is that all there is to being a girl?" Look
between the ears! . . . She said, "You've done a lot of work." And I thought,
"What did I do? I went shopping! In my own closet!"

This anecdote clearly reveals the arbitrary judgments to which transsexuals
are subjected when they request hormones. It also indicates the implicit
sexism of the doctor, who judged "women" and "men" almost exclusively
based on their physical appearance. The information gathered in this study
confirms other research in the field, which illustrates that transsexuals are
judged according to sexist and stereotypical gender concepts by medical
personnel.[10]

Most transsexuals and transgenderists I interviewed wanted to work
with doctors to monitor their health. They took an active role in the main-
tenance of their own bodies. To be monitored while on hormones was justified for both physical and psychological reasons. The two quotations below are from MTF transsexuals who were taking hormones through an
underground market. One subject had her hormones mailed to her from
the United States, while another bought them from a transsexual friend.
Both emphasize the important psychological benefits of being monitored
by a doctor on hormones:

> About two, three weeks, a month after I decided to [start hormones], I
> went to see a doctor, 'cause I wanted to have it [my health] normalized,
> 'cause . . . I felt very unstable and scared about going through all that and
> I wanted things to be well done, 'cause I thought it's scary enough like that,
> and I don't want to be all fucked up.

> I really wanted to get on hormones from a doctor. [Q: Right. So you could
> be monitored?] Yeah. I . . . I wanted it just from an internal sense of wanting
> to be legitimate, like I tried hard to get some physician to help me. I saw a
> bunch of them, I explained my situation, I was always completely honest,
> and I always, I always told them that I'd already gone to see . . . other
> doctors and they'd said no, but I hope that they'd [prescribe hormones] . . .
> but they'd always just look at me and say, "Well, I'm not qualified. I don't
> know anything about this."

Interestingly, both of these transsexual women emphasize the psychological
aspects of seeing a doctor—"I wanted to have it normalized"; "wanting to

be legitimate"—rather than a strictly biomedical approach. This suggests that the barriers transsexuals face in accessing hormones can have serious psychological repercussions. The stress associated with initiating a transition can be compounded by the refusal of doctors to support that decision. When doctors deny requests for hormones, and especially when they express no interest in learning about this issue, transsexual men and women feel that they are being judged. By being forced outside the formal institution of health care, TS/TG people are erased from the social world in and through the daily practices of general practitioners who refuse to work with them.

Finding a doctor who is TS/TG-positive is even more difficult for individuals located outside of large urban centers. In order to preserve their privacy, transgendered and transsexual people who live in small towns often tolerate two- or three-hour commutes for their health care needs. One transsexual woman living in southwestern Ontario described her efforts in finding a doctor to start her transition:

> I had a heck of a time. . . . I didn't want it to get back to my family physician. . . . I was afraid that it would get back to my family . . . and I didn't want anybody to know. I started calling doctors . . . I would call a receptionist. I would say that I was a transsexual, that I wanted to be on hormones, and would these doctors consider doing it. Most of them would say no. Eventually I found one that would do it. So I went to see him.

Even though the transsexuals and transgendered people I interviewed told one another about doctors that would prescribe hormones, these doctors' large caseloads often make them unable to accept new patients. Thus even when transsexuals are interested in working with doctors to monitor their health, most cannot find a sympathetic caregiver to work with.

> Doctors won't take new patients, either—especially if they're transgendered. They're just so naive about it all. So they don't want to take anybody else on. 'Cause I've tried to refer a few of the [TS/TG] girls, that were close friends of mine, to my doctors. They will not take them.

Other barriers can prevent honest, direct communication between many transsexual patients and their caregivers. Transsexuals expressed their fear that their doctors would discontinue their hormones if they told them everything about their lives. Several individuals interviewed admitted that they took more hormones than the prescribed dosage. Some obtained hormones from their doctors as well as from an underground market, but only spoke about their "legitimate" hormones in the health care setting. Other people did not tell their physicians if they had stopped taking their hormones. They feared that if they divulged such information, their doctors would judge them to be unbalanced, or not "true" transsexuals, and they would be without a source of hormones in the future, should they wish to take them again. One interviewee commented that she would start and stop hormones based on how she felt she was being treated in her primary relationship:

> I'd go on and off. On one week and off the next. It was all emotional decisions, based on my boyfriend, how I was getting treated and perceived.

The same interviewee withheld this information from her doctors:

> I tended not to tell them, because I wanted them to renew the prescriptions and not freak out about my stability. So I tended not to tell them.

The difficulties transsexuals experience accessing hormones and quality medical care can thus compromise an open relationship among doctors and transgendered clients.

## Knowledge of Hormones and Their Side Effects

Many of the transsexuals and transgendered people I interviewed were extremely well-informed about hormones and their effects on the body. They were invested in learning more about hormones for a variety of reasons. They wanted to change their bodies, and sought information about the most effective means of doing so. People were generally familiar with the medical literature on hormones, particularly with reference to transsexuals. Furthermore, transsexuals and transgenderists would speak with one another about the various hormones available. In fact, many of the people I interviewed asked me what I had learned about different hormones during the course of this research. Transsexuals also realized that an extensive knowledge of hormones aided their relations with their caregivers. As one respondent asserted, doctors can be less reluctant to prescribe hormones if a patient had demonstrated knowledge about the drug and its effects on the body: "I had to prove that I knew what the drugs were, what the drugs did, what the side effects were. I went in extremely knowledgeable." Many transsexuals also stated that they were far more knowledgeable about hormones than their doctors:

> I haven't found people very knowledgeable or accommodating. The best I could do was look up information, photocopy it, and hand it to my doc-

tors, and then they would say, "Well, this is in print, this is a paper, O.K."
I had to look it all up myself.

She [an endocrinologist] said she had never done it [prescribed hormones
to an MTF transsexual]. I said, "Well, I've got information for you."

The doctors I find are not very connected to, they are not really aware
of the side effects [of hormones]. And if, sometimes, they are aware of the
side effects, they are aware, but in relationship to genetic women, not to
transsexuals.

Interviewees also indicated that they needed to be continually informed
about different hormones, in case their treatment regimen had too many
negative side effects, or if they wished to change regimens for better results. Thus, transsexuals often educate their doctors about hormones at the
beginning of the patient-doctor relationship as well as throughout their
treatment.

As one of the above quotations indicates, many doctors have very little
knowledge of hormones with specific reference to transsexual women
and transsexual men. One interviewee summarized the biases of medical
professionals that prevent adequate health care for transsexuals:

I had asked him [my doctor] before . . . to have injectable estrogen and he
rejected the idea, he said that there was not such a thing. So you see, I
taught him that, and now he has all his transsexuals on estrogen, on injectable estrogen. But the point is he doesn't really do research about it
[hormones and transsexual health care]; he doesn't learn about it. He says
things like, if you ask him, "I'd like to have progesterone," [he says] "Well
you don't need it because you don't have a uterus." [He says this] without
knowing, well, what does progesterone/Provera do in people who don't
have a uterus? It may still have some effects on their body.

In certain instances, a lack of education on transsexual health care and
endocrinology has profound implications for the general physical and mental state of transsexuals. One interviewee recounts an experience with a
doctor who did not ensure the administration of a proper, regular dose of
testosterone. Still, this transsexual remained with his physician for quite
some time, since he did not know of another doctor from whom he could
obtain hormones:

She wasn't giving them to me properly. I would go six months without a
hormone. And my body would go through withdrawal. And that kept me
in depression. . . . [She was] saying that my hormones had nothing to do

with my state of being, when in actual fact it had everything to do with it. . . . No wonder I was in depression all the time, off and on. 'Cause I was not consistent.

## Medical Follow-up and Maintenance

The subjects I interviewed also revealed that their caregivers frequently neglected to do blood work to verify blood sugar and cholesterol levels or liver functions. One person who has been taking hormones for more than sixteen years commented that "No one [doctor] has ever insisted that I have blood tests." Another stated that she gets her blood work done only periodically, "and I have to bug him [my doctor] about it." An interesting finding of my research relates to the possibility of breast cancer in the case of MTF transsexuals. One medical issue raised by the administration of female hormones in genetic males is a possible increased risk in cancer.[11] To that end, I asked the MTF transsexuals and transgenderists I interviewed if their doctors examined their breasts, and whether they performed breast self-examinations. About a quarter of the respondents indicated that these issues had been addressed by their doctors. More than half replied that they did not do breast self-examinations, justifying that their breasts were too small anyway or claiming that they planned to do so at some unspecified time in the future. At least five people expressed surprise at the question: they were unaware of the theory that MTF transsexuals are at increased risk for cancer and had no knowledge of preventative health care. One interview subject stated that her "hormone doctor never once asked if there was a family history" of cancer. The question of breast cancer in MTF transsexuals clearly indicates that TS/TG people routinely receive inadequate health care from their primary care physicians.

One MTF transsexual did regularly examine her breasts. When she thought she found a lump and consulted medical personnel, however, she learned that they had very little knowledge of MTF transsexual bodies and cancer:

> I don't do it [breast self-examination] every time; I used to check it out and I used to always have little lumps and I would rush to the doctor and panic, and then he would examine it and say, "Well, it's hard to know, I think it's fine. It's probably because [MTF] transsexuals get those lumps." Both women and men doctors told me that several times, because I used to get a lot of lumps. And they used to tell me, "Oh, that's normal. [MTF t]ranssexuals get that when they're on hormones." And the question I used to ask was, "Yeah, but how are you going to know when it's a *bad*

lump, or just a normal one?" They would never have an adequate answer to that, so I just eventually stopped panicking about it, and went, "Well, that's it!" [laughter]

This anecdote reveals the lack of knowledge of transsexual bodies within the medical establishment, as well as a remarkable lack of interest among medical personnel in learning more about this issue. Furthermore, it illustrates how and why many transsexuals opt for less active roles in their primary health care, since the questions they pose cannot be answered by their treating physicians.

Although the sample population of this research study was predominantly MTF transsexuals and transgenderists, FTM transsexuals experience similar health care problems, particularly concerning gynecological issues. One of the FTM transsexuals I interviewed informed me that he had only one gynecological exam in more than thirteen years with the same physician.

Transsexual and transgendered people face tremendous obstacles and systemic discrimination in trying to gain access to hormones. Relations with doctors and medical personnel are far from ideal: transsexuals know more about hormones than many of their doctors and must often educate them about the specificity of transsexual bodies. The discrimination to which TS/TG people are subjected is even more visible in their interactions with the police. The next section addresses this problematic.

## RELATIONS WITH THE POLICE

As a general rule, most respondents indicated that they had experienced few difficulties with the police. The subject, however, had certainly crossed their minds. In the words of one interviewee: "I don't even want to get a traffic ticket until I get this finished. [Q: Why?] Well, what I'm doing is not illegal. I just wouldn't want them to call me 'sir.'" The trepidation expressed by this woman is certainly not unfounded. One métis transgendered person I interviewed told me about her encounter with the police in northern Ontario, where, in her opinion, "you don't get much more redneck." Driving in her car, she was pulled over for a broken headlight. Upon discovering that she was transgendered, however, the police changed their dealings with her—from a routine situation of a warning or a ticket to one of blatant harassment. They arrested her (without just cause) and locked her in the local jail. One of the arresting officers commented that "People like you should all be killed at birth."

While most of the transgendered people I interviewed were fortunate enough not to be subjected to similar situations, *all* of the prostitutes I spoke with recounted stories of police harassment, intimidation, and verbal abuse. Verbal abuse consisted of uniformed police officers yelling "faggot" and "queers" at sex trade workers in areas known for TS/TG prostitutes. In addition to such insults, police officers would harass the prostitutes in a variety of ways. Participants reported that police officers would stand right next to them on the street corner where they were working, thus preventing any client from approaching. Officers would also follow prostitutes down the street in their cars, keeping pace with them as they walked. Some officers would also take Polaroid photographs of prostitutes, telling them that they would keep their pictures on file. This tactic was particularly used against the young sex trade workers I interviewed; it may have been employed to scare the individuals from prostitution.

The interactions between police officers and transgendered prostitutes offer additional evidence of police harassment, both subtle and overt. Officers would ask MTF transsexuals for their male names, even when these individuals had their documentation legally changed. They would then refer to the transsexual woman by her male name. At all times, police officers would designate MTF transsexuals with male pronouns. Indeed, transgender sex trade workers stated that police officers seemed to make a point of calling them "sir," "boy," and "guy." At times, police officers would refer to transsexuals as objects. One MTF prostitute I interviewed told me that she was ridiculed by her arresting officers. When her mother arrived at the police station to post bail, they shouted, "Its mother is here to bail it out."

Transgendered prostitutes who had been assaulted said that the police officers they sought on the street refused to take a report of the incidents. They told me that the officers said things such as, "Well, what did you expect in the big city?" and "Well, you shouldn't have gone out looking like that." Sex trade workers were also told that violence against prostitutes was not important enough to file a report: "If something happens to us [prostitutes], though, they don't do anything. I got assaulted three weeks ago, and they told me they can't do anything with that guy because I was a prostitute." One black transgendered prostitute told me about an incident in which she was being held against her will by a client. She called the police, who responded rapidly. Their attitude changed, however, when they arrived at the scene and learned that she was transgendered: "And the minute they found out I was a transie, they were like . . . their attitude was like, 'This is what we came here for?' kind of thing." In addition to scorn, ridicule, and harassment, police officers may intimidate transgendered people with whom they come in contact. One interview subject, a post-operative prostitute, related an incident in which she was working in an area close to a transgendered sex trade zone (she worked in an area with nontranssexual women). Two uniformed police officers drove by and yelled, "Hey guy! You better watch what you're doing!" She replied that she was not a guy. One of the officers then asked her what she had under her skirt. She lifted it, exposing her vagina. The officers tried to intimidate her, telling her that they were going to arrest her for indecent exposure. She calmly stated that if they did so, she would tell the judge why she exposed her genitals. The officers departed.

One transgendered youth described a different sort of police intimidation. This person was assaulted with a group of friends. They called the police, and two of them agreed to drive in the police cruiser to look for the assailants. Shortly after entering the police car, they realized they had made a mistake:

> Basically, this is what they said, they go, "O.K., come with us, we'll drive around and look for them, and you can tell us the story." So we did, and then they just started harassing us. As soon as the car drove away from all my friends . . . they totally changed and became like real assholes. And it really upset us large, because we couldn't get out. [Q: Yeah, right. Because you were in the back (of the police cruiser)?] Exactly. And so we couldn't get out. We couldn't say nothing, or they'd like do something. We were real scared they were gonna gaybash us or something. The police in this city don't like gays, let alone transsexuals! That's worse! 'Cause then they're like, "Oh, this fucking faggot [sic] is becoming a girl! He can't make up his fucking mind!"

According to the respondent, the police drove these individuals around the city for more than an hour. They refused to take a report, stating that the area where the assault occurred was "a trannie prostitute area." The officers also made disparaging comments about the individuals, such as "What are you? Are you a guy or a girl? We don't like these fucking half-breeds."

Some TS/TG prostitutes told me about beatings by police officers. According to one individual, the police chased and beat her because they merely suspected her of a crime:

> Just before I went into jail, actually, they said that I was, I had a warrant out for my arrest, O.K.? And I didn't have no warrants out! I was clean, my record was clean and everything. It's not that my record was clean, I just had no charges, outstanding charges. So next thing I know, I'm running

from them, right? I ran from them, and when they caught me they broke my nose, they blackened both my eyes, my face was scraped all along here, because what they did was they grabbed my face and *shoved* it right into the cement. And then they put me in the back of the cop car with handcuffs on and found that I didn't have no warrants. So they let me go.

Stories like this one parallel those of visible minorities, who also face police violence. A community inquiry into policing practices in Toronto revealed that native people would be driven down to Cherry Beach, stripped of their clothes, thrown in Lake Ontario, and/or beaten.[12] Interestingly, the TS/TG prostitutes I spoke with also mentioned Cherry Beach: "I've been taken down to Cherry Beach, and literally beaten by them [police officers], and told to walk back." Prostitutes claimed that it was futile to file complaints against the police, because it would make their working conditions even worse:

> You have to [forget police violence]. You got no choice. I mean, if you're trying to make a living out here, you can't be fucking charging the cops or whatever.
>
> And if I would have charged them for what they did to me [police violence], I'd just, I'd never be able to forget it, because I'd be out here trying to make money, and they'd just hassle me, right?

Many of the TS/TG prostitutes I interviewed did not trust the police. They did not report any assaults because they believed the police would blame them for the incidents. For example, one prostitute had been badly beaten by her boyfriend when he discovered that she was transsexual:

> I couldn't phone the police. What am I going to say? "Oh, I had my boyfriend here and he just found out I had a penis and almost killed me"?! They would have just humiliated me, you know. It would have been a big joke.

A native transgendered person who was assaulted refused to report the incident because she had already experienced harassment and ridicule from uniformed police officers:

> My friend said, "Well, the cops are fucking right across the street." And I was like, "What the fuck do I want cops for?" I said, "I don't want to involve any fucking cops." I said, "Forget it; it's not worth it to me." She said, "Well, they're fucking sitting right there!" I said, "I don't fucking care! Let's just

get the fuck home, and I want to go home and clean my fucking face, you know? Fucking lick my wounds. Fuck it."

This individual's distrust of police officers is informed by her dealings with the police as a transgendered person of color and a prostitute. In their everyday dealings with transsexual and transgendered prostitutes, police engage in verbal abuse, ridicule, harassment, and intimidation. My findings about the conduct of police officers confirm other research in this domain, which documents the discrimination faced by sex trade workers, homeless people, and visible minorities.[13]

The harassment, intimidation, abuse, and uncooperative actions of certain police officers against TS/TG people are primarily directed against prostitutes. This is not to suggest that transgendered people who are not sex trade workers will experience no discrimination or abuse in their dealings with the police, as the example from the métis transgendered woman testifies. But it does underline a conjuncture of harassment and discrimination directed against TS/TG people who work in the sex trade; people who are subject to police abuse because of their work, their transgendered status, and in many cases, their nonwhite skin color. Remember that the discriminatory actions of some police officers described in this study—clearly directed against transgendered prostitutes—take place in a Canadian political context in which prostitution is legal.

The subject of relations with police officers indicates a significant division within transgender communities. All twelve of the transgendered prostitutes I interviewed recounted stories of police harassment. In contrast, only one of the twenty-one individuals who were not involved in the sex trade had experienced police harassment or abuse. This difference is obviously more than mere coincidence and explains why transgendered prostitutes do not use the services of the city's police department. As the interviewees made clear, they choose not to report the violence directed against them to the police, whether that violence is perpetrated by the police themselves, a client, a lover, or a stranger. Their decision to decline accessing police services is informed by their previous dealings with the police, as well as a need to maintain harmonious working conditions on the street.

Given the discrimination they must face in their dealings with police, TS/TG prostitutes decide to negotiate the world without recourse to this social service. In this manner, the workings of a specific institution (a discriminatory police department) marginalize transsexual people and, indeed, render them invisible. The next section expands on this theme, through an analysis of shelters for homeless youth and women.

## HOMELESS SHELTERS

There are few resources for transsexuals and transgenderists who are homeless. This section of the research documents the lack of staff training on transgender issues, the omission of TS/TG people from antidiscrimination policies, and some of the attitudes and beliefs that underlie the exclusion of transsexual and transgendered women from youth and homeless shelters.

Since some work has already been carried out on the subject of transsexual and transgendered women in women's shelters,[14] this chapter focuses on youth shelters, shelters for homeless women, and drop-ins for street people. Whereas the previous sections of this chapter have relied exclusively on interviews with transsexual and transgendered people, this section also appeals to interviews with social service providers.[15] The data reveal some of the policies and administrative practices that exclude TS/TG women from an established social service network.

### Homeless Youth

Representatives of shelters and agencies that work with homeless youth generally demonstrated an ignorance of transgendered people. In several cases, staff members asked for a clarification of the term "transgender." As the following quotation demonstrates, staff at agencies that work with homeless youth have very little training on transgender issues:

> We do outreach with street kids—that's our mandate. We don't serve them [transgender youth]. Well, I guess maybe some of the kids are like that [transgendered]. I don't know.

Moreover, staff members are often unaware of the way compulsory sex/gender relations can make home, school, and traditional work environments unsafe places for transgendered youth, leaving the street and prostitution as places where they can live their bodies as they choose. One person I spoke with claimed that transgender identity "is a case for people in their twenties."

When I asked about the situation of transgender clients, representatives of these agencies told me that anyone was welcome to use their services. I was informed that these shelters were environments "free from oppression," that people were "asked to keep their prejudices to themselves," and that "discrimination is not tolerated here." But none of the agencies I contacted had a written antidiscrimination policy that includes transgendered people.

Furthermore, only one agency indicated that it sought out training on transgender issues. In this case, I was informed that the shelter invited outside facilitators to do presentations on transgender issues. I inquired as to the names of these people, since I was interested in speaking with them, and since I imagined I would already know them. The names were not offered. Likewise, this person could not tell me where he obtained the written information on transgendered youth that he claimed to distribute to staff members of his agency. A staff member of a different youth shelter stated that education on transgender issues was "not a training priority."

Youth shelters have different areas segregated according to gender. Staff informed me that transsexuals would be housed according to their biological sex, not the gender in which they live. In discussing a hypothetical situation of an MTF transgendered person using the services of the shelter, however, the staff member I interviewed admitted that perhaps the shelter would not be a safe place: "youth with gender issues might not feel that this is a safe place for them . . . [with regard to] how the other men would act." I also spoke with several individuals in homeless shelters about the situation of FTM transgender youth. If MTF people were located on male floors and residences due to their biology, I asked whether FTM youth—who lived, identified, and interacted as men—would be housed with young women. Unfortunately, I did not receive an answer to this question; I spent a great deal of time trying to explain the concept of FTM transsexuality to the staff in homeless youth shelters. This line of inquiry must remain an avenue for future research.

The experiences of transgendered youth contradict the official policies of nondiscrimination espoused by homeless shelters. In her research on the treatment of lesbian and gay youth in group homes and youth shelters, Carol-Anne O'Brien documents the difficulties of MTF transgendered youth in such organizations.[16] O'Brien demonstrates that youth hostels are also reluctant to accept transgendered people, citing the refusal of one hostel to accommodate a cross-dressing Aboriginal youth:

> This one hostel said, "It's best that we don't let you in here for your own good. It's best to just go elsewhere. We don't want any trouble here. We don't want you to get hurt either." I said, "You can't do that, you know. I need a place to stay tonight. So if something happens, it's my fault. I can take care of myself. Just give me a bed." They just can't do that.
>
> Q: So they wouldn't let you in?
>
> A: No.[17]

The justification for denying this person admittance into the shelter is interesting. Staff claimed that the issue was one of "trouble" and potential violence. Paradoxically, by forcing a homeless transgendered youth back onto the street, these staff members claimed to be protecting this individual's safety! The comment that "We don't want any trouble here" also implies that the "trouble" is directly associated with the cross-dressing Aboriginal youth, rather than the shelter residents who might attack this person. This shifts the focus of the situation profoundly, from a social service agency offering its services to a client causing "trouble." In this way, transgendered youth are blamed for any confrontations or violent situations that could result from their presence in a shelter. It is especially noteworthy that even when transgendered people accept this situation ("So if something happens, it's my fault"), they are still refused services.

In the event that a transgendered youth is admitted into a shelter, staff demand strict adherence to their idea of masculinity and femininity. O'Brien discovered that staff members enforce normative sex/gender codes. "They said, 'No makeup, no nothing . . . Try to dress as masculine as you can.'"[18] Youth shelters are segregated according to gender, with sections for females and sections for males. Because transgendered youth challenge traditional gender boundaries they are not made to feel welcome in youth shelters:

> There's nowhere to put me. In the female section or the male section. So they put me in the hall. . . . Basically people like me don't go there. They go elsewhere, or on the street to try to make their own way, trying to make enough money to get hotel rooms.[19]

O'Brien's findings were confirmed in my own research. The transgendered youth I spoke with informed me that shelters were generally unsympathetic to them. One youth recounted the following incident:

> The staff [of a shelter for homeless youth] just looked at my [MTF cross-dressing] friends and went, "Hmmmph!" [Q: Did they say anything?] They just kind of looked at them and went, "Hmmmph! Oh great, look who's here now" type of look. My friends said they felt really out of place, really uncomfortable, but it was a place for them to stay for the night. So they were, like, kind of freaked out about it. And I felt bad for them.

Clearly, shelters can be unsafe and even hostile places for transgendered youth. Staff members refuse them access, tell them how to dress, act, and carry their bodies, subject them to unfair treatment (e.g., placing them in hallways), and implicitly blame them for any confrontations or violent incidents that arise from transphobic residents of these shelters. For all of these reasons, transgendered youth only use these services as a last resort.

The prostitutes I interviewed who work the street rarely considered shelters as an option for safe, temporary housing. The following quotation is an excerpt from a conversation I had with four TS/TG prostitutes. I asked them whether they had ever used the services of a women's, youth, or homeless shelter:

A: No. You go to the bathhouse.

B: Exactly. The saunas.

C: Someone else's house.

D: Exactly. Or the crack house.

A: If there's girls that need places to stay, though, a lot of the other girls help them out.

TS/TG prostitutes explored one of several alternatives: the bathhouse (this was true for the drag queens and MTF transsexuals interviewed), a crack house, or a friend's place. This data supports the conclusions based on the police: given the discriminatory treatment they receive, transsexual and transgender prostitutes do not locate themselves within the institutional network of health care and social services and prefer to fulfill their health care and social service needs on their own. This information provides further evidence as to the erasure of TS/TG people from the social world, through the daily work of health care and social service institutions.

### Homeless Women

Staff members of the shelters and drop-ins for homeless women I contacted were generally more familiar with transgender issues than individuals working with homeless youth. Many of the people I interviewed told me that they had worked with transsexual clients in their agency. Some people even noted that the question of MTF transsexuals in shelters for homeless women had been raised as an important issue in recent years.

In general, the shelters I spoke with held one of at least three different positions on the question of transsexual women in homeless women's shelters: outright refusal to admit; acceptance if the individual was postoperative; and acceptance if the individuals could provide documentation that they were undergoing a gender transition (e.g., a letter from the gender identity clinic at the Clarke Institute of Psychiatry or a doctor). In certain situations, a MTF transsexual would be housed in a motel room. This addresses the immediate needs of a particular transgendered person, but it is obviously only a short-term solution.

There are different reasons for accepting, or challenging, each of the positions outlined above. In the case of outright rejection of transsexual women, it is useful to reflect on one of the basic tenets of feminist theory and practice: that one's biological sex and one's social gender are not the same thing. Assuming that women's shelters emerged from the feminist movement, a mere rejection of an individual based on biological origins seems to be a flagrant contradiction of this feminist axiom.

The justification of post-operative status can also be questioned on these grounds. The representatives of shelters that accept only post-operative transsexual women frequently cited the safety and comfort of the other women residents. The presence of a pre-operative transsexual woman, it was claimed, would create a remarkably stressful situation for all women involved, since rooms and bathrooms are shared. It is interesting to note the slippage between the *penis* of a transsexual woman and her *gender* identity: this woman would not be welcome, nor would other women feel safe (I was repeatedly told), due to the presence of her penis. This position suggests that one's genitals and one's gender are the same. According to this logic, FTM transsexuals could use the services of a women's shelter, since they have vaginas (at least those individuals who have not had phalloplasty). And yet the safety and comfort level of women residents would most probably be challenged with the presence of a man, albeit a man with a vagina. Quite simply, genitals and gender are not the same, and it is inappropriate to formulate feminist social policy based on their equation.

My findings with regard to shelters for homeless women parallel research done on transsexuals and women's shelters. In her research on shelters for women, Mirha-Soleil Ross discovered that the refusal of services to a pre-operative or non-operative transsexual woman was justified on the grounds of the "safety" and comfort level of the other women residents. Ross argues that this concern over "safety" does not extend to transsexual women: "If I have fear and concerns for anyone's safety in a shelter, it is for an isolated TS woman, not for a non-transsexual who doesn't have to prove to anyone that she is a woman."[20]

As Ross so eloquently explains, this rationale absolves shelters of their responsibility in educating themselves and their residents about the diversity of women's lives:

Even the argument that TS women should be excluded for their own safety is not acceptable on a long term basis. Just like any other form of prejudice and discrimination, if some non-transsexual women are threatening the safety of a TS woman because she is a transsexual, it should be dealt with immediately and efficiently. The non-transsexual women should be confronted about their own ignorance and violence. I don't see why TS women should be restricted from access to such vital services because of somebody else's transphobia and hatred.[21]

Like the policies in homeless youth shelters, the transgendered person in question is singled out as the "cause" of this "problem," or the reason non-transsexual women in the shelter will not feel safe. This focuses attention on the transgendered person and neglects the real issue at hand: the provision of services to those in need.

The acceptance of post-operative transsexuals in women's shelters is questionable for four other reasons. First, it ignores the financial expenses associated with sex reassignment surgery (SRS); such a procedure costs approximately $8,000 in Canada through private surgeons and can cost up to $25,000 elsewhere. Moreover, in 1995 (when this research was conducted) the only way to have health insurance in Ontario pay for SRS was to enroll in a gender identity clinic. As Ross points out, these clinics treat prostitutes and individuals with criminal records with disdain.[22] The requirement that transsexual women be post-operative works against transsexual sex trade workers and those with criminal records. A policy that only accepts post-operative transsexual women in a woman's shelter also neglects the everyday realities of transgendered people of color and those who are poor. Second, this position assumes that all transsexual and transgendered women want to have genital surgery. This is belied by the fact that many women live quite happily for decades with their penises. Third, most surgeons will not operate on transsexuals who are seropositive.[23] Thus, a shelter for homeless women that only accepts post-operative transsexual women excludes seropositive transgendered people. And fourth, gender identity clinics do not recommend individuals for surgery who are younger than twenty-one. We have already observed the unfair treatment of MTF transgendered people in youth shelters; they are routinely denied access to these places. Consequently, the insistence that transsexual women be post-operative before accessing the services of a shelter for homeless women forces young MTF transgendered people to live on the street.

Some of the agencies I contacted stated that they accepted pre-operative transsexual women. These individuals, however, had to document their commitment to a transgender lifestyle. A letter from the Clarke Gender Identity Clinic or a doctor would fulfill this requirement. Although the acceptance of a pre-operative or non-operative transsexual woman is an improvement over her outright rejection, this policy remains disconnected from the everyday realities of many transgendered people. As I demonstrated earlier, access to hormones and supportive, knowledgeable medical personnel is difficult at the best of times. To require written documentation from a doctor as to one's transgender identity thus ignores the broader social relations of health care for transsexual and transgendered people. Moreover, doctors generally charge fees to provide written documentation of a patient's medical status. To force transsexual women to pay such fees in order to find shelter creates an undue stress on them. One of the reasons they are homeless, of course, is because they are also poor. Consequently, a policy that requires transsexuals to provide medical proof actively discriminates against them and their limited financial resources.

One of the interesting things that came up in my conversations with staff members of shelters for homeless women relates to the physical appearance of transsexual women. I was informed that an MTF transsexual would be accepted into some shelters "if the person doesn't come across as too terribly masculine." Staff people claimed that the physical appearance of transsexual women was related to their ability to "fit in." These comments illustrate the judgments to which transsexual women are subjected when they attempt to access social services. Other people decide if a transsexual woman is "feminine" enough, if she is "really" a woman, if her presence will be "disruptive," and if she has the right to the services offered to women. We might ask whether staff members judge all their clients on this basis, or just those who are known to be transsexual.

Moreover, the arbitrary criterion of physical appearance is (once again) disconnected from the everyday realities of transgendered women—especially those who are poor and living on the streets. One of the permanent ways MTF transsexuals can rid themselves of their facial hair is through electrolysis. This service costs anywhere from $35 to $75 an hour; most transsexuals need at least one hundred hours (often much more) for lasting results. If a transsexual woman has no money for a roof over her head, she probably cannot afford electrolysis. Therefore, it is quite likely that some transsexual women who present themselves to shelters for homeless women will have visible facial hair.

Many MTF transsexuals seeking shelter have recently been incarcerated. If arrested, MTF transsexuals who are pre-operative are jailed with men and will likely have their hormones taken away.[24] During incarceration, then, an individual who identifies and lives as a woman will undergo physical processes of masculinization. Upon her release, she may not look as "feminine" as she once did, since she has been denied hormones in jail.

Given these realities, it thus makes little sense to only accept transsexual women who look like genetic women; this does not acknowledge the complexity of their situations as poor, homeless, and/or ex-prisoner transsexual women. Moreover, the psychological effects of being refused admittance to a woman's shelter should not be underestimated. Transsexual and transgendered women want to change their bodies, and work to do so actively. To be refused admittance into a woman's shelter on the basis of one's physical appearance can reinforce the hatred that transsexuals feel for their bodies. This rejection can also lead to low self-esteem, increased alcohol and drug consumption, and even attempts at suicide. In this complex way, the denial of services to transsexual women has repercussions that range beyond their immediate housing needs.

The research on shelters for homeless youth demonstrates that transgendered people do not access these services, except as a last resort. Transgendered people espouse a similar mistrust of women's and homeless shelters. One MTF transsexual I interviewed informed me that although she was homeless for a few months upon her arrival in Toronto, she did not even attempt to access shelter services because of her gender presentation:

> When I first came down . . . , I was homeless. I didn't have much money. I didn't dare go near any shelters because I knew I'd have a lot of trouble, being a TV [transvestite]. I just didn't dare. I would just sleep in the park, that kind of stuff.

The current policies and practices of shelters for abused women, homeless women, and youth clearly do not address the needs of transgendered and transsexual women. Agencies deny transgendered people services with the rationale that other shelter residents will not feel safe, with no sustained consideration of safety issues for MTF transgendered people, whether in a shelter or on the street. In many instances, the gender of transsexuals and transgenderists is decided by someone other than the transgendered person—a gender identity clinic, a doctor, or staff members of these organizations. And finally, policies that accept post-operative transsexual women for admittance into a shelter do not serve the most disenfranchised transgendered people: those who are poor, prostitutes, ex-convicts, and/or seropositive. This type of discrimination is never acceptable. It is particularly ironic that such exclusionary practices continue in social service agencies designed to aid people with few resources.

What is perhaps most remarkable is that this issue is consistently addressed on a case-by-case basis. Staff have little or no training on transgender issues, and shelters do not have written anti-discrimination policies that include transgendered people. When the "problem" is individualized in this manner, a particular transgendered person is perceived as the root of this issue. Although many staff people of shelters stated that their facilities would not be safe for transgendered people, few people addressed the responsibility of the agency in creating, providing, and maintaining a safe space for a transsexual in need of assistance.[25] On the subject of providing services to TS/TG people, a staff member of a drop-in for homeless women remarked, "No one thinks it's their responsibility."

The research conducted on shelters for youth, the homeless, and women reveal three significant themes: safety; conditional acceptance; and an individualizing of the "problem." The notion of *safety* functions differently according to the type of shelter in question. Within youth shelters, staff members refuse admittance to transgendered people in an apparent concern for their safety, with respect to the potentially violent behavior of other shelter residents. Interestingly, this discourse of "safety" does not begin with the position of the transgendered client, nor does it consider questions of safety for this individual working or living on the street. In the context of women's shelters, the notion of safety refers to the psychological and physical space of non-transsexual shelter residents and staff members. As transsexual activists point out, this discourse does not concern itself with the physical safety of a transsexual or transgendered woman, or with her psychological well-being.[26] Paradoxically, a refusal of services to transsexuals and transgenderists creates a situation in which TS/TG women remain isolated; a position that is both easily encouraged and exploited by those who batter and abuse women. In this manner, the institutional workings of women's shelters may actually function to consolidate a cycle of violence against MTF transsexuals and transgenderists.

The theme of *conditional acceptance* designates the criteria to which transsexuals and transgenderists must respond in order to access shelter. Within youth shelters, conditional acceptance is contingent upon one's gender presentation (no males in makeup; no "cross-dressing") or willingness to accept inappropriate shelter arrangements (placing transgendered youth in the hallway). Within the context of women's shelters, conditional acceptance is usually dependent upon surgical status or documentation that attests to an individual's transgendered nature. Acceptance into a women's shelter is also often based on conditional criteria that are, in the final analysis, completely arbitrary: the assessment of shelter workers as to whether individuals are "really" transgendered; whether their physical appearance or behavior will be considered "disruptive" to shelter residents and the staff. These various conditional criteria do not account for the reality of many transgendered people, perhaps especially of those who are most in need of shelter services. Paradoxically, the institutional administration of women's shelters excludes transgendered people who are poor, ex-convicts, seropositive, young, and/or prostitutes.

The final theme that emerges from the data with respect to shelters centers around an individualization of the "problem" in finding shelter for transgendered people. No agencies in this study had written antidiscrimination policies that specifically referred to transgendered people.[27] Nor was there any concerted effort on the part of agencies within Toronto or Ontario to develop a citywide, regional, or provincial policy on this issue. Transsexuals who were refused services from one agency were not referred to another place for shelter. The refusal of services to transgendered clients solves the "problem" for the agency in question by the returning the responsibility to the transgendered person who is seeking shelter. In so doing, these agencies absolve themselves of their collective responsibility in working with all kinds of women, men, and youth—not just the women, men, and youth with whom they choose or prefer to work.

Shelters for women, the homeless, and youth work to effectively exclude transsexuals and transgendered people. Not surprisingly, transgendered people report that they do not make use of these services, preferring instead to crash in a park, a sauna, a shooting gallery, a crack house, or to make more money on the street to pay for an inexpensive room. The organization of shelters marginalizes MTF TS/TG people from the institutional world. This marginalization reinforces a lack of clear institutional policy for working with TS/TG people; it is difficult to articulate the need for guidelines when members of a particular population are invisible. My discussion of shelters refers, for the most part, to interviews with service providers. Most of the MTF transsexual and transgendered people I interviewed would not even consider going to shelters for youth or homeless women.

The final section of this chapter returns to the voices of transsexual and transgendered people through an exploration of their experiences with alcohol and drug rehabilitation programs.

## Alcohol, Drug, and Substance Use

Many of the people I interviewed spoke at great length about the long and difficult process through which they came to terms with their gender identities. Some used alcohol and drugs as a way to escape their confusion, pain, and suffering. This should not surprise to people familiar with questions of alcohol and substance use.[28] What my research further reveals, however, are the barriers transgendered people face once they attempt to access alcohol and drug rehabilitation programs.

Several individuals stated that the traditional forms of support available for people dealing with substance abuse were not welcoming of transsexuals. One subject recounted her experience with Alcoholics Anonymous (AA) in a small city. She had been attending meetings regularly and received a great deal of support. When it was discovered that she was transsexual, however, AA members were less than hospitable: "This is AA, where they're all supposed to hug and shake your hand. There were actually people that walked away from me when I went up to shake their hand." Other transgendered people recounted even more violent reactions at AA meetings. After discovering that one MTF was transsexual, an AA participant declared, "I'm going to fucking kill that thing after the meeting." The interviewee reports that she immediately withdrew from AA to protect her physical safety: "And I just got up and walked out."

Transsexuals who enrolled in more formal alcohol and drug rehabilitation program, reported feeling alone and isolated. Several of the individuals I interviewed went through rehabilitation programs in the gender assigned to them at birth (i.e., MTFs with men, FTMs with women). This made the process of their recovery even more difficult and stressful: "There was nobody in the group that I could relate to in the least." In many situations, transsexuals did not feel safe or comfortable enough to speak about their gender issues. A FTM transsexual who underwent treatment with women said, "Here I am . . . and I can't even say why I was drinking. Because at bottom it's this [transsexuality]." MTF transsexuals who went through recovery with men were also forced to deny their transsexuality: "I just kept it [transsexuality] my little secret"; "I wasn't quite ready to bring this issue up on the table at an all men's discussion meeting."

Things were not necessarily much better for transsexuals who received services in their chosen gender. One MTF transsexual I spoke with was housed in a women's detoxification program. Although no one denied her services outright as a woman, she overheard the staff make disparaging comments about transsexuals. An FTM transsexual I interviewed went through a recovery program with men. He explains the stress of hiding his transsexuality, both in terms of day-to-day life and in the counseling and group therapy context:

> It [the treatment facility] was all men. So I had to become very sensitive to the fact, when I took a bath [at] certain hours, when I went to the bathroom, when I went to bed, you know? And nobody knew. We shared rooms and whatnot. I was more sensitive to that, protecting myself. And I didn't want to bring up my gender issue because I knew that they would isolate me, make me feel different. I really believe that they would have looked at me differently. And I didn't want that to be there when I was dealing with alcoholism.

It is noteworthy that transsexuals deny their transsexuality both when they go through treatment in the gender assigned to them at birth and when they seek assistance in their chosen gender. In neither situation is it safe to declare one's transsexual status.

Most existing alcohol and drug rehabilitation agencies are clearly unsympathetic to transsexual and transgender issues. Counselors working in this area are also uninformed. One FTM transsexual I interviewed was referred to a service for alcohol and drug counseling. From the beginning, he was uneasy with this agency: "To tell you the truth, I didn't want to go there, 'cause it's for women." This man further stated that although his counselor was pleasant, she was quite ignorant of transsexuality:

> She's very nice, even if she doesn't think I should do this [transition]. . . . She thinks I'm trying to mutilate my body. I said, "Dear, I have scars all over me. I'm trying to take care of me now. I don't want to do that anymore."

Many transsexuals face similar dilemmas when they go for counseling. The FTM transsexual had to educate his counselor about the ways in which his addiction and gender issues are related: in living as a woman, he hated his body and how he was perceived, and so used alcohol to deal with that pain. His decision to live as a man decreased this anxiety, and thus lessened a need to consume alcohol. This is not to suggest that when transsexuals with addiction issues begin a transition, they will suddenly no longer have any drinking or substance abuse problems. But it is essential for caregivers to understand some of the reasons why some transsexuals may use drugs or alcohol.

Unfortunately, many transsexuals spend their time educating their counselors on transsexuality rather than exploring their addiction issues. Consider again the FTM transsexual's relationship with his counselor:

> She said she'll support me [to transition and live as a man], but she doesn't want me to do this. We've had long talks about it, like she just, it freaks her out. She wants me to try and just be gay. [laughter]

As this passage indicates, the FTM spent much of his time in the counseling context informing his caregiver about transsexuality. In particular, he had to explain the difference between sexual orientation and gender identity.

Finding an addiction treatment program or a counselor who is transgender-positive is a formidable challenge. Indeed, locating resources that accept transsexuals is difficult enough. Finding support where the staff have knowledge of transsexual and transgender issues is even less likely. These problems of access are compounded when questions of race and ethnicity are considered. Locating addictions counselors or recovery programs for Aboriginal transsexuals, or those of South Asian descent, seems an insurmountable task at the present time.

Interviews with TS/TG people indicate that these people face tremendous obstacles with respect to alcohol and drug recovery programs. A lack of services, open hostility to TS/TG individuals, a denial of transsexual/transgendered identity, and the education of service personnel are among the principal problems encountered. These difficulties explain how and why many TS/TG people withdraw from addiction recovery programs.

## CONCLUSION

The transsexual and transgendered people cited in this chapter describe numerous situations in which they are refused access to health care and social services. Such discrimination is more than a collection of isolated incidents, however. This mistreatment is a function of how health care and social service agencies are administered. The strategy of institutional ethnography offered here illustrates how health care and social services actually work on a daily basis. This method begins with the experiences of transgendered people not as a case study or an example to be generalized to the entire health care and social service network, but as a point of entry into the quotidian administration of the social world.

The information presented here has been primarily descriptive, offering a preliminary documentation of how transsexual and transgendered people situate themselves within, or outside, health care and social service agencies. Notwithstanding the importance of such description, it is useful to reflect on some of the conceptual and institutional relations that order and organize the discrimination faced by these individuals: abuse; noncooperation of social service personnel; judgment of transsexual or transgendered identity based on physical appearance; access to health care as facilitated through information on transsexuality; social policies that do not account for the everyday realities of poor TS/TG people; a lack of social policy in this domain; the denial of transsexual status; and a redefinition of the health care context. Instead of service provision to TS/TG clients, the clients become responsible for educating their service providers on TS/TG issues.

Abuse of TS/TG people is evidenced through both verbal insults and physical attacks. Examples of this institutional practice include the police officers who assault transsexual prostitutes and the shelter workers overheard making disparaging comments about transsexuals. A noncooperation of social service personnel is illustrated through police officers who refuse to take reports of sexual assault from TS/TG prostitutes. The judgment of TS/TG identity based on physical appearance is amply documented in the section of the chapter on hormones, which described doctors reluctant to prescribe hormones to transsexuals who did not fit their stereotyped visual images of men and women. The acceptance or rejection of transsexuals within certain women's shelters also appeals to the physical appearance of a TS/TG individual, thereby establishing a crucial link between an individual's gendered appearance and the ability to access social services. Interviews with TS/TG people indicate that access to health care is facilitated when the individual provides information about transsexuality to the health care provider. Many transsexuals are well-informed about the biomedical effects of hormones and offer this information freely to their doctors as a means of obtaining a prescription. Transsexuals are often more familiar than their primary care physicians about transsexual health care: the logical conclusion of a systemic relation in which access to health care is secured through the provision of information to medical personnel. In many instances, TS/TG people are excluded from institutions as a result of social policies that do not account for their everyday lives. This is especially noteworthy in the domain of shelters, in which one's genital status, physical appearance, or prior relations to the medical establishment determine acceptance into a shelter. These conditional criteria do not address the realities of poor, ex-convict, prostitute, and/or seropositive TS/TG people. While in certain instances social policies function to exclude TS/TG people from services, in other circumstances these individuals are refused admittance because of a lack of social policy. This absence of policy leads to an individualization of the "problem" of transsexuality and shifts the focus from one of an agency delivering appropriate services to a client (e.g., shelter, primary medical care, or information) to one of a TS/TG client finding an agency that will deal with them. Because of the profound discrimination to which TS/TG people are subjected, many choose not to disclose a TS/TG status within the health care and social service network. My interviews with participants indicate that this situation prevents TS/TG individuals from receiving comprehensive health care, since an integral aspect of their lives and their identities is neglected. Within alcohol/drug recovery programs, for instance, transsexuals reported that they could not address the relations between their addictions and their gender identities. Finally, interviewees explained how a lack of knowledge about transsexuality redefines the health care context, such that transsexuals are responsible for educating their service providers before they can receive appropriate services, referrals, and information.

Participants reported tremendous obstacles in finding health care and social service personnel willing to work with them. This systemic problem reveals how the attitudes of individual workers are linked to the evaluation of an individual's transsexual identity, which in turn is related to access to health care: a situation that is especially evident in the absence of social policies specific to a TS/TG clientele. In this regard, the attitudes of service providers determine the extent to which transsexuals will obtain services. This finding parallels other research in the area of government bureaucracy, which illustrates the central role the attitudes of government and service representatives play in the delivery of services to the public.[29]

The institutional relations discussed in this chapter are specific to transsexual and transgendered people. Indeed, these problems are constituted in the invisible workings of different agencies, through the policies they have adopted, the absence of policy in this domain, and the actions of health care and social service personnel. Importantly, these issues explain how and why transsexual and transgendered people do not appeal to an established health care and social service network. Many TS/TG individuals take hormones without being monitored by a physician because they cannot find a sympathetic doctor with whom to work. TS/TG youth find forms of temporary housing other than shelters, prostitutes do not report harassment from the police for fear of reprisal, and transsexuals deny their transsexual status while enrolled in alcohol and drug recovery programs. TS/TG people choose to address their health care and social service needs on their own rather than subject themselves to the judgment, harassment, or discrimination of health care and social service agencies. Since no one wants to deal with them, TS/TG people organize themselves outside of the institutional world to fulfill their own health care needs. The sale of hormones on an underground market constitutes the most clear example of this problematic.

Significantly, the refusal of services and the conditional acceptance criteria of many social service agencies exclude the most marginal individuals among transsexual and transgendered people: those who are seropositive, prostitutes, in prison, poor, young, and/or homeless. This division within TS/TG communities is remarkable, as evidenced by the research on police. All twelve of the TS/TG prostitutes I interviewed recounted stories of police harassment. In contrast, only one of the twenty-one individuals who were not involved in prostitution had experienced police harassment or intimidation. *Attention to the refusal of services must recognize that this exclusion is most noteworthy in the case of transsexual prostitutes.*

The results of this chapter explain how transsexuals and transgendered people are erased from the institutional world as a function of specific policies and administrative practices in health care and social services. Dorothy Smith's method of institutional ethnography proves especially pertinent in this investigation, since it offers a way to make sense of how everyday experience is ordered through social institutions. While Smith outlines institutional ethnography as a general strategy, the practical work of conducting an institutional ethnography can be carried out through a variety of qualitative research methods.[30] The findings presented in this chapter illustrate the relevance of interviews with transsexual and transgendered people. Because TS/TG people are obliterated from the social text, critical research methods that allow these people to speak, to make sense of their lives on their own terms, are urgently needed. Interviews offer one strategy for TS and TG people to articulate their own concerns and to explain how they are made to disappear.

# 8

## CLINICAL RESEARCH

## OR COMMUNITY HEALTH?

### Transsexual Perceptions of Gender Identity Clinics

In chapter 7, I examined how the institutional workings of health care and social services render TS/TG people invisible. This chapter extends this argument through a detailed consideration of how TS/TG people in Canada situate themselves with respect to gender identity clinics. Drawing on interviews with TS/TG people as well as service providers, I examine how the experience of gender identity clinics is ordered through the administrative practices of these institutions. The organization of gender identity clinics has important implications for the general health care needs of transsexuals and transgendered people. While chapter 7 explored some of the institutional relations of health care that prevent transsexuals and transgendered people from seeking services, this chapter examines the workings of a deep conflict among transsexuals and psychiatrists. This conflict reinforces the institutional exclusion of transsexuals and transgendered people, offering additional insight into how the erasure of TS/TG individuals is organized at a micrological level.

This chapter presents data culled from my interviews with TS/TG people in Toronto, with particular reference to their perceptions of the Gender Identity Clinic of the Clarke Institute of Psychiatry.[1] Like transsexuality, gender identity clinics are a recent phenomenon. They emerged in the late 1960s, in large part as a response to increased demand for hormonal and surgical sex reassignment by TS/TG people. Gender clinics have assumed at least two roles with respect to transgendered people: first, psychiatrists affiliated with such clinics offer their assessment of an individual's gender dysphoria; and second, the clinics can, upon a diagnosis of gender dysphoria and/or transsexualism, provide an individual with hormones and make a recommendation for sex reassignment surgery (SRS).

The very notion of gender clinics is not without controversy, however, both within the medical establishment and within TS/TG communities. Some medical personnel object that transsexualism is a mental illness that should be treated as such, rather than offering individuals the opportunity to change their bodies through hormones and surgery.[2] In a different manner, many transgendered people protest that gender identity clinics are not concerned with the health of transgendered people, but are only interested in their own professional research programs.[3] Given these suspicions from both the medical establishment and transgendered people, the research conducted at gender identity clinics can be subject to intense scrutiny, analysis, and debate.

The controversy surrounding gender identity clinics was especially marked in the United States in the late 1970s, following the publication of a study conducted at the gender clinic associated with Johns Hopkins University in Baltimore, Maryland—the institution where the first gender identity clinic in the United States was established. Researchers Meyer and Reter concluded that genital surgery offers "no objective advantage in terms of social rehabilitation."[4] Despite the neutral language of this research, this study was used as a justification to cease sex reassignment surgeries at Johns Hopkins Hospital. Since similar clinics across the country had modeled themselves on the Johns Hopkins program, it is not surprising that gender clinics affiliated with other universities also reconsidered their practice of performing sex reassignment surgeries subsequent to the publication of this research.

The Meyer and Reter study has been criticized for its lack of methodological rigor.[5] Moreover, there is speculation that a variety of factors apart from the Meyer and Reter study influenced the decision to cease SRS at Johns Hopkins, including the internal politics at Johns Hopkins Hospital.[6] I do not intend to chronicle the history of gender identity clinics in the United States[7] or offer an in-depth analysis of the events surrounding the Meyer and Reter study in this chapter. Reflection on the controversy associated with the publication of this study, however, raises some important questions about the relations between knowledge and action.

The Meyer and Reter research was used to inform the policy of Johns Hopkins Hospital with respect to SRS, with international implications for the types of health care services available to TS/TG people. Given this relation between research and practice, an examination of the methodological approach employed by Meyer and Reter is in order. Their study focused on the "successful" adjustment of post-operative transsexuals, establishing a link between "success" and the validity of SRS as a procedure. Meyer and Reter relied on variables like happiness and improved job stability to determine the successful outcome of genital surgery.

Significantly, the measure of these outcomes was conducted by psychiatrists and professionals associated with the Johns Hopkins gender clinic.

In this manner, the research established a tautology of clinical practice, scholarly investigation, and social policy: the gender identity clinic would diagnose whether an individual was transsexual; the clinic would offer hormones and surgery in the event of a diagnosis of transsexualism; and the clinic would subsequently determine if the sex reassignment surgery of this person contributed to an improved quality of life. Such an institutional practice is, in effect, a circular loop of psychiatric assessment and the provision of health services to TS/TG people.

Yet the voices, experiences, and interpretations of transgendered people are absent from this research. Professional literature in this domain rarely concerns itself with how transgendered people perceive the policies of gender identity clinics. And as transgendered activist Dallas Denny illustrates, psychiatrists exhibit attitudes of condescension, disrespect, and contempt for transgendered people in their "professional" publications.[8]

Inadequate attention to the experiences and interpretations of TS/TG people with respect to gender identity clinics is underscored by debates over the compromised relations among psychiatrists and their TS/TG clients. Both transgendered people and professionals active in the field of gender dysphoria acknowledge that TS/TG people are avid readers of the psychiatric and clinical research written about them.[9] Transgendered people read what psychiatrists write about them—who they are, how they live, why they are transsexuals—in order to facilitate their access to hormones and/or SRS. They analyze the case studies and theoretical positions of prominent psychiatrists so that they can enter the clinical setting, present the "classic" transsexual narrative, and receive the health care and medical technology they desire. In this way, the information gathered on transsexuals and transgendered people is incomplete, because it reflects the bias of the clinical research setting in which it was collected. Such bias is exposed in the research of anthropologist Anne Bolin, who studied a group of middle-class MTF transsexuals in the United States.[10] Located outside of both gender identity clinics and transsexual communities, Bolin observed how MTF transsexuals presented only certain aspects of their lives to their psychiatric and psychological caregivers.

The skewed nature of interactions among transgendered people and their caregivers is amply illustrated in the sociological literature. Ethnomethodologist Harold Garfinkel presented the case of Agnes, a biological male who presented herself to the UCLA Neuropsychiatric Clinic in the late 1950s with a scrotum, penis, and breasts, and who both lived and identified as a woman.[11] Garfinkel's research illustrates how gender is not an abstract social fact, but rather a social relation that is realized and repeated through its constant iteration: through voice, speech patterns, mannerisms, and the presentation of self. While Garfinkel's principal concern in the Agnes case was an analysis of the "seen but unnoticed" phenomena of everyday life, the case study further demonstrates the complex issues involved with respect to the relations among transsexuals and the psychiatrists and professionals who evaluate them and accord health care based on this evaluation.

Agnes insisted that she was a natural female, albeit one with a penis. She wished to receive SRS from the clinic; she may have learned about its medical and technological viability from the publicity surrounding the case of Christine Jorgensen, an American MTF transsexual who had SRS in Denmark in 1953. Yet Agnes never identified herself as a transsexual, nor did she wish to meet other transsexuals or transgendered people. Rather, she presented her condition as a medical aberration.

Her physicians and psychiatrists agreed with Agnes's self-diagnosis. Through comprehensive medical tests, her caregivers ruled out the possibility that Agnes obtained female hormones surreptitiously. Based on a diagnosis of her intersexuality, the personnel at UCLA recommended Agnes for surgery to construct a vagina.

Several years following her surgery, Agnes revealed that she had been ingesting estrogen since the age of twelve. This new information shed additional light on her case. Agnes had carefully constructed her presentation of self to the doctors, psychiatrists, and other professionals at UCLA, understanding that a diagnosis of intersexuality would facilitate her access to vaginal constructive surgery. She was not, however, a "true" intersexed individual, despite the conferral of that label to her case by prominent American psychiatrists. Agnes was a transsexual.

Mary Rogers's feminist interpretation offers some valuable insights on the power relations involved in the Agnes case. She points out that when Agnes presented herself to UCLA, she was young, had few financial resources and marginal job skills, and was living away from home. She had to participate in the research in order to obtain the surgery she desired. Rogers recognizes the vulnerable position in which Agnes was located in relation to Garfinkel. Rogers considers how Garfinkel directed his conversations with Agnes, as well as the fact that he offered no commentary on her relationship with her boyfriend Bill, a relationship in which Agnes was to assume a self-sacrificing role.[12] Rogers demonstrates that despite his insistence that gender is a result of social processes, Garfinkel was blind to his own role as a researcher in reproducing stereotypical relations between men and women in the 1950s. An appeal to the concept of "point of view" is central to Rogers's argument. Through a detailed analysis of Garfinkel's own reflections on the Agnes case, Rogers shows how his assessment of her gender identity relied on unwritten sex-typed criteria. She points out, for instance, Garfinkel's emphasis on Agnes's femininity, beauty, and measurements, rather than on an absence of facial hair. Rogers exposes the implicit masculinist bias of the research situation:

> Given the presence of an insistently masculine voice in the text—given, indeed, a text that both concerns gender and is itself gendered—this document may thus be read as a report of "cultural events" constitutive not only of Agnes's femininity in the research situation but also of Garfinkel's and Stoller's and Bill's masculinity relative to that situation. They all were passing.[13]

Rogers concludes that while the everyday "feminine" interactions of Agnes were subject to intense scrutiny, the everyday "masculine" positions of Garfinkel or the psychiatrists involved in her assessment were not considered. Masculinity thus functions as an unmarked norm within the research setting.

In light of these relations among gender, research, and social policy within gender identity clinics, this chapter attempts a somewhat ambitious undertaking. Drawing on the interviews conducted with transsexuals and transgendered people in the Project Affirmation research, I seek to document and analyze how TS/TG individuals perceive and interpret their experiences within gender identity clinics and, more broadly, within the institutional relations of psychiatry. This research is valuable for two reasons. First, it offers a sustained, comprehensive analysis of how TS/TG people situate themselves with respect to the practices of gender identity clinics. Although the dissatisfaction with gender clinics is widely known within transgender and transsexual communities,[14] there has been no systematic attempt to collect data based on this experience outside of the clinical research setting. (Bolin's study stands out as a partial exception here. Nevertheless, while she clearly illustrates the mistrust of psychiatrists and psychologists among MTF transsexuals, many members of her sample population were not specifically enrolled in university-based gender identity clinics.) The second contribution of this chapter relates to social policy. The research of gender clinics is used to formulate policy concerning eligibility, and therefore who has access to hormones and SRS. Yet we have already observed that this research reflects a clinical bias and does not adequately consider the perspective of TS/TG people. A study that outlines how transgendered people locate themselves within the institutional apparatus of gender identity clinics can thus inform the development of social policy that addresses the health care needs and concerns of TS/TG individuals.

## METHODOLOGY: INTERVIEWS WITH CLIENTS AND SERVICE PROVIDERS

Only nineteen of the initial thirty-three interviewees in the Project Affirmation study were enrolled or had at one time been enrolled in the Clarke Gender Identity Clinic. The results from this chapter are thus taken from a population of nineteen individuals: seventeen MTF and two FTM transsexual or transgendered people.[15] Like I pointed out in chapter 7, this study is limited concerning the experiences of FTM transsexuals and transgenderists. Some additional data is presented from a community-based needs assessment of transsexuals and transvestites with regard to HIV in Québec.[16] Although the sample population of the Québec research is different from that of the Project Affirmation study conducted in Ontario, the results provide a clear indication of the discrimination against prostitutes in gender identity clinics. Given a dearth of studies on the experiences of prostitutes with gender identity clinics, this data is included in the present chapter.

In the first part of this book, I suggested that a poststructuralist sociology needs to understand that transsexuals and transgendered people are produced through an objectivist discourse preoccupied with gender identity and genital status. Because the questions asked of transgendered people generally position us as an object of fascination, they limit themselves to debates around the etiology of transsexualism or the aesthetic or physical functions of reconstructed genitals. Such questions do not begin with the lived experience of TS/TG people, but rather satisfy the curiosity of non-transsexual men and women. To conduct a research study on TS/TG health care that does not raise these issues begins from the mundane assumption that TS/TG people are a regular part of everyday life, and that we merit consideration not because we have decided to live in a gender other than the one to which we were assigned, but because we have specific concerns with respect to health care and social services. Practically speaking, if academics wish to understand how transsexuals and transgendered people are situated in the world without reverting to a discourse of gender identity or genital status, they need to formulate interview questions that focus on social institutions, and how they are experienced by the research participants. Such a starting point is even more significant in the psychiatric context. As outlined above, gender identity clinics assess people who name themselves transsexual (or, more recently, transgendered) and rely on this assessment in their decision to offer the individual hormones and/or recommend them for surgery. In other words, the institutional workings of psychiatry relate debates about who is or is not transsexual to the health services TS/TG individuals obtain. My research did not ask interviewees to speak about how they perceived themselves in terms of sex/gender. In this way, it was hoped that the information they offered would be as comprehensive and as accurate as possible, because they would focus on the topics of health care and social services rather than providing a classic transsexual narrative.

In addition to my interviews with TS/TG people who were or had been enrolled in the Clarke Institute of Psychiatry Gender Identity Clinic (GIC), I interviewed several representatives of the GIC staff. In the initial stages of the project, I contacted the GIC for an overview of the services they offered and how they were administered. Once I had conducted several interviews with participants, I began to examine the data with particular attention paid to their perceptions of the GIC and its role in TS/TG health care. Several common themes emerged from the interviews, notably a lack of information from the GIC on hormones and a dissatisfaction with the "real-life test."[17] I was thus able to develop precise questions to ask representatives of the GIC with respect to these issues. Such a strategy enabled a critical view of the administration of TS/TG health care, beginning from the issues TS/TG people identified as important.

It is customary, in qualitative research, to omit any references to specific institutions and individuals in order to preserve the confidentiality of participants. This protocol was not possible for the purposes of this research, since the Clarke GIC was the institutional site responsible for making a recommendation to the Ontario Health Insurance Programme (OHIP) that an individual be approved for SRS in Ontario. Given the GIC's unique role in making such recommendations, it would be futile to attempt to hide the identity of the institution through vague or nuanced language. However, it remains necessary to preserve the confidentiality of the service providers and TS/TG people interviewed. The question of confidentiality is especially important for service providers, since the information revealed in this chapter could affect how TS/TG people relate to particular service providers, professionals, and psychiatrists associated with the GIC. I interviewed a variety of individuals who work with the GIC in different capacities. The people I contacted will not be identified to avoid compromising their working relationships with TS/TG clientele. The professional functions and genders of service providers will only be specified when it is directly relevant to the discussion at hand; for example, in an examination of sexism within a diagnostic process, or the role of clinical researchers in the provision of health care. Many TS/TG people in this study express profound dissatisfaction with the services of the GIC at the Clarke Institute of Psychiatry. By protecting the identity of individual service providers, it is hoped that this research focuses on the policies and administration of the GIC.

The information contained in this chapter was gathered during the summer of 1995. The report I produced for Project Affirmation, however, did not contain most of the data presented here. The section of the report concerning the GIC limited itself to primarily two topics: the perception that the GIC did not share information on hormones and transsexuality with TS/TG people, and debate about the real-life test. I omitted the other controversial topics presented in this chapter, such as sexism in the assessment process, because of the political climate of health care in Ontario during the time of the research process. In June 1995, a conservative government won a provincial election. Shortly after coming to power, as part of their massive restructuring of health care in Ontario, the government announced that it intended to defund sex reassignment surgeries.[18] This situation created a moral and political dilemma for me as a community-based researcher. I had informed potential interviewees that I was to act as their voice, to document and summarize how they experienced health care and social services in Ontario. Participants agreed to talk with me based upon this understanding of my role. Many people were highly critical of the services offered at the GIC and hoped that my role as a researcher would provide legitimacy to their perceptions and experiences. I did not want to betray this trust, yet I feared that if my final report reflected all of the information I gathered with respect to the GIC, the provincial government could use my research as justification for defunding SRS. For this reason, I decided to withhold much of the information collected during the research process. This was not an easy decision, but one that attempted to acknowledge that research is not just a static thing in the world, its product a report that sits on a shelf. Research is, rather, an activity embedded in social relations of power and access. In some instances, these social relations require that researchers withhold information that can be used against the members of the community under study. As Sandra Kirby and Kate McKenna argue,

> The destination of the research information is critical to people in the margins. If there is any question that the information could be used to their detriment, or if it could be used to organize their experience so that it can be further [controlled], it should not be released. The researcher's

responsibility is to take direction about the destination of the research information from the participants and collaborators.[19]

Most of the participants in my study clearly indicated that they were dissatisfied with the services at the GIC. Yet the political context of health care in Ontario at the time of the research prevented a comprehensive discussion of this situation.[20]

With respect to the services and policies of the Gender Identity Clinic at the Clarke Institute of Psychiatry, the participants I interviewed identified four themes: debate over the concept and function of the real-life test; sexism in the diagnostic process; service providers' lack of training and sensitivity to sex work and prostitution among MTF transgendered people; and a refusal to provide TS/TG people with information, knowledge, and resources directly related to their bodies and lives. Before examining each of these topics in depth, a brief overview of health care for transgendered people in Ontario, and the GIC's central role therein, is warranted.

Having documented the perceptions of research participants with regard to the above topics, this chapter offers some reflection on the specific institutional relations at work that explain this conflict between transsexuals and the psychiatric establishment. I conclude with a brief discussion of how this knowledge could inform political action in this domain.

## HEALTH CARE IN ONTARIO AND THE GENDER IDENTITY CLINIC

The Clarke GIC plays an important role in the lives of transsexuals in Ontario. Individuals who wish to have SRS covered through provincial health insurance must have an assessment and recommendation by the GIC.[21]

The Clarke GIC has an active client list of approximately three hundred patients, meaning that about three hundred people consult them at least once a year. Staff of the GIC informed me that, on average, they see one new patient every week. The GIC has established guidelines for their patients to be eligible for SRS. The individual must live in the chosen gender (the "opposite sex") full-time for at least two years. The GIC requires that this person provide written documentation supporting this claim. People can work, study, or do volunteer work full-time in order to meet this requirement. People can also engage in a variety of these activities (e.g., studying part-time and working part-time), as long as the total is equivalent to full-time work or school. This requirement is commonly referred to as the real-life test.

After one year of cross-living, the individual becomes eligible for hormones. An endocrinologist associated with the GIC monitors the health of clients who obtain their hormones through the GIC. After two years of cross-living, the individual becomes eligible for surgery. Before being recommended for surgery, however, a candidate must fulfill several other conditions: be legally divorced, if once married; be at least twenty-one years of age; have no evidence of psychosis; and have no recent record of criminal activity.[22]

Strictly speaking, the GIC does not "approve" people for surgery. It merely certifies that the individual in question has been assessed, is of sound mind, is diagnosed to be transsexual, and will not suffer any adverse effects from SRS. The GIC makes this recommendation to OHIP, who in turn decides whether the procedure will be covered through provincial health insurance plans. (A representative at OHIP stated that this was a rubber-stamp procedure, since they always followed the recommendation of the GIC.[23]) Staff at the GIC reported that approximately six or seven individuals are recommended for surgery each year; OHIP confirmed this information.[24]

Transgendered people who wish to have the cost of their sex reassignment surgeries covered under provincial health insurance, then, must enroll in the GIC program. Without the recommendation of the GIC, a transgendered individual is personally responsible for the costs of reassignment surgery.

## THE REAL-LIFE TEST

A majority of the interviewees objected to both the nature and function of the real-life test. Access to hormones was a central component of transgendered people's misgivings about this policy, because the GIC specifies that an individual cross-live for one year before beginning hormone treatment. Staff at the GIC provided a number of reasons to justify this policy. They stated that the administration of hormones to female-to-male transsexuals has profound and lasting effects. Thus, they wanted to be sure that the individual in question was truly committed to living in the chosen gender. It would be unfair to require that FTMs wait one year before obtaining hormones while MTFs could get hormones after an initial diagnosis. Staff at the GIC also expressed concern about the possible health risks involved in taking hormones, as well as about a "snowball effect" in individuals who begin hormones too soon (in the opinion of staff at the GIC) and become heavily invested in having surgery soon thereafter.[25]

Maxine Petersen and Robert Dickey, two researchers associated with the

Clarke GIC, studied the policies of gender identity clinics around the world. They surveyed nineteen different gender identity clinics in Canada, the United States, and Europe. On the subject of hormones, they learned that thirteen clinics delayed estrogen treatment (in the case of MTF transsexuals) even when a diagnosis of transsexualism had been made. Most of these clinics had the same policies for MTF and FTM transsexuals. One clinic claimed to be more cautious with FTMs, due to the irreversible effects of the hormones (e.g., voice change). Another clinic cited a longer delay in the administration of hormones to MTFs because its staff felt more certain about the diagnosis of transsexuality in their FTM clients.[26]

The contribution of Petersen and Dickey is important, and their interpretation of these policies is even more interesting. They conclude with a discussion of emerging transgender activism—notably, prominent American transgender and transsexual activists who seek to facilitate access to hormonal treatment and surgical sex reassignment.[27] In Petersen and Dickey's view,

> it may not be overstating the case to describe their view of hormonal and surgical reassignment as a "right" and their goal as achieving surgical reassignment on demand, i.e., by treating it as any other cosmetic surgery.[28]

Petersen and Dickey maintain that the internationally recognized Standards of Care of the Harry Benjamin International Gender Dysphoria Association (HBIGDA) contradict this approach. Their argument is valid in the case of SRS; the Standards of Care are certainly designed to ensure that individuals are well-informed and prepared to undergo such surgery. But the case of hormonal treatment is somewhat different, since the Standards of Care do not contraindicate the administration of hormones to an individual who is diagnosed as transsexual.[29] It is unfortunate that Petersen and Dickey collapse hormones and surgery in their discussion; the availability of hormones and the availability of SRS are distinct, yet related, issues.

Petersen and Dickey's discussion of these issues is especially noteworthy for the types of opposition it perpetuates. On one side are gender identity clinics, whose function is "to protect individuals from making precipitous decisions of such an irreversible character";[30] on the other side are transsexual rights advocates, who fight for surgery and hormones on demand. It is curious that Petersen and Dickey neglect to mention the work of the American Educational Gender Information Service (AEGIS), which strikes a balance between these positions. AEGIS notes that the administration of hormones can be used quite effectively as a diagnostic tool for transvestites;

many male transvestites begin hormones and learn that they are not interested in pursuing surgery. Moreover, AEGIS argues that a policy of cross-
living without hormones can bring on unnecessary stress, since it requires
that an individual inform lovers, coworkers, and landlords she or he is undergoing a gender transition. AEGIS suggests, in contrast, that an individual
begin hormone therapy while still living in the gender assigned to them at
birth. A full-time gender transition can occur at a later date. While the
Clarke GIC justifies the delay in hormone therapy in part due to health
reasons, AEGIS raises the important point that "health" includes one's psychological state:

> The result of failed hormonal therapy is at worst some physical charac-
> teristics which run counter to type and which may be difficult for the in-
> dividual to explain. The result of a failed real-life test is a life in shambles.
> Family, friends, and employers cannot be un-told about transsexualism,
> marriages and family life are unlikely to be resumed, and lost employment
> is unlikely to be regained. A non-passable appearance, which is likely if the
> individual has not been on hormones for a significant period, can be highly
> stigmatizing, and can place the individual in danger in this era of hate
> crimes. Furthermore, a failed real-life test can result in a high potential for
> self-destructive behavior, including suicide.[31]

Two additional factors should be mentioned. The first concerns the
ways in which people access hormones. The information I presented in
chapter 7 clearly shows that transsexuals and transgenderists are creative,
resourceful, and informed individuals who will go to great lengths in order
to obtain their hormones. The staff of the GIC I spoke with estimated that
30 to 50 percent of their clients received their hormones outside the GIC.[32]
Interestingly, the GIC does not expel individuals engaged in the first year
of their real-life test who obtain hormones on their own.[33] Thus, the GIC
does not enforce its own policy that individuals cross-live for a year without
hormones when patients initiate hormone treatment outside of the GIC
during this period. Also noteworthy is the fact that the gender identity
clinic in Vancouver—which performs the same functions of assessment,
diagnosis, and treatment as the GIC of the Clarke—does not delay hormones to individuals diagnosed as transsexuals. This policy, moreover, fol-
lows the international Standards of Care of the HBIGDA. Contrary to what
Petersen and Dickey imply, this has not created a situation of "surgery on
demand."

The subjects I interviewed who were familiar with the GIC—both MTF and FTM—objected to the one-year delay in hormone treatment. Transsexuals made a point of telling me that they understood the necessity of ensuring an individual was serious about undergoing a gender transition. They did not agree, however, with a delay in hormone treatment once a diagnosis had been made. In the words of one interviewee:

> I think hormones should go to anyone who can give informed consent, an informed decision. As long as they know what they're [hormones] for, what the side effects are, I think that an intelligent adult should be given access to hormones. Period.

My research indicates that transsexuals and transgenderists who objected to the GIC's hormone policy were informed not only about how transsexuality is administered in Toronto, but how health care is organized for transsexuals elsewhere. This finding parallels the research of Dallas Denny and Jan Roberts, who learned that most transsexuals and transgenderists were overwhelmingly aware of the Harry Benjamin International Gender Dysphoria Association, its policies, and its procedures.[34]

## SEXISM IN THE DIAGNOSTIC PROCESS

The previous discussion of Agnes and her clinical context indicates that, certainly within the context of 1950s psychiatry, stereotypes of femininity helped Agnes secure SRS. The research also exposes the implicitly masculinist frame of reference of the assessment process: a situation in which Agnes was considered to be a "natural" female because she appeared attractive to her male caregivers, and in which her position as a transsexual (intersexed) individual was subject to close scrutiny and analysis, while the genders of the clinical staff warranted no reflection or consideration within the research. This case study amply indicates the workings of gender relations within the clinical context. More recent research reveals that the masculinist bias of caregivers remains an integral component of the health care process for many TS/TG people.[35] This finding is confirmed in my study of TS/TG people in Toronto.

In their ethnomethodological study of gender, Kessler and McKenna discovered that some male clinicians relied on their own conceptions of masculinity and femininity in their assessment of a transsexual client:

> [One clinician stated that] he was more convinced of the femaleness of a male-to-female transsexual if she was particularly beautiful and was

capable of evoking in him those feelings that beautiful women generally do. Another clinician [revealed] that he uses his own sexual interest as a criterion for deciding whether a [MTF] transsexual is really the gender she claims.[36]

Anne Bolin's study of MTF transsexuals in the United States supports the evidence that the diagnostic process of transgendered people is marked by sexism. She notes that psychiatrists and medical personnel often had the unwritten expectation that MTF transsexuals would present themselves as "hyper-feminine."[37] This expectation created difficulties for MTF transsexuals who were more comfortable wearing jeans and T-shirts or similar unisex clothes.

Bolin's findings about the importance of apparel were paralleled in my research. Several MTF transgendered interviewees who presented to the GIC in jeans and a T-shirt reported that the staff inquired about their dress, suggesting to them that a more gender-marked appearance was in order. Most MTF transgendered people interviewed, however, admitted that they carefully constructed their outfit, accessories, and makeup when visiting the GIC.

The GIC's policy with respect to the legal names of transgendered people also reveals a sexist bias. When individuals who wish to undergo a gender transition have a name that could function in both genders (such as "Robin" or "Dale"), the GIC advises that they replace the name with one that confirms the chosen gender:

> For the altered documentation to be meaningful, and to prevent any circumventing of the spirit of the criteria of full-time cross-living, the choice of the new name becomes important. To this end, we encourage patients to select a first name that clearly and unambiguously reflects the new gender role. Patients should not, in other words, choose a name such as *Robin,* which is equally common among men and women and thus provides no clue to the sex of its bearer. Patients whose original given names were of the unisex type are encouraged to replace them with more clearly sex-typed names such as *John* or *Mary.*[38]

An interview in the transgendered magazine *Chrysalis Quarterly* [CQ] with one Canadian transsexual reveals that, while the authors of the policy on name change merely "encourage" a transgendered person with an androgynous name to adopt a sex-typed name, the actual practices of gender clinics *require* such an initiative:

CQ: Didn't you have a name that worked in both genders?

A: Yes. My first name was Lonnie—I had started to spell it Loni—and my middle name worked, too. But the clinic told me I had to change it.

CQ: Wasn't it just a suggestion?

A: No, they told me I had to change it or forget about the program.[39]

This individual's experience illustrates the difference between what is written on paper—that it is productive to "encourage" those people with unisex names to adopt gender-marked names—and what actually happens in the administration of gender identity clinic programs: transgendered people believe that they must comply with these "encouragements" or risk losing access to hormones and SRS. Moreover, the suggestion that an individual with an androgynous name replace it does not account for the experience of that TS/TG person. Presumably, if an individual has a name that works equally well in either gender, then changing it to one marked by a specific gender will not necessarily aid the individual in "passing." If TS/TG people pass already, there is no need to change their name. If they do not pass, this situation will not be resolved upon adoption of a sex-typed name.[40]

Sexism in the assessment process can thus be observed in administrative attitudes concerning the physical stature of TS/TG clients; their clothing; and their names, particularly if before transition they had an "androgynous" name. All of these examples illustrate the gendered expectations of clinicians involved in diagnosing transgendered people. My research provides further support to other studies in this area.[41]

An additional area of inquiry in my study concerns the issue of sexual harassment. Many of the transgendered people I interviewed spoke about the Clarke GIC staff's gendered expectations concerning dress, beauty, and mannerisms. Several interviewees, however, recounted incidents in which staff behaved inappropriately given their professional capacities, making nuanced reference to sexual behavior. One MTF interviewee described the remarks of a male staff member prior to her SRS in England: "'Well when you come back . . . I want to examine you myself for vaginal depth.'" The interviewee maintained that she was incredibly uncomfortable with this situation, but she did not challenge the clinician: she thought this procedure might have been necessary to determine the success of the surgery. She did remark, however, that a post-surgical examination was never explained to her as part of the program at the GIC. In her interpretation, the clinician did not speak about this examination from a medical standpoint.

Another interviewee described an incident that reveals a similar dynamic between MTF transgendered patients and some male care providers: "The last time I was there . . . he kept talking to me and he kept . . . he just kept staring at my breasts . . . it just didn't feel good." This person also did not confront the staff member, for she did not wish to jeopardize her chance at obtaining a recommendation for SRS.

While MTF transsexuals felt themselves to be the objects of sexual harassment, FTMs I interviewed reported that they were required to uphold marked stereotypes of rugged masculinity. A FTM transsexual who is shy and reserved described his interaction with a GIC staff member:

> One of the things that really flipped me out was like he took me to a private room and he said, "Hey, what do you want to do with a woman?" Can you imagine?

> Q: How did you respond?

> A: "Can I get out of here?!" No, I didn't say that! . . . He was like, it was sort of like a stag party or something. It was weird, you know? . . . I didn't know if I thought it was really appropriate or not, 'cause it sort of freaked me out. I think he was trying to shock me . . . I was embarrassed . . . it had been years since I'd talked about it [transsexuality] to anyone . . . it was real hard. Basically, I cried . . . I'm a very decent person, and modest. And I don't like vulgar [talk and behavior]. . . . That experience was very unpleasant.

This encounter indicates how the sexism of some care providers affects FTM transsexuals in the clinical context. While MTF transgendered people are positioned as objects of sexual desire within such a discourse, FTM transsexuals are expected to uphold codes of gratuitous sexuality. Unfortunately, these patients feared that if they complained about such incidents, they would jeopardize their access to hormones and surgery.

## PROSTITUTION AMONG MTF TRANSSEXUALS

In a historical overview of gender clinics in the United States, Dallas Denny maintains that biased selection criteria determined which transgendered people had access to hormones and SRS. She argues that researchers and professional staff placed a high value upon an individual's gender presentation. This criterion facilitated access to gender clinics for those people who were skilled in makeup and self-presentation. In Denny's view, this situation "resulted in the acceptance of flocks of drag queens and street hustlers, who were generally skilled at appearing as women, but who often were not transsexual."[42]

Denny further contends that prostitutes were overrepresented within sample populations of people enrolled in gender identity clinic programs:

> The clinics viewed sex reassignment as a last-ditch effort to save those with whom other therapies and interventions had failed. Those who were accepted for treatment were often prostitutes, were profoundly depressed, and often placed clinicians under duress by threatening autocastration or suicide. They and others who were considered "hopeless"—i.e., were likely to die, anyway—were accepted. It was a classic misapplication of the triage method, with those most likely to benefit from intervention being turned away, and the terminal cases receiving treatment.[43]

Denny's argument is certainly worthy of consideration, particularly with regard to the generalizability of the sample populations of gender clinics. Nevertheless, her position assumes that most "true" transsexuals are not involved in prostitution and/or street life. Denny also suggests that transgendered people who were not involved in street culture were most likely to benefit from treatment. While she raises some important questions with respect to the selection of candidates for gender clinic programs, her comments indicate a general ignorance of the culture and diversity of street-involved TS/TG individuals.

The research project upon which this chapter is based focuses on the experiences of TS/TG people—including prostitutes—with health care and social services in Ontario. My research in this domain indicates that prostitutes are certainly not overrepresented among TS/TG clients enrolled in the Clarke GIC. Moreover, the representatives of the GIC I interviewed expressed negative attitudes about prostitution in general and TS/TG prostitutes in particular.

As previously discussed, the GIC requires that all individuals enrolled in its program undergo the real-life test; that is, that they work, go to school, or volunteer full-time in their chosen gender. When I asked whether an individual who had decided to work as a prostitute would be considered for acceptance into their program, one clinic representative responded in the following manner:

> Well that's [prostitution] a problem because it can't be documented. . . .
> We don't say that "This is something that cannot be done" because they're
> [prostitutes] going to do it anyway. But it doesn't meet our criteria, and if
> you want to meet our criteria and go through this program you have to get

a "regular" job or go to school or do volunteer work, and sex trade workers are not volunteers.[44]

The response of this service provider is of an administrative order.[45] Documentation required to prove that one is cross-living successfully, such as one's yearly tax revenue statements, cannot be offered in the case of transsexual prostitutes. Yet other forms of documentation can serve as proof that prostitutes are living in their chosen genders. Many transsexual prostitutes advertise their services in the paper, often including their photographs in the advertisements. A collection of such documents over the course of a year would indicate that prostitution was indeed the job of this person.

The service provider's comment that "sex trade workers are not volunteers" reflects an ignorance of prostitute communities, because it does not consider all of the volunteer efforts of prostitutes and other sex trade workers with regard to legal reform, AIDS activism, and health promotion. Such an oversight seems particularly ironic given the regional location of the GIC in Toronto. Toronto is home to Maggie's, a peer-run drop-in and referral center for prostitutes, where TS and TG people have been active. The national chapter of the Canadian Organization for the Rights of Prostitutes (CORPS) is also located in Toronto. Given the strong presence of prostitute activists in Toronto, I presented a hypothetical situation to this service provider. I asked this person to imagine a MTF transsexual who paid for their rent, clothes, entertainment, electrolysis, and other expenses through prostitution, but who also volunteered twenty-five hours a week at a local community group (thereby meeting the criteria for the real-life test). I asked whether such a person would be eligible for enrollment in the GIC program, and specifically for a recommendation for SRS. The service provider replied that prostitution per se was not a contraindication for recommendation for surgery. Significantly, however, this clinic representative *implied* that the individual in question would be at risk for contracting HIV:

> We would be concerned [about this person] simply because it's [prostitution] a health risk as well, in these times, but beyond that . . . I think that that would not color our assessment if they met the other criteria.[46]

The assumption that transsexual prostitutes are at risk for contracting HIV simply due to their work ignores the scholarly literature that amply demonstrates that prostitutes are well-informed individuals who protect both themselves and their clients from the transmission of HIV and other sexually transmitted diseases.[47] Moreover, the service provider employed conditional terminology ("I think") and subjunctive verbs ("would not color").

This response indicates that the GIC has no clear policy with respect to transsexuals who work as prostitutes but who may do volunteer work to meet the criteria of the GIC's real-life test. Given the absence of such a policy, one wonders how the volunteer activities of transsexual prostitutes would be interpreted, particularly in the case of those who volunteered their time fighting to improve working conditions for prostitutes. Would such activity fulfill the GIC's criteria for cross-living?

Because this interview revealed misconceptions and ignorance about prostitutes (e.g., the assumption that prostitutes transmit HIV and are not active as volunteers), I decided to include this topic within my interviews with other clinic staff. A researcher presented with the hypothetical situation outlined above expressed negative opinions about transsexual prostitutes. His initial response to the situation attempted to dismiss its relevance to the GIC. He began by stating that an individual with a recent criminal record would be ineligible for a recommendation for SRS. I pointed out that within the current Canadian legal context, prostitution per se is not illegal; it is the act of communicating for the purposes of prostitution that is criminalized. This GIC representative subsequently raised the issue of HIV, suggesting that the GIC would be cautious with respect to recommending an HIV-positive person for SRS. I rebutted with the suggestion that it was inappropriate to assume that all transsexual prostitutes are HIV-positive. Finally, the GIC representative stated that prostitutes constituted only a minority of transsexual communities, that they made up "the bottom 10 percent" of the population, and that they were located on the "lower rungs of the ladder." This person contrasted transsexual sex trade workers with "professional" transsexuals, noting that some of the nonprostitute individuals enrolled in the GIC earned over $100,000 a year.[48]

This valorization of professional status and income is evidenced in the comments of Dr. Pierre Assalian, a psychiatrist who works with the Gender Identity Clinic of the Montréal General Hospital, on the talk show *Montréal Today:*

> it [transsexuality] can happen to anybody, it can happen to any culture, any profession, there is, it's not necessarily, some will say that they are bums, or they are, unfortunately some of them and they are not necessarily been [sic] operated, they give a bad image to the transsexuals when they go on Ontario Street soliciting sexual relationships, this are not the typical kind. The typical transsexuals are people that are, we have clients who are surg[eons], who are physicians, who are lawyers, uh, all kinds of, of social strata.[49]

Assalian's comments establish the legitimacy of transsexuality through an appeal to professional occupations. Like the statements made by the GIC representative, this position discriminates against prostitutes, since it does not consider prostitution to be a valid form of work.

My interviews with service providers at the GIC illustrate a general ignorance of transsexual prostitutes. One clinic staff member noted that most of these individuals did not enroll in the program.[50] This claim is substantiated within my research. Although twelve of the thirty-three individuals in the sample population worked as prostitutes, only four were enrolled in the GIC program. This data clearly indicates the underrepresentation of prostitutes within the GIC at the Clarke Institute of Psychiatry. Yet while staff at the GIC are certainly aware that transsexual prostitutes do not make use of their facilities, they have not conducted any research that would address why this is the case.

My interviews with TS/TG prostitutes offer insight into some of the factors that inform their decision to access hormones and SRS independently of the Clarke GIC. Two of the four prostitutes who were enrolled in the GIC did not reveal to the clinic that they were prostitutes. One said, "I knew that [prostitution] would disqualify me right away." Transsexual prostitutes who were honest about their occupations, however, recounted the negative attitudes of their service providers. When one individual was arrested for soliciting, she reported that staff at the GIC told her she had to quit working as a prostitute. They informed her that if she was "caught one more time" they wouldn't help her. Since prostitution was her main source of income, she decided to withdraw from the program. Reflecting on the situation, she commented that their criteria for a real-life test did not account for her poverty and lack of job skills. In her words, "They thought I was crazy. I thought they were crazy." She believes that the antiprostitute attitudes of the GIC were used to deny her access to hormones and SRS.

Another transsexual prostitute said that in order to meet the criteria for the real-life test, she stopped working as a prostitute and obtained a low-paying job in the service industry. She worked there for a year, the length of time required before she could be considered eligible for hormones and eventually surgery. After a year working in the service industry, at a level of pay significantly lower than that to which she was accustomed as a prostitute, the GIC evaluated her and asked that she work another year before initiating hormone treatments. The interviewee perceived this dynamic as a power imbalance, where evaluation and treatment could be delayed indefinitely. She expressed frustration that the GIC staff did not appreciate the profound adjustments she had made in her work to demonstrate her commitment to SRS. Prostitution was, according to staff at the GIC, an "easy way out." Because she did not feel that the clinic staff understood her situation, she withdrew from the clinic to begin saving the necessary funds for surgery:

> I told them to go to hell . . . if nothing's going to be done about it [a recommendation for SRS], I'm going to go back to sucking dick for a living. I can get a *lot* further ahead doing that. And I did it. I did it.

Data from research I conducted in Québec reveals a similar institutionalized discrimination against prostitutes.[51] Professionals associated with gender identity clinics in Québec maintained that they needed to verify the social integration of TS/TG people. They appealed to the HBIGDA "Standards of Care," which require social integration of transsexual individuals. Practically speaking, full-time work or studies attest to this social integration. The Standards of Care do not explicitly exclude transsexual prostitutes; this is merely the interpretation offered by psychiatrists and clinic staff, who do not consider prostitution a legitimate form of work.[52] Prostitute interviewees in Québec told me that the staff of gender identity clinics refuse to evaluate them:

> Le docteur tenair absolument à savoir ou avoir une preuve de, de mes revenus. Là quand j'ai dit que c'était de la prostitution, la thérapie a été interrompue jusqu'à temps que j'prouve que j'travaillais. [Q: Y voulait pas, y voulait que tu continuais ta thérapie?] Tant et aussi longtemps que je continuais la prostitution, au moins que, que j'prouve que, avec un talon de chèque de paie, que je travaillais. [The doctor absolutely insisted on knowing or on having proof of my income. And then when I said it was from prostitution, the therapy was discontinued until I could prove that I worked. (Q: He didn't want you to continue the therapy?) For as long as I worked as a prostitute, at least until I could prove, with a pay stub, that I was working.]

> Il y a beaucoup de discrimination là, et du moment où ils savent que tu fais de la prostitution, ils vont te mettre à la porte. Ils veulent avoir un élite, des gens choisis, des, ils veulent pas de moutons noirs, tsé. [There's a lot of discrimination there, and the moment they know you work as a prostitute, they will kick you out. They want an elite, the chosen people, they don't want any black sheep, you know.][53]

My interviews with prostitutes clearly indicate the discrimination to which they are subject in gender identity clinics. This information was confirmed through my interviews with clinic staff and psychiatrists. When I asked whether a transsexual working as a prostitute could use their services, one Québec City professional contended that prostitution only occurs in Montréal:

> [Q: Comme vous savez, y a beaucoup de transsexuelles qui font de la prostitution, hum, si quelqu'un fait de la prostitution, est-ce que cette personne-là peut avoir recours à vos services ici?] On a pas eu encore. Parce que Québec est un petit ville en? [Hum hum.] C't'une ville de province alors c'est euh, c'est différent de de de grande ville comme Toronto, Montréal, euh Vancouver. [(Q: As you know, many transsexuals work as prostitutes. If someone works as a prostitute, could that person use your services here?) We haven't yet had that. Because Québec is a small city. (Hum hum.) It's a city in a rural region, so it's different than a big city like Toronto, Montréal, um Vancouver.]

My research challenges this assumption, since I interviewed transsexual prostitutes who lived in Québec City and who had already used the services of the institution where this professional works.

In certain instances, the psychiatrists I interviewed associated prostitution with transvestism, but not with transsexualism:

> C'est peut être . . . parce que on se restreint au traitement des per, au suivi des personnes transsexuelles et non pas des personnes travesties, est-ce que c'est pour ça qu'on a pas été confrontés au problème de prostitution ou de la drogue, je le sais pas. [Maybe it's . . . because we limit ourselves to the treatment of, to following transsexuals and not transvestites, is why we haven't been confronted with the problems of prostitution and drugs, I don't know.] [54]

This interviewee not only associates transvestism and prostitution, but subsequently links both to the use of drugs. Other professionals interviewed claimed that prostitution can be observed through the clothing and mannerism of individuals:

> Mais c'est vrai de de moins en moins on va voir ce ce genre de transsexuel [une prostituée]. Nous allons en voir encore, c'est tellement de transsexuels qui viennent nous voir mais qui nous disent, qu'on soupçonne un peu de la façon dont ils sont habillés ou se comporter ou que c'est des gens que qui font la prostitution ou qui font euh euh un genre de spectacle . . . [But it's true that less and less, we see this type of transsexual [prostitute]. We will still see some, there are so many transsexuals who come to see us who

say, well we suspect a bit by the way they dress or their behavior, that these are people who are involved in prostitution or who do a kind of show . . . ] [55]

This professional continues in associating prostitution with HIV, stating that transsexuals enrolled in their program are at less risk for the transmission of HIV:

Et c'est pour cela si vous me dites que les études ont démontré qu'il y a une augmentation des HIV [chez les personnes transsexuelles], vous savez c'est des gens qui ont des relations sexuelles à risque ou non-protégées, ça m'étonnerait de la majorité de notre groupe disons, des transsexuels, évidemment ça existe là pis on est très conscients de de de ce problème. [Q: Pouvez-vous élaborer là-dessus? Pourquoi est-ce que ça vous étonneriez?] A cause de, de euh de la stabilité sociale de ces gens-là. Quand on voit ces transsexuels qu'on voit euh . . . on a plusieurs qui sont mariés là-dans, ou qui qui étaient mariés, qui ont des enfants, euh, qui sont des professionnels, alors ils sont très conscients euh du risque de de d'une relation sexuelle non-protégée. [And that's why if you tell me that studies have indicated an increase in HIV (among transsexuals), you know these are people who are having risky or unprotected sex, it would surprise me that that would include the majority of our group, let us say the transsexuals, obviously it exists and we are very conscious of this problem. (Q: Could you elaborate on that? Why would that surprise you?) Because of, of the social stability of these people. When you see the transsexuals that we see, um, we have many who are married, or who were married, who have children, um, who are professionals, so they are very conscious of the risk of an unprotected sexual relation.] [56]

These examples illustrate several misconceptions about prostitutes: that "real" transsexuals are not prostitutes; that prostitution can be discerned through dress and mannerisms; and that professional transsexuals are more aware of HIV and its transmission than transsexual or transvestite prostitutes. Furthermore, my interviews with service providers reveal the circular logic of their positions: they refuse to evaluate prostitutes, claim that "real" transsexuals are not prostitutes, and subsequently claim that transsexuals are not at great risk for HIV, as evidenced through their work with non-prostitute "professional" transsexuals.

The research conducted in Québec confirms the findings of my interviews with service providers at the Clarke Institute of Psychiatry GIC in Toronto. Discriminatory attitudes toward prostitutes, as well as an implicit valorization of "professional" transsexuals, contribute to the institutional marginalization of transsexual prostitutes.

## LACK OF INFORMATION AND RESOURCES ABOUT TRANSSEXUALITY

The transgendered people I interviewed stated that they did not receive sufficient information from the Clarke GIC about transsexuality, hormones, and how transition would affect their lives. Much of the dissatisfaction among TS/TG clients related to information about hormones, their side effects, and the appropriate dosages required. Several MTF transsexuals reported that service providers at the GIC actually refused to supply them with the information they requested:

> I asked about getting information [on hormones] and they [the GIC] were really evasive about it, like they wouldn't let me go into their library . . . at the Clarke, I couldn't get in.

> The Clarke's [GIC] not . . . I can't get much information from them [about hormones], they're not that helpful in that department.

> I wanted to know about different kinds of hormones, and it's [the GIC response] like, "This is the one we think you should be on."

> I'm not sure if I'm on the right thing [type of hormone and dosage]. . . . I'm just taking what they want me to take, you know? But I'd like to do research and find out what is really, what I should be on.

Some of the interviewees noted that despite being uncomfortable with a lack of information on hormones available through the GIC, they did not search for alternative sources of hormones. This decision was primarily influenced by the GIC's monopoly regarding recommendations for surgery. Transsexuals feared that if they procured hormones outside of the GIC, they would not receive a favorable assessment from the clinic:

> No they [the GIC] won't talk about it. [My doctor affiliated with the GIC] says, "You've got to be on this [type and dosage of hormone]." And that's it. [My doctor] is hard to get along with. If I had a choice, I would probably pick another doctor, but I'm stuck with [mine] because it's with the Clarke and I'm in the [gender identity] program there. But you know, if I went out and I picked another doctor, they [the GIC] might cut me off [from hormones and a recommendation for surgery]. I don't know what's going to happen. I don't want to take any chances. You know how it is.

This quotation illustrates that transsexuals regularly compromise the kind of health care they desire, or deserve, because they believe they have no choice with respect to selecting service providers ("*If* I had a choice . . . "). This less than adequate situation results from how health care was administered for transsexuals in Ontario in 1995, in which only the Clarke GIC was authorized to make recommendations for surgeries that would be covered under provincial health insurance. Transsexuals in Ontario in 1995 who wished to have their sex reassignment surgeries covered through provincial health insurance did not have the right to a second opinion.

While the subject of hormones was addressed by many of the interviewees in the research on the GIC, others stated that they did not receive sufficient information regarding the actual process of SRS:

> The only thing the Clarke didn't supply was enough information about what the whole experience over there [England] is like. Not like, actually physical . . . it would have been nice if they gave me—I didn't realize some of the things that were going to happen that did, like needles in the stomach for ten days, tubings . . . [information about these medical procedures] would have been nice. I'm the type of person that likes to know *everything.*

This post-operative transsexual woman, who was recommended for surgery by the GIC, indicates that ample information about the surgery is essential for an individual's psychological preparations. She notes that such information is particularly important because the surgery is performed in England, where patients are isolated from their support network of family, lovers, and friends.

Participants in the research also maintained that they lacked information about living in their gender of choice: what clothes to wear, how to interact, and how to apply their makeup, as well as some of the unwritten rules governing gender in Western culture. MTF transsexuals stated that they required knowledge about makeup, walking, and voice, and lamented the fact that there was no structure through the GIC to provide such information or facilitate its acquisition (such as group discussions or courses). In the words of one interviewee, "They [the GIC] should be able to provide access to these types of things. Because for a lot of people, it would make their lives easier." FTM transsexuals indicated a similar need for information and resources about how to live in their chosen gender. One FTM interviewee revealed that it was painful for him to bind his breasts, and he did not know where to buy special garments and bandages that could aid in this process: "They [the clinic staff] didn't help me, in that sense. I was very much alone."

214

MTF transsexuals and transgenderists raised the issue of violence in their discussions about passing and the need to acquire information on dress, mannerisms, and voice. They noted that the consequences for a MTF transgendered person who did not "pass" could include verbal abuse and physical assault. The information and resources they sought with respect to dress, manner, and voice were thus in part important for their personal safety.

Interestingly, MTF transgendered people I interviewed noted that the issue of violence was not resolved for those MTF transgendered people who "pass" undetected as transgendered, since they are subject to the same harassment and threat of sexual assault as all women in our culture. Indeed, interviewees remarked that the threat of violence and sexual assault against women was unique regarding transgendered women for two reasons. First, such people could be subject to brutal beatings in addition to verbal abuse and/or sexual assault if their aggressor(s) discovered that they were transgendered (this was especially the case for pre-operative or non-operative MTF individuals). Second, although transgendered women may live as women in this culture, most have not grown up as women and thus have not acquired the strategies many women learn to negotiate or diffuse potentially violent or intimidating situations brought on by men. MTF transsexuals often lack the background knowledge of living with sexual harassment on a daily basis when they begin to live as women, a knowledge that non-transgendered women have acquired through years of living as women.

Some MTF interviewees felt that, given a culture of sexual harassment of women, MTF transsexuals needed focused discussions and practical activities to live both successfully and safely as women. Interviewees suggested several different formats to address this issue: discussion within the clinical context; community meetings with focused discussion and exchange; and self-defense courses prepared specifically for transsexuals. They believed that, by sponsoring such programs, the GIC could play a crucial role in supporting an individual's decision to live in a gender other than the one to which they were assigned at birth. Such interviewees stated regrettably, however, that the GIC did not subscribe to such a comprehensive approach to health care for transsexuals. When asked whether the GIC had ever offered a self-defense course, for instance, one MTF exclaimed, "You've got to be kidding!" Her reaction represents the perspective of many TS/TG people, who do not believe that the GIC offers them the kind of information and resources they need to undergo a gender transition.

The issue of violence was central to the research participants, since most TS/TG people have experienced hostility and the very real threat of physical aggression due to a perceived incongruity between sex and gender. Given the importance accorded to violence as an issue that warrants specific programs and activities for TS/TG people, the interviewees offered highly critical interpretations of the GIC's real-life test, particularly the requirement that individuals live in their chosen gender for one year before hormone therapy.

Many interviewees maintained that except in rare circumstances, individuals will not be able to pass undetected as transgendered until they have been on hormones for some time. This situation is especially true for MTF transgendered people, according to interviewees. A policy that demands cross-living without hormones and with no supplementary support (tips on passing, dress, self-defense), therefore, puts TS/TG people at serious risk of verbal abuse and physical assault. For these reasons, TS/TG people did not feel that the GIC's one-year cross-living requirement prior to hormones addresses their psychological or physical well-being. Participants expressed strong reactions to social policy that ignores the violence permeating their everyday lives:

> You can't expect people to go through this [a gender transition] without survival skills [dealing with violence].

> [The GIC's real-life test functions to say,] "Let's see if you can suffer getting beat up a lot. Then, if you really can, if you really want to do it still [transition], then you really must be a transsexual."

> The thing is, the Clarke says, "Well, put on a dress and a skirt and go out," you know? And that's it . . . like throwing you to the wolves, kind of thing. You can't do hormones, you can't have this . . . just go out. And if you fail, well, it proves you're not a transsexual. And then if you do succeed, the first year or so, [the GIC replies] "Well, we *might* put you on hormones. We *might*, we *might*." Or eventually they do . . .

> I think there are flaws in the way they [the GIC] see this [transsexuality]. They see this as some kind of psychosis, which they're going to treat with aversion therapy—which to me is what the real-life test is, it's aversion therapy. Send some guy with a deep voice out into the street [dressed as a woman] . . . and hope they survive.

> It's not real life. This is cruel and unusual punishment. We wouldn't do this to the worst sex offender . . . yet we're [transsexuals] forced to live this way.

Transgendered people's daily experiences of violence constituted the basis of their objections to the GIC's policy with respect to cross-living. The

216

clinic's policy, moreover, does not account for the different ways in which transgendered people live. An individual who is able to transition at the workplace, who lives in a detached house and who uses her/his own car to work, shop, go to the bank, and engage in leisure activities will have a very different experience of passing than an individual who is assaulted in their workplace, who lives in a high-rise apartment building (having to take an elevator to leave), and who relies on public transportation. Although the first individual may experience the threat of violence as she/he shops for groceries or stands in line at the bank, and while such an experience is not to be dismissed, cross-living may be even more dangerous for those regularly negotiating social spaces that make them particularly vulnerable to assault—the confined space of an elevator, or the stark lighting of the subway.

## PSYCHIATRIC HEALTH CARE SPECIFIC TO TRANSSEXUALS

The data presented above provides ample documentation of a deep conflict between transsexuals and psychiatric service providers. This conflict is fostered and reinforced through the institutional relations of psychiatric health care that are specific to TS/TG people. My research identifies three major issues in this domain: (1) conflicting definitions of "health" between transsexuals and psychiatrists; (2) the process through which informed consent is obtained in the delivery of psychiatric evaluation and services; and (3) a link between employment and health, such that employment is required as a condition of accessing a psychiatric evaluation as well as health services. Furthermore, these institutional relations contribute to the expulsion of transsexuals from the institutional world, demonstrated by many of the transsexuals and transgendered people I interviewed who choose to address their hormonal and SRS needs without recourse to a gender identity clinic. Such actions constitute a worthwhile illustration of the institutional erasure of transsexuals, understanding the notion of "erasure" here in terms of exclusion. Attention to the institutional relations of psychiatric health care specific to TS/TG people, then, can help explain how and why some TS/TG individuals situate themselves outside the health care system established to provide them services.

### Conflicting Definitions of "Health"

Research in the field of health care must confront the theoretical problem of defining its terms of reference—that is, articulating what is meant by the concept of "health." For some scholars and service providers, the notion of "health" encompasses the biomedical, psychological, and social needs of particular individuals and/or populations. The World Health Organization, for instance, defines "health" through an appeal to these interrelated aspects of wellness: "Health is a state of complete physical, mental and social well-being and not merely the absence of disease or infirmity." [57] While some scholars advocate such a broad perspective on health, others limit the scope of health as a category, and therefore of what is relevant for health services and health research. A common objection to the WHO definition of health is that it is too broad and that its general character prevents an adequate understanding of the specifically biomedical aspects of health. [58] This position often suggests restricting definitions of "health" to its physical and bio-medical components.

The experiences of transsexuals and transgendered people indicate that they have a different understanding of "health" than psychiatrists and personnel associated with gender identity clinics. This tension is most apparent in the objections to the real-life test, particularly those put forward by AEGIS. In elaborating their position that one year of cross-living before the prescription of hormone therapy is too severe, AEGIS draws on the complex elements of a transsexual individual's life: job, family, friends, lovers, housing, the threat of violence directed against a visibly transsexual person, and mental health. In this manner, AEGIS appeals to a broad scope of elements that constitute "health," including physical, psychological, and social domains.

This appeal to the social and psychological aspects of health is further evidenced in transsexual objections to the current administration of the GIC. Participants cited the need for information and resources on a wide variety of issues related to transsexualism, including tips on passing successfully and dealing with the threat of violence. MTFs stated the need for discussion and education regarding potentially violent situations, while an FTM maintained that the GIC impeded his own gender transition by not sharing information regarding how to strap his breasts. These objections to the GIC program emerge from a particular understanding of "health," which includes its biomedical, psychological, and social components.

One participant emphasized the importance of psychological support for transsexuals beginning a transition. Subsequent to making an appointment for an assessment, she received no information about transsexuality from the GIC. She contends that this practice ignores the mental health of transsexuals:

When someone's transgendered, you can't . . . treat it as a case where it's like, "I'm transgendered" and they [service personnel] say, "Oh, O.K., wait three months." When someone says they're suicidal, you don't make an appointment to see a doctor and then, he says, "O.K., in three months, you can see this doctor." You get at least *something* immediately. . . . I can't think it's very healthy to be there without care. Once you realize you're a transsexual, you need information immediately.

This comment illustrates the different definitions of health held by transsexuals, who are interested in a comprehensive approach to physical, mental, and social well-being; and those held by the staff of a GIC, who confine their activities to psychiatric evaluation and assessment.

Some interviewees noted that when they were admitted directly to the Clarke Institute of Psychiatry (rather than the GIC) and attempted to address their gender issues as part of their general mental health, they did not obtain the assistance of staff members of the GIC. One MTF transgendered person recounted an incident in which, following suicidal and self-destructive behavior, she was admitted into the Clarke. When she asked to meet with representatives of the GIC, however, she was refused. A representative of the clinic told her, "As long as you're in crisis, I'm not prepared to talk to you."

The response of this service provider appeals to the diagnostic role of the GIC, in which the clinic exists to assess transsexual, transgendered, and/or gender dysphoric individuals. The transgendered person in question, however, sought assistance in the form of a counseling context that would be supportive of her transgendered status. The clinic did not respond to this need because, according to an administrative representative, such a practice was not interpreted to be within the mandate of the program. This situation illustrates the different understandings and expectations of the GIC on the part of transgendered people and the clinic staff. Representatives of the GIC see their role in terms of diagnosis and assessment, whereas transgendered people approach the GIC in search of comprehensive health care, understanding "health" in terms of its biomedical, psychological, and social components.

The experiences of an FTM transsexual parallel the situation outlined above, suggesting that it is not an isolated incident. This individual had been recommended by the GIC for hormones and a double mastectomy. Several years after his surgery and his transition, he attempted suicide. He returned to the gender clinic because, in his opinion, his suicide attempt was directly related to a low self-esteem resulting from his transsexuality. This man reports that the clinic staff were concerned about the possible negative impact of his suicide attempt on the reputation of the clinic, since they had recommended him for hormones and surgery. The psychological well-being of this FTM was secondary. He recounts the following interaction with a clinic representative:

> [He said] "We can't have any more of that [attempted suicide], because it just doesn't look good on us [the GIC]." But there wasn't any like, "What's going on in your mind?" kind of thing. [Q: Did he talk to you about resources, of other people you could talk to, places to go, help?] No. Absolutely not. They should have talked to me a little bit, like why I'd done this [attempted suicide]. Like, I hadn't seen them for ages, there was no asking what had gone on in my life since then.

Like the debate over the real-life test and the experiences of the MTF individuals discussed above, this anecdote indicates the conflicting understandings of the role and function of a gender identity clinic between TS/TG people and GIC representatives.

## Informed Consent

In addition to different understandings of health, transsexuals and psychiatrists conceive of the relations between patient and professional in unique ways. The notion of informed consent illustrates this problematic.

Within biomedical ethics, the concept of "consent" refers to a patient's understanding of the risks associated with a particular treatment, condition, and/or disease.[59] Patients need to be apprised of any and all risks accompanying particular treatment regimens. From the perspective of hospital administration, this understanding is required in order to protect against malpractice lawsuits. From the perspective of patients, individuals need to have all of the relevant information about their health and potential treatment options in order to make the best possible decision as to their care.

The provision of information is central to obtaining consent from a patient. Given the inherently social nature of this process, some researchers and policy makers in the field of biomedical ethics emphasize that informed consent can only be acquired within a social context in which patients are active participants in their health care. Within such a model, the notion of informed consent refers not to the simple reading and signing of a form, but rather to an interactive context between patients and medical professionals characterized by exchange and negotiation. In the United States, for instance, the Presidential Commission for the Study of Ethical Problems in Medicine and Biomedical and Behavioral Research concluded in 1982 that

> [e]thically valid consent is a process of shared decision-making based upon mutual respect and participation, not a ritual to be equated with reciting the contents of a form that details the risks of particular treatments.[60]

In this framework, patients receive information from physicians as to the known and unknown risks associated with different treatment options. Furthermore, patients have the opportunity to express their concerns and uncertainties to the physician. Patients and physicians then work together toward a course of action amenable to both parties. Informed consent thus reflects an interactive process in which information is exchanged, discussed, and interpreted.

The experiences of transsexuals and transgenderists enrolled in the Clarke GIC indicate that they cannot easily obtain information about hormones and their side effects through the GIC. Information is not readily shared between medical and psychiatric personnel and TS/TG clients. In this regard, the institutional relations of a psychiatric evaluation of transsexuals do not reflect a process wherein informed consent is truly achieved, since a developed understanding of informed consent demands a social context in which information is accessible to patients. A similar dynamic is at work in the case of SRS. Some research participants lament the lack of information regarding the biomedical procedures accompanying SRS. One post-operative MTF transsexual, for instance, was unaware of the post-operative care required immediately following her vaginoplasty. This lack of information is symptomatic of a broader institutional context, in which transsexuals are not provided with the appropriate information needed to make an informed decision about their treatment.

The failure of obtaining informed consent in the case of transsexual health care is directly related to the inadequate information provided. Debates in the field of biomedical ethics and informed consent also emphasize the *exchange* of information between patients and their care providers. The transsexuals interviewed report that they did not discuss information about their health care with service providers at the GIC for fear of losing access to hormone therapy or being denied a recommendation for SRS. In 1995, the administrative structure of transsexual health care in Ontario—in which the recommendation of the GIC was required for the public funding of SRS—created an institutional context that compromised informed consent. Since the GIC was the only body authorized to make a recommendation for SRS, transsexuals accepted an institutional context in which they were not active participants with their health care providers.

Transsexual experiences of the assessment process raise additional questions regarding informed consent. Many of the interviewees in the sample population protested the presence of interns and residents in their assessment interviews. Because the GIC is located within the Clarke Institute of Psychiatry, a teaching hospital affiliated with the University of Toronto, it is used as a practical training ground for medical and psychiatric professionals interested in issues of gender dysphoria. Interviewees felt that this emphasis on teaching other professionals redefined the health care context, so that their concerns as clients were secondary. One MTF transsexual in this study specifically objected to the presence of psychiatric/medical personnel whom she did not know:

> What really annoys me is that they have these little internees [sic] who show up to talk to you. The Gender Clinic also trains future psychiatrists in how to interview and assess transsexuals, and how to give noncommittal answers, and how to refer them to the Clarke . . .

This transsexual woman continues, recounting her own experience of assessment. She specifically objects to the presence of psychiatric/medical personnel whom she did not know:

Q: So you walk in for your assessment . . .

A: . . . and there were a few people present, two people here [gestures to the left] and three people here [gestures to the right].

Q: Had you been informed that they were going to be present?

A: I was informed, at one point, that only one other doctor would be present.

Q: And had you signed a consent form?

A: To have other people in the room?

Q: Right.

A: No. No consent form was mentioned or authorized.

Another interviewee's description of her assessment interview is even more alarming:

I wasn't told this, but I wound up being a lecture subject. He [a clinical psychiatrist] had other people in the room . . . the room was full of people. [Q: This is for your assessment?] Yeah. I wasn't told about this. This is illegal. He's supposed to tell me in advance. Nothing. I'm supposed to sign a release form. No release was signed. I tried to say that I wasn't comfortable with this. He said, "Fine. We'll reschedule. It'll take about six months to get another meeting, and then you'll get your assessment in about a year." I said, "Excuse me, this is blackmail!" And he said, "No it isn't; that's just the way things work around here." So I went through with it. I went through with it. He talked to me for a minute and a half, asked me inane questions . . . and then spends most of his time lecturing to the assembled cast, and just ignored me. I was just some, some prop for his lecture.

TS/TG people I interviewed objected strongly to the presence of unknown medical and psychiatric personnel in their assessment interviews. They noted that the presence of such individuals did not facilitate an open communicative context, since they were forced to speak about their genders, bodies, genitals, and sexualities in front of complete strangers. Moreover, interviewees maintained that the others' presence revealed a lack of sensitivity toward the feelings and experiences of transsexuals on the part of service providers at the GIC. Interviewees felt quite powerless and vulnerable during their assessment interview, because they understood that their assessment would be directly linked to the possibility of hormones and surgery. The presence of additional medical and psychiatric personnel, according to the interviewees in my sample population, increased this sense of isolation and vulnerability.

The TS/TG people I interviewed suggested that the presence of unknown medical and psychiatric personnel in their assessment interviews compromised their relations with their care providers, preventing an interactive context of health care in which they could be active participants. These transsexuals thus endorse a conception of informed consent that advocates reciprocity, exchange, and negotiation.

My interviews with psychiatric personnel reveal different understandings of informed consent. One professional presented with transsexual objections to the assessment process, notably the presence of unknown medical and psychiatric personnel, maintains that the evaluation procedure itself does not require the signature of a consent form or discussion of informed consent. This provider maintained that since the assessment process does not involve "experimental treatment," it does not raise issues of consent.

Questioned specifically on the presence of interns, the representative of the clinic explained:

Q: And how does it work in terms of consent of um, for instance, of someone's assessment?

A: Well they would understand that they're being assessed by, certainly the ones in the uh, uh generally yeah they understand that it is a student.

Q: And do they sign like a consent . . .

A: [cross-talk] It's not, it's not, no, it's not a consent, it's not a consent issue. I mean, they're getting, . . . they're not getting any kind of experimental treatment, they're getting the same interview that [Interviewer: Right.] you know, . . . that they would get from a social worker or whatever. And no one is interviewed only by a psychology student, there are always, . . . so there is no need for a signature, I don't think.[61]

This perspective limits consent to situations in which biomedical treatment is involved, excluding the social process in which information is exchanged.

The mistrust of psychiatrists among many transsexuals, which emerges from conflicting definitions of health as well as understandings of informed consent, contributes to a context filled with misinformation. Many participants, for example, told me that the GIC restricted the number of individuals in Ontario who would be recommended for surgery each year. My interviews with OHIP contradict this assumption; a representative of OHIP explained that there is no quota system in place and that the number of transsexuals recommended for surgery varies from one year to the next.[62] A second myth circulating in transsexual communities related to the services of the Gender Identity Clinic in Vancouver. Many participants claimed that the clinic in Vancouver was more community-based than the clinic in Toronto; that the Vancouver clinic, for instance, had free electrolysis and offered makeup sessions. An interview with a representative of this clinic contradicts this assumption: in 1995, the Vancouver clinic had not offered any makeup sessions and did not employ an electrologist.[63] This clinic did state their plans, however, to have a private electrologist affiliated with the clinic in the future.

These unsubstantiated rumors need to be situated in relation to a broader institutional context of health care, in which transsexuals have difficulty obtaining information from service providers, in which their comprehensive psychological and social health needs remain unaddressed, and in which psychiatrists reduce the process of informed consent to the signing of a form for experimental treatment. While the generation of myths among transsexuals with respect to gender identity clinics is lamentable, such a practice is indicative of an institutional relation in which transsexuals receive little information about their health care from the health service network established to deal with them.

## Employment and Health Care

In order to be considered as a candidate for SRS, transsexuals enrolled in the GIC must fulfill the criteria of the real-life test, criteria that demand that an individual be employed full-time or be enrolled in school. According to GIC staff, this requirement is designed to ensure that an individual is integrated in society as a member of their chosen gender.[64] One of its consequences, however, is the denial of an evaluation to unemployed transsexuals. Since access to hormones and surgery are linked to psychiatric assessment, this administrative regulation effectively creates a situation in which access to health care is secured through employment. The experiences of prostitutes illustrate this problematic. Prostitutes are refused a psychiatric evaluation from staff of the GIC, with the justification that prostitution is not considered to be a valid form of work for the purposes of the real-life test. This refusal thus forces prostitutes to seek their hormones and their SRS outside of the GIC, on the private market. Since they must pay for their SRS themselves (a vaginoplasty can cost between $8,000 and $20,000), these individuals often remain in prostitution because it is a lucrative form of work. In this manner, while a GIC excludes prostitutes from an assessment because of their work, this exclusion is ongoing. Forced outside of the institution established to serve them as transsexuals (the GIC), prostitutes remain outside of the institutional world because they are ineligible for the public funding of their sex reassignment surgeries.

An interpretation of the Standards of Care that eliminates prostitution as a valid form of work creates a social relation in which a transsexual's access to health care is secured through employment. This creates a two-tiered system of health care for transsexuals, in which employed individuals are eligible for SRS funding, while transsexuals without full-time jobs who are not in school must pay for their surgeries themselves. This structure is especially difficult for transsexual youth, who may not have a stable employment history or consolidated job skills. Indeed, the experiences of an

MTF transsexual who begins a transition at the age of forty-five and who has worked in a unionized position with the federal government for twenty years will be markedly different from those of a sixteen-year-old MTF transsexual who has been ridiculed and bullied at school, was expelled from the home of her biological family, and lacks a legal employment history. Given these diverse realities, we ought to question the implications of social policies that link employment and access to health care, particularly for poor transsexuals, transsexual youth, and transsexuals without secondary education.

That employment facilitates access to health care for transsexuals is further evidenced in my interviews with staff of gender identity clinics in Canada. One representative I questioned about the enrollment of transsexual prostitutes in that clinic remarked that these individuals were a small minority of the transsexual community. Transsexual prostitutes were contrasted with transsexuals with professional careers and high incomes. Psychiatric professionals associated with the Clarke GIC implied that prostitutes are at increased risk of contracting HIV. A representative of a different clinic was even more direct, stating that real transsexuals are not prostitutes. This institutional discrimination against prostitutes is intimately linked to the assessment process. One Québec psychiatrist, for instance, associated prostitution with transvestism (as well as the excessive use of drugs and alcohol) but not with transsexuality. In a wonderful illustration of circular logic, another clinic representative stated that real transsexuals are not prostitutes, that their clinic does not evaluate prostitutes, and that their position is evidenced by a sample population of nonprostitute transsexuals enrolled in their clinic.

The institutional relations of psychiatry link employment and access to health care for transsexuals in two ways. First, a transsexual individual must be working or studying full-time in order to be evaluated. Second, the interviews with clinic staff demonstrate an implicit valorization of transsexuality through income and professional status: an individual's transsexual identity is secured through his or her paid work. These links between employment and access to health care also demonstrate the conflict between transsexuals and the psychiatric establishment. Access to hormones and SRS, achieved through a psychiatric evaluation and diagnosis of a GIC, are contingent on a transsexual individual's employment. The evidence presented from prostitutes clearly indicates that without stable employment deemed acceptable to clinic staff, transsexuals are refused an evaluation and thus access to health care.[65]

## Transsexual Responses to Psychiatry: Privatized Health Care

Transsexuals are in conflict with their psychiatric service providers as a function of specific institutional relations: dissenting definitions of "health," divergent perspectives on the concept and practice of informed consent, and administrative policies that conjoin health care and employment. These institutional relations create a situation in which many TS/TG people choose to obtain their health care without the assistance of a gender identity clinic. They can obtain recommendations for SRS from psychiatrists unaffiliated with a gender identity clinic, but they must pay for such surgery themselves. The following comments from interviewees who decided to access hormones and surgery outside the GIC offer significant insight into some of the reasons for such decisions:

> Avoid the Clarke at all costs, and do the other route. It might be longer to do . . . but it's less heartache.

> Oh who would bother with that foolishness?

> I found that their [the GIC's] willingness to share information was really minimal, so I . . . that's why I didn't stay with them [to transition]. . . . It was more than just what the hormones were, it was the attitude, you know? [Q: What was the difference between the other doctor and the (GIC at the) Clarke?] Well for one thing, they took a really direct interest in my life, whereas the Clarke, maybe they did, but they certainly didn't show it to me. . . .

Since they are interested in addressing their comprehensive biomedical, psychological, and social needs, these transsexuals have chosen not to locate themselves within an institutional context that is only set up to provide a psychiatric evaluation of their gender identity.

These perceptions of transsexuals are in stark contrast to how service providers of the GIC understand their administration of health care for TS/TG people. In my interviews with service providers, psychiatrists and professionals acknowledge that many TS/TG individuals choose not to follow the program of the GIC. They describe this situation as one wherein transsexual or transgendered people choose to "select themselves out." [66] One service provider claimed that the GIC will provide an assessment to anyone: "There's no such thing as not having access. We will assess anyone." [67] This citation illustrates that GIC staff understand their role as one of assessment and diagnosis. A different representative of the GIC also raised the question of clients who "select themselves out" of the program:

I don't think what we asked for was unreasonable, but it set definite standards by which most people selected themselves out. Our clinic never said to anybody, well not in the past ten or fifteen years, "you're not suitable for surgery." What it always said was, "If you want to pursue surgery, this is what you have to do." And basically patients then selected for or against surgery by choosing or not choosing to meet the criteria.[68]

My research indicates that many TS/TG people do not enroll or continue in the GIC program precisely due to this exclusive focus on psychiatric evaluation and assessment. While clinic staff contend that transsexuals "select themselves out" because they are not interested in fulfilling specific administrative criteria, my research illustrates that transsexual prostitutes object to the discriminatory aspects of these criteria, which do not respect their work. Moreover, transsexuals I interviewed sought health care services that encompassed much more than a psychiatric evaluation. In this manner, many transsexuals in Canada are located—and locate themselves—as consumers of privatized medical care. Their actions need to be interpreted with regard to the specific psychiatric institutional practices. The ideas of defining health, informed consent, and an implicit link between employment and access to health care offer insight into this conflict between transsexuals and psychiatrists.

The institutional relations of psychiatric health care for transsexuals reiterate and consolidate some of the most significant problems transsexuals experience in accessing health care. In chapter 7, I examined how the practices of health care and social services exclude the most marginal of transsexuals through inappropriate social policies (or the lack of social policy). A similar dynamic is at work in the case of gender identity clinics, since the interpretation of the Standards of Care offered by psychiatrists associated with a GIC eliminate prostitutes and unemployed transsexuals from the assessment process. In the case of social services as well as a gender identity clinic, transsexuals choose to address their health care needs outside of an established organizational context. The marginalization of transsexuals from both health care institutions and gender identity clinics support and reinforce each other, creating a global situation in which transsexuals are deeply mistrustful of professional health care and psychiatric services.

## IMPLICATIONS AND APPLICATIONS OF THIS RESEARCH

The results of this research provide insight into contemporary debates on health care and psychiatry for transsexuals. Given the contested nature of these debates, as well as a dearth of studies on how transsexuals and transgendered people perceive psychiatric services, it is useful to consider how these results can be used in the development and delivery of health care services to transsexuals.

The information presented in this chapter differs significantly from many English-language writings on the relations between transsexuals and the psychiatric establishment. Some sociologists and feminists, for instance, examine how transsexuals are created by medicine and psychiatry and argue that transsexuals can only exist in and through the relations of psychiatry and medicine.[69] The practices of medicine and psychiatry with regard to transsexuals are thus interpreted to be regressively normative, aligning the biological sexes of individuals who live outside prescribed sex/gender norms. In this manner, sociologists and feminists examine the institutional production of transsexuals in order to expose the sexist underpinnings of medical and psychiatric practices.

English-language transsexuals have examined the relations between transsexuals and psychiatrists to advance a different agenda. While some sociologists and feminists would advocate the virtual elimination of transsexuals (since transsexuals are figured to be the dupes of gender[70]), many U.S. transsexual activists argue that transsexuals are not well treated by psychiatrists and deliberately misrepresent themselves in the clinical context.[71] Some U.S. transsexuals extend this line of thought in an attempt to liberate transsexuals from a psychiatric evaluation or diagnosis.[72]

The information presented throughout this chapter could be deployed to support either of these arguments. Sociologists and feminists could cite the TS/TG people in this chapter to claim that medicine and psychiatry produce transsexuals (see chapter 2). And the experiences of the individuals I interviewed can support the claim of U.S. transsexual activists that the evaluation and diagnosis of transsexualism is detrimental to transsexual people. In both instances, critics make sense of the organization of health care and psychiatry in order to advance a particular argument about transsexuals: that transsexuals should not exist, or that we should be able to determine our own destiny without the authorization of psychiatric personnel.

The research presented in this chapter offers a different understanding of these issues. One of the important claims of this chapter is that an evaluative model orders the experience of transsexuals within gender identity clinics. According to interviews I conducted, psychiatrists see their role as one of assessment and evaluation. TS/TG people, however, envision a

much more comprehensive role: the provision of information and resources, as well as psychological and social support.

A focus on the health care needs identified by transsexuals and transgendered people enrolled in gender identity clinics is a notable absence in
the literature on this issue. As discussed earlier, some sociologists and feminists examine the psychiatric production of transsexuals to make the political argument that transsexuals should not exist. Yet a critical investigation
of how psychiatry produces transsexuals does not need to subsequently
claim that transsexuals have no right to be in the world. Comparatively, one
could analyze how the administrative practices of social work produce individuals as poor: how the evaluative process functions to name some individuals as poor while excluding others.[73] This inquiry is useful because it
explores how experience is ordered through administration. But it requires
a huge leap in logic to claim that these individuals are not really "poor"
because poverty is *only* enacted through the operations of social work practices. Nor should one claim that the individuals who are not deemed to be
poor by an administrative apparatus are financially secure, well-off,
wealthy, or anything other than poor. In other words, such a study does
not need to invalidate the experiences and existence of individuals without
money, capital, or financial resources. A similar problematic is at work in
the case of transsexuals: we can understand how a psychiatric relation of
evaluation determines the experience of TS/TG people with gender identity
clinics without arguing that transsexuals ought not to exist, or that transsexuals can *only* exist through psychiatry.[74] While some sociologists and
feminists examine the practices of medicine and psychiatry in order to advance a political argument about the very existence of transsexuals, my research studies the workings of psychiatry as a means for TS/TG people to
identify the gaps in the existing services: to articulate their own health
care needs. Unlike objectivist sociology, this research program takes it for
granted that TS/TG people live in the world and asks these individuals
what kinds of services and programs they desire.

The results of this chapter also challenge U.S. transsexual activism,
which seeks to eliminate "gender identity disorder" from the psychiatric
establishment. In Ontario in 1995, SRS was funded by provincial health
insurance upon the recommendation of the GIC at the Clarke Institute of
Psychiatry. These transsexuals and transgendered people thus needed a diagnosis from the GIC.[75] This institutional structure of health care, which
linked the GIC and provincial health insurance, reveals the limitations of
activism (especially activism that misnames itself as international) designed

to remove transsexualism and gender identity disorder from psychiatric classification. The TS/TG people cited throughout this chapter were not interested in challenging the fact that their surgeries could be reimbursed through provincial health insurance—quite the contrary. Their objections to the gender identity clinics emerge not from the status of expert conferred to them, nor to the diagnostic process per se. *Transsexuals and transgendered people I interviewed object to the practices of gender identity clinics to the extent that they do not fulfill their comprehensive biomedical, psychological, and social needs.*

Finally, my empirical research illustrates how TS/TG people situate themselves outside of institutions like the GIC. In some instances, this location is a result of overt discrimination—the gender identity clinics in Québec that refuse to evaluate prostitutes, for example. In other instances, a refusal to negotiate these institutions is explained through discrimination of a more subtle nature: the negative attitudes of service providers at the GIC with regard to prostitutes, attitudes that undermine the confidence of prostitutes in the health care and social service network. In still other cases, transsexuals and transgendered people establish themselves outside of gender identity clinics because they object to an exclusive focus on psychiatric assessment and evaluation. This information expands on that presented in chapter 7, which shows how and why transsexual prostitutes do not make use of shelters and social services. The erasure of TS/TG people occurs in the daily work of institutions such as *gender identity clinics.*

English-language scholarship on transsexuals and psychiatry is fundamentally concerned with articulating a political argument about transsexuals: that we are ideological dupes, or that we should have the right to change our bodies without the authorization of psychiatrists. Within this framework, the experiences of transsexuals are only cited to the extent that they confirm the particular argument proposed. The research presented in this chapter offers a markedly different approach. A focus on a psychiatric context of evaluation allows us to understand the unmet health care needs of TS/TG people, as identified by them. This information provides a fresh approach to the relations among transsexuals and the psychiatric establishment. Indeed, by maintaining a focus on these institutional relations, the weaknesses of both academic and activist positions on this debate are exposed.

Objectivist sociological studies on transsexuals and psychiatry, exemplified in the work of Raymond, and Billings and Urban, offer a comment on transsexuality as a moral issue. The particular health care needs of transsexuals, however, remain outside this scope of inquiry, since it begins from the position, a priori, that transsexuals do not and should not exist. This literature is centrally concerned with transsexuality as a moral issue, not as a question of health.

American transsexual activism, in contrast, works for the depsychiatrization of transsexualism, the move to a consumer model of health care. Like the objectivist social studies, this position does not concentrate on issues of health care. Classifying SRS as a cosmetic procedure would not challenge the institutional relations that determine how transsexuals experience health care. Debates over breast implants for both nontranssexual and transsexual women, for instance, raise important questions about the provision of information to health care consumers, as well as the practice of informed consent. Within this controversy, many women object that they had not been informed of all of the potential risks associated with this procedure, which clearly indicates that medical practices reflect narrow definitions of health and informed consent.[76] Since breast augmentation is classified as a cosmetic procedure, it is useful as a comparative example for the discussion at hand. While a consumerist health model for SRS could lessen the social stigma associated with this procedure, it does not transform the institutional relations of health care with respect to defining health and informed consent. Moreover, a politico-economic classification of SRS as cosmetic surgery reinforces a connection between employment and health, since only transsexuals with financial resources could afford genital surgery. Furthermore, my research demonstrates that some transsexuals in Canada are situated as consumers of health services as a function of the current administration of gender identity clinics; this is especially the case for prostitutes, who are refused a psychiatric evaluation and thus access to hormones and SRS.[77] An activist position that argues for the classification of SRS as a cosmetic procedure does not understand or reflect on the institutional exclusion of transsexual prostitutes. A consumer model of health care for transsexuals refuses to challenge a psychiatric institutional relation in which access to health care is facilitated through employment, preferably professional employment. In summary, an American transsexual activist discourse that advocates a consumerist paradigm neglects the unique institutional relations of psychiatry and health care for transsexuals. Like objectivist sociology, U.S. transsexual activists frame transsexuality as a moral question and not as a matter of health care.

Given the political problems evidenced in the existing scholarship and activism on transsexualism and psychiatry, what is the appropriate course of action? How can this research inform the development of programs and the delivery of services for transsexuals? In answering these questions, it is crucial that we maintain a focus on the institutional relations of health care and psychiatry for transsexuals. The integration of transsexuals into the institutional world demands services that respond to the concerns outlined by research participants. What is required, in other words, are programs that function with a comprehensive definition of "health," encompassing its biomedical, psychological, and social components. Social services that offer information to TS/TG people, and that encourage them to use this information in their decisions about their health care and body changes, are equally important. Finally, programs for TS/TG people need to place a political priority on issues of poverty, understanding how transsexual prostitutes, unemployed transsexuals, and poor transsexuals are marginalized in the existing network.

Examples of this approach can be found within community-based organizations that work with a TS/TG population. The Meal-Trans program in Toronto, for instance, offers nutritious meals once a week to primarily low-income TS/TG people.[78] Program activities also include information sessions on topics as diverse as makeup for MTFs, passing tips for both FTMs and MTFs, safety and legal issues for MTF prostitutes, and genital reassignment surgery. By providing people with information, welcoming the participation of prostitutes and addressing their particular needs, offering a healthy meal for poor transsexuals who may not have eaten well in the past week, and creating a social space for TS/TG people to exchange ideas, experiences, and information, Meal-Trans challenges a narrow definition of "health," helps to create a truly reciprocal process of informed consent, and intervenes in a fusion of employment and access to health care for transsexuals. In this way, the activities of Meal-Trans transform transsexuals' relations to the institutional world.

The work of PASTT, a community-based health care project for transsexuals and transvestites in Paris, is another program that transforms the institutional relations of health care and psychiatry specific to transsexuals and transvestites.[79] PASTT provides services and resources to transsexual prostitutes working in the Bois de Boulogne: condoms, clean needles, information. The project also offers legal advice, accompaniment in the health care and social service network, assistance in changing identity papers, support for transsexuals in conflict with immigration, and orientation with respect to hormone therapy and SRS. By offering information on the complex elements of the lives of transsexuals, PASTT advocates a broad definition of "health" and fosters a social context in which transsexuals work with service providers to make informed decisions about their health care. Importantly, PASTT begins its work by acknowledging the validity of prostitution as a form of work for transsexuals. Through the presence of a minibus in the Bois de Boulogne, as well as information nights held in bars and restaurants frequented by transsexuals and transvestites, PASTT respects the work of transsexual prostitutes. In this way, the project does not require that a transsexual work outside the field of prostitution in order to obtain access to health care and social services.

To date, debates about transsexuality and psychiatry frame the issue in terms of morality. The results of my research suggest that this debate does not actually address the situation of transsexuals in terms of health care. Through interviews with TS/TG people enrolled in some Canadian gender identity clinics, this chapter offers an important first step in understanding the tension between transsexuals and psychiatrists, and explains why many transsexuals do not make use of the GIC services. The conflict between transsexuals and psychiatric service providers emerges from particular institutional relations of defining health, informed consent, and a link between employment and access to health services. A political program that seriously considers the health care needs of transsexuals must address these institutional relations.

Innovative interventions in the domain of transsexual health care, however, are not evidenced or explained by either objectivist social science or prominent American transsexual activism. Rather, it is in examining the unremarkable labor of community-based programs for TS/TG people that we can reflect on the kinds of services and activities that integrate transsexuals into the health care network. This work is actually far removed from debates on transsexuality and psychiatry, since it frames the question at hand in terms of health services and not as a moral concern. Interviews with transsexuals enrolled in Canadian gender identity clinics elucidate the absences and limitations of their health care, broadly defined. The challenge now is to organize to fulfill these needs.

Beginning with a documentation of the problems with gender identity clinics as identified by Canadian transsexuals, this chapter has sought to understand some of the relations that explain a conflict between transsexuals and psychiatrists. My research shows that TS/TG people are excluded from the institutional world as a function of conflicting definitions of health, the social process through which consent is obtained, and an implicit link between employment and health care. Continuing this focus on the administrative erasure of TS/TG people, the following chapter presents a case study of how institutions in Québec manage—or neglect—transsexual legal identity, civil status, and health care.

# ❈ 9 ❧

# THE ADMINISTRATION OF ERASURE

## The Bureaucracy of Legal Sex, a Vicious Circle
## of Administration, and HIV/AIDS in Québec

*Why is it that nobody thought to do a study of transsexuals and AIDS? Nobody could care less, nobody knows about it. It is easy to ignore a community that you don't know.*—Diane Gobeil

Chapters 7 and 8 outlined how transsexuals are excluded from the institutional world, relying on data collected from interviews with transsexuals and transgendered people. Taking seriously a poststructuralist commitment to investigating the textual organization of social life, a pre liminary documentation of how TS/TG individuals experience the institutional world enables a critical appreciation of the social policies (or lack of policies) that order this experience.

This chapter extends this line of inquiry, examining another aspect of the administration of transsexual health care in Québec. The research emerges out of a community-based needle exchange program in Montréal of the agency CACTUS (le Centre communautaire auprès des toxicomanes utilisateurs de seringues). Diane Gobeil, an outreach worker of CACTUS, identified the need for both research and community programs specifically geared to a TS/TG population. In the fall of 1996, she organized a meeting among TS/TG people with officials from regional, provincial, and national health programs. Out of that meeting emerged a CACTUS project specifically focused on the health care needs of transsexuals and transvestites: ASTT(e)Q (Action Santé: Travesti(e)s et Transsexuel(le)s du Québec). In 1997, ASTT(e)Q received funds from Health Canada to produce a resource directory of services available to TS/TG people in Montréal. The Centre Québecois de Coordination sur le SIDA, a provincial HIV/AIDS coordinating body associated with the Ministry of Health and Social Services, provided funding for a provincial needs assessment of TS/TG people in Québebec with respect to HIV/AIDS.[1]

This chapter presents a modified version of the final report of that needs assessment. As such, it is a revised version of an applied sociology research project focused on HIV/AIDS. Empirically, it illustrates how the institutional and administrative apparatus of transsexual lives and health care results in the social marginalization of these people, a marginalization that creates conditions of vulnerability to HIV/AIDS. Theoretically, the chapter offers an excellent case study of how transsexual people disappear from view; indeed, of how TS/TG people are produced through erasure. The chapter also illustrates just how complicated the everyday world is for TS/TG individuals: complications that preempt any kind of neat theoretical overview of transsexual lives as offered by critics in queer theory or objectivist sociology. An applied sociological research program exemplifies the messy nature of reflexive research and theory, because they emerge from a social world that is chaotic, disorderly, and inconsistent. Such an intellectual practice also demonstrates the necessity of institutional collaboration. This focus on HIV/AIDS is, in part, a function of how the research was funded. A researcher who wishes to be situated in the everyday world must take this risk of institutional complicity, because the alternative can only offer a theory that may interest or dazzle academics but that remains irrelevant and/or destructive to the people designated to be objects of inquiry (and that assumes the university is not an institution). The political and methodological challenge for an applied sociologist is to acknowledge such institutional complicity and to use it in the interests of the research subjects. In doing this research, and in writing this chapter, I am not interested in the articulation of a theoretical program that is pure. I accept the parameters of HIV/AIDS funding as one strategy to make policy interventions in Québec society for transsexuals and transvestites.

Like the previous chapters, I use the term "erasure" to indicate the exclusion of transsexuals from the institutional world: how agencies deny services to these people, as well as why transsexuals decide not to make use of such organizations. Furthermore, this chapter illustrates how this erasure is organized at a micrological level, through the use of specific documents of juridical identity and civil status. Beginning from a poststructuralist understanding of the textual organization of social life, I explore the use and function of documents as central to the realization of sex/gender relations in the institutional world. My analysis concerns itself both with the administrative procedures through which documents of sexed identity are produced, as well as the social and economic consequences of living without such papers. The vulnerability of TS/TG people with regard to HIV/AIDS in Québec must be understood in relation to conferral of sexed civil status.

## LITERATURE REVIEW: HIV/AIDS AND TS/TG PEOPLE

Existing studies on HIV/AIDS indicate that TS/TG people are quite vulnerable to HIV/AIDS. Research on MTF transsexuals and transvestites who are prostitutes reveals an HIV seroprevalence rate that is, without exaggeration, astronomical. A study in Atlanta, for instance, found a seropositive rate of 68 percent, while researchers in Rio de Janeiro present a rate of 63 percent, and a project in Rome revealed a rate of 74 percent among MTF transgendered prostitutes who were intravenous drug users. Comparative studies claim that transgendered prostitutes have a higher seroprevalence rate than prostitutes who are not transgendered. Demographically speaking, the high percentage of people of color and members of ethnocultural communities ought to be noted. Furthermore, the literature correlates seropositive status with frequenting a transgendered milieu, as well as the reclamation of a transvestite or transsexual identity.[2]

A variety of factors explain a raised seroprevalence rate among MTF transgendered people. In developing countries, a lack of knowledge about HIV/AIDS as well as an association of HIV/AIDS with foreigners contribute to the adoption of unsafe behaviors with respect to HIV transmission.[3] In industrialized countries, unsafe behaviors with respect to HIV transmission for MTF transgendered people are related to four factors: (1) self-esteem and a stigma of AIDS;[4] (2) unsafe sexual relations with clients or lovers;[5] (3) alcohol and drug use, which can prevent the adoption of safe sexual practices;[6] and (4) the injection of intravenous drugs with a shared needle or syringe.[7] Two other factors are specific to transgendered people with regard to HIV transmission. First, transgendered people may inject their hormones in a muscle: if sterile needles are not available, there is an increased likelihood of HIV transmission if these people share their needles.[8] Moreover, these syringes are intramuscular and are often unavailable within needle exchange programs for intravenous drug users, thus marginalizing transgendered people from the existing health care and social service network.[9] Second, the injection of silicone to give a more feminine image to MTF transgendered people can also increase the risk of HIV transmission and other health problems such as hepatitis, an abscess, or bodily inflammations.[10]

To date, most studies on transgendered people have focused on MTF individuals. An innovative program at the Boston Department of Public Health, however, has addressed the specific needs of FTM transgendered people with respect to HIV.[11] Participants identified several factors that put them at risk for HIV transmission, notably self-esteem and a fear of rejection related to one's TS/TG body.

Previous chapters have demonstrated the distrust among TS/TG people of health care and social service institutions. This marginalization of transsexuals from the health care network prevents the dissemination of information on HIV/AIDS and safe behaviors and forces transsexuals to rely on an informal network to fulfill their unique medical, psychological, and social needs.[12]

Studies concerning the impact of HIV/AIDS upon TS/TG people are essential in order to develop appropriate programs and services for this population. Nevertheless, there are significant absences within the literature, notably a lack of data on the experiences of FTM transgendered people, as well as a lack of attention to transgendered people who are not prostitutes.[13]

Most of the existing studies on transgendered people and HIV focus on the behaviors of members within this population: particular behaviors (unsafe sex, sharing needles) are explained through the notion of risk factors. Within this framework, the concept of "risk" is individualized—risk concerns what individuals do with their bodies in their sexual relations or use of drugs. Rather than focusing on individual risk behaviors, this chapter adopts a sociological orientation concerned with the political, economic, juridical, and administrative factors that create conditions of vulnerability to HIV transmission in Québec. A summary of the 1996 International Conference on AIDS in Vancouver explicates such an orientation:

> Although some efforts beyond the provision of information and the targeting of individual decision-making were described, there continues to be a great deal of interest, particularly shown in media attention during the conference, on the psychological and individual factors determining "risk," rather than social and economic factors that create conditions for vulnerability.[14]

A focus on the social factors that create conditions of vulnerability to HIV, moreover, is in keeping with the orientations of Québec's HIV/AIDS strategy, which recognizes the importance of qualitative social science research methods in the collection of data on marginalized populations in Québec.[15]

The data was gathered through interviews with twenty-seven MTF and FTM transsexuals and transvestites from the cities of Montréal, Québec, and Hull.[16] Health care and social professionals were also interviewed to supplement an understanding of the administration of transgendered health care in Québec. In particular, this study examines how the marginalization of transsexuals in Québec is a function of access to health care and civil status administration. The interviews covered a variety of topics with participants: hormone therapy, addictions, identity papers, ethnocultural minorities, attitudes with respect to HIV/AIDS, the specific needs of FTM transgendered people, gender identity clinics, the situation outside of Montréal and in the regions of Québec, and prisons. A variety of conceptual categories emerged from the resulting data that explain how transgendered people are marginalized from the health care network, thus increasing their vulnerability to the transmission of HIV. Many of the participants in the study attended three sessions held in Montréal, Hull, and Québec City to present the preliminary results of this data; they expressed confidence that the research and the conceptual categories presented summarized their experience in accessing health care and social services. In this way, interviewees were involved not only in recounting their experiences to a researcher, but were also active in validating how that research was interpreted. A methodological strategy that consults transsexuals and allows them to validate (or modify) the research findings is particularly significant given that transgendered people are seldom consulted in the studies, articles, monographs, and books written about them. It is extremely rare that they are given the opportunity to approve how the data of their lives is interpreted.[17] Although the data yielded a rich framework and a variety of conceptual categories, this chapter will limit itself to two issues: the administration of identity papers for TS/TG people in Québec, and the administrative practices of different Québec institutions (with regard to TS/TG health care) that contradict one another, effectively denying access to health care for many—if not most—transsexuals.

In chapter 3, Diane Gobeil and Mirha-Soleil Ross illustrated that transsexuals are ignored within many AIDS service organizations because of the legal classification of the sex of transsexual individuals. This chapter looks more closely at how that classification works in the Québécois legal and administrative context, as well as how the institutional operations of name and sex change affect transsexuals' experiences with other institutions, such as health care. Once an examination of such administrative practices is completed, I return to the question of an erasure of TS/TG people from the social text. By way of example, this chapter argues that a poststructuralist sociology that seeks to offer a grounded, reflexive inquiry must begin its analysis with a detailed exposition of how this erasure functions, as well as the social, political, juridical, and economic consequences of this obliteration for TS/TG people.

## IDENTITY PAPERS: THE ADMINISTRATIVE
## PRACTICES OF LEGAL SEX

*Certaines administrations de la fonction publique refusent d'identifier certains de leurs citoyens."*—"Jackie"

*Ne me demandez pas qui je suis et ne me dites pas de rester le même: c'est une morale d'état civil; elle régit nos papiers.*—Michel Foucault

Transsexuals and transgendered people who live in a sex other than the one assigned to them at birth have to confront the question of their legal identity papers. Documents such as health care cards, drivers' licenses, birth certificates, banking cards, immigration certificates, and passports constitute an integral part of everyday life: they prove one's membership in a given society, demonstrating legal citizenship and civil status. These documents are required to negotiate a variety of different institutions: health care, the courts, banks, and customs and immigration. To say that people require documents that attest to their membership in a given society is to state the obvious. But what happens when individuals cannot or do not produce these documents? Or, to frame this question within a specifically transsexual context, what happens when the name and/or the sex inscribed on a given document do not correspond to the physical appearance of the person to whom the document was issued? How does an FTM transsexual who lives, identifies, and appears as a man present himself to an institution with identity papers that claim his name is (for instance), Marie-Pierre Tremblay? And what administrative procedures are required to change the name and sex of transgendered people?

According to TS/TG people in Québec, the administrative procedures of Québec's institutions with respect to name and sex changes prevent their social integration to the extent that there is a gap between their legal sex and their social gender. This gap creates problems for TS/TG people on a variety of levels: education, employment, and health care. In order to understand better this process of marginalization, as well as its relation to HIV/AIDS, it is necessary to provide an overview of this situation.

### Rules, Regulations, and Protocols

The administrative processes required for name and sex changes vary according to the institution in question. In general, for transgendered people in Québec, a name change can be accomplished relatively easily within federal institutions. For example, passports and social insurance numbers are assigned by federal jurisdictions governing citizenship and employment. Once these documents have been changed, individuals can modify the name that appears on their credit cards, their bank accounts, and other personal papers. These modifications, however, do not affect the sex designation on these documents. In order to change the sex, a person has to provide a change of sex certificate from the *Direction de l'état civil* (Office of Civil Status) or the Vital Statistics Office of her or his province. These institutions require medical certificates that attest to the success of the surgical interventions with regard to the change of sex.

The administrative procedures are different in the Québécois legal context, where the change of name and the change of sex occur at the same time, from those of English Canada, where a change of name can happen at the request of an individual. Québec's law concerning the change of name and the change of sex stipulates that individuals who have undergone medical treatment and surgical intervention to structurally change their genital organs (*organes sexuels*), in which these modifications are intended to change their visible sexual character, can modify their sex designation and/or their forename on their birth certificate.[18]

Moreover, the law requires that a person be single, have resided within Québec for at least one year, have Canadian citizenship, and be eighteen years old to be eligible for a sex-designation change. Québec's *Code civil* does not specify the surgeries that attest to "une modification structurale des organes sexuels." According to the Direction de l'état civil, in the case of MTF transsexuals, a vaginoplasty is required.[19] The situation of FTM transsexuals, in contrast, requires the reconstruction of male genital organs ("reconstruction des organes sexuels mâles").[20]

In Québec, the change of name can occur in the event that an individual demonstrates a "serious motive" in this regard.[21] A name that has negative or inappropriate connotations, is too difficult to pronounce or write in its original form, or does not correspond to the name inscribed on the birth certificate of the individual constitute serious motives. The *Direction de l'état civil* does not consider transsexualism to be a serious motive for the change of name.[22]

The administrative procedures in English Canada and Québec reflect two different legal contexts: English Canada adopts a common law approach wherein the name of a person can be changed at will, while Québec makes recourse to a civil code. Other jurisdictions that rely on a civil code— France, Belgium, Luxembourg, and Portugal—follow a similar logic. The change of name does not occur as easily within civil code jurisdictions as within common law countries, because civil status in inscribed as inalienable.[23]

The experiences of research participants offer important information not only with respect to the legal or administrative justifications of these policies, but also their social consequences for transsexuals. In the first instance, interviewees did not make a distinction between documents associated with the federal government and those related to the province of Québec. Several individuals did not try to change their names on their social insurance number cards, because they had failed to change their names on their baptismal certificates in Québec. In general, participants were not well-informed about the procedures or costs involved in the change of name and the change of sex on their personal documents.

## Problems of Social Integration Related to Identity Papers

Transsexuals interviewed claimed that the current situation creates many problems for them in the everyday world, since there is a disjuncture between their visual image and the legal documents. At the bank and the post office, for instance, transsexuals are suspected of fraud:

> Les banquiers croient qu'il s'agit d'un cas de fraude, quand ils voient un nom qui n'est pas identique avec un visage. [Bankers think it's a case of fraud when they see a name that doesn't correspond to a face.][24]

Legal documents also impede a job search if the name of the individual has not been changed. One participant summarized the unspoken discrimination to which transsexuals are subjected in the job search process:

> J'veux dire on m'fait chier, j'veux dire J'peux pas faire autrement, je vis en femme, tsé au moment donné, j'veux dire va voir madame X là, j'veux dire dans tel ministère, pis tout ça, c'est "sortez moi donc votre pièce d'identité" ou encore tu viens pour chercher un emploi, "t'es t'un gars," les employeurs de nos jours là, y'ont le choix tu penses-tu toué, quecqu'part j'veux qu'au moment donné y vont m'prendre moué? Y'ont pas droit à la discrimination mais entre trois p'tits points en? Tsé veux dire. Ha, la feuille à s'égare subitment dans filière 13 pis, "ha ben excusez-nous madame, on a trouvé quelqu'un d'autre." Ni vu, ni connu. [I mean, they drive me nuts, I can't do otherwise. I live as a woman, you know? So it's like, go see Ms. X in such and such a Ministry, and all that, it's like, "Show me your ID" or else you go to look for a job, "You're a man!" Employers these days, they have the

choice, you know? Do you think that they're going to take me? They can't discriminate, but dot dot dot. You know the deal. The form disappears quickly in file number 13 and it's like, "Oh, excuse us, miss, we found somebody else." Neither seen nor heard.] [25]

If it is true that transgendered people in Québec can change their names on their social insurance numbers, which allows them access to employment in their chosen gender, significant barriers remain for transgendered people looking for work in Québec. In the event that an employer requires a medical exam, for instance, or a school transcript, the individual's transgendered status will be revealed through the names inscribed on these documents. Furthermore, a change of name on these documents requires a certificate from the Direction de l'état civil. Even if transgendered people can change their names on their social insurance numbers, they risk being labeled as transsexuals if the recruitment process of the employer requires documents issued by provincial institutions.

A similar situation exists with respect to loans and bursaries for transgendered people in Québec. Consider, for example, an MTF transgendered person who applies for a loan to attend college. The Ministry of Education, a provincial institution, appeals to the Direction de l'état civil for a change of name certificate. Without such a certificate, the ministry will issue the loan and/or bursary in her legal name. The check will be issued in her old name and sent directly to her educational institution. Obviously this presents a problem if she is registered in her new name, perhaps with the assistance of her social insurance card, and has changed the name on her bank account. In other words, individuals who have not undergone the surgeries stipulated by the Direction de l'état civil as required for a change of name and who enroll in an educational institution do not have the right to keep their transgendered status private if they wish to receive loans and bursaries from the Ministry of Education.

Without considering the question of loans and bursaries, registration in an educational institution itself poses difficulties for transgendered people in Québec, since it demands the provision of previous school records and transcripts, documents that can only be modified with a change of name certificate from the Direction de l'état civil. As in the case of loans and bursaries, the TS/TG status of the individual is eventually revealed. Since transgendered people do not have the right to privacy within educational institutions in Québec, many decide to abandon their studies rather than be known as transgendered. As one participant declares, this situation is incredibly stressful for transsexuals:

pis si on serait, si si tout ça tout ce que tu fais pis tout ce qu'on serait capable de faire peut changer ça pour les prochains, ben tant mieux. Tant mieux. Parce que qui faut que ça change. Ça pas de bon sens. J'viens d'avoir un flash de tout ce que je viens de subir ces derniers mois pis j'te le dis que ça pas de bon sens. Cette partie-là a été la pire de ma transition. D'être obligé d'abandonner l'école pis tu vois c'est, c'est c'est incroyable. [And if we could, if what you're doing and everything that we can do could change that for the next ones, well all the better. All the better. Because it has to change. It makes no sense. I just had a flash of what I've gone through these last few months and I'm telling you, it makes no sense. This part was the worst part of my transition. To be forced to drop out of school, you know, it's, it's, . . . it's incredible.] [26]

The administrative difficulties faced by transgendered people in educational institutions are mirrored in the health care network. Like other provincial jurisdictions, the provincial health insurance agency, RAMQ (le Régime d'assurances maladie du Québec) will not issue a new health care card (change of name and/or sex) for a transgendered person without the authorization of the Direction de l'état civil. [27] Thus the birth name and sex stated on their health care documents do not correspond to their physical appearance. Participants declared, for the most part, that this situation forces them to live in a state of stress and anxiety each time they have to access any kind of health care. Each time a transgendered person consults medical, pharmaceutical, or hospital personnel, he or she will be confronted by a lack of understanding or an overt contempt of their transgendered body and identity. One transsexual recounts her experience in a waiting room:

et pis je demandais à l'infirmière, "Madame, s.v.p., moi je suis transsexuelle. S.v.p. ne m'appelle pas sur ce nom là, moi je suis transsexuelle," j'ai montré tous les papiers, je lui ai dit, "Appelle-moi sous ce nom là, c'est le nom que j'utilise couramment. Moi j'utilise pas du tout ce nom là, il, il est dans ma carte d'assurance soleil parce qu'ils veulent pas le changer. Moi j'ai fait tous les démarches, mais ils veulent pas. Alors, s.v.p. appelle-moi sous ce nom là." Il y avait des infirmières qui étaient très ouvertes, qui étaient très gentilles et pis qui m'appelaient madame, mais il y avait les autres qui étaient vraiment, alors c'est vraiment des connards, qui t'appellent, qui faisaient pas attention, ils le faisaient exprès. "Monsieur," en hommes, tsé. Moi je me levais pas, même pas du tout, je restais assise et pis je passais le tour, je laissais passer les autres patients avant moi, et après je me levais et je disais, "Moi, ce nom là, je t'avais dit de ne pas dire ça." Et puis des fois je m'en allais, je suis tellement fâchée, je vais dans les, la consultation, sans même pas passer. [And so I asked the nurse, "Miss, please, I'm transsexual. Please call me by this name here, I'm a transsexual," I showed all my papers, I told her, "Call me by this name, it's the name I use all the time. The other name I don't use, it's on my health care card because they don't want to change it. I've tried everything, but they don't want to. So, please, call me by this name." There have been some nurses who were really open, who were really nice and who called me Miss, but others were total bitches, who called you, who didn't pay attention, or who did it on purpose. "Mister," as a man, you know. Me, I didn't get up, not one little bit, I let the other patients go before me, and then after I got up and I said, "I told you, don't use that name there." And sometimes I just take off, I'm so pissed off, I just leave without seeing anybody.] [28]

This anecdote raises a variety of issues: the educative role played by transsexuals within the health care network, the stress involved for the transgendered person, and the ultimate result, a nondelivery of health care service to a TS/TG clientele. Another interviewee describes how health care documentation can play a detrimental role in TS/TG individuals' perceptions of their own identity:

Alors, pour prendre des hormones aussi, à la pharmacie, si tu paies, ça prend ton nom de femme, mais si c'est la carte d'assurance maladie qui paie, c'est ton nom de garçon. Alors, dans ton . . . le petit pot, c'est ton nom, en gros comme ça. Alors tsé, ça choque beaucoup. Parce que tu peux pas l'utiliser, c'est ton identité qui est en jeu, tu sais, toi tu veux rien savoir de ton nom de garçon, tu te sens femme, tu veux un nom de femme, tu sais. [So to get your hormones, too, at the pharmacy, if you pay, it's your female name, but if your health care card pays, it's your male name. So on your . . . little bottle, it's your name like that. So it freaks you out, you know? Because you can't use it, it's your identity in question, you know, you don't want anything to do with your male name, you feel like a woman, you want a female name, you know.] [29]

The respect of a transgendered person's gender identity is especially important in a hospital context. One MTF transsexual recounted her experience in a hospital:

le fait que plusieurs employés m'appelaient au masculin. J'ai fait des plaintes. Et puis j'ai dit de, de me respecter dans, dans mon état. Et par la suite, en ayant fait des plaintes j'ai mentionné mon prénom féminin pis qu'j'aimerais qu'on m'appelle par ce nom . . . mais plus on dirait pas

l'choix, j'crois qu'ils auraient mieux aimé m'appeler par mon prénom masculin juste pour peut-être, je l'sais pas, m'embêter. J'peux pas comprendre,
quand tu vois une personne malade, tu veux juste seulement que, qu'elle
soit bien, tsé. [The fact that several employees referred to me by my male
name. I made complaints and I said to respect me as I was. And then,
having made complaints I mentioned my female name and that I would
like to be called by this name . . . and they didn't have any choice, but I
think some of them would have preferred to call me by my male name just
to maybe, I don't know, bother me. I can't understand it, when you see
someone who is ill, you just want the person to feel good, you know.] [30]

Because of such negative experiences, several transgendered people interviewed—male-to-female and female-to-male—refuse to present their
health care cards. They prefer to pay cash for the services they need, so long
as their gender identity will be respected:

Je me suis dit, moi je ne veux pas m'en servir de la carte, je vais payer avec
mon argent. [I said to myself, I'm not going to use my card, I'm going to
pay cash.]

Moi je dis que j'en ai pas de carte soleil, que j'en veux pas, que de toute
façon je m'ai toujours privé, ça me dérange pas. [Q: Faques tu paies argent
comptant?] Oui. [Q: Au lieu de présenter ta carte?] C'est ça. [Me, I say that
I don't have a health care card, that I don't want one, that anyway I've
always done without one, it doesn't bother me. [Q: OK. So you pay cash?]
Yes. [Q: Instead of presenting your health care card?] That's right. [31]

A decision to live without a health care card has consequences beyond the
health care network The presentation of a Québec health care card also
serves to establish Québécois identity within everyday life, such as when
one picks up a registered letter at the post office or becomes a member of a
video club. If transgendered people in Québec do not use this card within
the health care network, they won't use it within everyday life either. Several
participants thus had no legal Québec identity, functioning in the world
only with federal documents. As we have observed, this strategy means that
the person will not have the right to receive loans and bursaries, or even to
study. Transsexuals in Québec sacrifice these rights in order to have their
gender identities respected.

These quotations accurately describe the stress to which transgendered
people are subjected, others' lack of understanding of their identities, and
the negative social consequences of the current law with respect to name

changes for transgendered people. To avoid these problems, and especially to facilitate social integration, several transgendered people interviewed— MTF and FTM—falsified their documents. According to these interviewees, it was easier to live under an assumed name and a fraudulent identity than to cope with documents indicating a disjuncture between their physical appearance and civil status. This option remains popular for transgendered people: of the twenty-seven people interviewed, five admitted to having falsified their identities. These individuals either obtained their papers through an underground market or created their own documents; and at least one participant convinced her pastor to issue a new baptismal certificate with a feminine sex and name! Furthermore, I observed one young MTF transsexual buy false papers in a TS/TG bar in Montréal: with these papers, she obtained both a female and an adult identity.[32] Remarkably, the individuals who falsified their papers were willing to repeat specific educational and credentialing programs (like driver's licenses) for their new identities, even if they already had these skills in their legal identity. In these cases, gender identity is privileged above legal identity: transsexuals would rather repeat courses to live in a chosen gender than receive credit for previous training by divulging a transsexual identity.

Participants who falsified their papers claimed they had no other choice; they criticized the Québec government for administrative practices that prevent their social integration:

La fausse identité tout ça là, si j'me ramasse là moué, j'veux dire avec un dossier criminel pour usurpation d'identité, dans l'fond-là, qui c'est qui est vraiment coupable en arrière de ça? Moué ou ben le gouvernement? Si on prend ça à la source là . . . j'aurais pas faite de faux papiers, j'aurais eu mes papiers avec mon identité féminine toute, on en parle pus. Ben non. Non, y'ont préférés, y'ont préférés m'faire plus de misère, pis ch't'obligée de prendre des moyens illégals. Apres ça on vient m'dire, "Ah oui, mais transsexuels, c'est sûr, y t'rentrent tout l'temps du bord d'illégalité." Ben oui, be on a tu l'choix? Si y nous laissent le choix, c'est ça que j'reproche au gouvernement. [False identity and all that, if I end up with a criminal file for fraudulent identity, well who's really responsible for that, in the end? Me or the government? If we go back to the source, you know . . . I wouldn't have falsified my papers, I would have had my papers with a female name and that's it, we don't talk about it anymore. But no. No, they preferred, they preferred . . . to cause me more misery, so I had to revert to illegal means. And then after that they come and say to me, "Ah yes, but transsexuals, it's true, they're always living beyond the law." Well yes, do we have any choice? They leave us no choice, that's why I blame the government.][33]

As this woman explains, it is rather ironic that the administrative practices of the Direction de l'état civil, a service associated with the Ministry of Justice, create a situation in which transgendered people falsify their legal identities.

The difficulties of transgendered people with respect to their civil status in Québec confirm other research in this domain, most particularly in relation to countries with a civil code. In 1992, for instance, France was condemned by the European Court of Human Rights with respect to Article 8 of the European Human Rights Convention, which assures the right to a private life. The judgment declared that France's refusal to modify the civil status of its transsexual citizens forced them to live with the discrimination of French society resulting from identification papers that indicated only their names and sexes at birth.[34] Portugal's laws prohibit changes of sex, so transsexuals cannot modify their papers at all—neither name nor sex.[35] Luxembourg has no protocol for name or sex changes for transsexuals.[36] Transsexuals in Belgium are allowed to change their forenames, but the modification of civil status after surgery remains a question for legislators, jurists, and administrative clerks.[37] Furthermore, Germany, although not a civil code country, proposes two related procedures for the administration of transsexual identity: the minor solution or the change of name, and the major solution or the change of sex.[38] My research offers a valuable contribution to these European studies, all of which clearly illustrate the juridical problems faced by transsexuals in civil code countries. TS/TG people who cannot modify their identity papers will always have difficulties in the health care network, particularly when a forename cannot be changed.

### Inconsistent Applications and Interpretations of the Law

My research further indicates that the laws and procedures affecting transgendered people are much more complex than mere administrative directives. How these laws are interpreted and applied in Québec is extremely inconsistent. This variable situation demands a close attention to the administrative practices that frame the application and interpretation of the law concerning change of name and change of sex for transgendered people. The ad hoc nature of government administration in this area is amply illustrated in the case of FTM transsexuals. As we have observed, the law stipulates that a person must have undergone permanent modification to their sexual organs. For FTM transsexuals, this phrase is interpreted as the reconstruction of male sexual organs. Yet the Direction de l'état civil does not specify how it interprets this criteria. FTM transsexuals interviewed claimed that prior to 1996, the surgeries required for change of name and change of sex included hysterectomy, mastectomy, and oovarectomy.[39] Since 1996, however, the Direction de l'état civil modified its application of the law, in interpreting it in a different manner. In January 1998, the Direction de l'état civil required a vaginectomy (the closure of the vagina) of FTM transsexuals to change their names and their sexes.[40] The justification for this criteria, however, is not evident. In any case, this new interpretation results from a change in administrative procedure at the Direction de l'état civil and neither as a result of a consultation among FTM transsexuals nor medical experts in the field (such as surgeons and professionals associated with gender identity clinics). One FTM transsexual recounts his experience upon discovery of this new interpretation:

Bon. Vaginectomie. Quand j'ai reçu cette lettre-là, j'ai dit, Mon Dieu, qu'est-ce qu'une vaginectomie? J'veux dire depuis toute cette transition-là, je sais quelles sont les opérations à subir pour en arriver. Pis j'ai dit la prochaine opération c'est une phalloplastie, mais c'est quoi ça une vaginectomie? Faque j'ai pris rendez-vous avec le medecin qui m'avait opéré. Faque finalement, le medecin il dit, c'est impossible. On pratique pas des vaginecomies sur des transsexués. C't impossible, ça c'est pratiqué seulement, c'est une opération pratiquée seulement sur des cas de cancer extrêmes. Pis primièrement, ils peuvent pas tout enlever parce qu'y ont besoin be certains tissus, docteur [nom propre] a besoin de certains tissus pour faire, pour reconstituer, . . . pour faire la phalloplastie. Faque il a réécrit cette lettre-là, qui dit justement, ça fait vingt-cinq ans qu'y pratique ces opérations-là, pis c'est la première fois qu'une demande comme ça est demandé pour un cas comme ça. [O.K. Vaginectomy. When I got that letter, I said, My God, what's a vaginectomy? I mean, since this whole transition thing began, I've known the operations required to complete it. And the next operation is a phalloplasty, but what's a vaginectomy? So I made an appointment with the doctor who operated on me. And then finally the doctor said, well that's impossible. We don't do vaginectomies on transsexuals. It's impossible, it's only done, it's an operation that's only performed in extremely rare cases of cancer. And first of all, they can't take everything away because they need certain tissues, Doctor [proper name] needs certain tissues to do, . . . to do the phalloplasty. So he wrote this letter here, which says that

it's been twenty-five years that he's performed these operations, and this is
the first time in a case like this that there is a request for that.][41]

The Direction de l'état civil told this transsexual that he could be exempted
from a vaginectomy due to health reasons, with a medical authorization.
Although he wrote a letter to this effect, which outlined that he was not
going to have a vaginectomy due to health reasons, his request for a change
of name and a change of sex was denied. According to this FTM transsexual, the criteria of vaginectomy had been replaced by that of a phalloplasty: "[La Direction de l'état civil] a changé d'idée. C'était plus une vaginectomie, c'était une phalloplastie. [They had changed their minds. It was
no longer a vaginectomy, it was a phalloplasty.]"[42]

As this quotation from an FTM transsexual makes clear, expert surgeons in the field recognize the biomedical reasons to reject the criteria of
vaginectomy, notably the need for tissues so that surgeons can perform a
phalloplasty.[43] Moreover, a judgment rendered in Germany rejected the criteria of vaginectomy for the legal change of sex in FTM transsexuals. The
judges pointed out that a vaginectomy can create further health complications, such as intestinal and bladder problems. They also declared that because a vaginectomy adds nothing to the appearance of genital organs, it
cannot be considered in a law that requires a structural modification to the
appearance of genital organs.[44]

Surgeons, representatives of gender identity clinics, and FTM transsexuals were not consulted in the implementation of a criteria of vaginectomy
for the change of name and the change of sex for FTM transsexuals in Québec.[45] An FTM transsexual informed his surgeon as well as a gender identity
clinic about this criteria and this new interpretation of the law. The Direction de l'état civil did not communicate this information to the professionals responsible for gender identity clinics in Québec, including surgeons.

In April of 1998, the Direction de l'état civil changed its interpretation
and its application of the law once more, this time requiring the reconstruction of male sexual organs but not specifying what surgeries were necessary
to attest to this reconstruction.[46] The Direction de l'état civil told me that in
addition to having male genital organs, a transsexual must be able to urinate
standing up, in order to be legally recognized as a man. When I questioned
the justification for this criteria, however, representatives of the Direction
de l'état civil could not explain the link between a person's legal sex and
their behavior in a washroom.[47]

My consultations yielded nonetheless important information. The Direction de l'état civil told me, for instance, that FTM transsexuals dream of

going to the bathroom standing up.[48] Yet since no FTM transsexuals were ever consulted in this matter, this "dream" and the pertinence of this hypothesis for determining their legal sex are questionable.[49] The Direction de l'état civil also explained the need to ensure that the body modifications undertaken by transsexuals are permanent and that a sex change is irreversible. According to one representative, an FTM transsexual who ceases his hormone therapy could easily begin to live again as a woman.[50] This example illustrates a lack of understanding of FTM transsexuals and their bodies: the administration of testosterone in genetic females has *permanent effects,* such as facial hair and a deepening of the voice.[51] In other words, the representative of the Direction de l'état civil lacked proper training and information about FTM bodies. Considering that the policies and directives used to effect a change of name and a change of sex refer to these same bodies, it seems that current interpretations of the law in Québec are based on false or misguided information. Finally, my research suggests the Direction de l'état civil's unwillingness to learn about transsexual bodies and lives. My offer of information and/or training on transsexuality was firmly rejected.[52]

The lack of adequate information and the attitudes of individual bureaucrats at the Direction de l'état civil are directly linked to administrative practices that refuse the conferral of male civil status to FTMs without "male sexual organs" and that consequently prevent FTMs from integrating into Québec society. Studies in Québécois administration contend that the attitudes of individual government bureaucrats are indispensable to the delivery of services.[53] The perspectives and opinions of a government representative are important not just with regard to how individuals receive services, but are central to the kinds of services and information that are rendered. My research demonstrates this dynamic within a specifically transsexual context. The following quotation from an immigrant MTF transsexual demonstrates the ad hoc nature of Québécois bureaucracy and the important role that the attitudes of government bureaucrats play in granting juridical identity to transsexuals:

> Ha mais, on m'appeleait monsieur X, et c'était tellement gênant parce que il y avait tellement de monde dans la salle d'audience. Parce qu'on demande la citoyenneté à beaucoup de monde en même temps. Mais moi j'étais avec . . . un nom d'homme. Et puis on m'a appelé monsieur X, . . . je tremblais, . . . je suis nerveuse. Un moment donné ça tremblait, c'était la sueur dans la main, moi j'ai pris mon courage et je me suis levée et j'ai regardé comme ça. Et puis j'ai pris mon papier de citoyenneté, je l'ai

regardé. Après j'ai dit à la madame que je voulais changer le nom pour ce nom de femme, mais elle ne voulait pas avant que l'État civil l'autorise. L'État civil ne veut pas avant le changement du sexe alors là c'est compliqué. Jusqu'au moment où on va trouver quelqu'un à l'État civil qui est ouvert et qui va dire, oui, ça marche. Tsé, parce que c'est comme ça qu'ça marche ici.

[Oh, and so they called me Mr. X, it was so embarrassing because there were so many people in the room. Because they grant citizenship to lots of people at the same time. But me, I had . . . a man's name. And so they called me Mr. X, I was shaking, I had, and me I'm nervous. So I was shaking, my palms were sweating, and so I gathered my courage and I got up and looked like this. And I took my citizenship paper and I looked at it. After I said to the lady that I wanted to change the name for this woman's name, but she didn't want to do it until the Office of Civil Status authorized it. But Civil Status doesn't want to do this until after the sex change, so it's complicated. Until the day you find someone at Civil Status who is open and who will say, yes, this can be done. You know, that is how things work here.] [54]

This anecdote reveals the important role played by the attitudes of government bureaucrats in the delivery of services to transsexuals.

As in the case of a vaginectomy, the criteria of a reconstruction of male genital organs was not established as a result of a consultation with FTM transsexuals. The Direction de l'état civil informed me that this criteria was based on the opinion of expert surgeons in this area.[55] However, they only referred to surgeons who perform these surgeries on FTM transsexuals in private. The question of a conflict of interest must be raised at this point. Without questioning the expertise and the professionalism of these private surgeons, how can they decide which surgeries FTM transsexuals must undergo in order to change their names and their sexes, if these surgeons perform these same surgeries? This process presupposes that these surgeons represent the opinions of all the experts in this area. In fact, the Direction de l'état civil staff told me that to their knowledge, there exists no other surgeon in Québec who is an expert in this area and who does not share the opinion of the surgeons to whom they referred.[56] My research contradicts this claim: they did not consult at least one surgeon: the one who objected to the criteria of vaginectomy. Furthermore, since this surgeon protested this policy in a letter to the Direction de l'état civil, it seems odd that the Direction de l'état civil claims to not know of his existence. The consultation undertaken by the Direction de l'état civil in this matter is incomplete. The opinions of representatives from gender identity clinics, FTMs, and the expertise of other surgeons are not taken into consideration.[57] In this light, the interpretation of the law concerning FTM transsexuals only appraises the opinions of certain experts in the field, neglecting the contribution of other experts. The administrative process used to arrive at this interpretation is arbitrary.

My research confirms not only a lack of clear information with regard to the policy of change of name and change of sex for transgendered people, but also an interpretation and a subsequent application of the law that is inconsistent. In a consultation in October 1997, the Direction de l'état civil could not specify which surgeries constitute a structural modification of genital organs: "Je ne peux pas vous énumerer des opérations. Chaque cas est différent. [I can't list the operations for you. Each case is different.]"[58] In January 1998, however, vaginoplasty was specified as required for MTF transsexuals, while FTMs needed to undergo a hysterectomy, an oovarectomy, a mastectomy, and a vaginectomy.[59] In April 1998, the same information was confirmed with respect to MTF transsexuals, but I was informed once again that a list of the surgeries required for FTM transsexuals was not possible since each case was studied separately.[60] The many changes within a relatively short period of time in the policies and interpretations of sex and name change laws for transgendered people illustrate a lack of clear directives and protocols in this area. The experiences of FTM interviewees and my own interviews demonstrate that the Direction de l'état civil justifies its interpretation and its application of the law for FTM transsexuals according to diverse and contradictory reasons: vaginectomy, a partial vaginectomy, the absence of a vaginectomy due to health reasons, phalloplasty, and the reconstruction of male sexual organs.

This lack of protocol also affects MTF transsexuals. One MTF transsexual informed me that after her surgery, she submitted all the required documentation to change her name and sex (i.e., a letter from her surgeon and an additional medical certificate). But because all of the medical treatments and surgeries were not specified in the first letter, this transsexual was required to provide a second letter, thus coordinating information and communication between her surgeon and the Direction de l'état civil.[61] The process indicates the need for an explanatory document that clearly outlines the medical treatments and surgeries required for the change of name and the change of sex. Without it, the administrative work of bureaucrats at the Direction de l'état civil, transsexuals, surgeons, and doctors will continue to be unnecessarily duplicated.

It is important to consider the administrative practices of the Direction de l'état civil, rather than simply reading the laws concerning name and sex changes. As my research indicates, the problems faced by FTM transsexuals in Québec in terms of their civil status are a result of how the law is *interpreted*. A study that only considers the text of the law could conclude that both the name and the sex of transsexuals can be changed in Québec. However, an inquiry that examines how this change occurs on an administrative level offers us important information. FTM transsexuals in Québec have difficulties in modifying their identity papers because policies and protocols in this field do not exist, change regularly, or are interpreted differently. The complexity of this situation is a direct result of how it is currently administered. As sociologists in the field of administration contend, government bureaucracy frequently lacks order. Grant Jordan's remarks about Britain are equally pertinent for the practices of the Direction de l'état civil in Québec:

> Where one might expect bureaucratic rigidity there is *ad hoc* improvisation. British public administration is made up by Governments as they go along. It is characterized by features that might be least expected: uncertainty, inconsistency, disorder.
>
> It is surprisingly difficult to prove this. An account of confusion reads very much like a confused account. Since there is no ordered pattern to British administration, the more detailed knowledge that is gathered serves to emphasize the weakness of our understanding.[62]

The information presented above illustrate the problem described by Jordan. At the Direction de l'état civil, the administrative process to interpret the law concerning the change of name and the change of sex for FTM transsexuals is partial, arbitrary, and incomplete.

A legal case against the Direction de l'état civil in 1998–99 addressed its arbitrary policies. An FTM who had completed the surgeries for change of name and sex required prior to 1996 brought legal action against this body.[63] The case was settled out of court, and the man was granted a new name and sex designation.[64] However, only a few months later, my research indicates that another FTM who had completed the same operations as this individual was refused a change of name and a change of sex.[65] But since the resolution of the situation with the legal case occurred out of court, no legal precedent had been set. For this reason, it is crucial that a reflexive sociology examine the practices of administration through which name and sex change are effected for transsexuals. Indeed, despite the lawsuit against the Direction de l'état civil, there remains no clear protocol in this domain and the administration continues to be of an arbitrary nature.

The current policies regarding change of name and change of sex for transsexuals in Québec assume that all transsexuals are interested in genital surgery. The results of the provincial needs assessment, however, describe a very different situation. Many individuals prefer to take hormones without undergoing surgery. In the current context, however, these people cannot legally change their names without surgical intervention. Interestingly, in countries that allow such a choice, a significant percentage of transgendered individuals opt to change only their forenames. In one German longitudinal study, within a sample population of 1,422 transgendered people, between 20 percent and 30 percent of the participants decided to live in a gender other than that of their birth sex by changing only their names and identity papers, without any subsequent genital surgery.[66] If Germany had the same law as Québec, between 284 and 426 people would live with a legal identity that does not correspond to their psychological or social identity. The participants in my research clearly indicated that that they would live their bodies as they choose to live them, with or without the approval of the Direction de l'état civil.

The social consequences of this current situation are dramatic. An individual who cannot or will not produce documents attesting to their legal identity cannot negotiate the institutions of everyday life: health care centers, schools, social service agencies. For transgendered people in Québec, the solution is obvious: to live one's life with no legal Québécois identity, no documents whatsoever that betray one's birth sex. The strategies employed to mitigate these circumstances are varied: the decision to pay for health care personally rather than using a health care card; obtaining false papers in order to study or go to school; working as a prostitute. Since transgendered people cannot produce appropriate documentation that offers them a legal identity in their chosen sex, many choose to live completely underground.

## THE VICIOUS CIRCLE OF ADMINISTRATION: "LA ROUE QUI TOURNE"

My research clearly illustrates that transgendered people in Québec have difficulties integrating into the social world as a function of how civil status is administered. My interviews with transsexuals and transvestites, as well as those with health care professionals and government bureaucrats, yield important information about how everyday life is shaped by the institutions we all negotiate. This project offers an engaging case study of Smith's framework of institutional ethnography, in which the sociologist considers how experience is ordered through specific institutional relations. Yet Smith's method of institutional ethnography limits itself to a detailed consideration of one particular institution, as do most scholars who apply her methods. George Smith's analysis of AIDS policies in Ontario, for instance, examines the lack of infrastructure for HIV/AIDS treatment in Ontario's health ministry of the late 1980s.[67] In their exploration of state security, Gary Kinsman and Patrizia Gentile analyze the concrete workings and texts of the Royal Canadian Mounted Police as a means of understanding how lesbians and gays in the Canadian government experienced issues of state security in relation to their sexual identities.[68] Roxana Ng's study of immigrant women workers begins with the daily workings of an employment agency in order to comprehend how the state mediates labor market demands through nonprofit agencies.[69] The strength of this focus on a single institution is a detailed, micrological appreciation of how specific social and historical relations manifest themselves in everyday life. Yet such a circumscribed inquiry may also present some methodological dangers by neglecting other important aspects of the everyday world. If institutional ethnography is valuable precisely because it shows how the world works, its greatest weakness for a general social theory may be its restriction to one institution.

The research conducted on HIV/AIDS in Québec brings these questions into sharp relief. My interviews with both transsexuals and transvestites, as well as representatives of health care services and government bureaucracy, clearly indicate the need for a more nuanced understanding of how institutions work. One of the greatest problems faced by transgendered people in Québec is not just negotiating with one particular institution, but entering into relations within a complex array of institutional sites. Each site has its own specific policies and protocols with regard to transgendered people, and these do not always accord with the directives of others. Indeed, my research reveals that an institution such as health care administers its affairs with little or no consideration of how they correspond to the policies and workings of a related institution, such as prisons. Such administration is equally negligent of the impact of this situation on the lives of the people who are situated within such different institutional networks. For transgendered people in Québec, the consequences of these administrative differences are important: the requirements of one institution exclude an individual from another, with the end result that transgendered people find themselves shut out from several institutional sites at once, perpetually lost in an administrative abyss.

Several examples illustrate this problematic. Federal prisons in Canada and Québec require that a transsexual individual be evaluated and monitored by a recognized gender identity clinic in order to obtain access to hormones and surgery.[70] Yet my research indicates that prostitutes in Québec are refused a psychiatric evaluation from these clinics because of their work (see chapter 8). Since they cannot access these clinics, this effectively means that prostitutes within federal correctional institutions cannot receive hormones and sex reassignment surgery. A second example from the research further exemplifies the discordance among different establishments and institutions. My interviews with representatives of gender identity clinics in Québec revealed that transsexuals with addiction issues are not evaluated until they have completed drug and alcohol recovery programs. Yet such programs generally do not address the question of gender identity within their services, and their staff rarely have the appropriate training, resources, and expertise in this area. Moreover, some addiction programs have inappropriate and discriminatory admission requirements for transgendered clients, such as the insistence that individuals dress and present themselves according to their biological sex. In this regard, a transgendered person who enrolls in an addiction recovery program will not necessarily find support and encouragement to explore his or her gender identity. What results is transsexuals and transvestites in Québec being refused services both by gender identity clinics and by alcohol and drug recovery programs: in neither institutional site can they address how their gender identity and their addictions may or may not be related.

Conflicting administrative practices of different Québec institutions are most evident in the general social integration of transgendered people. The Direction de l'état civil requires that an individual surgically modify their genitals in order to change their name and their sex. Yet in order to be authorized for surgery, psychiatrists and professionals associated with gender identity clinics demand that individuals prove their social integration, a fact usually established through full-time employment or studies. As I have shown, however, access to employment or school frequently requires official documents that declare an individual's transsexual status. As long as they cannot find work, or study with the aid of loans and bursaries, they will not be authorized for surgery. As long as they are not authorized for surgery, they cannot change their name legally. Without an appropriate name change, they cannot find work or go to school, which in turn prevents access to surgery. In this manner, TS/TG people in Québec are caught in a vicious circle of administration that prevents them from living as integrated members of society, and that may also prevent them from changing their bodies. It is this kind of administrative dynamic that creates social and economic conditions in which transsexuals in Québec are vulnerable to the transmission of HIV.

The policies of these different institutions may have some internal legitimacy. Psychiatrists and staff of gender identity clinics, for instance, claim that it would be inappropriate to perform genital surgery on individuals who have not demonstrated that they are well-adapted. This policy makes recourse to the Harry Benjamin International Gender Dysphoria Association's Standards of Care for the treatment of transsexuals, which tries to ensure the best possible adaptation for transsexual individuals.[71] The directives of the Direction de l'état civil also want to ensure administrative efficiency and enhanced social adjustment. Individuals need to undergo surgery before modifying their name and the sex as one means to demonstrate the seriousness of their intent and commitment to live in a chosen sex. And educational institutions are unwilling or reluctant to change the names on the files of their students without some formal authorization from the government department that administers these affairs, in this instance the Direction de l'état civil. In all of these institutional sites, the justifications for the policies and procedures have some validity. But when these policies and administrative practices are considered alongside one another, as they necessarily are by the transsexuals in Québec who negotiate these institutions, the global result is one of administrative chaos and institutional discordance—summarized succinctly by one research participant:

> Ça se résume très simple, le gouvernement met pas ses culottes. Tu pars du, du processus, tu commences l'opération tout ça, tu commences le processus pour te rendre à l'opération, t'arrives, te, même si t'es OK, le gouvernement paie pas, j'veux dire, y'a pas de chirurgiens fait que, t'es obligée d'aller voir un chirurgien au privé, mais un chirurgien au privé y faut que tu paies pour. Qu'est-ce qui te reste à faire? Tsé, pas de travail, pas rien, problème d'identité, tout ça, quecqu'part là, au moment donné ça, ça roue qui tourne. Faut qu't'ailles, pis là t'as besoin d'argent rapidement parce que là tu dis, "Aie calvas!" Qu'est-ce qui te reste à faire? Toué tu veux danser, mais danser avec un pénis, c'est "ruff" en chien, en. Donc, qu'est-ce qui te reste? Prostitution. Tu peux pas faire d'la prostitution longtemps, sans arriver pis commencer à prendre d'la drogue. Résultat, t'es obligée de prendre d'la drogue pis là, ben tu t'enlise. Tu peux pas t'rendre à l'opération, là quand tu r'viens dans le circuit pour demander d'l'aide, "Ha ben non. T'as

fait d'la prostitution." Tu vois ça? [It's really quite simple. The government is fucking the dog. You begin the process, the process to get your operation, you get there, and like even if you're all right, the government doesn't pay, I mean there are no surgeons, so you have to go see a private surgeon, but a private surgeon you have to pay for. So what're you gonna do? You know, no work, problems with your papers, all that, at a certain point, it's a vicious circle. You really need money fast and then you go, "Oh shit!" What're you gonna do? You want to dance, but dancing with a cock is a bit complicated, eh? So what's left? Prostitution. You can't do prostitution for very long without ending up taking some drugs. The result is that you have to take drugs, and then you get hooked. You can't get your operation, and then when you go back into the system to ask for help, "Oh no. You're a prostitute." Do you see how it works?] [72]

A critical examination of health care for TS/TG people in Québec must understand the workings not just of one institution, be it a gender identity clinic or the Direction de l'état civil, but the functions, procedures, and relations of several institutions. Transsexuals in Québec are marginalized from the social world as a result of a complex, interinstitutional process. Practically speaking, it is in examining how different institutional sites connect—or do not connect, as is more often the case—that transgendered people find themselves refused health care services, juridical identity, and the social status of person. This refusal both creates and reinforces conditions in which TS/TG people are vulnerable to HIV/AIDS.

The discordance among different institutional policies, moreover, engenders a two-tiered system of health care and social services for transsexuals. Gender identity clinics demand that an individual work or study full-time as a means to demonstrate social adaptation in a chosen gender. Yet as we have observed, full-time work or studies frequently demands the production of documents that divulge an individual's transgendered status. To the extent that a person is prevented from working or going to school, they will not be eligible for surgery and consequently will not be able to change their name. These policies function differently for different transgendered people. Individuals who begin transition with established careers, a work history, a unionized job, or a position in the federal or provincial government are frequently able to transition on the job. In this way, they can enroll in the program of a gender identity clinic, become eligible for surgery if evaluated to be transsexual, and change their personal documents. An MTF transgendered youth who works as a cashier at a grocery store, however, may not have the same kind of job security when she decides to transition. If she is fired, finding another job may be a challenge—particularly given her identity papers. If she remains unemployed, or begins to work as a prostitute, she will not be eligible for surgery via the authorization of a gender identity clinic, and thus will not be able to change her name. In this complex way, the current administration of health care and identity papers for transsexuals in Québec favors individuals who have stable, secure employment. Transgendered youth may find themselves to be among the most marginalized people within TS/TG communities.

## CONCLUSION

Reflection on the administration of legal sex in Québec illustrates the central role that documents play in everyday life, from situations as mundane as renting a video to those of a more formal nature—consulting a doctor at a community health clinic or presenting one's identification at the request of a police officer. The practical work of institutions is textually organized through documents.[73] Official documents—birth certificates, marriage licenses, immigration cards—function to establish a fact. As Don Zimmerman argues, the establishment of facts through authorized documents situates the "essentially *un*problematic character of official documents."[74] In the case of transsexuals, the production of a birth certificate or a change of name certificate establishes the facticity of sex. In this manner, documents are central in naming and sexing the subject.

Within ethnomethodology, it is well recognized that documents are themselves produced in highly specific and regulated contexts: not just any piece of paper can establish an individual's citizenship. The case study offered in this chapter reveals the importance of attending to the administrative process through which documents are produced. Transgendered people in Québec have no involvement in the administrative process through which sex is legally changed: the criteria used are based on misconceptions of individual bureaucrats at the Direction de l'état civil, a flagrant absence of policy and protocol in this area, and the opinions of certain surgeons and medical experts in Québec. Ethnomethodology further demonstrates that documents are required to negotiate most institutions; they are fundamental to the work of organizations. The absence of documents for transsexuals in Québec thus deprives these individuals from achieving the status of person in society. The social relations of sex and gender are institutionally organized and reproduced through the use of documents. Transsexuals respond to this situation by refusing to produce such papers:

a response that illustrates the systemic exclusion of transsexuals from the institutional world. It is in and through such erasure that transsexuals in Québec are vulnerable to the transmission of HIV/AIDS.

What this chapter has demonstrated beyond these observations, however, are the consequences of living without documents of one's legal sex: consequences that marginalize transgendered people and prevent social integration in the realms of employment, education, and health care. Further, the chapter illustrates that many of the current policies and administrative procedures with respect to change of name and change of sex in Québec are based on misinformation. Finally, TS/TG people have no voice or representation in the policy and bureaucratic decisions that determine how their documents will be issued and changed, factors that in turn define how transsexuals will experience their everyday lives.

In addition to the administration of legal sex, this chapter emphasizes the discordant policies of different institutions central to the lives of TS/TG people in Québec, which results in the exclusion of transsexuals from institutional sites and a subsequent further marginalization of these individuals from the social world. The administrators of these institutions can only offer bureaucratic justifications for their policies and procedures. A representative of the Direction de l'état civil, for instance, claimed that they could not take into consideration the social or economic consequences of how they interpreted the law with respect to name and sex changes.[75] A spokesperson for a gender identity clinic had no knowledge of how transsexuals in Québec change their name and sex, stating that such was not the role of a gender identity clinic.[76] And a representative of the Ministère de la Santé et des Services Sociaux declared that the ministry had not considered the issue of name and sex change for TS/TG people because this matter was about the law, not about health.[77] Indeed, what is remarkable about all of these responses is their common appeal to the terms of their institution: the Direction de l'état civil states that it is only mandated to apply the law, gender identity clinics function to evaluate transsexual candidates, and the Ministère de la Santé et des Services Sociaux limits its administration to a biomedical definition of health. Each institution can only make sense of the social world through its internal codes, terms, and definitions. Everything else may be interesting and important, but nonetheless remains outside of a scope of inquiry, excluded from the practical work of administration. Indeed, while particular institutions consider specific fields as relevant to transsexuals (jurisprudence, biomedical health, psychiatric evaluation), it appears that only TS/TG people need to consider the complex array and interplay of the economic, social, juridical, and administrative factors of their lives. Transsexuals cannot think about their change of name in exclusive relation to Québec's law, for instance, since the name inscribed on their legal documents has profound and immediate implications for their health care. Given these complex problems with identity papers, education, and employment, TS/TG people manage their lives as best they can, often living for decades outside of an institutional network designated to serve them. My research further confirms a gendered division of labor with respect to how marginalized transsexuals survive: many MTFs work as prostitutes, while some FTMs devote themselves to professional theft.[78] The exclusion of TS/TG people from Québec's institutions thus prevents social integration. As sociologist André Turmel remarks, institutions are fundamental in the constitution of social actors:

> Parmi les éléments constitutifs d'une société, les plus marqués sont les institutions. Elles sont notamment caractérisées par un haut degré de permanence; elles sont de plus cristallisées, voir sédimentées, dans l'histoire d'une société. A vrai dire, les institutions sont le point nodal de la constitution des personnes en acteurs sociaux; c'est par et à travers les institutions qu'une personne devient un acteur social doté d'habilités et de capacités pouvant en faire un membre actif dans une société. [Among the fundamental elements of a society, the most important are institutions. They are characterized by a high degree of permanence: they are crystallized, even rooted, in the history of a society. Indeed, institutions are the lynchpin of the constitution of people into social actors; it is in and through institutions that a person becomes a social actor decreed with the ability and capacity to become an active member of society.][79]

Diane Gobeil offers one important reason for the dearth of studies on transsexuals and AIDS: the classification of transsexuals according to their biological sex before surgery, and according to their chosen sex after surgery, a classification process that can only consider nontranssexual men and women. The results presented in this chapter offer an additional explanation. No one has thought about transsexuals because the institutions of the social world function to exclude us completely, with the result that we live our lives outside them, as evidenced by the actions of TS/TG people in Québec: functioning under assumed names or choosing to pay cash instead of presenting a health care card. Through the daily workings of institutions, as well as a significant discordance among institutions, TS/TG people are inscribed as impossible, quite literally eliminated from the social text. *Transsexuals are produced through erasure.*

Chapters 7 and 8 demonstrate how social service and health care agencies function to exclude TS/TG people. The research presented in this chapter illustrates that the erasure of transsexuals from the institutional world is much more than marginalization or exclusion. The sexed production of bodies produces only men and women. Transsexuals do not, and cannot exist, from a legal standpoint. The implications of this impossibility are immense with respect to health care and social integration. And while these issues may be most evident for transsexual individuals who live in their chosen gender but have not yet had genital surgery, these difficulties persist throughout their lifetimes, even after their legal papers have been changed. Post-operative transsexual women who need to have their prostate examined, or transsexual men who need to ensure proper gynecological care, represent two such examples. In this manner, the impossibility of imagining transsexuality (its legal absence) is directly linked to how transsexuals choose to locate themselves outside institutions. Transsexuals are produced through erasure to the extent that civil status and juridical identity foreclose transsexual possibilities, authorizing only nontranssexual men and women as citizens.

A critical sociological research agenda needs to understand how the erasure of TS/TG people is organized, as well as its consequences. This chapter offers a point of departure for such an inquiry: an investigation into how TS/TG people are rendered invisible, based upon a micrological analysis of how this obliteration is realized in specific administrative practices and social relations. Smith's framework of institutional ethnography offers a productive framework to make sense of the world as it is lived and experienced by TS/TG people. The results of this research process offer some valuable insights into the practice of institutional ethnography as a research method: social subjects negotiate a variety of different institutions at one and the same time. Sociology can provide an analysis of how a particular institution functions, as well as how it arranges the world of social subjects. But an engaged inquiry—one that begins with the everyday world as lived and interpreted by members of the research population—ought also to consider how various institutions of daily life intersect, connect, or diverge, and how these functions of association or separation are integral to the ordering of experience. In this way, this chapter demonstrates how documents of civil status and juridical identity are central to the organization of sex and gender relations in the institutional world.

# CONCLUSION

*Et si je dois passer par les chemins tortueux de la prostitution, je suis prêt. Des gens qui me ressemble, je n'en ai vu nulle part ailleurs qu'ici, sur le trottoir, ou accrochés à la nuit de Montmartre. Je n'en ai rien vu dans les facultés, ni dans les salons bourgeois, les usines. Ils ne sont ni boucher, ni contrôleur d'autobus, ni général, ni balayeur.*

*Ils sont là, "dans la pègre," dirait mon père. Ils sont coiffeurs ou danseuses, dirait ma mère. Et moi je dis: ils vivent ce qu'ils peuvent, là où ils peuvent. Ils sont dans des camps de concentration minuscules, dont les autres, les normaux, ne voient même pas les barbelés et les miradors. Ils sont interdits de séjour en société. Prisonniers de leur peau. Comme moi. Alors, qu'on me laisse choisir ma peau.*
—Maud Marin and Marie-Thérèse Cuny

The kind of poststructuralist sociological inquiry I outlined in chapter 3 informs my analysis throughout this book. I am specifically interested in understanding how transsexual and transgendered people are located in the everyday cultural and institutional world, the potential contribution of a reflexive sociology to further our understanding of the experiences of TS/TG individuals, and the concrete, practical relevance of this knowledge for policy interventions and social change.

Given the kinds of theoretical and political commitments I outline in part 1, I insist on a specifically social inquiry. Although many Anglo-American social scientists maintain that a commitment to social inquiry requires a rejection of poststructuralism, discourse analysis, and rhetorical theory, I demonstrate in part 2 their pertinence for any critical examination. In chapters 4 and 5, a focus on text advances a conception of language as social semiotic, as a form of social action. The theoretical frameworks of discourse analysis and rhetoric provide a means to appreciate how macrological social relations of gender are realized and reinforced in micrological linguistic, semiotic, and rhetorical operations. Chapters 6 through 9 continue this social focus through empirical case studies of how transgendered and transsexual people are located within, or excluded from, different institutional sites. While the culture and research sections each offer unique contributions to making sense of the social world from a transsexual/transgendered perspective, their approaches are quite complementary. Indeed, the chapters that focus on the cultural inscription of MTF transsexual and transgendered people illustrate how gendered discourse excludes TS/TG people from the realm of representation. This textual negation reveals the pertinence of specific qualitative social science research methods—such as interviews, oral history, and institutional ethnography—as crucial tools in the collection of data on transsexual and transgendered people unavailable through legal, psychiatric, and medical texts. If the functions of discourse and rhetoric erase the presence and possibility of TS/TG people, critical inquiry needs to rely on data collection techniques that challenge this erasure. In this regard, discourse analysis and qualitative research methods offer an engaging conjunctural analysis of social life.[1]

Taking up a poststructuralist concern with the *production* of subjects, the empirical studies in this book offer specific cases to examine how transsexual and transgendered people are produced—that is, erased—in different sites: antiviolence activism, health care, gender identity clinics, civil status. By focusing on some of the most significant institutions with which TS/TG people must negotiate in everyday life, I reject an exclusive focus on the production of transsexuals within the medical and psychiatric establishment. As outlined in chapters 2 and 3, scholarship that limits itself to locating transsexuals within medicine and psychiatry brings with it theoretical, methodological, and political dangers: notably the virtual reduction of transsexuals to medical and psychiatric discourse. This theoretical position assumes transsexuals are only produced within these sites and ignores the construction of sex and gender in a variety of institutional locations. A methodological focus on the inscription of TS/TG people outside of medicine and psychiatry is further significant given my argument that transsexual and transgendered people are produced through erasure. If scholars limit their inquiry to the sites wherein transsexuals and transgendered people are most visible, their research programs will reinforce a more general obliteration of TS/TG people from the social world. In this case, the knowledge generated functions to produce TS/TG people in select sites, thereby circumscribing our understanding of who these people are and how they live. A truly reflexive sociology demands an inquiry that is much more engaged, because it recognizes that knowledge constructs its own object.

Erasure is the most significant social relation in which transsexuals and transgendered people are situated. The data presented throughout this book illustrates three related conceptions of erasure: the reduction of transsexual and transgendered people to the merely figural; the institutional exclusion of TS/TG individuals; and the production of knowledge and conceptual frameworks in which transsexuality is virtually inconceivable and impossible. Yet this erasure functions differently for distinct transgendered individuals. Nonprostitute MTF transsexuals, for instance, are erased through the use of rhetoric in mass culture. They are reduced to a mere figure, made visible only to indicate some other phenomenon; represented as stereotypical caricatures only to disappear as human beings. FTM transsexuals, in contrast, are erased in the bureaucratic administration (and bunglings) of social and legal institutions. As the data presented from Québec illustrates, frequently FTM transsexuals and transgendered people cannot be inscribed within the social text. Institutions such as the Direction de l'état civil cannot confer the legal status of male to an individual who does not have a penis. MTF prostitutes, however, are erased from the social and institutional world in a manner different than either FTM transsexuals or nonprostitute MTF transsexuals. The empirical research presented throughout this book provides ample documentation of how MTF prostitutes are ignored and neglected in everyday life: antiviolence activism that precludes an adequate conceptualization of gender and violence, especially violence against prostitutes; shelters for women and the homeless that do not acknowledge the poverty in which many transsexual prostitutes live; police officers who refuse to accept reports of sexual assault from prostitutes; gender identity clinics that do not respect the work of prostitutes and therefore refuse to evaluate them; health care policies of Canadian federal prisons that, in appealing to the expertise of gender identity clinics, effectively deny treatment to prostitutes. These specific institutional practices function to exclude transsexual and transgendered prostitutes from the social world. The findings presented throughout this book further indicate that many transsexual and transgendered prostitutes refuse to negotiate with these institutions because of subtle or overt discrimination against prostitutes. In all of the instances cited above, TS/TG people are rendered invisible. Yet the practical workings of this erasure vary according to the different TS/TG people one considers. If a reflexive poststructuralist sociology needs to understand that TS/TG people are produced through erasure, it must also appreciate that not all transsexual and transgendered people are erased in the same way.

TS/TG people disappear in the unseen work of discourse, rhetoric, and institutions. Given this erasure, the immediate question for the social scientist is how to collect data. The research presented throughout this book offers some methodological orientations that may prove useful in future research studies. For instance, I suggest that social scientists recognize that there is not one large "transgendered community," but rather several small networks of transsexual and transgendered people, as well as many TS/TG people unaffiliated with other individuals like them. (This insight thus cautions against the simplistic use of the word "transgendered," since this umbrella term may erase the specificity of different transgendered, and especially transsexual, individuals.) My research also draws on a wide variety of sources and texts: transsexual media, interviews with transsexuals and transvestites, institutional policies, and briefs presented to government bodies. If Anglo-American discussions about transsexual and transgendered people are limited to the extent that they draw on a narrow range of sources (almost exclusively the writings of Leslie Feinberg, Riki Ann Wilchins, and Kate Bornstein), critical research needs to base its analysis upon a more extensive sample. In terms of the practical gathering of information, interviews offer an excellent occasion for the social science researcher to collect knowledge. Moreover, the process of validating the interpretation of research data remains a crucial component of any reflexive sociological practice. In chapter 9, I described the public forums I organized with TS/TG people explicitly to present them with the preliminary results and to validate my interpretations, but there are certainly other ways for transsexual and transgendered people to offer feedback on the interpretations of their lives proposed by academics. For example, Deborah Feinbloom used a collective contract of rights and responsibilities with a transvestite research population. Feinbloom negotiated the right to interpret their lives and behaviors according to sociological theory, but she also offered them the opportunity to voice their objections.[2] In a parallel manner, sociologist Henry Rubin presents data from his interviews with FTM transsexuals that contradict his theoretical argument: a respect for how FTM transsexuals locate themselves within the world.[3] Unfortunately, an accountability to the people under study is flagrantly absent in most queer theory and objectivist sociology. Indeed, given that transsexuals and transgendered people are always reduced to an object of study (whether the object is deemed to be fascinating, horrific, tragic, or transgressive), I suggest that we demand that researchers on transsexual and transgendered people tell us how TS/TG people validated their interpretations, findings, and conclusions. Transsexuals and transgendered people must be actively involved in the construction of academic knowledge about our bodies and our lives: anything less advocates a position wherein knowledge is produced, in the first and last instance, for the institution of the university.

In part 1, I argue that our knowledge of transsexual and transgendered people reflects the process through which data has been gathered and interpreted. I caution against the assumptions prevalent within English-language theory and activism on transgendered people, especially within the context of the United States. This literature is preoccupied with questions of identity and habitually extends its discussion of identity to speak about collective action and social movements. Such a position is articulated by Judith Halberstam, who claims, "We are at present in the midst of a Foucauldian 'reverse discourse' on transsexuality and transgenderism."[4] While there is certainly an increased visibility of some transsexual and transgendered people in the English-speaking United States, we ought to reflect carefully on this claim of an emerging specifically transgendered social movement. An exclusive focus on the visibility of TS/TG individuals takes for granted the ability to represent oneself within social institutions, an assumption that implicitly presumes that transsexuals have access to health care. My research contradicts this assertion by showing that this is not the case for all, or even most, transsexual people. A celebration of recent U.S. transgender visibility—evidenced through certain media representations, activist positions, and academic debates—does not consider the experiences of a diverse group of transsexual and transgendered people: the MTF transsexual in prison who cannot access hormones; the seropositive transsexual who cannot find a surgeon willing to perform sex reassignment surgery; the fifteen-year-old female who identifies as a man, who wants hormones, and who is without resources; the transsexual who cannot change his legal identity, and thus cannot find work or go to school without divulging his transsexual status. While certain academics contend that there is an increased representation of transsexual and transgendered people in North America in recent years, I maintain that some transsexuals are more invisible than ever.

Furthermore, English-language transgendered theory and activism in the United States habitually assumes that transsexuals should be politically aligned with American lesbian and gay communities. Again, my research challenges this claim. In many instances, lesbians and gay men are responsible for an erasure of transsexual and transgendered people: for example, academic critics like Schwartzwald who reduce transgendered people to mere tropological figures; antiviolence activists who cannot acknowledge the presence or realities of transsexual street prostitutes; lesbian therapists who counsel their FTM clients to live as lesbian women. These examples complicate any easy coalition among transsexuals and mainstream lesbian and gay communities. Moreover, the different case studies presented throughout this book suggest that transsexuals and transgendered people are perhaps better aligned with prostitute activists than with lesbians and gay men. Systemic and institutionalized discrimination against prostitutes impedes and prevents their access to health care and thus the ability of many transsexuals to live their bodies as they choose. Such discrimination is evident in numerous locations: gender identity clinics, prisons, and health care and social service agencies. It is discrimination against prostitutes that orders the experiences of many transsexuals—especially MTF transsexuals—within the institutional world. How relevant is a "transgendered" social movement that does not make the decriminalization of prostitution a political priority?

This remains the most severe limitation of Anglo-American scholarship on transgendered and transsexual people: *there is no sustained analysis of how TS/TG people are situated (and/or situate themselves) outside institutions.* Since Anglo-American activists and academics frequently base their claims to transgendered social movements and collective action upon such limited knowledge, the political programs they advance are equally insufficient. This is a methodological issue familiar to the critical social scientist: information taken from an institutional population cannot be generalized to a noninstitutional population.[5] A process of data collection that moves beyond the United States, and the English language, has much to offer in critical reflection on how transsexual and transgendered people organize themselves individually and collectively.

The results of my research force a reconsideration of the absences within recent scholarship and activism on transsexual and transgendered individuals. My research clearly demonstrates the institutional exclusion of transsexuals and transgendered people: how different administrative practices and social policies (or the lack of social policies) marginalize these individuals, as well as why many TS/TG people choose not to make use of the existing services. Yet this exclusion functions differently for different transsexual and transgendered people: most pre-operative or non-operative seropositive MTF transsexuals cannot access women's shelters due to policies that accept only post-surgical transsexual women; all of the TS/TG prostitutes I interviewed recounted incidents of police harassment and abuse, compared to only a small minority of nonprostitute transsexuals; prostitutes are not evaluated by gender identity clinics and are thus ineligible for access to hormones and sex reassignment surgery via these clinics; and the employment and professional status of a transsexual individual facilitates a positive evaluation of their transsexual identity, which is in turn linked to access to health care. In all of these instances, we can observe important differences among transsexual and transgendered people. Current administrative practices and social policies actually function to create a two-tiered system of health care for transsexuals, such that poor transsexuals, ex-convicts, seropositive individuals, the unemployed, and prostitutes are regularly refused services.

Attention to these divisions among transsexual and transgendered people is important in the development of appropriate theory and politics. The consumer model of health care proposed by some American transsexual activists, for instance, reinforces a link between employment and access to health care, thus bolstering the invisibility of poor transsexuals. In a parallel manner, an American transgender theory that exalts increased transgender visibility perpetuates a vision of the social world in which the everyday lives of transsexual immigrants and transsexual prostitutes are eclipsed. American transgender theory and politics need to be challenged on two levels: their insensitivity to the wide diversity of TS/TG people, and how an absence of poor transsexuals within these discourses legitimates the institutional exclusion of such individuals.

Attention to the erasure of poor transsexuals is especially important at this historical moment, given a marked fascination in transsexual and transgendered phenomenon in the mainstream and alternative media. Indeed, transsexual and transgendered people and characters have become objects of fascination for journalists, playwrights, filmmakers, cultural producers, and academics. Critical theory and activism must consider the extent to which these inscriptions of TS/TG people are complicit with the virtual erasure of transsexual bodies and lives. More often than not, cultural representations about transgendered phenomena have nothing whatsoever to do with the everyday lives of transsexuals and transvestites, especially the lives of prostitutes, immigrants, and the working poor.

Scholarship and activism on TS/TG people that seeks to offer an innovative and practically relevant contribution to the existing knowledge base needs to account for and intervene in the erasure of transsexual and transgendered people in the cultural and institutional world. To neglect how such erasure is organized on a micrological level perpetuates such obliteration, making the theory produced deeply complicit with the social world it set out to understand. The dangers of such unacknowledged complicity are amply illustrated in both queer theory and mainstream social science. As Jay Prosser contends, queer theory's entire program relies upon the transgendered figure: a reliance that reinforces a reduction of transgendered people to the figural dimensions of discourse.[6] Given that mass culture inscribes MTF transsexual and transgendered people purely as rhetorical figures, queer theory is actually bound within a more general social relation that denies the possibility of transsexual subjectivity. That the framework cannot acknowledge this dynamic reveals its absolute failure for critical inquiry. Mainstream social science, in contrast, limits its analysis of TS/TG people to questions deemed interesting to the academic sociologist. Preoccupied with gender identity, this perspective ignores issues of labor, everyday life, and institutions, thereby producing transsexuals within a narrow field of reference. The selection and interpretation of evidence obscures the complexity of TS/TG bodies and lives. Knowledge that does not reflect upon or intervene in the effacement of TS/TG people legitimates the very cultural meanings, social relations, and institutional practices it needs to understand and challenge.

The transsexuals and transvestites cited throughout this book describe the systemic discrimination they confront on a daily basis in the social world: in the mass media, in lesbian and gay communities, in the health care network, in gender identity clinics, in the Direction de l'état civil. A reflexive sociological practice seeks to document this discrimination as experienced and interpreted by the transsexuals and transvestites who live it. Moreover, critical sociology relates this experience to how the world is organized through institutions, texts, and documents. In this regard, the practice of sociology can offer a valuable contribution to improving the everyday lives of transsexuals. It is hoped that this book provides an engaging illustration of the role that sociology can play in the production of knowledge, the elaboration of meaningful social policy, and the work of social change.

# NOTES

## Notes to Introduction

1.  The definitions offered here are necessarily partial and incomplete, perhaps especially because many of these terms and identities are constantly being redefined. The designations I attribute here, then, should not be read as the ultimate statement on transsexual and transgendered lives, but rather as a clear delineation of the referents invoked by my use of these terms throughout this book.

2.  I have no intentions of erasing the specificity of transsexuals, but as a kind of shorthand, I use "transgendered people" throughout the book, despite the fact that where I live and work in Québec, the term "transgender" does not exist in French. I use the term to refer to male-to-female transsexuals, female-to-male transsexuals, transsexuals who are not interested in genital surgery, drag queens, transgenderists, people who take hormones and who may live in a gender other than the one assigned to them at birth, females who live as men, cross-dressers, and other individuals who live outside normative sex/gender relations. I am increasingly uneasy with an Anglo-American use of the term "transgender" to the extent that it ignores transsexual individuals. For this reason, I employ two strategies: (1) I refer to transsexuals and transvestites, but with the understanding that my use of the term "transsexual" denotes individuals who change their bodies in some way (for example, through the use of hormones but not necessarily through genital surgery). Used in this way, the phrase "transsexuals and transvestites" is a direct translation of the French terms "les personnes transsexuelles et travesties." (2) I specify "transsexual and transgendered people" [TS/TG people] throughout this book. (Some activists suggest using the term "trans-" as one strategy of inclusive language.) This question will be discussed further in chapter 3.

3.  I am a male-to-female transsexual. That being said, I am not interested in situating myself personally within this book. There are a variety of reasons to justify my position. First, autobiography is the only discourse in which transsexuals are permitted to speak. An academic text on transsexuality and the institutional world that does not address the transsexual author's persona history, then, is a critical intervention in the existing knowledge paradigm. Moreover, I do not endorse the position common in Anglo-American milieux that knowledge can only be founded on experience. If the information in this book is judged to be productive and useful, or limited and of questionable value, I believe that this derives from the process through which the knowledge was gathered, interpreted, and analyzed, not as a result of my own personal history. While I do believe my own transsexual identity

and access to the field is an important issue, this subject remains an avenue
for future research.

## Notes to Chapter 1

1. For some of the central texts in queer theory, see Judith Butler, *Gender
   Trouble: Feminism and the Subversion of Identity* (New York: Routledge, 1990);
   Butler, "Performative Speech Acts and Gender Constitution: An Essay in Phe-
   nomenology and Feminist Theory," *Performing Feminisms: Feminist Critical
   Theory and Practice,* ed. Sue Ellen Case (Baltimore: John Hopkins University
   Press, 1991), 270–82; Butler, *Bodies That Matter: On the Discursive Limits of
   "Sex"* (New York: Routledge, 1993); Marjorie Garber, *Vested Interests: Cross-
   Dressing and Cultural Anxiety* (New York: Routledge, 1992); Carole-Anne
   Tyler, "Boys Will be Girls: The Politics of Gay Drag," in *Inside/Out: Lesbian
   Theories, Gay Theories,* ed. Diana Fuss (New York: Routledge, 1991), 32–70;
   Michael Moon and Eve Sedgwick, "Divinity: A Performance Piece. A Dossier.
   A Little-Understood Emotion," *Discourse* 13, no. 1 (fall–winter 1990–1991):
   12–39.
2. An examination of the placement (and often, refusal) of male-to-female transsexuals within women's shelters is available in Mirha-Soleil Ross, "Investigating Women's Shelters," *Gendertrash* 3 (winter 1995): 7–10. This issue is further discussed in chapter 7.
3. Butler, *Gender Trouble,* 130, emphasis in original.
4. Within the context of Montréal, the exclusion of male-to-female transsexuals
   and transgendered people within gay male bars dates back further than the
   late 1980s. See Bernard Courte and Jean-Michel Sivry, "Les espaces du cuir,"
   *Le Berdache* 16 (December 1980–January 1981): 29–30.
5. For an investigation of the gendered construction of gay male sexuality, see
   Seymour Kleinberg, "The New Masculinity of Gay Men, and Beyond," in *Beyond Patriarchy: Essays by Men on Pleasure, Power, and Change,* ed. Michael
   Kaufman (Toronto: Oxford University Press, 1987), 120–38.
6. Moon and Sedgwick, "Divinity," 19.
7. I discuss these events in more detail in Ki Namaste, "Fighting Back with Fashion: Pride Day Perversions and the Tyranny of the Homogeneous," *Fuse* 16,
   no. 2 (fall 1992): 7–9.
8. One bisexual transgendered political speaker scheduled to talk at Divers/Cité
   in 1994 was eliminated due to "time constraints." Numerous lesbian and gay
   political speakers, however, addressed the crowd that day.
9. Interview with author, October 12, 1994.
10. Historical research on these questions reveals that while gender transgressions
    on the stage were often tolerated, this acceptance rarely extended to individu-
    als who cross-dressed in everyday public space. See, for instance, George
    Chauncey Jr.'s discussion of a straight-identified navy man who was arrested
    for being involved with a female impersonator in "Christian Brotherhood or

Sexual Perversion? Homosexual Identities and the Construction of Sexual Boundaries in the World War I Era," in *Hidden from History: Reclaiming the Gay and Lesbian Past,* ed. Martin Duberman, Martha Vicinus, and George Chauncey Jr. (New York: New American Library, 1989), 294–317. As his defense, the man claimed that he did not find his partner to be "peculiar" (i.e., queer) since his partner wore "women's" clothes for his stage role. Chauncey points out that, in some instances, the impersonation of femininity on the stage was permissible, even to the extent that some of the female impersonators wore "women's" clothes in their everyday lives. Also see Chauncey's discussion of drag cultures in pre–World War I New York, in which he demonstrates that drag balls provided a socially acceptable occasion to cross-dress. Chauncey, *Gay New York: Gender, Urban Culture, and the Making of the Gay Male World, 1890–1940* (New York: Basic Books, 1994), 298. Vern Bullough and Bonnie Bullough demonstrate that cross-dressing was sanctioned and even encouraged during certain seasonal celebrations and festivities—an acceptance that can be witnessed in the contemporary celebration of Halloween. Bullough and Bullough, *Cross-Dressing, Sex, and Gender* (Philadelphia: University of Pennsylvania Press, 1993), 66, 75. For an examination of performance drag, see Sara Maitland, *Vesta Tilly* (London: Virago Press, 1986). For a more detailed study of cross-dressing on stage in the British context, see J. S. Bratton, "Irrational Dress," *The New Woman and Her Sisters: Feminism and Theatre 1850–1914,* ed. Vivien Gardner and Susan Rutherford (Ann Arbor: University of Michigan Press, 1992), 77–91. The legal restrictions on transvestism are also discussed in Rudolf Dekker and Lotte van de Pol, *The Tradition of Female Transvestism in Early Modern Europe* (New York: St. Martin's Press, 1989).

11. Butler, *Bodies That Matter,* 131.
12. It is significant that Butler refers to Extravaganza throughout her manuscript by her first name—"Venus." This appellation suggests either a familiarity with Extravaganza and other Latina transsexual prostitutes, or reduces her to a mere character in a movie (rather than a living person in a documentary). A decision to name Extravaganza "Venus" is particularly ironic given Butler's own objections to being called "Judy" when an individual asked, "What about the materiality of the body, Judy?": "I take it that the addition of 'Judy' was an effort to dislodge me from the more formal 'Judith' and to recall me to a bodily life that could not be theorized away. There was a certain exasperation in the delivery of that final diminutive, a certain patronizing quality which (re)constituted me as an unruly child, one who needed to be brought to task" (Butler, *Bodies That Matter,* ix). Although Butler objects to the appellations that do not invoke her formal name (appellations generally required in an academic context), she does not extend the same courtesy to Extravaganza. The semantic organization of Butler's discourse reinforces the absolute disrespect and erasure of transsexual prostitutes' lives that pervades her discussion of *Paris Is Burning.* Following academic conventions of citing individuals in documentaries, I will refer to Venus Extravaganza as "Extravaganza."

13. Butler, *Bodies That Matter*, 131.
14. For a discussion of how the city of Houston's cross-dressing ordinance was revoked, see Phyllis Frye, "Repeal of the Houston Crossdressing Ordinance," *Proceedings from the First International Conference on Transgendered Law and Employment Policy* (Houston, Tex.: International Conference on Transgender Law and Employment Policy, 1992), 104–7. See also Mary Dunlap, "The Constitutional Rights of Sexual Minorities: A Crisis of the Male-Female Dichotomy," *Hastings Law Journal* 30 (March 1979): 1132–49. My thanks to Judith Marshall for the latter reference.
15. Ibid., 17.
16. Ibid., 116.
17. Ibid., 57.
18. For a discussion of DeAundra Peek, see Gabriel Gomez, "DQTV: Public Access Queers," *Fuse* 17, no. 1 (fall 1993): 8–10. The video work of Vaginal Creme Davis is presented in Matias Viegener, "'The Only Haircut That Makes Sense Anymore': Queer Subculture and Gay Resistance," in *Queer Looks: Lesbian and Gay Perspectives on Film and Video*, ed. Martha Gever, John Greyson, and Pratibha Parmar (New York: Routledge, 1993), 116–33. For a useful summary of Joan Jett Blakk's activities, consult Joe Jeffreys, "Joan Jett Blakk for President: Cross-Dressing at the Democratic National Convention," *Drama Review* 37, no. 3 (fall 1993): 186–95.
19. For a more developed critique of Tyler's essay, see Michael du Plessis, "Queer Pasts Now: Historical Fiction in Lesbian, Bisexual, Transgender, and Gay Film," Ph.D. diss., University of Southern California, 1993. Du Plessis emphasizes the ways in which Tyler's analysis lacks historical and cultural specificity.
20. For a useful introduction to poststructuralism, see Pauline Rosenau, *Post-Modernism and the Social Sciences: Insights, Inroads, and Intrusions* (Princeton, N.J.: Princeton University Press, 1992).
21. René Descartes, *Oeuvres philosophiques* (Paris: Garnier, 1963).
22. Michel Foucault, *L'Histoire de la sexualité*, vol. 1, *La volonté de savoir* (Paris: Gallimard, 1976) [translated to English by Robert Hurley under the title *The History of Sexuality, volume 1, An Introduction* (New York: Random House, 1978)], 134 [15].
23. Foucault, *La volonté de savoir*, 134; Foucault, *The History of Sexuality*, 101.
24. Here, Derrida is drawing on the semiotic concept of value, in which the meaning of a term can only be generated and interpreted with regard to that which it is not. In more theoretical terms, value is only secured through difference. For more on these theoretical issues, see Derrida's discussion of the Swiss linguist Ferdinand de Saussure in *De la grammatologie* (Paris: Éditions de Minuit, 1967), 42–108. Also see de Saussure, *Cours de linguistique générale* (Paris: Payot, 1972 [1913]).
25. Derrida, *De la grammatologie*.
26. Derrida, *La dissémination* (Paris: Éditions du Seuil, 1972).
27. For Derrida's work on the concept of invagination, see "La loi du genre," *Glyph* 8 (1980): 176–201. For an interesting reading of this use of a feminine

metaphor in Derrida, see Gayatri Chakavorty Spivak, "Displacement and the Discourse of Woman," in *Displacement: Derrida and After,* ed. Mark Krupnick (Bloomington: Indiana University Press, 1983): 169–95.

28. Derrida, *L'Écriture et la différence* (Paris: Éditions du Seuil, 1967).

29. Derrida, "Limited Inc. abc," Glyph 2 (1977): 162–254.

30. Claude Lévi-Strauss, *Tristes tropiques* (Paris: Plon, 1955).

31. Derrida, *De la grammatologie,* 157–73. Derrida's critique of Lévi-Strauss is also evident in "La structure, le signe et le jeu dans le discours des sciences humaines," *L'Écriture et la différence,* 409–28.

32. For more on the historical emergence of queer theory, see Jeffrey Escoffier, "Inside the Ivory Closet: The Challenges Facing Lesbian and Gay Studies," *OUT/LOOK* 10 (fall 1990): 40–48; Michael Warner, "Introduction: Fear of a Queer Planet," *Social Text* 29 (1991): 3–19; and Steven Seidman, "Symposium: Queer Theory/Sociology: A Dialogue," *Sociological Theory* 12, no. 2 (July 1994): 166–77.

33. Fuss, "Inside/Out," in *Inside/Out: Lesbian Theories, Gay Theories,* ed. Diana Fuss (New York: Routledge, 1991), 1–10.

34. Garber, *Vested Interests,* 17.

35. Butler, "Imitation and Gender Insubordination," in *Inside/Out: Lesbian Theories, Gay Theories,* ed. Diana Fuss (New York: Routledge, 1991), 13–31.

36. Escoffier, "Inside the Ivory Closet"; Seidman, "Symposium"; and Warner, "Fear of a Queer Planet."

37. Lorna Weir, "Preliminary Observations on the Relations between Queer Theory and Social Sciences," presentation at Queer Sites: Bodies at Work, Bodies at Play, University of Toronto, May 13, 1993.

38. The neglect of social relations within the field of queer theory is amply illustrated in a recent anthology: *Queer Theory/Sociology,* ed. Steven Seidman (Cambridge, Mass.: Blackwell, 1996).

39. Butler, *Bodies That Matter,* 132.

40. For a more developed argument on the centrality of a transgendered trope to the field of queer theory, see Jay Prosser, *Second Skins: The Body Narratives of Transsexuality* (New York: Columbia University Press, 1998), 21–60.

41. This argument has been most forcefully made by Donald Morton, "The Politics of Queer Theory in the (Post)Modern Moment," *Genders* 17 (1993): 121–50.

42. On the formulaic application of deconstruction in the Anglo-American university, see Vincent Leitch, *Deconstructive Criticism: An Advanced Introduction* (New York: Columbia University Press, 1983), 262.

## NOTES TO CHAPTER 2

1. Harold Garfinkel, *Studies in Ethnomethodology* (Englewood Cliffs, N.J.: Prentice-Hall, 1967).

2. Suzanne Kessler and Wendy McKenna, *Gender: An Ethnomethodological Approach* (New York: John Wiley and Sons, 1978).

3. Suzanne Kessler, "The Medical Construction of Gender: Case Management of

Inter-Sexed Infants," *Signs* 16, no. 1 (1990): 3–26. Also see Deborah Findlay, "Discovering Sex: Medical Science, Feminism and Intersexuality," *Canadian Review of Sociology and Anthropology* 32, no. 1 (February 1995): 25–52.

4. Esther Newton, *Mother Camp: Female Impersonators in America* (Englewood Cliffs, NJ: Prentice-Hall, 1972). See also Colette Piat, *Elles . . . "les Travestis": La vérité sur les transsexuels* (Paris: Presses de la Cité, 1978).

5. Newton, *Mother Camp,* 41–58.

6. Ibid., 45.

7. Ibid., 51.

8. For an introduction to ethnography, see David Fetterman, *Ethnography: Step by Step* (London: Sage, 1989); and James Spradley, *The Ethnographic Interview* (New York: Holt, Rinehart and Winston, 1979). For contemporary debates on ethnography, see Margery Wolf, *A Thrice-Told Tale: Feminism, Postmodernism, and Ethnographic Responsibility* (Stanford, Calif.: Stanford University Press, 1992); and Martin Hammersley, *What's Wrong with Ethnography? Methodological Explorations* (New York: Routledge, 1992).

9. Anne Bolin, "Transcending and Transgendering: Male-to-Female Transsexuals, Dichotomy, and Diversity," in *Third Sex, Third Gender: Beyond Sexual Dimorphism in Culture and History,* ed. Gilbert Herdt (New York: Zone Books, 1994), 213–39; and Bolin, *In Search of Eve: Transsexual Rites of Passage* (South Hadley, Mass.: Bergin and Garvey, 1988).

10. Bolin, "Transcending and Transgendering," 460. For a similar argument, see Deborah Feinbloom, Michael Fleming, Valerie Kijewski, and Margo Schulter, "Lesbian/Feminist Orientation among Male-to-Female Transsexuals," *Journal of Homosexuality* 2, no. 1 (fall 1976): 59–71. Also note the work of Eli Coleman, Walter Bockting, and Louis Gooren, "Homosexual and Bisexual Identity in Sex-Reassigned Female-to-Male Transsexuals," *Archives of Sexual Behavior* 22, no. 1 (1993): 37–50; and Holly Devor, "Sexual Orientation Identities, Attractions, and Practices of Female-to-Male Transsexuals," *Journal of Sex Research* 30, no. 4 (November 1993): 303–15.

11. Bolin, "Transcending and Transgendering," 461.

12. Although Bolin is writing as an anthropologist, one can imagine similar critical work located outside this discipline. For instance, Sandy Stone elaborates a politics of "posttranssexuality," which displaces traditional definitions of transsexualism. Stone, "The *Empire* Strikes Back: A Posttranssexual Manifesto," in *Body Guards: The Cultural Politics of Gender Ambiguity,* ed. Julia Epstein and Kristina Straub (New York: Routledge, 1991), 281–304.

13. One of the most common oppositions to transsexualism (usually expressed under the banner of "feminism") is the assumption that it reinforces sexist stereotypes. The sociological literature that advances this position is discussed later in this chapter.

14. Bolin, "Transcending and Transgendering," 462.

15. Ibid., 478–82.

16. Bullough and Bullough, *Cross Dressing, Sex, and Gender* (Philadelphia: University of Pennsylvania Press, 1993).

17. Ibid., 203–23. See also Gert Hemka, "'A Female Soul in a Male Body': Sexual Inversion as Gender Inversion in Nineteenth-Century Sexology," in *Third Sex, Third Gender,* 213–39.

18. Magnus Hirschfeld, *The Transvestite: An Investigation of the Erotic Desire to Cross-Dress,* trans. Michael Lombardi (Buffalo, N.Y.: Prometheus Books, 1991 [1910]).

19. Bullough and Bullough, *Cross Dressing, Sex, and Gender;* and Ines Orobio de Castro, *Made To Order: Sex/Gender in a Transsexual Perspective* (Amsterdam: Het Spinhuis, 1993).

20. Bolin, *In Search of Eve;* Bolin, "Transcending and Transgendering."

21. For an introduction to conversation analysis, see D. Silverman, *Interpreting Qualitative Data: Methods for Analyzing Talk, Text, and Interaction* (Newbury Park: Sage, 1993); D. Watson, "Ethnomethodology, Conversation Analysis and Education: An Overview," *International Review of Education* 38, no. 2 (1992): 257–74; and Paul Drew, "Conversation Analysis: Who Needs It?" *Text* 10, nos. 1–2 (1990): 127–35.

22. Brian Fay, *Social Theory and Political Practice* (London: Allen and Unwin, 1975), 92–111.

23. Ibid., 110.

24. Seidman, "The End of Sociological Theory: The Postmodern Hope," *Sociological Theory* 9, no. 2 (fall 1991): 131.

25. Leon Pettiway, *Honey, Honey, Miss Thang: Being Black, Gay, and On the Street* (Philadelphia: Temple University Press, 1996).

26. Ibid., xl.

27. Ibid., xxiv.

28. Pettiway's reference to prostitution as "sex work" is immediately undermined in this phrase, when he writes that these individuals "commit sex work." The connotations of the term "commit," of course, imply that prostitution is a criminal offense. By qualifying these activities with the word "commit," Pettiway does not view prostitution as a form of work. (Presumably, he would not state that university professors "commit" lectures.)

29. For research that frames prostitution as work rather than a crime, see Frances Shaver, "The Regulation of Prostitution: Avoiding the Morality Trap," *Canadian Journal of Law and Society* 9 (spring 1994): 123–45. For an analysis of drug use as a health issue, as opposed to a criminal one, see Alex Wodak and Peter Lurie, "A Tale of Two Countries: Attempts to Control HIV among Injecting Drug Users in Australia and the United States," *Journal of Drug Issues* 27, no. 1 (1996): 117–34.

30. Pettiway, *Honey, Honey,* xxx.

31. Nowhere in the introduction does Pettiway even acknowledge that transgendered people may read his book. At one point, he goes so far as to state: "In the end we can feel fortunate that our lives are by comparison ordinary and mundane" (xli). This use of the pronoun "we" and the possessive pronoun "our" assumes that the researcher and the readers are not poor, transgendered, or prostitutes.

32. The issue of access to hormones is addressed in greater detail in chapter 7.
33. On the systemic discrimination TS/TG prostitutes experience with respect to social services, see Mirha-Soleil Ross, "Investigating Women's Shelters," *Gendertrash* 3 (1995): 7–10; Christine Tayleur, "Racism and Poverty in the Transgender Community," *Gendertrash* 4 (1995): 17–20; and Ki Namaste, "Access Denied: A Report on the Experiences of Transsexuals and Transgenderists with Health Care and Social Services in Ontario" (Toronto: Project Affirmation, 1995). Report available from the Coalition for Lesbian and Gay Rights in Ontario, P.O. Box 822, Station A, Toronto, Ontario, M5W 1G3, Canada, (416) 533–6842. This question is explored in greater detail in chapters 7 and 8.
34. Richard Ekins, *Male Femaling: A Grounded Approach to Cross-Dressing and Sex-Changing* (London: Routledge, 1997).
35. Ibid., 71–85.
36. Ibid., 166.
37. Jeanne B. in *Whore Carnival*, ed. Shannon Bell (Brooklyn: Autonomedia, 1995): 141.
38. For an engaged and respectful inquiry concerning how FTM transsexuals perceive their identities and bodies, see Henry Rubin, "Phenomenology as Method in Trans Studies," *GLQ: A Journal of Lesbian and Gay Studies* 4, no. 2 (1998): 263–81. See also Rubin, *Always-Already Men: Female to Male Transsexual Subjectivity and Embodiment* (University of Chicago Press, forthcoming).
39. Glaser and Strauss, *The Discovery of Grounded Theory: Strategies for Qualitative Research* (Chicago: Aldine Press, 1967).
40. Pettiway, *Honey, Honey*, xxx.
41. Janice Raymond, *The Transsexual Empire: The Making of the She-Male* (Boston: Beacon, 1979).
42. Dwight Billings and Thomas Urban, "The Socio-Medical Construction of Transsexualism: An Interpretation and Critique," *Social Problems* 29, no. 3 (February 1982): 266, emphasis in original. Interestingly, in a reprinted version of the essay, the term "only" has not been italicized. See Billings and Urban, "The Socio-Medical Construction of Transsexualism: An Interpretation and Critique," in *Blending Genders: Social Aspects of Cross-dressing and Sex-changing*, ed. Richard Ekins and Dave King (London: Routledge, 1996), 99.
43. Billings and Urban, "The Socio-Medical Construction of Transsexualism," 273.
44. Ibid., 272.
45. Raymond, *The Transsexual Empire*, 116; Billings and Urban, "The Socio-Medical Construction of Transsexualism," 273.
46. Billings and Urban, "The Socio-Medical Construction of Transsexualism," 273.
47. Bernice Hausman, *Changing Sex: Transsexualism, Technology, and the Idea of Gender* (Durham, N.C.: Duke University Press, 1995): xi.
48. Hausman, *Changing Sex*, 140.
49. Raymond, *The Transsexual Empire*, 178.
50. Fay, *Social Theory and Political Practice*, 31.
51. Ibid., 47.
52. Billings and Urban, "The Socio-Medical Construction of Transsexualism," 277.

53. See Christine Burnham with Patricia Diewold, *Gender Change: Employability Issues* (Vancouver: Perceptions Press, 1994); and Viviane K. Namaste, "Évaluation des besoins: Les travesti(e)s et les transsexuel(le)s au Québec à l'égard du VIH/Sida" (Montréal: report submitted to the Centre Québécois de Coordination sur le Sida, May 1998). Available from CACTUS, 1626 rue Saint-Hubert, Montréal, Québec, Canada, H2L 3Z3.

54. A nice critique of Billings and Urban is available in Dave King, *The Transvestite and the Transsexual: Public Categories and Private Identities* (Brookfield, Vt.: Avebury, 1993), 49–50, 185–90.

55. Fay, *Social Theory and Political Practice*, 97, 101.

56. See Rubin's excellent critique of Hausman in "Phenomenology as Method in Trans Studies," *GLQ: A Journal of Lesbian and Gay Studies* 4, no. 2 (1998): 264–66.

## Notes to Chapter 3

1. The relevance of poststructuralism and a micrological/macrological juncture is cogently argued in Paul Thibault, *Social Semiotics as Praxis: Text, Meaning-Making, and Nabokov's Ada* (Minneapolis: University of Minnesota Press, 1991).

2. For more on the relevance of a micrological/macrological distinction within social theory, see Ian Craib, *Modern Social Theory: From Parsons to Habermas* (New York: St. Martin's Press, 1984).

3. Dorothy Smith, *The Everyday World as Problematic: A Feminist Sociology* (Toronto: University of Toronto Press, 1987); and Marie L. Campbell and Ann Manicom, eds., *Knowledge, Experience, and Ruling Relations: Studies in the Social Organization of Knowledge* (Toronto: University of Toronto Press, 1995).

4. Brian Fay, *Social Theory and Political Practice* (London: Allen and Unwin, 1975).

5. Mirha-Soleil Ross, "Reaching Out to the Unreachable: An Interview with Diane Gobeil from CACTUS Montréal," *Gendertrash* 4 (spring 1995): 11–16.

6. Catherine Hankins, letter to Diane Gobeil, October 30, 1996. The Montréal needle exchange CACTUS (Centre d'action communautaire auprés des toxicomanes utliisateurs de seringues) uses the categories of "Homme," "femme," and "autre" to collect demographic data on its clients. See Catherine Hankins, Sylvie Gendron, Thang Tran, "CACTUS-MONTRÉAL: Profil comportemental de la clientèle et prévalence de l'infection par le VIH, 1 octobre 1994–7 février 1995, rapport numéro 6" (Montréal: Direction de la santé publique, 1995).

7. Hankins, letter to Diane Gobeil, October 30, 1996.

8. P. Gattari, L. Spizzichino, C. Valenzi, M. Zaccarelli, and G. Reeza, "Behavioural Patterns and HIV Infection among Drug Using Transvestites Practising Prostitution in Rome," *AIDS Care* 4, no. 1 (1992): 83–87.

9. Public Health in Montréal recently has begun consulting transsexuals concerning these administrative categories.

10. Ellen Faulkner (edited by Karen Baldwin and Deborah Hierlihy), *Anti-Gay/ Lesbian Violence in Toronto: The Impact on Individuals and Communities* (Ottawa: Department of Justice, Research and Statistics Division, Policy Sector, 1997), 13.

11. In her extensive bibliography, Dallas Denny notes the clinical bias of the literature on transgendered people: *Gender Dysphoria: A Guide to Research* (New York: Garland, 1994). I discuss this issue in more detail in chapter 6.

12. But see, for instance, Christine Burnham, in consultation with Patricia Diewold, *Gender Change: Employability Issues* (Vancouver: Perceptions Press, 1994).

13. Ross, "Reaching Out to the Unreachable," 14–15.

14. D. Smith, *The Everyday World as Problematic.*

15. George Smith, "Political Activist as Ethnographer," *Social Problems* 37, no. 4 (November 1990): 629–48; and "Accessing Treatments: Managing the AIDS Epidemic in Ontario," in Campbell and Manicom, *Knowledge, Experience, and Ruling Relations* 18–34.

16. D. Smith, *The Everyday World as Problematic,* 173.

17. O'Brien, "The Social Organization of the Treatment of Lesbian and Gay Youth in Group Homes and Youth Shelters" (master's independent inquiry project, Carleton University, Ottawa, May 1992), 2. Also see O'Brien, "The Social Organization of the Treatment of Lesbian, Gay and Bisexual Youth in Group Homes and Youth Shelters," *Canadian Review of Social Policy* 34 (winter 1994): 37–57.

18. Roxana Ng, *The Politics of Community Services: Immigrant Women, Class, and the State* (Toronto: Garamond, 1988), 11.

19. Ibid., 85.

20. G. Smith, "Political Activist as Ethnographer," 639.

21. Campbell and Manicom, introduction to *Knowledge, Experience, and Ruling Relations,* 7–8.

22. Joan Scott, "Experience," in *Feminists Theorize the Political,* ed. Butler and Joan Scott (New York: Routledge, 1992), 22–40.

23. For an example of this argument, see Christina Crosby, "Dealing with Differences," in ibid., 130–43.

24. Fay, *Social Theory and Political Practice,* 98–110.

25. Campbell and Manicom, introduction to *Knowledge, Experience, and Ruling Relations,* 8–9.

26. See, for instance, Bryan Palmer's *Descent Into Discourse: The Reification of Language and the Writing of Social History* (Philadelphia: Temple University Press, 1990).

27. D. Smith, *The Everyday World as Problematic,* 17.

28. Rubin astutely challenges the extent to which Hausman theorizes transsexuals as produced by medical and psychiatric discourse in "Phenomenology as Method in Trans Studies," *GLQ: A Journal of Lesbian and Gay Studies* 4, no. 2 (1998): 264–66. For a more general overview of these theoretical difficulties in the context of poststructuralism in the social sciences, see Pauline Rosenau,

*Postmodernism and the Social Sciences: Insights, Inroads, Intrusions* (Princeton, N.J.: Princeton University Press, 1992).

29. See Peter Berger and Thomas Luckmann, *The Social Construction of Reality: A Treatise in the Sociology of Knowledge* (New York: Anchor Books, 1967).

30. Unlike much of the research on transsexuals and transgendered people concerned with identity, Henry Rubin's phenomenological research offers an important methodological intervention concerning identity as it is lived, experienced, and interpreted by transsexual and transgendered people. See "Phenomenology as Method in Trans Studies" and *Always-Already Men: Female to Male Transsexual Subjectivity and Embodiment* (forthcoming, University of Chicago Press).

31. The historical emergence of transsexuals and transgendered people is presented in a variety of sources: Pat Califia, *Sex Changes: The Politics of Transgenderism* (San Francisco: Cleis Press, 1997), 52–85; Hausman, *Changing Sex*, 110–140; Raymond, *Transsexual Empire;* Bullough and Bullough, *Cross Dressing, Sex, and Gender*, 203–23; and King, *The Transvestite and the Transsexual*, 34–68.

32. In a recent article, Judith Halberstam draws such a parallel: "We are at present in the midst of a Foucauldian 'reverse discourse' on transsexuality and transgenderism." "Transgender Butch: Butch/FTM Border Wars and the Masculine Continuum," *GLQ: A Journal of Gay and Lesbian Studies* 4, no. 2 (1998): 301.

33. Sandy Stone similarly points out that in a psychiatric context, transsexuals must define themselves as "women" or "men," remarking that "it is difficult to generate a counterdiscourse if one is programmed to disappear." Stone, "The Empire Strikes Back: A Posttranssexual Manifesto," in *Body Guards: The Cultural Politics of Gender Ambiguity*, ed. Julia Epstein and Kristina Straub (New York: Routledge, 1991), 295.

34. Interestingly, recent bisexual theory has also made the argument that critical inquiry needs to understand precisely how bisexual identities, bodies, and practices are inscribed as *impossible*, a move that requires a theoretical perspective other than that of lesbian and gay theory. See *RePresenting Bisexualities: Subjects and Cultures of Fluid Desire*, ed. Donald Hall and Maria Pramaggiore (New York: New York University Press, 1996).

35. Michel Foucault, *L'Archéologie du savoir* (Paris: Gallimard, 1969).

36. It is significant that I appeal to Foucault's earlier work elaborated in *L'Archéologie du savoir*. Indeed, I am not the only transsexual scholar to do so. Henry Rubin refers to Foucault's *Les mots et les choses: Une archéologie des sciences humaines* in his research on FTM transsexuals. In fact, a critical reading of Foucault's early work avoids a formulaic application of his ideas elaborated in *L'Histoire de la sexualité*. This is especially significant given the central role *L'histoire de la sexualité* plays in Anglo-American lesbian and gay studies. By not referring to this text, scholars avoid the mistake of metonymically associating transsexuals with lesbians and gay men, as well as the unspoken assumption that lesbian/gay theories are appropriate for making sense of transsexual bodies and lives. More radically, a return to Foucault's early corpus

represents an engagement with the shift in his ideas from phenomenology to discourse analysis. Given the complete and utter obliteration of transsexual identity in the current English-language scholarship, an appeal to a theoretical framework that does not nullify how transsexuals experience their bodies and the social world is warranted. For more on this shift from phenomenology to discourse analysis (and later, genealogy) in Foucault, see M. Hannah, "Foucault on Theorizing Specificity," *Environment and Planning D; Society and Space* 11 (1993): 349–63. See also Rudi Visker, *Genealogie als kritiek: Michel Foucault* (Munich: Wilhelm Fink Verlag, 1991); and Manfred Frank, *Was ist Neostruckturalismus?* (Frankfurt-am-Main: Suhrkamp Verlag, 1984).

37. Thibault, *Social Semiotics as Praxis.*
38. On this issue, see Margaret Deidre O'Hartigan's excellent pamphlet "'Transgender' as Borg" (February 1997; available from P.O. Box 82447, Portland, OR 97282). Previously published as "Are You Transgender?" *Bay Area Reporter* 27, no. 9 (February 27, 1997): 6; and "Assimilate or Die? The Transgender as Borg," *San Diego Update* (February 19, 1997): A19–20. O'Hartigan pointed out to me that transsexual objections to the use of the term "transgender" are not a recent phenomenon and date back to the mid-1970s in the context of the United States. O'Hartigan, letter to the author, August 1, 1998.
39. Teresa de Lauretis, "Gender Symptoms, or, Peeing Like a Man," *Social Semiotics* 9, no. 2 (August 1999): 261.
40. Cited in O'Hartigan, "'Transgender' as Borg," 2.
41. Ibid., 3.
42. Max Valerio, "Speaking Truth—Sade, Leslie Feinberg and David Harrison," *Transsexual News Telegraph* 7 (summer 1997): 40–3.
43. Ross, "Review of *Transgender Warriors*," *Siren* 1, no. 5 (December 1996–January 1997): 20–21.
44. The intertext here is Monique Wittig's famous declaration that the discourses of heterosexuality prevent lesbians and gay men from speaking unless they express themselves in heterosexist terms. See Wittig, "The Straight Mind," trans. Mary Jo Lakeland and Susan Ellis Wolf, *Feminist Issues* 1, no. 1 (1980): 103–11.
45. Rubin, "Phenomenology as Method in Trans Studies," 263–81.
46. Ibid., 276.
47. Ibid.
48. Halberstam, "Transgender Butch," 287–310.
49. Ibid., 306–7.
50. Khartini Slamah, "Developing Effective HIV/AIDS Programs for Transsexuals Working as Sex Workers," presentation at the XI International Conference on AIDS, Vancouver, July 1996; Helen, "Police Entrapment," *ON TOP* [Ongoing Network—Transsexual Outreach Project] 1 (1992): np. (The Transsexual Sex Industry Workers' newsletter, TOP, is available from P.O. Box 11-412, Manners Street, Wellington, New Zealand, or P.O. Box 68-509, Newton, Auckland, New Zealand.)
51. Bornstein, *Gender Outlaw: On Men, Women, and the Rest of Us* (New York:

Routledge, 1994); Wilchins, *Read My Lips: Sexual Subversion and the End of Gender* (Ithaca, N.Y.: Firebrand, 1997); and Feinberg, *Transgender Warriors: Making History from Joan of Arc to RuPaul* (Boston: Beacon, 1996).

52. Margaret Deirdre O'Hartigan makes the important point that Bornstein, Wilchins, and Feinberg all share the same lesbian publicist and are frequently booked to speak to lesbian audiences. Her analysis is especially insightful because it underlines the institutional aspects of discourse; what circulates in the media is directly connected to specific social and institutional relations. See O'Hartigan, "Our Bodies, Your Lies: The Lesbian Colonization of Transsexualism" (December 1997), 7. (This pamphlet is available from Margaret Deidre O'Hartigan, P.O. Box 82447, Portland, OR 97282).

53. Two notable exceptions to this absence are Roberta Perkins, *The 'Drag Queen' Scene: Transsexuals in Kings Cross* (Hemel Hempstead: Allen and Unwin, 1983) and Pettiway, *Honey, Honey, Miss Thang.*

54. See, for instance, Giovanni Sciuto, *Le Petit livre rouge des: Travestis pas comme les autres: Le 4me sexe* (Evry: Éditions du Sénart, 1974); Elisabeth Salvaresi, *Travelo: Enquête sur la prostitution travestie* (Paris: Presses de la Renaissance, 1982); Colette Piat, *Elles . . . "les Travestis": La vérité sur les transsexuels* (Paris: Presses de la cité, 1978). Also see Daniel Welzer-Lang, Odette Barbosa, and Lilian Mathieu, "Prostitution et (post)-modernité: un brouillage des signes et des identités?" in Welzer-Lang, Barbosa and Mathieu, *Prostitution: Les uns, les unes, les autres* (Paris: Éditions Métailié, 1994): 174–87; and Lilian Mathieu and Daniel Welzer-Lang, "Des transgenders. Le brouillage des identités sur le marché de la prostitution," *Revue Sexologique* 2, no. 2 (1996): 170–74. The fact that transsexual and transvestite prostitutes are recognized by francophone scholars does not, however, necessarily mean that their identities and lives are respected by them. For a critical review of Welzer-Lang and Mathieu's position, see Claudette Isabelle, "Quand une proposition ne convainc pas vraiment," *Revue sexologique* 2, no. 2 (1996): 174–77. A recognition of transsexual/transvestite prostitution is equally recognized within some French-language (mainstream) media and journalism. See the dossier "Mineurs, Travestis, SIDA, Drogue: Prostitution: Tout a changé," *Le Nouvel observateur,* June 24–July 4, 1990, 4–11. Also see Hélène Hazera, "Les soeurs du boulevard," *Têtu* 35 (June 1999): 8–21.

55. Mirha-Soleil Ross, presentation at Queen's University, Kingston, Ontario, June 1998.

56. Patricia Elliot and Katrina Roen, for instance, expose some of the limitations of U.S. transgendered discourse as a framework to make sense of the lives of individuals such as Babe, a FTM transsexual from the Pacific Islands studying in New Zealand. Addressing an American transgendered discourse that is critical of individuals invested in genital reassignment surgery, they write: "it is important to ask just how relevant and fair it is to apply (predominantly white) U.S. transgenderists' arguments to this man who faces the possibility of going back to his home island and being told by Christian family members that he is a woman because that is the body God gave him, and he cannot use

the (communal) men's toilets because if he does it will become obvious to the men there that he has not got a penis." Elliot and Roen, "Transgenderism and the Question of Embodiment: Promising Queer Politics?" *GLQ: A Journal of Lesbian and Gay Studies* 4, no. 2 (1998): 250.

57. See Daniel Carrière, "L'empire transsexuel," *Le Berdache* 25 (November 1981): 50–51. Also see Collectif Androgyne meeting minutes, September 7, 1980 (available for consultation at Archives gaies du Québec, 4067 Saint-Laurent, Bureau 202, Montréal).

58. Janice Raymond, *The Transsexual Empire: The Making of the She-Male* (Boston: Beacon, 1979).

59. Guy Simoneau, director, *Plusieurs tombent en amour* (Montréal: Crépuscule, 1980).

60. See Thérèse Limoges, *La prostitution à Montréal; comment, pourquoi certaines femmes deviennent prostituées: Étude sociologique et criminologique* (Montréal: Éditions de l'homme, 1967); and Catherine Texier and Marie-Odile Vézina, *Profession, Prostituée: Rapport sur la prostitution au Québec* (Montréal: Libre Expression, 1978).

61. Catherine Hankins and Sylive Gendron, *Projet Prostitution: Rapport sur les entretiens de groupes réalisés à la maison Tanguay,* (Montréal: Centre d'études sur le sida, Unité de santé publique, Hôpital général de Montréal, May 8, 1994).

62. For more on the inclusion of MTF transsexuals within the MWMF, see Riki Ann Wilchins, "The Menace in Michigan" in *Read My Lips: Sexual Subversion and the End of Gender* (Ithaca, N.Y.: Firebrand, 1997), 109–114; and "TS Women Enter MWMF," *Gendertrash* 3 (winter 1995): 13–14.

63. Moreover, this issue has been the subject of academic research, illustrated in the sociological inquiry of Holly Devor, Monica Kendel, and Nancy Strapko. Monica Kendel, "Lesbian-Feminist Opinions about Transsexuals," presentation at Learned Societies, Canadian Sociological and Anthropological Association, Montréal, June 1995.

64. Anglo-American debates on the place of prostitutes within feminism are available in Laurie Bell, ed. *Good Girls/Bad Girls: Sex Trade Workers and Feminists Face to Face* (Toronto: Women's Press, 1987); and F. Delacoste and P. Alexander, eds., *Sex Work: Writings by Women in the Sex Industry* (San Francisco: Cleis Press, 1987).

## NOTES TO CHAPTER 4

1. Joan Scott, *Gender and the Politics of History* (New York: Columbia, 1988); Denise Riley, *"Am I That Name?" History and the Category of "Women"* (Minneapolis: University of Minnesota Press, 1989); Gayatri Spivak, *In Other Worlds: Essays in Cultural Politics* (New York: Routledge, 1988); Spivak, "Can the Subaltern Speak?" in *Marxism and the Interpretation of Culture,* ed. Cary Nelson and Lawrence Grossberg (Chicago: University of Illinois Press, 1988), 271–313.

2. Scott, *Gender and the Politics of History,* 88.

3. Ibid., 138.

4. Foucault, *L'Archéologie du savoir*, 133; *The Archaeology of Knowledge*, trans. A. M. Sheridan Smith (New York: Harper and Row, 1972), 101. (Hereafter the corresponding page numbers of Smith's translation appear in brackets.)

5. Ibid., 138 [105].

6. Ibid., 65 [47–48]. Emphasis in original.

7. A more developed discussion of the juncture between macrological and micrological relations, as well as the import of Foucault's methodology in theorizing this site, is available in Thibault, *Social Semiotics as Praxis*.

8. Yves Mallette, "Punks et skins envahissent les rues," *Photo Police!* 25, no. 5 (June 26–August 3, 1992): 16–17.

9. Corinne Sorin, "Quand les punks fréquentent les aînés," *Nouvelles Centre-Sud* 3, no. 19 (13 July 13, 1992): 1.

10. Ibid. English translation mine.

11. Foucault, *L'Archéologie du savoir*, 141 [107].

12. Ibid.

13. Ibid., 48 [65].

14. Angela McRobbie, *Feminism and Youth Culture* (London: Macmillan, 1981).

15. Joanne Gottlieb and Gayle Wald, "Smells Like Teen Spirit: Riot Grrrls, Revolution and Women in Independent Rock," in *Microphone Fiends: Youth Music and Youth Culture*, ed. Andrew Ross and Tricia Rose (New York: Routledge, 1994), 250–74.

16. Matias Viegener, "'The Only Haircut That Makes Sense Anymore': Queer Subculture and Gay Resistance," in *Queer Looks: Perspectives on Lesbian and Gay Film and Video*, ed. Martha Gever, John Greyson, and Pratibha Parmar (New York: Routledge, 1993), 116–17.

17. Viegener, "The Only Haircut," 131 n. 2.

18. The opposition put forward by Viegener is direct: punks are misogynist and homophobic, such that the emergence of "queer-punks" is both significant and innovative. Moreover, despite an appeal to drag practices to support his argument, Viegener continually collapses the diversity of "queer" identities back into a lesbian/gay framework.

19. Larry Grossberg, "Is There Rock After Punk?" *Critical Studies in Mass Communication* 3, no. 1 (1986): 50–74.

20. Jon Savage, "Tainted Love: The Influence of Male Homosexuality and Sexual Divergence on Pop Music and Culture since the War," in *Consumption, Identity, Style*, ed. A. Tomlinson (London: Comedia/Routledge, 1990), 165.

21. Ibid.

22. Jacques Attali, *Noise: The Political Economy of Music* (Minneapolis: University of Minnesota Press, 1985), 243.

23. Julie Burchill and Tony Parsons, *The Boy Looked at Johnny: The Obituary of Rock and Roll* (London: Pluto Press, 1978), 16.

24. Dick Hebdige, *Subculture: The Meaning of Style* (London: Methuen, 1979), 121, 123, 108.

25. Mike Brake, *The Sociology of Youth Culture and Youth Subculture* (London: Routledge and Kegan Paul, 1980), 81–82.

26. Burchill and Parsons, *The Boy Looked at Johnny*, 35.
27. Greil Marcus, *Lipstick Traces: A Secret History of the Twentieth Century* (Cambridge: Harvard University Press, 1989), 36, 75.
28. Burchill and Parsons, *The Boy Looked at Johnny*, 74-84.
29. Ibid., 49
30. Marcus, *Lisptick Traces*, 80.
31. Ibid., 80.
32. Brake, *Sociology of Youth Culture*, 152.
33. Burchill and Parsons, *The Boy Looked at Johnny*, 13.
34. New York Dolls, "Personality Crisis," *Lipstick Killers* (Lille, France: ROIR [Reach Out International Records], no date.)
35. Ibid.
36. T. Rex, "Rip-Off," *Electric Warrior* (Canada: Reprise Records, 1971).
37. The Sweet, "Blockbuster," *Glam Rock* (USA: Virgin Music Video, 1988 [1973]).
38. T. Rex, "Solid Gold Easy Action," *Glam Rock* (USA: Virgin Music Video, 1988 [1972]).
39. For an astute interpretation of the central role bisexuality played in glam rock, see the film *Velvet Goldmine,* written and directed by Todd Haynes, Zenith/ Killer Productions, 1998. Also note the Sweet's 1973 song "A.C.D.C.," whose lyrics include the line: "She's A.C./D.C. / She's got / Some other woman as well as me." *Desolation Boulevard* (London: Capitol Records, 1973).
40. Hebdige, *Lipstick Traces,* 25; Brake, *Sociology of Youth Culture,* 80.
41. *Horses* (USA: Arista, 1976).
42. Cited by Donny the Punk in G. B. Jones and Bruce LaBruce, "Don't Be Gay: Or, How I Learned to Stop Worrying and Fuck Punk Up the Ass," *Maximum Rock and Roll* 71 (April 1989, "Sexuality Issue"), 54.
43. Ibid.
44. Siouxie Sioux and the Banshees, "Dear Prudence," *Nocturne* (London: Polydor, 1983).
45. The Buzzcocks, "Orgasm Addict," *Singles Going Steady* (Scarborough, Ontario: A&M Records of Canada, 1977).
46. The Vibrators, *Pure Mania* (London: CBS Records, 1977).
47. Jones and LaBruce, "Don't Be Gay," 53.
48. "The Dicks [interview]," *Maximum Rock and Roll* 6 (May-June 1983), 14.
49. For accounts of MTF transgendered people in early punk, see Bambi Lake with Alvin Orloff, *The Unsinkable Bambi Lake: A Fairy Tale Containing the Dish on Cockettes, Punks, and Angels* (San Francisco: Manic D Press, 1996). Also see her interview in the fanzine *Tantrum* (spring 1993): 32-42.
50. Jayne County with Rupert Smith, *Man Enough To Be a Woman* (London: Serpent's Tail, 1995), 110.
51. Jon Savage, *England's Dreaming: Sex Pistols and Punk Rock* (London: Faber, 1991), 183.
52. Ibid.
53. For more information about the Club 82, see Julian Fleischer, *The Drag*

*Queens of New York: An Illustrated Field Guide* (New York: Riverhead Books, 1996). The book offers little information about the intersections of punk and transsexualism, however.

54. Clinton Heylin, *From the Velvets to the Voidoids: A Pre-Punk History for a Post-Punk World* (New York: Penguin, 1993), 188.
55. Ibid., 183.
56. Letter to the author, August 4, 1998.
57. Savage, *England's Dreaming*, 45–103.
58. Ibid.
59. Quoted in Savage, *England's Dreaming*, 259.
60. Savage, *England's Dreaming*, 260.
61. Burchill and Parsons, *The Boy Looked at Johnny*, 74; Simon Frith, *Sound Effects: Youth, Leisure, and the Politics of Rock 'n' Roll* (London: Constable, 1983), 244.
62. Charles Young, "From Altar Boys to the Dead Boys," *Rolling Stone* 253 (December 1, 1977): 20.
63. Jones and LaBruce, "Don't Be Gay." Note their argument that this move to a "basic" punk look was an effort to avoid capitalist co-optation.
64. According to comments in the fanzine *Anarcho-Homocore-Nite-Club* (Toronto: circa 1993), the "hardcore" aesthetic emerged in Washington, D.C. and in Southern California in the early 1980s.
65. Jones and LaBruce, "Don't Be Gay," 52.
66. *High School Fag* 4 (1992): 14.
67. Foucault, *L'Archéologie du savoir*, 133 [101].
68. Hebdige, *Subculture*, 121.
69. Brake, *Sociology of Youth Culture*, 81–82.
70. Hebdige, *Subculture*; Brake, *The Sociology of Youth Culture*; Burchill and Parsons, *The Boy Looked at Johnny*.
71. Viegener, "The Only Haircut," 131 n. 2.
72. Hebdige, *Subculture*.
73. Marcus, *Lipstick Traces*; Burchill and Parsons, *The Boy Looked at Johnny*.
74. Burchill and Parsons, *The Boy Looked at Johnny*, 74; Frith, *Sound Effects*, 244.
75. Foucault, *L'Archéologie du savoir*, 138 [105].
76. For an examination of the semiotic strategies employed to displace an opposition between transgendered people and punks, see Namaste, *Deconstructive Que(e)ries: Identity, Social Semiotics, and Queer-Punk Culture* (Ph.D. diss., Programme doctoral en sémiologie, Université du Québec à Montréal, 1995).

## Notes to Chapter 5

1. Mariana Valverde, "As If Subjects Existed: Analyzing Social Discourses," *Canadian Review of Sociology and Anthropology* 28, no. 2 (May 1991): 173–87.
2. Ibid., 179.
3. Ibid., 174. See her astute critique of how literary critic Jonathan Culler privileges rhetorical studies for literary language.

4. G. Lakoff and M. Johnson, *Metaphors We Live By* (Chicago: University of Chicago Press, 1980).
5. Weber's use of machine metaphors is discussed in G. Morgan, *Images of Organisation* (London: Sage, 1986). Also see F. Bealey, *Democracy in the Contemporary State* (Oxford: Clarendon, 1988); and Bryan Turner, *Max Weber: From History to Modernity* (New York, London: Routledge, 1992).
6. Jordan, *The British Administrative System: Principles versus Practice* (London: Routledge, 1994), 71–72.
7. For a specifically sociological understanding of metaphor, see Bryan Green, *Literary Methods and Sociological Theory: Case Studies of Simmel and Weber* (Chicago: University of Chicago Press, 1988). Green limits his analysis, however, to sociological theory without necessarily considering social life.
8. These five elements of rhetorical analysis, associated with Aristotle, are presented in Oswald Ducrot and Tzvetan Todorov, *Dictionnaire encyclopédique des sciences du langage* (Paris: Éditions du Seuil, 1972), 99–105.
9. Ibid.; Groupe $\mu$ [J. Dubois, F. Edeline, J. M. Klinkenberg, P. Minguet, F. Pire, H. Trinon], *Rhétorique générale* (Paris: Larousse, 1970); A. J. Greimas and J. Courtés, *Sémiotique: Dictionnaire raisonné de la théorie du langage* (Paris: Hachette, 1979); Jonathan Culler, *The Pursuit of Signs: Semiotics, Literature, Deconstruction* (Ithaca, N.Y.: Cornell University Press, 1981).
10. Max Black, *Models and Metaphors: Studies in Language and Philosophy* (Ithaca, N.Y.: Cornell University Press, 1962).
11. Ibid., 31.
12. Ibid., 35.
13. Ibid., 32–33.
14. For an introduction to catachresis in rhetorical theory, see Dumarsais, *Des tropes ou des différents sens* (Paris: Flammarion, 1988 [1730]); Pierre Fontanier, *Les figures du discours* (Paris: Flammarion, 1968 [1821]); Christine Klein-Lataud, *Précis des figures de style* (Toronto: Éditions du GREF, 1991); and Richard Lanham, *A Handlist of Rhetorical Terms* (Berkeley and Los Angeles: University of California Press, 1969).
15. Black, *Models and Metaphors,* 37.
16. Ibid.
17. Ibid., 40.
18. Ibid., 41.
19. Ibid.
20. For an ethnographic study of transsexuals and drag queens in Sydney, see the work of Roberta Perkins, *The "Drag Queen" Scene: Transsexuals in Kings Cross* (Hemel Hempstead: Allen and Unwin, 1983).
21. Monique Proulx, *Le sexe des étoiles* (Montréal: Québec/Amérique, 1987); Paule Baillargeon, director, *Le sexe des étoiles* (Montréal: Production Pierre Gendron et Jean-Roch Marcotte, 1993).
22. Proulx, *Le sexe des étoiles,* 17.
23. Ibid., 60. English translation mine.
24. Ibid., 144.

25. These comments address Proulx's novel. For a scathing critique of Baillargeon's film, see the brilliant intervention written by Mylène P. and Françoise L., "Star Wars: The Empire Strikes Back," *Gendertrash* 2, no. 1 (1993): 7–8. In particular, they contend that the decision to cast a masculine-looking man (Denis Mercier) to play the part of Marie-Pierre, rather than a woman or a transsexual, reveals the intentions of Proulx and Baillargeon to situate MTF transsexuals as cheap, ridiculous, impossible imitations of women.

26. Proulx, *Le sexe des étoiles*, 40–41. English translation mine.

27. Ibid., 123.

28. Paul Robert, *Le Petit Robert* (Paris: Le Robert, 1986), 2004.

29. Proulx, *Le sexe des étoiles*, 213–14.

30. Ibid., 213.

31. Ibid., 271–72.

32. Gilles Bibeau and Marc Perreault, *Dérives montréalaises: A travers des itinéraires de toxicomanies dans le quartier Hochelaga-Maisonneuve* (Montréal: Boréal, 1995).

33. Daniel Proulx, *Le Red Light de Montréal* (Montréal: VLB, 1997).

34. M. Proulx, *Le sexe des étoiles*, 318. English translation mine.

35. Mylène P. and Françoise L. offer insightful comments on these events, in pointing out how this metaphor relies on a conservative, reproductive model of sex and gender. As they eloquently declare, "Post-menopausal women are women, too." See "Star Wars," 8.

36. Baillargeon, quoted in Georges Privet, "L'étoile de fond," *Voir* (August 26–September 1, 1993): 9.

37. The film represents people of color within the transsexual bar in Montréal, but not within the everyday events of life in the suburbs.

38. Tremblay, *Hosanna*, translated by John van Burek and Bill Glassco (Vancouver: Talonbooks, 1974). Originally published as *Hosanna suivi de La Duchesse de Langeais* (Montréal: Leméac, 1973). Page references to the original edition appear in brackets following the English translation citations.

39. Tremblay, *Hosanna*, 9 [13].

40. See, for instance, Kenneth McRoberts and Dale Posgate, *Québec: Social Change and Political Crisis* (Toronto: McLellan and Stewart, 1980); and Denis Monière, *Le développement des idéologies au Québec: Des origines à nos jours* (Montréal: Éditions Québec/Amérique, 1977).

41. Jean-Guy Prince, "Rencontre avec Michel Tremblay," *Le Berdache* 25 (November 1981): 30. The original French text is somewhat more complex than the translation I offer here. The term "travestissement" refers to transvestism, but also to betrayal. Thus, Tremblay's collocation of "l'état de travestissement d'un pays" refers to both cross-dressing and an actual state (état) of betrayal.

42. Cited and translated by Schwartzwald, "From Authenticity to Ambivalence: Michel Tremblay's *Hosanna*," *American Review of Canadian Studies* (winter 1992): 502.

43. Ibid., 499–510; and Schwartzwald, " 'Symbolic' Homosexuality, 'False Feminine,' and the Problematics of Identity in Québec," in *Fear of a Queer Planet:*

*Queer Politics and Social Theory,* ed. Michael Warner (Minneapolis: University of Minnesota Press, 1993): 264–99; Schwartzwald, "(Homo)sexualité et problématique identitaire," in *Fictions de l'identitaire au Québec,* ed. Sherry Simon et al. (Montréal: XYZ éditeur, 1991), 117–50.

44. Tremblay, *Hosanna,* 102 [75].
45. Schwartzwald, "From Authenticity to Ambivalence," 500.
46. Ibid., 501.
47. Ibid., 507.
48. Tremblay, *Hosanna,* 60 [41].
49. The word "transgendered," of course, does not exist in French. Nor was this term commonplace in 1973, when Hosanna was written and produced.
50. Tremblay, *Hosanna,* 33 [27].
51. The name of one American transgendered magazine, for instance, is *Chrysalis.*
52. Tremblay, *Hosanna,* 39 [29].
53. Ibid., 98 [74].
54. While Tremblay clearly relies on the notion of gender inversion (not simply gay male sexuality) to advance the narrative of *Hosanna,* it is curious that scholars such as Schwartzwald have overlooked other writings that do establish a metaphorical connection between sexuality and Québec (and/or the city of Montréal). See, for instance, Stephen Schecter's novel *T'es Beau en écoeurant* (Montréal: Nouvelle Optique, 1984), in which an anglophone communist Jewish bisexual man from the ville Mont-Royal is involved with a francophone gay male anarchist from the plateau Mont-Royal.
55. Schwartzwald, "From Authenticity to Ambivalence," 500–501.
56. Schwartzwald, "'Symbolic' Homosexuality," 281.
57. Ibid.
58. André Montmorency, *De la ruelle au boulevard* (Montréal: Leméac, 1992).
59. Ibid., 171.
60. Ibid.
61. Schwartzwald, "From Authenticity to Ambivalence," 507–8.
62. For a historical analysis of Boulevard Saint-Laurent, see Aline Gubbay, *A Street Called "The Main"* (Montréal: Meridian Press, 1989). For a history of Saint-Laurent in relation to prostitution, see D. Proulx, *Le Red Light de Montréal.* Also see André Bourassa and Jean-Marc Larrue, eds., *Les nuits de la "Main": Cent ans de spectacles sur le boulevard Saint-Laurent (1891–1991)* (Montréal: VLB, 1993).
63. Tremblay, *Hosanna,* 60 [42].
64. Susan Stryker, "Renaissance and Apocalypse: Notes on the Bay Area's Transsexual Arts Scene," *Transsexual News Telegraph* 3 (summer 1994): 14–17.
65. Ibid., 15.
66. Ibid., 16.
67. Ibid.
68. Ibid.
69. Ibid.
70. Ibid.

71. Nathan Irvin Huggins, *Harlem Renaissance* (New York: Oxford University Press, 1971); Bruce Kellner, *The Harlem Renaissance: A Historical Dictionary of the Era* (Westport, Conn.: Greenwood, 1984).

72. Huggins, *Harlem Renaissance;* Kellner, *The Harlem Renaissance.*

73. For an analysis of institutionalized racism in Ontario's arts funding system, see Marlene Nourbese Philip, "The 'Multicultural' Whitewash," *Fuse* 47 (fall 1987): 13–22.

74. Stryker does remark on sex worker Christine Beatty's book *Misery Loves Company* (San Francisco: Glamazon Press, 1993), and notes that it is self-published, but she does not examine why Beatty might have been denied access to established publishing forums. Stryker, "Renaissance and Apocalypse," 15. (Beatty, *Misery Loves Company* [San Francisco: Glamazon Press, 1993], available from P.O. Box 423602, San Francisco, CA 94142.)

75. Stryker, "Renaissance and Apocalypse," 16.

76. Vincente Navarro, *The Politics of Health Policy: The U.S. Health Reforms, 1980– 1994* (Cambridge, Mass.: Basil Blackwell, 1994).

77. Leon Pettiway, *Honey, Honey, Miss Thang: Being Black, Gay, and on the Streets* (Philadelphia: Temple University Press, 1996); Christine Tayleur, "Racism and Poverty in the Transgender Community," *Gendertrash* 4 (1995): 17–20.

78. For an engaging historical analysis of how San Francisco has been ideologically positioned as a liberal city in the United States, see Nan Alamilla Boyd, "'Homos Invade S.F.!' San Francisco's History as a Wide-Open Town," in *Creating a Place for Ourselves: Lesbian, Gay, and Bisexual Community Histories,* ed. Brett Beemyn (New York: Routledge, 1997), 73–95. I read Stryker's article as a reiteration of this ideology rather than a critical exposition of its historical construction.

79. Martine Rothblatt, *The Apartheid of Sex: A Manifesto on the Freedom of Gender* (New York: Crown, 1995), xiii.

80. Steven Epstein, "Gay Politics, Ethnic Identity: The Limits of Social Constructionism," *Socialist Review* 17, nos. 3–4 (May–August 1987): 9–54. For a valuable critique of the ethnic identity model within lesbian and gay politics in the United States, see Steven Seidman, "Identity and Politics in a 'Postmodern' Gay Culture: Some Historical and Conceptual Notes," in *Fear of a Queer Planet,* ed. Warner, 105–42.

81. Michael du Plessis, "Blatantly Bisexual; Or, Unthinking Queer Theory," in *RePresenting Bisexualities: Subjects and Cultures of Fluid Desire,* ed. Donald Hall and Maria Pramaggiore (New York: New York University Press, 1996), 19–54.

82. Rothblatt, *The Apartheid of Sex,* 3.

83. Schwartzwald, "'Symbolic' Homosexuality."

84. Rothblatt, *The Apartheid of Sex,* 18.

85. Ibid., 168–69.

86. Navarro, *The Politics of Health Policy.*

87. See, for instance, Christine Tayleur, "Racism and Poverty in the Transgender Community"; Margaret Deidre O'Hartigan, "In Long Run My Sex-Change Surgery Saved Tax Dollars," *Minneapolis Star Tribune,* February 4, 1995, 17A.

Also see O'Hartigan, "G[ender] I[dentity] D[isorder] and the Greater Good," *Transsexual News Telegraph* 7 (summer 1997): 28–29; and her self-published 1996 pamphlet "A Transsexual Manifesto; The Transgender Movement's Dirty Little Secret: Just Another White Good Ol' Boy Network" (available from Margaret Deirdre O'Hartigan, P.O. Box 82447, Portland, OR 97282. Nancy Nangeroni summarizes these issues in "Are We All Crazy? The Controversy over Gender Identity Disorder: An Overview," *Transsexual News Telegraph* 7 (summer 1997): 26–27, 46. Also see James Nelson, "The Silence of the Bioethicists: Ethical and Political Aspects of Managing Gender Dysphoria," *GLQ: A Journal of Lesbian and Gay Studies* 4, no. 2 (1998): 213–30.

88. Susan Stryker, "A Taste of Our Own Medicine: The Health Law Project," *Transsexual News Telegraph* 2 (winter 1994): 14–15.

89. Ibid., 15.

90. Ibid.

91. Also see Rothblatt, "An American Perspective on Transgender Health Law," in *Transsexualism, Medicine, Law: Proceedings, XXIII Colloquy on European Law* (Strasbourg: Council of Europe, 1995): 189–202.

92. Rothblatt, *The Apartheid of Sex,* 168.

93. Rothblatt, "An American Perspective on Transgender Health Law," 200.

94. Stryker, "A Taste of Our Own Medicine," 15.

95. For a historical analysis of the concept of the individual in the context of the United States, see S. A. Marton, "Who Are 'The People'?: Gender, Citizenship, and the Making of the American Nation," *Environment and Planning D: Society and Space* 8 (1990): 449–58. Also see Gayatri Spivak, "Scattered Speculations on the Question of Culture Studies," in *Outside in the Teaching Machine* (New York: Routledge, 1993), 255–84.

96. For an excellent comparison between how the body is legally inscribed in common law versus civil law, see Robert Kouri, "Certain Legal Aspects of Modern Medecine (Sex Reassignment and Sterilization)" (Ph.D. diss., Institute of Comparative Law, McGill University, 1975).

## NOTES TO CHAPTER 6

1. The chapter limits itself to the literature on violence against lesbians and gay men, as well as a case study of antiviolence activism in Montréal. The scholarship on violence against non-transsexual women is not considered in my analysis.

2. Quoted in G. Valentine, "(Hetero)Sexing Space: Lesbian Perceptions and Experiences of Everyday Spaces," *Environment and Planning D: Society and Space* 11 (1993): 409.

3. National Gay and Lesbian Task Force, *Anti-gay/lesbian Violence, Victimization, and Defamation in 1993* (Washington, D.C.: NGLTF Policy Institute, 1994), 1.

4. Valentine, "(Hetero)Sexing Space"; Gary Comstock, *Violence Against Lesbians and Gay Men* (New York: Columbia University Press, 1991); and B. von Schultess, "Violence in the Streets: Anti-lesbian Assault and Harassment in San

Francisco," in *Hate Crimes: Confronting Violence Against Lesbians and Gay Men,* ed. G. Herek and K. Berril (London: Sage, 1992), 65–75.

5. Michael Hendricks, "Lesbian and Gay Community Relations with the M[ontréal] U[rban] C[ommunity] Police," brief presented for the group Lesbiennes et Gais contre la violence to the Québec Human Rights Commission, November 1993.

6. Briefs presented to the Québec Human Rights Commission include Hendricks, "Lesbian and Gay Community Relations"; Irène Demczuk, "Des droits à reconnaître. Hétérosexisme et discrimination envers les lesbiennes"; David Pepper, "Community Based Responses to Bias Crimes: Some Critical Steps;" SPCUM, "Mémoire sur la discrimination et la violence envers les gais et les lesbiennes"; and Ki Namaste, "Transgenders and Violence: An Exploration" (the brief upon which this chapter was based). Copies of these briefs are available from the Commission des droits de la personne et de la jeunesse, 360 Saint-Jacques, Montréal, Québec, H2Y 1P5 Canada.

7. D. Smith, *The Everyday World as Problematic: A Feminist Sociology* (Toronto: University of Toronto Press, 1987), 17.

8. "The Traffic in Women: Notes on the 'Political Economy' of Sex," in *Toward an Anthropology of Women,* ed. R. Reiter (New York: Monthly Review Press, 1975), 157–210; "Thinking Sex: Notes Towards a Radical Theory of the Politics of Sexuality," in *Pleasure and Danger: Exploring Female Sexuality,* ed. C. Vance (Boston: Routledge and Kegan Paul, 1984), 267–319; and "Of Catamites and Kings: Reflections on Butch, Gender, and Boundaries," in *The Persistent Desire: A Femme-Butch Reader,* ed. Joan Nestle (Boston: Alyson, 1991), 466–82.

9. Lévi-Strauss, *Les Structures élémentaires de la parenté* (Paris: Presses universitaires de France, 1949).

10. Rubin, "Thinking Sex," 308.

11. Ibid., 307.

12. Rubin, "Of Catamites and Kings," 475.

13. Ibid., 477.

14. Ibid., 474.

15. NGLTF, "Anti-gay/lesbian Violence," 16.

16. Marlene Mackie, *Exploring Gender Relations* (Toronto: Butterworths, 1983).

17. S. Ortner and H. Whitehead, eds., *Sexual Meanings: The Cultural Construction of Gender and Sexuality* (Cambridge: Cambridge University Press, 1981).

18. A. Kinsey, W. Pomeroy, and Clyde E. Martin, *Sexual Behavior in the Human Male* (Philadelphia: W. B. Saunders Company, 1948).

19. Rubin, "Thinking Sex," 307.

20. Joseph Harry, "Conceptualizing Anti-gay Violence," *Journal of Interpersonal Violence* 5 (1990): 350–58; Harry, "Derivative Deviance: The Cases of Extortion, Fag-Bashing and the Shakedown of Gay Men," *Criminology* 19 (1982): 546–63.

21. Harry, "Derivative Deviance."

22. Von Schultess, "Violence in the Streets."

23. Valentine, "(Hetero)Sexing Space," 409.

24. See, for instance, Shirley Ardener, *Defining Females: The Nature of Women in Society* (London: Croom Helm, 1978); E. Garmonikow, D. Morgan, J. Purvis, and D. Taylorson, *The Public and the Private* (London: Heinemann Educational Books, 1983); R. Sydie, *Natural Women, Cultured Men: A Feminist Perspective on Sociological Theory* (Toronto: Methuen, 1987); and Judith Walkowitz, *Prostitution and Victorian Society: Women, Class, and the State* (Cambridge: Cambridge University Press, 1980).
25. Ardender, *Defining Females*, 10.
26. Walkowitz, *Prostitution and Victorian Society*, 5.
27. Comstock, *Violence Against Lesbians and Gay Men*, 49.
28. Ibid., 49–50.
29. See Valentine, "(Hetero)Sexing Space," 410.
30. Comstock, *Violence Against Lesbians and Gay Men*, 65.
31. Valentine, "(Hetero)Sexing Space," 410.
32. While queerbashing is centrally concerned with policing the public presentation of gender and sexuality, it is noteworthy that many lesbians and gay men who are victims of violence have their personal property destroyed. For instance, in Kansas City, Kansas, the word "fag" was spraypainted on eight cars parked near a gay bar (NGLTF, *Anti-gay/lesbian Violence*, 24). In Ovett, Mississippi, local residents objecting to the presence of a feminist and lesbian retreat verbally harassed the women, placed a dead dog on their mailbox, and threatened their physical safety (ibid., 37). Despite the sanctity of private property within capitalist democracy, sexual minorities risk having their cars, homes, and possessions vandalized—an act of violence that attempts to regulate sexuality and gender within the *private* sphere.
33. Feinberg, *Transgender Warriors;* Ortner and Whitehead, *Sexual Meanings;* Gilbert Herdt, ed., *Third Sex, Third Gender: Beyond Sexual Dimorphism in Culture and History* (New York: Zone Books, 1994); Holly Devor, *Gender Blending: Confronting the Limits of Duality* (Bloomington: Indiana University Press, 1989); Bullough and Bullough, *Cross Dressing, Sex, and Gender.*
34. The issue of "passing" has been examined from an ethnomethodological perspective within sociology. See Harold Garfinkel, *Studies in Ethnomethodology* (Englewood Cliffs: Prentice-Hall, 1967); and Kessler and McKenna, *Gender: An Ethnomethodological Approach.*
35. Kessler and McKenna, *Gender: An Ethnomethodological Approach*, 151–52.
36. Devor, *Gender Blending,*133.
37. Brian Tully, *Accounting for Transsexuality and Transhomosexuality* (London: Whiting and Birch, 1992), 266.
38. NGLTF, *Anti-gay/lesbian Violence.*
39. Quoted in A. Enigma, "Livin' Large: Dorian Corey," *Thing* 8 (1992): 35–36.
40. The confusion of gender and sexuality manifests itself at the level of semantics, such that "faggot" is an insult with which many MTF transsexuals are familiar. The NGLTF report on violence includes the following incident: "A [MTF] transsexual activist for the homeless and people with AIDS was verbally abused in a hospital. As she sat in a wheelchair with a 103 degree fever,

a doctor and several hospital employees repeatedly called her an 'AIDS carry-
ing fucking faggot'" (NGLTF, *Anti-gay/lesbian Violence,* 26).

41. See Devor, *Gender Blending;* Bullough and Bullough, *Cross Dressing, Sex, and
Gender.*

42. For example, Brandon Teena, a FTM transsexual murdered in Humboldt, Ne-
braska, was assaulted and raped one week before his death. Details of this incident are discussed in the NGLTF, *Anti-gay/lesbian Violence,* 18. Also see
Aphrodite Jones, *All She (sic) Wanted* (New York: Pocket Books, 1996). For
insightful analyses of how U.S. lesbian and gay communities have misrepre-
sented Brandon Teena to be a lesbian rather than an FTM transsexual, consult
Kathleen Chapman and Michael du Plessis, "'Don't Call Me Girl': Lesbian
Theory, Feminist Theory, and Transsexual Identities," in *Cross-Purposes: Lesbians, Feminists, and the Limits of Alliance,* ed. Dana Heller (Bloomington: Indiana University Press, 1997), 169–85; and C. Jacob Hale, "Consuming the Living, Dis(re)membering the Dead in the Butch/FTM Borderlands," *GLQ: A
Journal of Lesbian and Gay Studies* 4, no. 2 (1998): 311–48.

43. Pat Califia, "The City of Desire: Its Anatomy and Destiny," *Invert* 2, no. 4
(1991): 14.

44. David Adkin, *Out: Stories of Lesbian and Gay Youth* (Montréal: National Film
Board of Canada, 1993).

45. For more on the geographic area of Montréal's red-light district, see Daniel
Proulx, *Le Red Light de Montréal* (Montréal: VLB, 1997); Danielle Lacasse, *La
Prostitution féminine à Montréal, 1945–1970* (Montréal: Boréal, 1994); and Li-
moges, *La Prostitution à Montréal.*

46. Montréal police entered Café Cléopâtra with a video camera, for instance, on
November 13, 1997. See Namaste, *Évaluation des besoins,* 61.

47. *Pocket Criminal Code of Canada* S.195.1 (Toronto: Carswell, 1987), 118–19.

48. Valerie Scott, "C-49: A New Wave of Oppression," in *Good Girls/Bad Girls: Sex
Trade Workers and Feminists Face to Face,* ed. Laurie Bell (Toronto: Women's
Press, 1987), 100–103.

49. Cathy, "Unveiling," in *Good Girls/Bad Girls,* 88–91.

50. Hankins and Gendron, *Projet Prostitution,* 4.

51. See, for instance, Hendricks, "Lesbian and Gay Community Relations with the
MUC Police."

52. Ibid., 3.

53. SPCUM, "Mémoire sur la discrimination et la violence envers les lesbiennes et
les gais," 10. English translation mine.

54. Ibid., 10–11.

55. Ibid., 11.

56. See Comstock, *Violence Against Lesbians and Gay Men;* NGLTF, *Anti-gay/lesbian
Violence.*

57. The human rights hearings were intended to address violence against lesbians
and gay men. Many lesbians, however, felt that the issues that concerned
them as women were not addressed within a gay male setting—a feeling that
led to the formation of a lesbian caucus (see Demzcuk, "Des droits à re-

connaître"). Following the hearings, the lesbian caucus officially withdrew from the community coalition, the *Table de concertation des lesbiennes et des gais du grand Montréal.* The caucus cited a lack of understanding of gender issues on the part of gay men as the primary reason for their departure. (Remarkably, neither lesbian or gay male activists met with representatives of transsexual communities to address the question of violence.)

58. These tactics parallel those of citizens in Vancouver who, in the mid-1980s, organized to evict sex workers from the city's prestigious West End. See S. Arrington, "Community Organizing," in *Good Girls/Bad Girls,* 104–8. For an excellent analysis of the ways in which right-wing extremists mobilized residents of *Centre-Sud,* consult the brief prepared by the Comité contre le racisme d'Hochelaga-Maisonneuve for the Québec Human Rights Commission. At one of their demonstrations, chants progressed from "dehors les putes" [whores out] to "dehors les gauchistes" [leftists out] to "plus de tapettes dans notre quartier" [no more fags in our neighborhood]. Comité contre le racisme d'Hochelaga-Maisonneuve, "Mémoire déposé à la Commission des droits de la personne dans le cadre de la consultation publique sur la discrimination et la violence envers les gais et les lesbiennes," brief presented to the Québec Human Rights Commission, Montréal, 1993.

59. Comstock, *Violence Against Lesbians and Gay Men,* 49–50.

60. See Arrington's insightful comments on the geopolitical situation in Vancouver's West End in the mid-1980s, when property-owning gay men instigated a drive to remove prostitutes (transgendered people among them) from the residential area. Arrington, "Community Organizing," 104–8.

61. Comstock, *Violence Against Lesbians and Gay Men,* 49–50.

62. Ibid., 49.

63. NGLTF, *Anti-gay/lesbian Violence,* 29.

64. Comstock, *Violence Against Lesbians and Gay Men,* 65.

65. For more on transgendered people in prison, see James Tee, *Health Issues of the HIV+ MTF Transgendered Prison Population* (Toronto: PASAN—Prisoners' AIDS Support Action Network [489 College St., Suite 405, Toronto, Ontario, M6G 1A5, 416-920-9567], 1997); Maxine Petersen, Judith Stephens, Robert Dickey, and Wendy Lewis, "Transsexuals within the Prison System: An International Survey of Correctional Services Policies," *Behavioral Sciences and the Law* 14 (1996): 219–29; and Ann Scott, "A Brief on HIV/AIDS in the Transgendered Prison Population," presentation at the International Foundation for Gender Education conference, Toronto, March 27, 1998. Also see Ann Scott and Rick Lines, "HIV/AIDS in the Male-to-Female Transsexual and Transgendered Prison Population: A Comprehensive Strategy. A Brief from PASAN" (Toronto, May 1999).

66. Documenting hate crimes against gays and lesbians is difficult because the violence must be clearly accompanied by anti-gay epithets. For instance, if a man is stabbed in the gay village and his wallet stolen, he will be considered the victim of a robbery unless the assailants called him derogatory insults relating to his perceived sexuality (see SPCUM, "Mémoire sur la discrimination et la

violence envers les gais et les lesbiennes"). In the case of violence against transgendered people, this criteria for documentation is questionable, since many MTF transsexuals are called "faggot." Programmatically, we should not have to wait until bashers decry transgendered people with the proper vocabulary before we have an adequate manner of recording such genderbashing incidents.

67. See Valentine, "(Hetero)Sexing Space"; von Schultess, "Violence in the Streets"; and Harry, "Conceptualizing Anti-gay Violence."
68. Arrington, "Community Organizing," 104–8.

## NOTES TO CHAPTER 7

1. Denny, *Gender Dysphoria.*
2. D. Smith, *The Everyday World as Problematic.*
3. I was responsible for the section of the research on transgendered people; this information was subsequently summarized by the project in their final report to Health Canada. Coalition for Lesbian and Gay Rights in Ontario, *Systems Failure: A Report on the Experiences of Sexual Minorities in Ontario's Health-Care and Social-Services System* (Toronto: CLGRO, 1997). (Copies of this report can be obtained by writing to the Coalition for Lesbian and Gay Rights in Ontario, Box 822, Toronto, Ontario M5W 1G3 Canada 416-533–6824.)
4. The study was publicized through advertisement in the transgendered press, word of mouth, and street outreach. Participants received a $20 honorarium, which facilitated access to the field. Access to prostitutes was greatly increased when outreach was conducted in the third or fourth week of the month, when TS/TG prostitutes had less disposable income as well as fewer clients.
5. Glaser and Strauss, *The Discovery of Grounded Theory.* For an exposition and application of grounded theory methods, see Sandra Kirby and Kate McKenna, *Experience, Research, Social Change: Methods from the Margins* (Toronto: Garamond, 1989).
6. The research also addressed experiences with hospitals and emergency rooms. The findings of this section revealed a lack of understanding of TS/TG issues among hospital staff, a disrespect of TS/TG individuals, and regular breaches of confidentiality of TS/TG status within the hospital environment. For more information, see Namaste, "Access Denied."
7. Sheila Kirk, *Hormones* (Wayland, Mass.: International Foundation for Gender Education, 1992), 80–84.
8. Ibid.
9. Walter Bockting, B.R. Simon Rosser, and Eli Coleman, *Transgender HIV/AIDS Prevention Program* (Minneapolis: Program in Human Sexuality, University of Minnesota, 1993); Kirk Elifson, Jacqueline Boles, Ellen Posey, Mike Sweat, William Darrow, and William Elsea, "Male Transvestite Prostitutes and HIV Risk," *American Journal of Public Health* 83, no. 2 (February 1993): 260–62.
10. Bolin, *In Search of Eve;* Kessler and McKenna, *Gender: An Ethnomethodological Approach.*

11. James Pritchard, Dan Pankowsky, Joseph Crowe, and Fadi Abdul-Karim, "Breast Cancer in a Male-to-Female Transsexual: A Case Report," *Journal of the American Medical Association* 259, no. 15 (April 1988): 2278–80.

12. Ontario Legal Aid Plan, *Uniform Treatment. A Community Inquiry into Policing of Disadvantaged Peoples* (Toronto: Ontario Legal Aid Plan, 1994), 8.

13. Ibid.

14. Ross, "Investigating Women's Shelters," 7–10; Allison Cope and Julie Darke, "Trans Accessibility Project: Making Women's Shelters Accessible to Transgendered Women," Kingston, Ontario, Violence Intervention and Education Workgroup, 1999.

15. I spoke with representatives of fourteen different agencies: four shelters for homeless youth in Toronto, six shelters and/or drop-ins for homeless women in Toronto, three shelters/drop-ins for youth in the Ottawa area, and one women's shelter in Ottawa. I asked staff members whether their organizations accepted transsexual and transgendered people, and whether TS/TG individuals had been or presently were among their clients. (Definition was supplied in the event that the individuals I contacted were unfamiliar with the terms "transsexual" and/or "transgender.") Furthermore, I inquired as to the existence of an antidiscrimination policy that includes transsexual and/or transgendered people. Finally, I asked people what kind of training the staff members received concerning TS/TG issues.

16. O'Brien, "The Social Organization of the Treatment of Lesbian and Gay Youth in Group Homes and Youth Shelters" (master's independent inquiry project, Carleton University, Ottawa, May 1992).

17. Ibid., 65.

18. Ibid., 76.

19. Ibid., 72.

20. Ross, "Investigating Women's Shelters," 9.

21. Ibid.

22. Ibid. The discrimination against transsexual prostitutes in gender identity clinics is explored in greater depth in chapter 8.

23. A. Neal Wilson, "Sex Reassignment Surgery in HIV Positive Transsexuals"; and Sheila Kirk, "Guidelines for Selecting HIV Positive Patients for Genital Reconstructive Surgery"; both in *International Journal of Transgenderism* 3, nos. 1–2 ( January–June 1999).

24. Laura Masters, *The Imprisoned Transgenderist* (St. Catherine's: TransEqual, 1993); Ann Scott, "A Brief on HIV/AIDS and the Transgendered Prison Population" (presentation at the International Foundation for Gender Education conference, Toronto, March 27, 1998); James Tee, "Health Issues of the HIV+ MTF Transgendered Prison Population" (brief prepared for PASAN [Prisoners' HIV/AIDS Support Action Network], May 9, 1997); Namaste, *Évaluation des besoins;* Maxine Petersen, Judith Stephens, Robert Dickey, and Wendy Lewis, "Transsexuals within the Prison System: An International Survey of Correctional Services Policies," *Behavioral Sciences and the Law* 14 (1996): 219–29.

25. This situation is changing. At the time of writing, TS/TG antidiscrimination policies of shelters have been adopted in Toronto by the Catholic Children's Aid Society (due in large part to the initiatives of Ann Scott), as well as the YWCA of Metropolitan Toronto.
26. Ross, "Investigating Women's Shelters," 9.
27. On the lack of written antidiscrimination policies with regard to transgendered people, also see Ross, "Investigating Women's Shelters," 7.
28. For an analysis of addiction issues for transsexuals, see Jay Stilz, "Transsexuals and Substance Abuse" (master's thesis, California State University, Dominguez Hills, 1986); Carlos Carceres and Jorge Cortinas, "Fantasy Island: An Ethnography of Alcohol and Gender Roles in a Latino Gay Bar," *Journal of Drug Issues* 26, no. 1 (winter 1996): 245–60.
29. Carolle Simard, *La place de l'autre: Fonctionnaires et immigrés au Québec* (Montréal: Fides, 1998).
30. G. Smith, "Political Activist as Ethnographer," 629–48.

## Notes to Chapter 8

1. The topics covered with respect to gender identity clinics were broad. Interviewees were asked open-ended questions about their interpretations of their treatment at the GIC of the Clarke Institute of Psychiatry. Subjects were also asked about specific areas of inquiry, notably the assessment process. An individual was asked relevant follow-up questions relating to a particular aspect of their encounter(s) within the GIC when they had emphasized its importance to them. For instance, if an interviewee stated that they could not access information on hormones through the GIC, and if they expressed frustration therein, I asked them to elaborate on this situation. Follow-up questions in such an instance included: "How did you feel, not being able to find the information for which you were looking?"; "Did they refer you to another agency or organization which could help you obtain the information you needed?"; and "How do you think things should be organized differently at the GIC, regarding information on hormones?" The follow-up questions were intended to gain further insight into how the transsexual or transgendered interviewees understood their situation. Although I would ask questions as an interviewer, areas of inquiry upon which to expand had already been identified as important by the transgendered people interviewed. In this manner, the interviewees played an active role in the interview situation, and thus in the research process.
2. For a more detailed discussion of medical objections of transsexualism, see Harry Benjamin, *The Transsexual Phenomenon* (New York: Julian Press, 1966); and Leslie Lothstein, *Female to Male Transsexualism: Historical, Clinical, and Theoretical Issues* (Boston: Routledge and Kegan Paul, 1983), 56–59.
3. Anne Bolin, *In Search of Eve: Transsexual Rites of Passage* (South Hadley, Mass.:

Bergin and Garvey, 1988); and Sandy Stone, "The *Empire* Strikes Back: A Posttranssexual Manifesto," in *Body Guards: The Cultural Politics of Gender Ambiguity*, ed. Julia Epstein and Kristina Straub (New York: Routledge, 1991), 281–304.

4. John Meyer and Donna Reter, "Sex Reassignment: Follow-up," *Archives of General Psychiatry* 36 (1979): 1015.
5. Ray Blanchard and Betty Steiner, eds., *Clinical Management of Gender Identity Disorder in Children and Adults* (Washington: American Psychiatric Press, 1990).
6. Ogi Ogas, "Spare Parts: New Information Reignites a Controversy Surrounding the Hopkins Gender Identity Clinic," *Baltimore City Paper* 9 (March 1994): 10, 12–15.
7. For an historical overview of gender identity clinics in the United States, see Dallas Denny, "The Politics of Diagnosis and a Diagnosis of Politics: The University-Affiliated Gender Clinics, and How They Failed to Meet the Needs of Transsexual People," *Chrysalis Quarterly* 1, no. 3 (winter 1992): 9–20. Also consult Bernice Hausman, *Changing Sex: Transsexualism, Technology, and the Idea of Gender* (Durham, NC: Duke University Press, 1995).
8. Dallas Denny, *Gender Dysphoria: A Guide to Research* (New York: Garland, 1994), x–xi.
9. Bolin, *In Search of Eve*; Stone, "The *Empire* Strikes Back"; Denny, *Gender Dysphoria*; Blanchard and Steiner, *Clinical Management of Gender Identity Disorder in Children and Adults*; and Leslie Lothstein, *Female-to-Male Transsexualism*.
10. Bolin, *In Search of Eve*.
11. Garfinkel, *Studies in Ethnomethodology* (Englewood Cliffs, N.J.: Prentice-Hall, 1967), 116–85, 285–88.
12. Rogers, "They All Were Passing: Agnes, Garfinkel, and Company," *Gender and Society* 6, no. 2 (June 1992): 179.
13. Ibid., 185.
14. Stone, "The Empire Strikes Back," 294; Bolin, *In Search of Eve*, 48–68.
15. Potential interviewees were contacted through a variety of strategies: street outreach, notices distributed through the gender identity clinic, community support groups, local social service agencies, and word of mouth. I also relied on snowball sampling, asking interviewees to refer me to a friend or two whom I could also contact for the research. One of the methodological limitations of snowball sampling is that it tends to produce a homogeneous sample, since every individual contacted is part of the same network. The data gathered through this process, then, cannot be easily generalized to be representative of an entire community or population under investigation. While it is important to consider this shortcoming, snowball sampling was only one strategy employed to locate research participants. The interviewees came from vastly different segments of the transgender communities. Several different informal networks of TS/TG people thus make up the sample population, which was further supplemented by individuals who were unaffiliated with any formal or informal transgendered networks. This diversity thus subverts

the potential criticism that the current study is limited due to its methodological shortcomings. Moreover, like chapter 7, this project attempts to write an institutional ethnography. Within such a framework, the interview data should be interpreted not as a case study to be generalized, but as a point of entry into how the social relations of health care are organized and experienced by TS/TG people.

16. Namaste, *Évaluation des besoins.* Additional data from this report are presented in chapter 9.
17. Leonard Clemmensen, "The 'Real Life Test' for Surgical Candidates," in *Clinical Management of Gender Identity Disorder in Children and Adults,* ed. Blanchard and Steiner, 119–35.
18. Jeff Harder, "Tories to Snip Sex Changes," *Toronto Sun,* July 13, 1995, 4.
19. Kirby and McKenna, *Research, Experience, Social Change,* 164.
20. SRS was defunded by the Ontario provincial government in the fall of 1998. See Jeff Harder, "Ontario Refuses to Pay for Sex Change," *Ottawa Sun,* October 3, 1998, 3.
21. Provincial health insurance in Ontario paid for SRS upon recommendation of the GIC in 1995. This practice was discontinued in 1998.
22. Clemmensen, 'Real Life Test' for Surgical Candidates," 124.
23. Interview with author, June 19, 1995.
24. Ibid.
25. Interviews with author, June 28 and July 18, 1995.
26. Maxine Petersen and Robert Dickey, "Surgical Sex Reassignment: A Comparative Survey of International Centers," *Archives of Sexual Behavior* 24, no. 2 (1995): 135–38.
27. Health Law Standards of Care, *International Conference on Transgender Law and Employment Policy, Inc.* (Houston, Tex.: ICTLEP, 1993).
28. Petersen and Dickey, "Surgical Sex Reassignment," 150.
29. See Paul Walker, Jack Berger, Richard Green, Donald Laub, Charles Reynolds, and Leo Wollman, "Standards of Care: The Hormonal and Surgical Sex Reassignment of Gender Dysphoric Persons," in *Gender Dysphoria: A Guide to Research,* ed. Dallas Denny (New York: Garland, 1994), 633–648.
30. Petersen and Dickey, "Surgical Sex Reassignment," 150.
31. American Education Gender Information Service (AEGIS), *Position Statement—Blanket Requirement for Real-Life Test Before Hormonal Therapy: In Our Opinion, Inadvisable* (Decatur, Ga.: AEGIS, 1992).
32. Interview with author, June 28, 1995. Also see Ray Blanchard, Robert Dickey, Maxine Petersen, and Judith Stephens, *Consumer Satisfaction Survey* (Report submitted to Gender Identity Clinic of the Clarke Institute of Psychiatry, Toronto, November 13, 1993).
33. Interview with author, June 28, 1995.
34. Dallas Denny and Jan Roberts, "Results of a Questionnaire on the Standards of Care of the Harry Benjamin International Gender Dysphoria Association," presentation at The International Congress on Cross Dressing, Gender, and Sex Issues, Van Nuys, Calif., February 23–26, 1995.

35. Bolin, *In Search of Eve;* Kessler and McKenna, *Gender;* and Denny, "The Politics of Diagnosis."

36. Kessler and McKenna, *Gender,* 118.

37. Bolin, "Gender Subjectivism in the Construction of Transsexualism," *Chrysalis Quarterly* 1, no. 3 (winter 1992): 25.

38. Clemmensen, 'Real Life Test' for Surgical Candidates, 123.

39. Denny, "The Politics of Diagnosis," 16. The Canadian gender identity clinic in which this patient was enrolled is not identified. That is, it is not known whether the clinic to which she refers is the GIC at the Clarke Institute of Psychiatry.

40. Clemmensen's choice of names—John or Mary—reveals an implicit cultural bias. Indeed, there is no discussion of transsexuals who may choose names that may not be easily gendered in a Euro-American frame of reference. Furthermore, many names unmistakably gendered to English-speaking people may be unisex to other linguistic groups—e.g., "Carole" and "Marie." Critical research has demonstrated the cultural bias of psychiatry. See, for instance, Peter Guarnaccia, Maritza Rubio-Stipec, and Glorisa Canino, "Ataques de Nervios in the Puerto Rican Diagnostic Interview Schedule: The Impact of Cultural Categories on Psychiatric Epidemiology," *Culture, Medicine, and Psychiatry* 13 (1989): 1223-1231; and Atwood Gaines, "From DSM-I to III-R: Voices of Self, Mastery and the Other: A Cultural Constructivist Reading of U.S. Psychiatric Classification," *Social Science Medicine* 35, no. 1 (1992): 3–24.

41. Kessler and McKenna, *Gender;* Bolin, *In Search of Eve;* and Bolin, "Gender Subjectivism in the Construction of Transsexualism."

42. Denny, "The Politics of Diagnosis," 12.

43. Ibid.

44. Interview with author, Gender Identity Clinic, Clarke Institute of Psychiatry, June 28, 1995.

45. At the International Foundation for Gender Education's conference held in Toronto in March 1998, Maxine Petersen of the Clarke Institute's Gender Identity Clinic reiterated the institution's refusal to accept the earnings of prostitutes as a form of self-employed income. Field notes, March 28, 1998.

46. Interview with author, Gender Identity Clinic, Clarke Institute of Psychiatry, June 28, 1995.

47. See, for instance, Lori Dorfman, Pamela Derish, and Judith Cohen, "Hey Girlfriend: An Evaluation of AIDS Prevention among Women in the Sex Industry," *Health Education Quarterly* 19, no. 1 (spring 1992): 25–40.

48. Interview with author, July 18, 1995.

49. Assalian, *Montréal Today,* CTV Network, 24 February, 1999. (To obtain transcript, call 514-273-6311.)

50. Interview with author, June 28, 1995.

51. This data is from a provincial needs assessment of transsexuals and transgendered people in Québec with respect to HIV/AIDS. It involved interviews with twenty-seven TS/TG people, as well as numerous service providers. See Namaste, *Évaluation des besoins.*

52. See "Standards of Care" in *Gender Dysphoria*, ed. Denny, 633–48.

53. Namaste, "Evaluation des besoins," 45.

54. Ibid., 46.

55. Ibid.

56. Ibid.

57. World Health Organization, "Preamble to the Constitution of the World Health Organization," in *Biomedical Ethics*, ed. Thomas Mappes and Jane Zembaty (Montréal: McGraw-Hill, 1986), 244.

58. Daniel Callahan, "The WHO Definition of Health," in *Biomedical Ethics*, ed. Mappes and Zembaty, 244–52.

59. See, for instance, Glenn Graber, Alfred Beasley, and John Eaddy, "Informed Consent," in *Ethical Analysis of Clinical Medicine: A Guide to Self-Evaluation* (Baltimore and Munich: Urban and Schwarzenberg, 1985), 40–53; Paul Ramsey, *The Patient as Person* (New Haven: Yale University Press, 1970); and American College of Legal Medicine Foundation, "Informed Consent," in *MedicoLegal Primer* (Pittsburgh: American College of Legal Medicine Foundation, 1991), 287–294.

60. Presidential Commission for the Study of Ethical Problems in Medicine and Biomedical and Behavioral Research, *Making Health Care Decisions*, vol. 1, *Report* (Washington, D.C.: U.S. Government Printing Office, 1982), 2–6; cited by Graber, Beasley, and Eaddy, "Informed Consent," in *Ethical Analysis of Clinical Medicine: A Guide to Self-Evaluation* (Baltimore and Munich: Urban and Schwarzenberg, 1985), 44.

61. Interview with author, July 18, 1995.

62. Interview with author, June 19, 1999.

63. Interview with author, July 11, 1995.

64. Interviews with author, June 28 and July 18, 1995.

65. In an official administrative sense, prostitutes are refused services from a GIC because they do not fulfill the conditions of a "real-life test," as set out in the international Standards of Care and interpreted by clinic staff. Psychiatrists and clinic staff may object that they do not actually refuse patients an evaluation; they merely make clear the administrative criteria required to be eligible for their clinic program. However, the prostitutes interviewed explain that they are refused both an evaluation and health care services because of their work. This situation is most evident in the case of a prostitute expelled from a GIC subsequent to the discovery of her occupation. While some psychiatrists and clinic staff may maintain that they merely uphold administrative criteria, and do not outright refuse an evaluation, transsexual prostitutes interviewed clearly interpret these criteria to be a direct refusal of services. To the extent that clinic staff exclude prostitution as a valid form of work for the purposes of the "real-life test," we can speak about the refusal of services to transsexual prostitutes in Canada.

66. Interviews with author, June 28 and July 18, 1995.

67. Interview with author, April 4, 1995. A similar position was articulated in a subsequent interview on June 28, 1995.

68. Interview with author, July 18, 1995.
69. See, for instance, Raymond, *The Transsexual Empire;* Billings and Urban, "The Socio-Medical Construction of Transsexualism," 266–82; and Hausman, *Changing Sex.*
70. Hausman, *Changing Sex,* 140.
71. Stone, "The *Empire* Strikes Back"; and Bornstein, *Gender Outlaw.*
72. *Health Law Standards of Care;* Nangeroni, "Are We All Crazy? The Controversy over Gender Identity Disorder," *Transsexual News Telegraph* 7 (summer 1997): 26–27, 46.
73. Don Zimmerman, "Fact as Practical Accomplishment," in *Ethnomethodology: Selected Readings,* ed. Roy Turner (Markham: Penguin, 1975), 128–43.
74. For a more developed argument on this question, see James Nelson, "The Silence of the Bioethicists: Ethical and Political Aspects of Managing Gender Dysphoria," *GLQ: A Journal of Lesbian and Gay Studies* 4, no. 2 (1998): 213–230.
75. Transsexuals also use the diagnosis of gender identity disorder to receive Family Benefits Assistance in Ontario, which provides more money than general welfare.
76. Lisa Parker, "Beauty and Breast Implantation: How Candidate Selection Affects Autonomy and Informed Consent," *Hypatia* 10, no. 1 (winter 1995): 183–201; Fabienne Darling-Wolf, "Framing the Breast Implant Controversy: A Feminist Critique," *Journal of Communicative Inquiry* 21, no. 1 (spring 1997): 77–97; and Kathryn Taylor and Merrijoy Kelner, "Informed Consent: The Physician's Perspective," *Social Science and Medicine* 24, no. 2 (1987): 135–143.
77. Since October 1998, SRS has not been covered by provincial health insurance, locating all transsexuals in Ontario as consumers with regard to their genital surgeries.
78. Meal-Trans, c/o 519 Community Centre, 519 Church St, Toronto, Ontario, Canada (416-392-6878).
79. PASTT—Projet Action Santé auprès des Travestis et Transsexuels, 94 rue Lafayette, 75010, Paris.

## Notes to Chapter 9

1. Namaste, *Évaluation des besoins*
2. Elifson et al., "Male Transvestite Prostitutes and HIV Risk," 260–62; James Inciardi and Hilary Stuart, "Male Transvestite Sex Workers and HIV in Rio de Janeiro, Brazil," *Journal of Drug Issues* 27, no. 1 (1997): 135–46; P. Gattari, L. Spizzichino, C. Valenzi, M. Zaccareli, G. Reeza, "Behavioural Patterns and HIV Infection among Drug Using Transvestites Practising Prostitution in Rome," *AIDS Care* 4, no. 1 (1992): 83–87; M. J. Gras, T. van der Helm, R. Schenk, G. J. van Deernum, R. A. Coutinho, J. O. van den Hoek, "HIV-infection en risicogedrag ander prostitute(e)s in de tippelzone te Amsterdam; annwijzigen voor een verhoogde HIV-prevalentie onder transvestieten/transseksuelen" ["HIV Infection and Risk Behaviour among Prostitutes in the

Amsterdam Streetwalkers' District: Indications of Raised Prevalence of HIV among Transvestites/Transsexuals"], *Nederlands Tidjschrift Geneeskunde* 141, no. 25 (June 21, 1997): 1238–41; Laura Spizzichino, P. Gattari, P. Casella, S. Venezia, M. Zaccareli, G. Deeza, "Immigrants and HIV Infection: The Role of Counselling," presentation at the XI International Conference on AIDS, Vancouver, July 1996; B. Modan, R. Goldschmidt, E. Rubenstein, "Prevalence of HIV Antibodies in Transsexual and Female Prostitutes," *American Journal of Public Health* 82 (1992): 590–92; D. F. MacFarlane, "Transsexual Prostitution in New Zealand: Predominance of Persons of Maori Extraction," *Archives of Sexual Behaviour* 13, no. 4 (1984): 301–9; Boles and Elifson, "The Social Organization of Transvestite Prostitution and AIDS," *Social Science Medicine* 39, no. 1 (1994): 85–93.

3. Khartini Slamah, "Developing Effective HIV/AIDS Programs for Transsexuals Working as Sex Workers," presentation at the XI International Conference on AIDS, Vancouver, July 1996; I. Lubis, J. Master, M. Bambang, A. Papilaya, and R. L. Anthony, "AIDS Related Attitudes and Sexual Practices of Jakarta WARIA (male transvestites)," *Southeast Asian Journal of Tropical Medicine and Public Health* 25, no. 1 (March 1994): 102–6.

4. Walter Bockting, B. R. Simon Rosser, and Eli Coleman, "Transgender HIV/ AIDS Prevention Program" (Minneapolis: Program in Human Sexuality, University of Minnesota, 1993); Theresa Mason, Margaret Connors, Cornelia Kammerer, "Transgenders and HIV Risks: Needs Assessment" (Boston: Massachusetts Department of Public Health, August 1995); San Francisco Department of Public Health, AIDS Office, "HIV Prevention and Health Service Needs of the Transgender Community in San Francisco: Results from Eleven Focus Groups" (San Francisco Department of Public Health, 1997).

5. Elifson et al., "Male Transvestite Prostitutes and HIV Risk," 260; Boles and Elifson, "The Social Organization of Transvestite Prostitution and AIDS," 85; Bockting et al., *Transgender HIV/AIDS Prevention Program*, 33.

6. Carlos Carceres and Jorge Cortinas, "Fantasy Island: An Ethnography of Alcohol and Gender Roles in a Latino Gay Bar," *Journal of Drug Issues* 26, no. 1 (winter 1996): 245–60; Elifson et al., "Male Transvestite Prostitution and HIV Risk," 260. An analysis of addictions with respect to transsexuals, which does not consider its relation to HIV, is available in Jay Stilz, "Transsexuals and Substance Abuse" (master's thesis, California State University, Dominguez Hills, 1986).

7. Gattari et al., "Behavioural Patterns and HIV Infection."

8. Ki Namaste, Sandra Laframboise, and Deborah Brady, "La transsexualité, le travestisme, et le VIH/Sida: Une introduction à la santé des personnes transsexuelles et travesties face au VIH et au Sida" (Vancouver: High Risk Project, 1996).

9. San Francisco Department of Public Health, "HIV Prevention and Health Service Needs of the Transgender Community in San Francisco."

10. S. Goihman, A. Ferreira, S. Santos, and J. L. Grandi, "Silicone Application as a Risk Factor for HIV Infection," presentation at the IX International Conference

on AIDS, Yokohama, Japan, August 1994; "Back Alley Transsexual Injections?" *San Francisco Bay Times* 14, no. 11 (February 25, 1993): 11; L. A. Farina, V. Palacio, M. Salles, D. Fernandez-Villanueva, B. Vidal, and P. Menendez, "Granuloma escrotal por aceite migrado desde la cadera en dos varones transexuales (lipogranuloma esclerosant escrotal)," *Archiva Espana Urologica* 50, no. 1 (Jan–Feb 1997): 51–53.

11. Doug Hein, "Education and Soul-Searching: The Enterprise HIV Prevention Group" (presentation to the Hero's Journey Conference, Boston, August 1997).

12. See the following presentations at the XI International Conference on AIDS (Vancouver, July 1996): Marsha Bennett, "An Ethnographic Study of HIV Infected Male-to-Female Transgendered Clients"; Tammi Tam Raymundo, J. M. Fleras, P. Resurrection, "Building Rapport with Transvestite Sex Workers: Enabling Easy Access to Health Information"; James Grimaldi and J. Jacobs, "HIV/AIDS Transgender Support Group: Improving Care Delivery and Creating a Community"; and Barbara Warren, John Capizuca, Birgit Pols, and Barbara Otter, "AIDS Prevention for Transgender and Transsexual Persons: A Collaborative Community-Based Program." See also Mason et al., "Transgenders and HIV Risk"; San Francisco Department of Public Health, *HIV Prevention*; Lloyd Siegal and Arthur Zitrin, "Transsexuals in the New York City Welfare Population: The Function and Illusion in Transsexuality," *Archives of Sexual Behavior* 7, no. 4 (July 1978): 285–290; and Namaste, "Access Denied."

13. But see Bockting et al., *Transgender HIV/AIDS Prevention Program.*

14. Prumina Mane et al., "Summary of Track D: Social Science: Research, Policy, and Action," *AIDS* 10 (supplement 3, 1996): S123–132.

15. "Stratégie québécoise de lutte contre le sida, Phase 4: Orientations 1997–2002" (Québec: Ministère de la Santé et des Services Sociaux, Direction générale de la santé publique, 1997).

16. For a more detailed demographic profile of the project participants, consult Namaste, *Évaluation des besoins.*

17. On a lack of consultation of transgendered people within health care, see Namaste, *Évaluation des besoins.* Also see Deborah Feinbloom, *Transvestites and Transsexuals: Mixed Views* (New York: Delacourte Press, 1976).

18. "La personne qui a subi avec succès des traitements médicaux et des interventions chirurgicales impliquant une modification structurale des organes sexuels, et destinés à changer ses caractères sexuels apparents, peut obtenir la modification de la mention du sexe figurant sur son acte de naissance, et, s'il y a lieu, de ses prénoms." *Code civil du Québec,* Section 71 S IV (Québec: Éditeur officiel du Québec, 1991), 28.

19. Interview with author, January 16, 1998.

20. Interview with author, April 28, 1998.

21. *Code civil du Québec,* Section 71 S III, 26.

22. Interviews with author, October 30, 1997, and January 16, 1998. In the 1970s Ethel Greffier reported that sex reassignment was considered to constitute a serious motive, but that bureaucrats at the Direction de l'état civil hesi-

tated to apply the law in this manner. See Greffier, "De certains aspects juridiques du transsexualisme dans le droit québécois," *Revue de droit Université de Sherbrooke* 6 (1975): 114–49.

23. See Michèle Rivet, "La vérité et le statut juridique de la personne en droit québécois," *Revue générale de droit* 18 (1987): 843–68. The relation between the civil code and transsexualism is explicit in the following works: Robert Kouri, "Comments on Transsexualism in the Province of Québec," *Revue de droit Université de Sherbrooke* 4 (1973): 167–83; Robert Kouri, "Certain Legal Aspects of Modern Medicine (Sex Reassignment and Sterilization)" (Ph.D. diss., Institute of Comparative Law, McGill University, 1975); Ethel Greffier, "De certains aspects juridiques"; D. Salas, *Sujet de chair, sujet de droit: La justice face au transsexualisme* (Paris: Presses universitaires de France, 1994).

For a consideration of the French influence on Québécois law, see Louise Langevin and Denise Pratt, "Du code civil du Bas Canada au nouveau Code Civil du Québec: L'Influence de la codification française," in *Droit québécois et droit français: Communauté, autonomie, concordance,* ed. H. Patrick Glenn (Cowansville, Québec: Éditions Yves Blais, 1993), 63–89; and H. Patrick Glenn, ed., *Droit québécois et droit français: Communauté, autonomie, concordance* (Cowansville, Québec: Éditions Yves Blais, 1993), 577–97.

24. Namaste, "Évaluation des besoins," 98 (my translation)
25. Ibid. (my translation).
26. Ibid. (my translation).
27. Interview with author, RAMQ, October 17, 1997.
28. Namaste, "Évaluation des besoins," 101 (my translation).
29. Ibid., 102 (my translation).
30. Ibid., 102–3 (my translation).
31. Ibid., 103 (my translation).
32. Field notes, October 10, 1997.
33. Namaste, "Évaluation des besoins," 105–6 (my translation).
34. A summary of this judgment is available in Louis-Edmond Pettiti, *Les transsexuels* (Paris: Presses universitaires de France, 1992).
35. Jorge Costa-Santos and Rosa Madeira, "Transsexualism in Portugal: The Legal Framework and Procedure, and Its Consequences for Transsexuals," *Medicine, Science, and the Law* 36, no. 3 (1996): 221–25.
36. Henri Delvaux, "Les conséquences juridiques du changement de sexe en droit comparé," presentation at the XXIII Colloque sur le droit européen, Vrije Universiteiet Amsterdam, Netherlands, April 14–16, 1993. Also see the published version of this presentation: Delvaux, "Legal Consequences of Sex Reassignment in Comparative Law," in *Transsexualism, Medicine, and Law* (Proceedings, XXIII Colloquy on European Law, Vrije Universiteit Amsterdam, Netherlands), [Strasbourg: Council of Europe, 1995]), 149–76.
37. V. Latter, O. Heymans, J. Lemaître, S. van Bree, and M. Isgour, "Transsexualisme et procédure," *Acta Urologica Belgica* 64, no. 4 (December 1996): 1–3.
38. Cordula Weitz and Suzanne Osburg, "Transsexualism in Germany: Empirical Data on Epidemiology and Application of the German Transsexuals' Act Dur-

ing Its First Ten Years," *Archives of Sexual Behavior* 25, no. 4 (1996): 409–25; F. Pfafflin, "Psychiatric and Legal Implications of the New Law for Transsexuals in the Federal Republic of Germany," *International Journal of Law and Psychiatry* 4 (1981): 191–98; Michael Will, "Legal Conditions of Sex Reassignment by Medical Intervention—Situation in Comparative Law," in *Transsexualism, Medicine, and Law* (Proceedings, XXIII Colloquy on European Law, Vrije Universiteit Amsterdam, Netherlands), [Strasbourg: Council of Europe, 1995]), 75–95.

39. Field notes, July 14 and September 19, 1997.
40. Interview with author, January 16, 1998.
41. Namaste, "Évaluation des besoins," 108–9 (my translation).
42. Ibid. (my translation).
43. J. J. Hage, "Medical Requirements and Consequences of Sex Reassignment Surgery," *Medicine, Science, and Law* 35, no. 1 (1995): 17–24; J. J. Hage, *From Peniplastica Totalis to Reassignment Surgery of the External Genitalia in Female-to-Male Transsexuals* (Amsterdam: VU Universiteit Press, 1992).
44. Will, "Legal Conditions," 75–95.
45. Field notes, May 5 and May 7, 1998.
46. Interview with author, April 28, 1998.
47. Interviews with author, April 28, 1998.
48. Interview with author, April 28, 1998.
49. Interviews with author, January 16 and April 28, 1998.
50. Interview with author, April 28, 1998.
51. Sheila Kirk, *Hormones*.
52. Interview with author, April 28, 1998.
53. Carolle Simard, *La place de l'autre: Fonctionnaires et immigrés au Québec* (Montréal: Fides, 1998).
54. Transcription of interview 20 for Namaste, "Évaluation des besoins," (my translation).
55. Interview with author, April 28, 1998.
56. Ibid.
57. Gender Identity Clinic, Montréal General Hospital, telephone interview with author, May 5, 1998; Gender Identity Clinic, Hôpital Hôtel Dieu, telephone interview with author, May 7, 1997; Centre Hospitalier de l'Université Laval, telephone interview with author, April 16, 1998.
58. Telephone consultation, Direction de l'état civil, October 30, 1997.
59. Interview, Direction de l'état civil, January 16, 1998.
60. Interview, Direction de l'état civil, April 28, 1998.
61. Field notes, April 27, 1998.
62. Grant Jordan, *The British Administrative System: Principles versus Practice* (London: Routledge, 1994), 2.
63. Philip Preville, "Real Men Don't Need Penises," *Montréal Mirror,* July 2–9, 1998, 13; Dominique Ritter, "Bending the Definition of Gender," *Montréal Mirror,* February 18–25, 1999, 4.

64. Field notes, August 5, 1999.
65. Field notes, August 5, 1999.
66. Weitz and Osburg, "Transsexualism in Germany."
67. Smith, "Accessing Treatment: Managing the AIDS Epidemic in Ontario," in *Knowledge, Experience, and Ruling Relations: Studies in the Social Organization of Knowledge,* ed. Marie Campbell and Ann Manicom (Toronto: University of Toronto Press, 1995), 18–34.
68. Gary Kinsman and Patrizia Gentile, *"In the Interests of the State": The Anti-gay, Anti-lesbian National Security Campaign in Canada—A Preliminary Research Report* (Sudbury: Laurentian University, April 1998).
69. Ng, *The Politics of Community Services,* 85.
70. Correctional Service Canada, Directive 800 (Health Services), articles 27–32. Individuals who receive a sentence of two years or more are incarcerated in federal prisons. Provincial prisons in Québec have no written policies with respect to transsexual prisoners. Interview with author, Établissement de détention de Montréal, February 2, 1998.
71. Paul Walker, Jack Berger, Richard Green, Donald Laub, Charles Reynolds, and Leo Wollman, "Standards of Care: The Hormonal and Surgical Sex Reassignment of Gender Dysphoric Persons," in *Gender Dysphoria: A Guide to Research,* ed. Dallas Denny (New York: Garland, 1994), 633–48.
72. Namaste, "Évaluation des besoins," 131–2 (my translation).
73. Smith, *The Everyday World as Problematic,* 209–10.
74. Don Zimmerman, "Fact as Practical Accomplishment," in *Ethnomethodology: Selected Readings,* ed. Roy Turner (Markham: Penguin, 1975), 133.
75. Interview with author, April 28, 1998.
76. Field notes, November 11, 1997.
77. Interview with author, November 22, 1998.
78. Field notes, September 12, 1997. Although I interviewed only five FTMs for this particular research study, it is perhaps noteworthy that at least two of these individuals had falsified their documents in order to work legally in the world. While MTFs may choose to work as prostitutes as a way to avoid the problems associated with their papers, FTMs may opt to live under an assumed name.
79. André Turmel, "Le retour du concept d'institution," in *Culture, institution, et savoir,* ed. André Turmel (Québec: Presses de l'université Laval, 1997), 2.

## Notes to Conclusion

1. Peter Manning, *Semiotics and Fieldwork* (Beverly Hills, Calif.: Sage, 1987); Dean MacCannell, "Semiotics and Sociology," *Semiotica* 61, nos. 3–4 (1986): 193–200.
2. Feinbloom, *Transvestites and Transsexuals* (see especially the appendix, "Ethical Implications of Field Work," 255–69).
3. Rubin, "Phenomenology as Method in Trans Studies," *GLQ: A Journal of Lesbian and Gay Studies* 4, no. 2 (1998): 263–81.

4. Halberstam, "Transgender Butch, 301.
5. For an examination of this methodological issue in the context of intravenous drug use, see John Watters, "The Significance of Sampling and Understanding Hidden Populations," *Drugs and Society* 7, nos. 3–4 (1993): 13–21.
6. Prosser, *Second Skins: The Body Narratives of Transsexuality* (New York: Columbia University Press, 1998).

# BIBLIOGRAPHY

Adkin, David. *Out: Stories of Lesbian and Gay Youth.* Montréal: National Film Board of Canada, 1993.

AEGIS [American Education Gender Information Service]. "Position Statement—Blanket Requirement for Real-Life Test Before Hormonal Therapy: In Our Opinion, Inadvisable." Decatur, Ga.: AEGIS, 1992.

American College of Legal Medicine Foundation. "Informed Consent." In *Medico-Legal Primer,* 287–94. Pittsburgh: ACLMF, 1991.

*Anarcho-Homo-Nite-Club* 1. Toronto, circa 1993 (fanzine).

Ardener, Shirley. *Defining Females: The Nature of Women in Society.* London: Croom Helm, 1978.

Arrington, S. "Community Organizing." In *Good Girls/Bad Girls: Sex Trade Workers and Feminists Face to Face,* ed. Laurie Bell, 104–8. Toronto: Women's Press, 1987.

Attali, Jacques. *Noise: The Political Economy of Music.* Minneapolis: University of Minnesota Press, 1985.

B., Jeanne, and Xanthra Phillippa. *Gendertroublemakers: Transsexuals in the Gay Community.* Toronto: Genderpress, 1993.

B., Jeanne. "Interview." In *Whore Carnival,* ed. Shannon Bell, 137–45. Brooklyn: Autonomedia, 1995.

"Back Alley Transsexual Injections?" *San Francisco Bay Times* 14, no. 11 (February 23, 1993): 11.

Baillargeon, Paule. *Le sexe des étoiles.* Montréal: Production Pierre Gendron et Jean-Roch Marcotte, 1993.

Bealey, F. *Democracy in the Contemporary State.* Oxford: Clarendon, 1988.

Beatty, Christine. *Misery Loves Company.* San Francisco: Glamazon Press, 1993. (Available from Glamazon Press, P.O. Box 423602, San Francisco, CA 94142.)

Bélanger, Jacques/Brigitte Martel. *Né homme comment je suis devenu femme.* Montréal: Éditions Québécor, 1981.

Bell, Laurie, ed. *Good Girls/Bad Girls: Sex Trade Workers and Feminists Face to Face.* Toronto: Women's Press, 1987.

Benjamin, Harry. *The Transsexual Phenomenon.* New York: Julian Press, 1966.

Bennett, Marsha. "An Ethnographic Study of HIV Infected Male-to-Female Trans-gendered Clients." Presentation at the XI International Conference on AIDS, Vancouver, July 1996.

Berger, Peter, and Thomas Luckmann. *The Social Construction of Reality: A Treatise in the Sociology of Knowledge.* New York: Anchor Books, 1967.

Bibeau, Gilles, and Marc Perreault. *Dérives montréalaises: A travers des itinéraires de toxicomanies dans le quartier Hochelaga-Maisonneuve.* Montréal: Boréal, 1995.

Billings, Dwight, and Thomas Urban. "The Socio-Medical Construction of Transsexualism: An Interpretation and Critique." *Social Problems* 29, no. 3 (1982): 266–82.

Black, Max. *Models and Metaphors: Studies in Language and Philosophy.* Ithaca: Cornell University Press, 1962.

Blanchard, Ray, and Betty Steiner, eds. *Clinical Management of Gender Identity Disorder in Children and Adults.* Washington, D.C.: American Psychiatric Press, 1990.

Blanchard, Ray, Robert Dickey, Maxine Petersen, and Judith Stephens. *Consumer Satisfaction Survey.* Toronto: Gender Identity Clinic, Clarke Institute of Psychiatry, November 13, 1993.

Bockting, Walter, B. R. Simon Rosser, and Eli Coleman. "Transgender HIV/AIDS Prevention Program." Minneapolis: Program in Human Sexuality, 1993.

Boles, Jacqueline, and Kirk Elifson. "The Social Organization of Transvestite Prostitution and AIDS." *Social Science Medicine* 39, no. 1 (1994): 85–93.

Bolin, Anne. "Gender Subjectivism in the Construction of Transsexualism." *Chrysalis Quarterly* 1, no. 3 (winter 1992): 23–26, 39.

———. *In Search of Eve: Transsexual Rites of Passage.* South Hadley, Mass.: Bergin and Garvey, 1988.

———. "Transcending and Transgendering: Male-to-Female Transsexuals, Dichotomy, and Diversity." In *Third Sex, Third Gender: Beyond Sexual Dimorphism in Culture and History*, ed. Gilbert Herdt, 213–39. New York: Zone Books, 1994.

Bornstein, Kate. *Gender Outlaw: On Men, Women, and the Rest of Us.* New York: Routledge, 1994.

Bourassa, André, and Jean-Marc Larrue, eds. *Les nuits de la "Main": Cent ans de spectacles sur le boulevard Saint-Laurent (1891–1991).* Montréal: VLB, 1993.

Boyd, Nan Alamilla. "'Homos Invade S.F.!' San Francisco's History as a Wide-Open Town." In *Creating a Place for Ourselves: Lesbian, Gay, and Bisexual Community Histories*, ed. Brett Beemyn, 73–95. New York: Routledge, 1997.

Brake, Mike. *The Sociology of Youth Culture and Youth Subculture.* London: Routledge and Kegan Paul, 1980.

Bratton, J. S. "Irrational Dress." In *The New Woman and Her Sisters: Feminism and Theatre 1850–1914*, ed. Vivien Gardner and Susan Rutherford, 77–91. Ann Arbor: University of Michigan Press, 1992.

Bullough, Bonnie, and Vern Bullough. *Cross Dressing, Sex, and Gender.* Philadelphia: University of Pennsylvania Press, 1993.

Burchill, Julie, and Tony Parsons. *The Boy Looked at Johnny: The Obituary of Rock and Roll.* London: Pluto Press, 1978.

Burnham, Christine, in consultation with Patricia Diewold. *Gender Change: Employability Issues.* Vancouver: Perceptions Press, 1994.

Butler, Judith. *Bodies That Matter: On the Discursive Limits of "Sex."* New York: Routledge, 1993.

———. *Gender Trouble: Feminism and the Subversion of Identity.* New York: Routledge, 1990.

———. "Imitation and Gender Insubordination." In *Inside/Out: Lesbian Theories, Gay Theories*, ed. Diana Fuss, 13–31. New York: Routledge, 1991.

———. "Performative Speech Acts and Gender Constitution: An Essay in Phenomenology and Feminist Theory." In *Performing Feminisms: Feminist Critical Theory and Practice*, ed. Sue Ellen Case. Baltimore: John Hopkins University Press, 1991, 270–82.

Califia, Pat. "The City of Desire: Its Anatomy and Destiny." *Invert* 2, no. 4 (1991): 13–16.

———. *Sex Changes: The Politics of Transgenderism*. San Francisco: Cleis Press, 1997.

Callahan, Daniel. "The WHO Definition of Health." In *Biomedical Ethics*, ed. Thomas Mappes and Jane Zembaty, 244–52. Montréal: McGraw-Hill, 1986.

Campbell, Marie, and Ann Manicom, eds. *Knowledge, Experience, and Ruling Relations: Studies in the Social Organization of Knowledge*. Toronto: University of Toronto Press, 1995.

Carceres, Carlos, and Jorge Cortinas. "Fantasy Island: An Ethnography of Alcohol and Gender Roles in a Latino Gay Bar." *Journal of Drug Issues* 26, no. 1 (winter 1996): 245–60.

Carrière, Daniel. "L'empire transsexuel." *Le Berdache* 25 (novembre 1981): 50–51.

Castillo, Otto René. *Let's Go! Vamanos patria a caminar*. Trans. Margaret Randall. London: Cape Goliard Press, 1971.

Cathy. "Unveiling." In *Good Girls/Bad Girls: Feminists and Sex Trade Workers Face to Face*, ed. Laurie Bell, 88–91. Toronto: Women's Press, 1987.

Chapman, Kathleen, and Michael du Plessis. "'Don't Call Me Girl': Lesbian Theory, Feminist Theory, and Transsexual Identities." In *Cross-Purposes: Lesbians, Feminists, and the Limits of Alliance*, ed. Dana Heller, 169–85. Bloomington: Indiana University Press, 1997.

Chauncey, George. "Christian Brotherhood or Sexual Perversion? Homosexual Identities and the Construction of Sexual Boundaries in the World War I Era." In *Hidden From History: Reclaiming the Gay and Lesbian Past*, ed. Martin Duberman, Martha Vicinus, and George Chauncey Jr., 294–317. New York: New American Library, 1989.

———. *Gay New York: Gender, Urban Culture, and the Making of the Gay Male World, 1890–1940*. New York: Basic Books, 1994.

Clemmensen, Leonard. "The 'Real Life Test' for Surgical Candidates." In *Clinical Management of Gender Identity Disorder in Children and Adults*, ed. Ray Blanchard and Betty Steiner, 119–35. Washington, D.C.: American Psychiatric Press, 1990.

Coalition for Lesbian and Gay Rights in Ontario. *Systems Failure: A Report on the Experiences of Sexual Minorities in Ontario's Health-Care and Social-Service Systems*. Toronto: CLGRO, 1997. (Copies of this report can be obtained by writing to the Coalition for Lesbian and Gay Rights at Box 822, Toronto, Ontario, M5W 1G3 [416-533-6824].)

*Code civil du Québec*. Québec: Éditeur officiel du Québec, 1991.

Coleman, Eli, Walter Bockting, and Louis Gooren. "Homosexual and Bisexual Identity in Sex-Reassigned Female-to-Male Transsexuals." *Archives of Sexual Behavior* 22, no. 1 (1993): 37–50.

Collectif Androgyne. Meeting minutes, September 7, 1980. (Available for consultation at Archives gaies du Québec, 4067 Saint-Laurent, Bureau 202, Montréal.)

Comité contre le racisme Hochelaga-Maisonneuve. "Mémoire déposé à la Commission des droits de la personne dans le cadre de la consultation publique sur la discrimination et la violence envers les gais et les lesbiennes." Brief presented to the Québec Human Rights Commission, November 1993. (Copy available for consultation at the Commission des droits de la personne et de la jeunesse, 360 Saint-Jacques, Montréal, Québec, H2Y 1P5.)

Comstock, Gary. *Violence Against Lesbians and Gay Men.* New York: Columbia University Press, 1991.

Cope, Allison, and Julie Darke. "Trans Accessibility Project: Making Women's Shelters Accessible to Transgendered Women." Kingston, Ontario, Violence Intervention and Education Workgroup, 1999.

Correctional Services of Canada. *Directive 800 (Health Services).* Ottawa: CSC, 1991.

Costa-Santos, Jorge, and Rosa Madeira. "Transsexualism in Portugal: The Legal Framework and Procedure, and Its Consequence for Transsexuals." *Medicine, Science, and the Law* 36, no. 3 (1996): 221–25.

County, Jayne, and Rupert Smith. *Man Enough To Be a Woman.* London: Serpent's Tail, 1995.

Courte, Bernard, and Jean-Michel Sivry. "Les espaces du cuir." *Le Berdache* 16 (December 1980–January 1981): 29–30.

Craib, Ian. *Modern Social Theory: From Parsons to Habermas.* New York: St. Martin's Press, 1984.

Crosby, Christina. "Dealing with Differences," in *Feminists Theorize the Political,* ed. Judith Butler and Joan Scott, 130–43. New York: Routledge, 1992.

Culler, Jonathan. *The Pursuit of Signs: Semiotics, Literature, Deconstruction.* Ithaca: Cornell University Press, 1981.

Darling-Wolf, Fabienne. "Framing the Breast Implant Controversy: A Feminist Critique." *Journal of Communicative Inquiry* 21, no. 1 (spring 1997): 77–97.

de Lauretis, Teresa. "Gender Symptoms, or, Peeing Like a Man." *Social Semiotics* 9, no. 2 (August 1999): 257–270.

de Saussure, Ferdinand. *Cours de linguistique générale.* Paris: Payot, 1972 [1913].

Dekker, Rudolf, and Lotte van de Pol. *The Tradition of Female Transvestism in Early Modern Europe.* New York: St. Martin's Press, 1989.

Delacoste, F., and Priscilla Alexander, eds. *Sex Work: Writings by Women in the Sex Industry.* San Francisco: Cleis Press, 1987.

Delvaux, Henri. "Les conséquences juridiques du changement de sexe de droit comparé." Presentation at the XXIII Collque sur le droit européen, Vrije Universiteit Amsterdam, Netherlands, April 14–16, 1993.

———. "Legal Consequences of Sex Reassignment in Comparative Law." In *Transsexualism, Medicine and Law* (Proceedings, XXIII Colloquy on European Law,

Vrije Universitiet Amsterdam, Netherlands, 14–16 April 1993), 149–76. Strasbourg: Council of Europe, 1995.

Demczek, Irène. "Des droits à reconnaître: Hétérosexisme et discrimination envers les lesbiennes." Brief presented to the Québec Human Rights Commission, November 1993. (Copy available for consultation at the Commission des droits de la personne et de la jeunesse, 360 Saint-Jacques, Montréal, Québec, H2Y 1P5.)

Denny, Dallas, ed. *Gender Dysphoria: A Guide to Research.* New York: Garland, 1994.

———. "The Politics of Diagnosis and a Diagnosis of Politics. The University-Affiliated Gender Clinics, and How They Failed to Meet the Needs of Transsexual People." *Chrysalis Quarterly* 1, no. 3 (winter 1992): 9–20.

Denny, Dallas, and Jan Roberts. "Results of a Questionnaire on the Standards of Care of the Harry Benjamin International Gender Dysphoria Association." Presentation at the International Congress on Cross Dressing, Gender, and Sex Issues, Van Nuys, Calif., 23–26 February 1995.

Derrida, Jacques. *De la grammatologie.* Paris: Éditions de Minuit, 1967.

———. *La dissémination.* Paris: Éditions du Seuil, 1972.

———. *L'Écriture et la différence.* Paris: Éditions du Seuil, 1967.

———. "The Law of Genre/La loi du genre." *Glyph* 8 (1980): 176–201.

———. "Limited Inc. abc." *Glyph* 2 (1977): 162–254.

——— "La structure, le signe, et le jeu dans le discours des sciences humaines." In *L'Écriture et la différence,* ed. Derrida, 409–28. Paris: Éditions du Seuil, 1967.

Descartes, René. *Oeuvres philosophiques.* Paris: Garnier, 1963.

deVille, Michelle. "Interview." *Fuzzbox* 1 (circa 1990): np.

Devor, Holly. *Gender Blending: Confronting the Limits of Duality.* Bloomington: Indiana University Press, 1989.

———. "Sexual Orientation Identities, Attractions, and Practices of Female-to-Male Transsexuals." *Journal of Sex Research* 30, no. 4 (November 1993): 303–15.

"The Dicks [interview]." *Maximum Rock and Roll* 6 (May–June 1983): 14.

Dorfman, Lori, Pamela Derish, and Judith Cohen. "Hey Girlfriend: An Evaluation of AIDS Prevention among Women in the Sex Industry." *Health Education Quarterly* 19, no. 1 (spring 1992): 25–40.

Drew, Paul. "Conversation Analysis: Who Needs It?" *Text* 10, nos. 1–2 (1990): 127–35.

du Plessis, Michael. "Blatantly Bisexual: Or, Unthinking Queer Theory." In *Re-Presenting Bisexualities: Subjects and Cultures of Fluid Desire,* ed. Donald Hall and Maria Pramaggiore, 19–54. New York: New York University Press, 1996.

———. "Queer Pasts Now: Historical Fictions in Lesbian, Bisexual, Transgender, and Gay Film." Ph.D. diss., Department of Comparative Literature, University of Southern California, 1993.

Ducrot, Oswald, and Tzvetan Todorov. *Dictionnaire encyclopédique des sciences du langage.* Paris: Éditions du Seuil, 1972.

Dumarsais. *Des tropes ou des différents sens.* Paris: Flammarion, 1988 [1730].

Dunlap, Mary. "The Constitutional Rights of Sexual Minorities: A Crisis of the Male-Female Dichotomy." *Hastings Law Journal* 30 (March 1979): 1132–49.

Ekins, Richard. *Male Femaling: A Grounded Approach to Cross-Dressing and Sex-Changing.* London: Routledge, 1997.

Elifson, Kirk, Jacqueline Boles, Ellen Posey, Mike Sweat, William Darrow, and William Elsea. "Male Transvestite Prostitutes and HIV Risk." *American Journal of Public Health* 83, no. 2 (February 1993): 260–62.

Enigma, A. "Livin' Large: Dorian Corey." *Thing* 8 (1992): 35–36.

Epstein, Steven. "Gay Politics, Ethnic Identity: The Limits of Social Constructionism." *Socialist Review* 17, nos. 3–4 (May–August 1987): 9–54.

Escoffier, Jeffrey. "Inside the Ivory Closet: The Challenges Facing Lesbian and Gay Studies." *OUT/LOOK* 10 (fall 1990): 40–48.

Farina, L. A., V. Palacio, M. Salles, D. Fernandez-Villanueva, B. Vidal, and P. Menendez. "Granuloma escrotal por aceite migrado desde la cadera en dos varones transexuales (lipogranuloma esclerosant escrotal)." *Archiva Espana Urologica* 50, no. 1 (January–February 1997): 51–53.

Faulkner, Ellen, Karen Baldwin, and Deborah Hierlihy. *Anti-Gay/Lesbian Violence in Toronto: The Impact on Individuals and Communities.* Ottawa: Department of Justice, Research and Statistics Division, Policy Sector, 1997.

Fay, Brian. *Social Theory and Political Practice.* London: Allen and Unwin, 1975.

Feinberg, Leslie. "Building Bridges." *Transsexual News Telegraph* 1 (summer 1993): 8–9.

———. *Transgender Liberation: A Movement Whose Time Has Come.* New York: World View Forum, 1992.

———. *Transgender Warriors: Making History from Joan of Arc to RuPaul.* Boston: Beacon, 1996.

———. Presentation at Second International Conference on Transgender Law and Employment Policy, Houston, Texas, August 1993.

Feinbloom, Deborah, Michael Fleming, Valerie Kijewski, and Margo Schulter. "Lesbian/Feminist Orientation among Male-to-Female Transsexuals." *Journal of Homosexuality* 2, no. 1 (fall 1976): 59–71.

Feinbloom, Deborah. *Transvestites and Transsexuals: Mixed Views.* New York: Delacourte Press, 1976.

Fetterman, David. *Ethnography: Step by Step.* London: Sage, 1989.

Findlay, Deborah. "Discovering Sex: Medical Science, Feminism and Intersexuality." *Canadian Review of Sociology and Anthropology* 32, no. 1 (February 1995): 25–52.

Fleischer, Julian. *The Drag Queens of New York: An Illustrated Field Guide.* New York: Riverhead Books, 1996.

Fontanier, Pierre. *Les figures du discours.* Paris: Flammarion, 1968 [1821].

Foucault, Michel. *L'Archéologie du savoir.* Paris: Gallimard, 1969. Translated by A. M. Sheridan Smith under the title *The Archaeology of Knowledge* (New York: Harper and Row, 1972).

———. *L'Histoire de la sexualité,* vol. 1, *La Volonté de savoir.* Paris: Gallimard, 1976. Translated by Robert Hurley under the title *The History of Sexuality,* vol. 1, *An Introduction* (New York: Random House, 1978).

Frith, Simon. *Sound Effects: Youth, Leisure, and the Politics of Rock 'n' Roll*. London: Constable, 1983.

Frye, Phyllis. "Repeal of the Houston Crossdressing Ordinance." *Proceedings from the First International Conference on Transgendered Law and Employment Policy*. Houston: ICTLEP, 1992, 104–7.

Fuss, Diana. "Inside/Out." In *Inside/Out: Lesbian Theories, Gay Theories*, ed. Diana Fuss, 1–10. New York: Routledge, 1991.

*Fuzzbox*. Montréal, circa 1990.

Gaines, Atwood. "From DSM-I to III-R: Voices of Self, Mastery and the Other: A Cultural Constructivist Reading of U.S. Psychiatric Classification." *Social Science Medicine* 35, no. 1 (1992): 3–24.

Garber, Marjorie. *Vested Interests: Cross-dressing and Cultural Anxiety*. New York: Routledge, 1992.

Garfinkel, Harold. *Studies in Ethnomethodology*. Englewood Cliffs, N.J.: Prentice-Hall, 1967.

Garmonikow, W., D. Morgan, J. Purvis, and D. Taylorson. *The Public and the Private*. London: Heinemann Educational Books, 1983.

Gattari, P., L. Spizzichino, C. Valenzi, M. Zaccareli, and G. Reeza. "Behavioural Patterns and HIV Infection among Drug Using Transvestites Practising Prostitution in Rome." *AIDS Care* 4, no. 1 (1992): 83–87.

Glaser, Barney G., and Anselm L. Strauss. *The Discovery of Grounded Theory: Strategies for Qualitative Research*. Chicago: Aldine, 1967.

Glenn, H. Patrick. "Droit québécois et droit français: Communauté, autonomie, concordance." In *Droit Québécois et droit français: Communauté, autonomie, concordance*, ed. H. Patrick Glenn, 577–97. Cowansville, Québec: Éditions Yves Blais, 1993.

Goihman, S., A. Ferreira, S. Santos, and J. L. Grandi. "Silicone Application as a Risk Factor for HIV Infection." Presentation at the X International Conference on AIDS, Yokohama, Japan, August 1994.

Gomez, Gabriel. "DQTV: Public Access Queers." *Fuse* 17, no. 1 (fall 1993): 8–10.

Gottlieb, Joanne, and Gayle Wald. "Smells Like Teen Spirit: Riot Grrrls, Revolution and Women in Independent Rock." In *Microphone Fiends: Youth Music and Youth Culture*, ed. Andrew Ross and Tricia Rose, 250–74. New York: Routledge, 1994.

Graber, Glenn, Alfred Beasley, and John Eaddy. "Informed Consent." In *Ethical Analysis of Clinical Medicine: A Guide to Self-Evaluation*, 40–53. Baltimore and Munich: Urban and Schwarzenberg, 1985.

Gras, M.J., T. van der Helm, R. Schenk, G. J. van Deernum, R. A. Coutinho, and J. O. van den Hoek. "HIV-infectin en risicogedrag ander prostitue(e)s in de tippelzone te Amsterdam; annwijzigen voor een verhoogde HIV-prevalentie onder transvestieten/transsekssuelen." ["HIV Infection and Risk Behavior among Prostitutes in the Amsterdam Streetwalkers' District: Indications of Raised Prevalence of HIV among Transvestites/Transsexuals."] *Nederlands Tijdschrift Geneeskunde* 141, no. 25 (June 21, 1997): 1238–41.

Green, Bryan. *Literary Methods and Sociological Theory: Case Studies of Simmel and Weber.* Chicago: University of Chicago Press, 1988.

Greffier, Ethel. "De certains aspects juridiques du transsexualisme dans le droit québécois." *Revue de droit Université de Sherbrooke* 6 (1975): 114–49.

Greimas, Algirdas Julien, and Joseph Courtés. *Sémiotique: Dictionnaire raisonné de la théorie du langage.* Paris: Hachette, 1979.

Grimaldi, James, and J. Jacobs. "HIV/AIDS Transgender Support Group: Improving Care Delivery and Creating a Community." Presentation at the XI International Conference on AIDS, Vancouver, July 1996.

Grossberg, Larry. "Is There Rock after Punk?" *Critical Studies in Mass Communication* 3, no. 1 (1986): 50–74.

Groupe μ. *Rhétorique générale.* Paris: Larousse, 1970.

Guarnaccia, Peter, Maritza Rubio-Stipec, and Glorisa Canino. "Ataques de Nervios in the Puerto Rican Diagnostic Interview Schedule: The Impact of Cultural Categories on Psychiatric Epidemiology." *Culture, Medicine, Psychiatry* 13 (1989): 1223–31.

Gubbay, Aline. *A Street Called "The Main."* Montréal: Meridian Press, 1989.

Hage, J. J. "Medical Requirements and Consequences of Sex Reassignment Surgery." *Medicine, Science, and Law* 35, no. 1 (1995): 17–24.

———. *From Peniplastica Totalis to Reassignment Surgery of the External Genitalia in Female-to-Male Transsexuals.* Amsterdam: VU University Press, 1992.

Halberstam, Judith. "Transgender Butch: Butch/FTM Border Wars and the Masculine Continuum." *GLQ: A Journal of Lesbian and Gay Studies* 4, no. 2 (1998): 287–310.

Hale, C. Jacob. "Consuming the Living, Dis(re)membering the Dead in the Butch/FTM Borderlands." *GLQ: A Journal of Lesbian and Gay Studies* 4, no. 2 (1998): 311–48.

Hall, Donald, and Maria Pramaggiore, eds. *RePresenting Bisexualities: Subjects and Cultures of Fluid Desire.* New York: New York University Press, 1996.

Hammersley, Martin. *What's Wrong with Ethnography? Methodological Explorations.* New York: Routledge, 1992.

Hankins, Catherine. Faxed letter to Diane Gobeil, October 30, 1996.

Hankins, Catherine, and Sylvie Gendron. *Projet Prostitution: Rapport sur les entretiens de groupes réalisés à la maison Tanguay.* Montréal: Centre d'études sur le sida, Unité de santé publique, Hôpital général de Montréal.

Hankins, Catherine, Sylvie Gendron, and Thang Tran. *CACTUS-Montréal: Profil comportemental de la clientèle et prévalence de l'infection par le VIH, 1 octobre 1994 – 7 février 1995. Rapport numéro 6.* Montréal: Direction de la santé publique, 1995.

Hannah, M. "Foucault on Theorizing Specificity." *Environment and Planning D: Society and Space* 11 (1993): 349–63.

Harder, Jeff. "Ontario Refuses to Pay for Sex Changes." *Ottawa Sun,* October 3, 1998, 3.

———. "Tories to Snip Sex Changes." *Toronto Sun,* Thursday, July 13, 1995, 4.

Harry, Joseph. "Conceptualizing Anti-gay Violence." *Journal of Interpersonal Violence* 5 (1990): 350–58.

———. "Derivative Deviance: The Cases of Extortion, Fag-Bashing and the Shakedown of Gay Men." *Criminology* 19 (1982): 546–63.

Hausman, Bernice. *Changing Sex: Transsexualism, Technology, and the Idea of Gender.* Durham, N.C.: Duke University Press, 1995.

Haynes, Todd, director and writer. *Velvet Goldmine.* Zenith/Killer Productions, 1998.

Hazera, Hélène. "Les soeurs du boulevard." *Têtu* 35 (juin 1999): 8–21.

*Health Law Standards of Care.* Houston: International Conference on Transgender Law and Employment Policy, 1993.

Hebdige, Dick. *Subculture: The Meaning of Style.* London: Methuen, 1979.

Hein, Doug. "Education and Soul-Searching: The Enterprise HIV Prevention Group." Presentation, Hero's Journey Conference, Boston, August 1997.

Helen. "Police Entrapment." *ON TOP* [Ongoing Network—Transsexual Outreach Project] 1 (1992): np. (Newsletter available from the Transsexual Sex Industry Workers, TOP, P.O. Box 11-412, Manners Street, Wellington, New Zealand; or P.O. Box 68-509, Newton, Auckland, New Zealand.)

Hemka, Gerdt. "A Female Soul in a Male Body: Sexual Inversion as Gender Inversion in Nineteenth-Century Sexology." In *Third Sex, Third Gender: Beyond Sexual Dimorphism in Culture and History,* ed. Gilbert Herdt, 213–39. New York: Zone Books, 1994.

Hendricks, Michael. "Lesbian and Gay Community Relations with the M[ontréal] U[rban] C[ommunity] Police." Brief presented to the Québec Human Rights Commission, November 1993. (Copy available for consultation at the Commission des droits de la personne et de la jeunesse, 360 Saint-Jacques, Montréal, Québec, H2Y 1P5.)

Herdt, Gilbert, ed. *Third Sex, Third Gender: Beyond Sexual Dimorphism in Culture and History.* New York: Zone Books, 1994.

Heylin, Clinton. *From the Velvets to the Voidoids: A Pre-Punk History for a Post-Punk World.* New York: Penguin, 1993.

*High School Fag* 4. Reading, Mass.: 1992 (fanzine).

Hirschfeld, Magnus. *The Transvestite: An Investigation of the Erotic Desire to Cross-Dress.* Trans. Michael Lombardi. Buffalo, N.Y.: Prometheus Books, 1991 [1910].

Huggins, Nathan Irvin. *Harlem Renaissance.* New York: Oxford University Press, 1971.

Inciardi, James, and Hilary Stuart. "Male Transvestite Sex Workers and HIV in Rio de Janeiro, Brazil." *Journal of Drug Issues* 27, no. 1 (1997): 135–46.

Isabelle, Claudette. "Quand une proposition ne convaic pas vraiment." *Revue sexologique* 2, no. 2 (1996): 160–64.

Jeffreys, Joe. "Joan Jett Blakk for President: Cross-Dressing at the Democratic National Convention." *Drama Review* 37, no. 3 (fall 1993): 186–95.

Jones, Aphrodite. *All She (sic) Wanted.* New York: Pocket Books, 1996.

Jones, G. B., and Bruce LaBruce. "Don't Be Gay: Or, How I Learned to Stop Worrying and Fuck Punk Up the Ass." *Maximum Rock and Roll* 71 (April 1989, "Sexuality Issue"): 50–54.

Jordan, Grant. *The British Administrative System: Principles versus Practice.* London: Routledge, 1994.

Kellner, Bruce. *The Harlem Renaissance: A Historical Dictionary of the Era.* Westport, Conn.: Greenwood, 1984.

Kendel, Monica, Holly Devor, and Nancy Strapko. "Lesbian-Feminist Opinions about Transsexuals." Presentation at Learned Societies, Canadian Sociological and Anthropological Association, Montréal, June 1995.

Kessler, Suzanne, and Wendy McKenna. *Gender: An Ethnomethodological Approach.* New York: John Wiley and Sons, 1978.

Kessler, Suzanne. "The Medical Construction of Gender: Case Management of Inter-Sexed Infants." *Signs* 16, no. 1 (1990): 3–26.

King, Dave. *The Transvestite and the Transsexual: Public Categories and Private Identities.* Brookfield, Vt.: Avebury, 1993.

Kinsey, Alfred C., Wardell B. Pomeroy, and Clyde E. Martin. *Sexual Behavior in the Human Male.* Philadelphia: W.B. Saunders Company, 1948.

Kinsman, Gary, and Patrizia Gentile. "'In the Interests of the State': The Anti-gay, Anti-lesbian National Security Campaign in Canada; A Preliminary Research Report." Sudbury: Laurentian University, April 1998.

Kirby, Sandy, and Kate McKenna. *Experience, Research, Social Change: Methods from the Margins.* Toronto: Garamond Press, 1989.

Kirk, Sheila. "Guidelines for Selecting HIV Positive Patients for Genital Reconstructive Surgery." *International Journal of Transgenderism* 3, nos. 1–2 (January–June 1999) (www.symposion.com/ijt).

———. *Hormones.* Wayland, Mass.: International Foundation for Gender Education, 1992.

Kleinberg, Seymour. "The New Masculinity of Gay Men, and Beyond." In *Beyond Patriarchy: Essays by Men on Pleasure, Power, and Change,* ed. Michael Kaufman, 120–38. Toronto: Oxford University Press, 1987.

Klein-Lataud, Christine. *Précis des figures du style.* Toronto: Éditions du GREF, 1991.

Kouri, Robert. "Certain Legal Aspects of Modern Medicine (Sex Reassignment and Sterilization)." Ph.D. diss., Institute of Comparative Law, McGill University, 1975.

———. "Comments on Transsexualism in the Province of Québec." *Revue de droit Université de Sherbrooke* 4 (1973): 167–83.

Lacasse, Danielle. *La Prostitution féminine à Montréal, 1945–1970.* Montréal: Boréal, 1994.

Lake, Bambi. "Interview." *Tantrum* (spring 1993): 32–42.

Lake, Bambi, and Alvin Orloff. *The Unsinkable Bambi Lake: A Fairy Tale Containing the Dish on Cockettes, Punks, and Angels.* San Francisco: Manic D Press, 1996.

Lakoff, G., and M. Johnson. *Metaphors We Live By.* Chicago: University of Chicago Press, 1980.

Langevin, Louise, and Denise Pratt. "Du code civil du Bas Canada au nouveau Code Civil du Québec: L'Influence de la codification française." In *Droit québécois et droit français: Communauté, autonomie, concordance*, ed. H. Patrick Glenn, 63–89. Cowansville, Québec: Éditions Yves Blais, 1993.

Lanham, Richard. *A Handlist of Rhetorical Terms*. Berkeley and Los Angeles: University of California Press, 1969.

Latter, V., O. Heymans, J. Lemaître, S. van bree, and M. Isgour. "Transsexualisme et procédure." *Acta Urologica Belgica* 64, no. 4 (décembre 1996): 1–3.

Leitch, Vincent. *Deconstructive Criticism: An Advanced Introduction*. New York: Columbia University Press, 1983.

Lévi-Strauss, Claude. *Les Structures élémentaires de la parenté*. Paris: Presses universitaires de France, 1949.

———. *Tristes tropiques*. Paris: Plon, 1955.

Limoges, Thérèse. *La prostitution à Montréal; Comment, pourquoi certaines femmes deviennent des prostituées: Étude sociologique et criminologique*. Montréal: Éditions de l'homme, 1967.

Lothstein, Leslie. *Female to Male Transsexualism: Historical, Clinical, and Theoretical Issues*. Boston: Routledge and Kegan Paul, 1983.

Lubis, I., J. Master, M. Bambang, A. Papilaya, and R. L. Anthony. "AIDS Related Attitudes and Sexual Practices of Jakarta WARIA (Male Transvestites)." *Southeast Asian Journal of Tropical Medicine and Public Health* 25, no. 1 (March 1994): 102–6.

MacCannell, Dean. "Semiotics and Sociology." *Semiotica* 61, nos. 3–4 (1986): 193–200.

MacFarlane, D. F. "Transsexual Prostitution in New Zealand: Predominance of Persons of Maori Extraction." *Archives of Sexual Behavior* 13, no. 4 (1984): 301–9.

Mackie, Marlene. *Exploring Gender Relations*. Toronto: Butterworths, 1983.

Maitland, Sara. *Vesta Tilly*. London: Virago Press, 1986.

Mallette, Yves. "Punks et skins envahissent les rues." *Photo Police!* 25, no. 5 (26 juin–3 juillet 1992): 16–17.

Mane, Prumina, Peter Aggleton, Gary Dowsett, Richard Parker, Geeta Rao Gupta, Sandra Anderson, Stefano Bertozzi, Eric Chevallier, Martina Clark, Noerine Kaleeba, Stuart Kingma, Geoff Manthey, Martina Smedberg, and Susan Timberlake. "Summary of Track D: Social Science: Research, Policy, and Action." *AIDS* 10 (supplement 3, 1996): S123–32.

Manning, Peter. *Semiotics and Fieldwork*. Beverly Hills, Calif.: Sage, 1987.

Marcus, Greil. *Lipstick Traces: A Secret History of the Twentieth Century*. Cambridge, Mass.: Harvard University Press, 1989.

Marin, Maud, avec la collaboration de Marie-Thérèse Cuny. *Le saut de l'ange*. Paris: Éditions j'ai lu, 1993 [1987].

Marton, S. A. "Who Are 'The People'?: Gender, Citizenship, and the Making of the American Nation." *Environment and Planning D: Society and Space* 8 (1990): 449–58.

Mason, Theresa, Margaret Connors, and Cornelia Kammerer. "Transgenders and

HIV Risks: Needs Assessment." Boston: Massachusetts Department of Public Health, 1995.

Masters, Laura. *The Imprisoned Transgenderist*. St. Catharines: TransEqual, 1993.

McRobbie, Angela. *Feminism and Youth Culture*. London: Macmillan, 1981.

McRoberts, Kenneth, and Dale Postgate. *Québec: Social Change and Political Crisis*. Toronto: McLellan and Stewart, 1980.

Meyer, John, and Donna Reter. "Sex Reassignment: Follow-up." *Archives of General Psychiatry* 36 (1979): 1010–15.

"Mineurs, Travestis, SIDA, Drogue . . . Prostitution: tout a changé." *Le nouvel observateur*, 24 juin–4 juillet 1990, 4–11.

Modan, B., R. Goldschmidt, and E. Rubenstein. "Prevalence of HIV Antibodies in Transsexual and Female Prostitutes." *American Journal of Public Health* 82 (1992): 590–92.

Monière, Denis. *Le développement des idéologies au Québec: Des origines à nos jours*. Montréal: Éditions Québec/Amérique, 1977.

Montmorency, André. *De la ruelle au boulevard*. Montréal: Leméac, 1992.

Moon, Michael, and Eve Sedgwick. "Divinity: A Performance Piece. A Dossier. A Little-Understood Emotion." *Discourse* 13, no. 1 (fall–winter 1990–1991): 12–39.

Morgan, G. *Images of Organisation*. London: Sage, 1986.

Morton, Donald. "The Politics of Queer Theory in the (Post)Modern Age." *Genders* 17 (1993): 121–50.

Namaste, Ki, Sandra Laframboise, and Deborah Brady. *La transsexualité, le travestisme, et le VIH/Sida: Une introduction à la santé des personnes transsexuelles et travesties face au VIH et au Sida*. Vancouver: High Risk Project, 1996.

Namaste, Ki. "Fighting Back with Fashion: Pride Day Perversions and the Tyranny of the Homogeneous." *Fuse* 16, no. 2 (fall 1992): 7–9.

Namaste, Ki. "Transgenders and Violence: An Exploration." Brief presented to the Québec Human Rights Commission, November 1993. (Copy available for consultation at the Commission des droits de la personne et de la jeunesse, 360 Saint-Jacques, Montréal, Québec, H2Y 1P5.)

Namaste, Ki. "Access Denied: A Report on the Experiences of Transsexuals and Transgenderists with Health Care and Social Services in Toronto, Ontario." Report submitted to Project Affirmation and the Coalition for Lesbian and Gay Rights in Ontario, Toronto, 1995.

Namaste, Ki. *Deconstructive Que(e)ries: Identity, Social Semiotics, and Queer-Punk Culture*. Ph.D. diss., Université du Québec à Montréal, 1995.

Namaste, Viviane. "Évaluation des besoins: Les travesti(e)s et les transsexuel(le)s au Québec à l'égard du VIH/Sida." Report submitted to the Centre Québécois de Coordination sur le SIDA, Montréal, May 1998. (A copy of this report is available through ASST(e)Q in care of CACTUS, 1626 rue Saint-Hubert, Montréal Québec H2L 3Z3.)

———. "HIV/AIDS and Female-to-Male Transsexuals and Transvestites: Results from a Needs Assessment in Québec." *International Journal of Transgenderism* 3, nos. 1–2 (January–June 1999) (www.symposion.com/ijt).

Nangeroni, Nancy. "Are We All Crazy? The Controversy over Gender Identity Disorder." *Transsexual News Telegraph* 7 (summer 1997): 26–27, 46.

National Gay and Lesbian Task Force (U.S.) Policy Institute [NGLTF]. *Anti-gay/lesbian Violence, Victimization, and Defamation in 1993.* Washington, D.C.: NGLTF Policy Institute, 1994.

Navarro, Vicente. *The Politics of Health Policy: The U.S. Health Reforms, 1980–1994.* Cambridge, Mass.: Basil Blackwell, 1994.

Nelson, James. "The Silence of the Bioethicists: Ethical and Political Aspects of Managing Gender Dysphoria." *GLQ: A Journal of Lesbian and Gay Studies* 4, no. 2 (1998): 213–30.

Nestle, Joan. *A Restricted Country.* Ithaca: Firebrand, 1987.

Newton, Esther. *Mother Camp: Female Impersonators in America.* Englewood Cliffs, N.J.: Prentice-Hall, 1972.

Ng, Roxana. *The Politics of Community Services: Immigrant Women, Class, and the State.* Toronto: Garamond, 1988.

O'Brien, Carol-Anne. "The Social Organization of the Treatment of Lesbian, Gay and Bisexual Youth in Group Homes and Youth Shelters." *Canadian Review of Social Policy* 34 (winter 1994): 37–57.

———. "The Social Organization of the Treatment of Lesbian, Gay and Bisexual Youth in Group Homes and Youth Shelters." Master's thesis, Carleton University, Ottawa, May 1992.

Ogas, Ogi. "Spare Parts: New Information Reignites a Controversy Surrounding the Hopkins Gender Identity Clinic." *Baltimore City Paper,* March 1994, 10, 12–15.

O'Hartigan, Margaret Deirdre. "GID [Gender Identity Disorder] and the Greater Good." *Transsexual News Telegraph* 7 (summer 1997): 28–29.

———. "In Long Run My Sex-Change Surgery Saved Tax Dollars." *Minneapolis Star Tribune,* February 4, 1995, 17A.

———. Letter to author, August 4, 1998.

———. *Our Bodies, Your Lies: The Lesbian Colonization of Transsexualism.* Pamphlet, 1997. (This and following pamphlets available from Margaret Deirdre O'Hartigan at P.O. Box 82447, Portland, OR, 97282.)

———. *'Transgender' as Borg.* Pamphlet, 1997.

———. *A Transsexual Manifesto: The Transgender Movement's Dirty Little Secret: Just Another White Good Ol' Boy Network.* Pamphlet, 1996.

Ontario Legal Aid Plan. *Uniform Treatment. A Community Inquiry into Policing of Disadvantaged Peoples.* Toronto: Ontario Legal Aid Plan, 1994.

Orobio de Castro, Ines. *Made to Order: Sex/Gender in a Transsexual Perspective.* Amsterdam: Het Spinhuis, 1993.

Ortner, S., and H. Whitehead. *Sexual Meanings: The Cultural Construction of Gender and Sexuality.* Cambridge: Cambridge University Press, 1981.

P., Mylène, and Françoise L. "Star Wars: The Empire Strikes Back." *Gendertrash* 2, no. 1 (fall 1993): 7–8.

Palmer, Bryan. *Descent into Discourse: The Reification of Language and the Writing of Social History.* Philadelphia: Temple University Press, 1999.

Parker, Lisa. "Beauty and Breast Implantation: How Candidate Selection Affects Autonomy and Informed Consent." *Hypatia* 10, no. 1 (winter 1995): 183–201.

Pepper, David. "Community Based Responses to Bias Crimes: Some Critical Steps." Brief presented to the Québec Human Rights Commission, November 1993. (Copy available for consultation at the Commission des droits de la personne et de la jeunesse, 360 Saint-Jacques, Montréal, Québec, H2Y 1P5.)

Perkins, Roberta. *The 'Drag Queen' Scene: Transsexuals in Kings Cross*. Hemel Hempstead: Allen and Unwin, 1983.

Petersen, Maxine, and Robert Dickey. "Surgical Sex Reassignment: A Comparative Survey of International Centers." *Archives of Sexual Behavior* 24, no. 2 (1995): 135–56.

Petersen, Maxine, Judith Stephens, Robert Dickey, and Wendy Lewis. "Transsexuals within the Prison System: An International Survey of Correctional Services Policies." *Behavioral Sciences and the Law* 14 (1996): 219–29.

Pettiti, Louis-Edmon. *Les transsexuels*. Paris: Presses universitaires de France, 1992.

Pettiway, Leon. *Honey, Honey, Miss Thang: Being Black, Gay, and on the Street*. Philadelphia: Temple University Press, 1996.

Pfafflin, F. "Psychiatric and Legal Implications of the New Law for Transsexuals in the Federal Republic of Germany." *International Journal of Law and Psychiatry* 4 (1981): 191–98.

Philip, Marlele Nourbese. "The 'Multicultural' Whitewash." *Fuse* 47 (fall 1987): 13–22.

Piat, Colette. *Elles . . . "les Travestis." La vérité sur les transsexuels*. Paris: Presses de la cité, 1978.

*Pocket Criminal Code of Canada*. Toronto: Carswell, 1987.

Presidential Commission for the Study of Ethical Problems in Medicine and Biomedical and Behavioral Research, *Making Health Care Decisions*. Vol. 1, *Report*. Washington, D.C.: U.S. Government Printing Office, 1982.

Preville, Philip. "Real Men Don't Need Penises." *Montréal Mirror*, July 2–9, 1998, 13.

Prince, Jean-Guy. "Rencontre avec Michel Tremblay." *Le Berdache* 25 (novembre 1981): 30–31.

Pritchard, James, Dan Pankowsky, Joseph Crowe, and Fadi Abdul-Karim. "Breast Cancer in a Male-to-Female Transsexual: A Case Report." *Journal of the American Medical Association* 259, no. 15 (April 1988): 2278–80.

Privet, Georges. "L'étoile de fond." *Voir*, 26 août–1 septembre 1993, 8–9.

Prosser, Jay. *Second Skins: The Body Narratives of Transsexuality*. New York: Columbia University Press, 1998.

Proulx, Daniel. *Le Red Light de Montréal*. Montréal: VLB, 1997.

Proulx, Monique. *Le sexe des étoiles*. Montréal: Québec/Amérique, 1987.

Ramsey, Paul. *The Patient as Person*. New Haven: Yale University Press, 1970.

Raymond, Janice. *The Transsexual Empire: The Making of the She-Male*. Boston: Beacon Press, 1979.

Raymundo, Tammi Tam, J. M. Fleras, and P. Resurrection. "Building Rapport with Transvestite Sex Workers: Enabling Easy Access to Health Information."

Presentation at the XI International Conference on AIDS, Vancouver, July 1996.

Riley, Denise. *"Am I That Name?" History and the Category of "Women."* Minneapolis: University of Minnesota Press, 1989.

Ritter, Dominique. "Bending the definition of gender." *Montréal Mirror,* February 18–25, 1999, 4.

Rivet, Michèle. "La vérité et le statut juridique de la personne en droit québécois." *Revue générale de droit* 18 (1987): 843–68.

Robert, Paul. *Le Petit Robert.* Paris: Le Robert, 1986.

Rogers, Mary. "They All Were Passing: Agnes, Garfinkel, and Company." *Gender and Society* 6, no. 2 (June 1992): 169–91.

Rosenau, Pauline. *Post-Modernism and the Social Sciences: Insights, Inroads, and Intrusions.* Princeton, N.J.: Princeton University Press, 1992.

Ross, Mirha-Soleil. "Investigating Women's Shelters." *Gendertrash* 3 (1995): 7–10.

———. "Reaching Out to the Unreachable: An Interview with Diane Gobeil from CACTUS Montréal." *Gendertrash* 4 (spring 1995): 11–16.

———. Review of *Transgender Warriors,* by Leslie Feinberg. *Siren* 1, no. 5 (December 1996–January 1997): 20–1

———. "Video and Performance Art as Transsexual Activism." Presentation to the Human Rights Office, Institute of Women's Studies, Department of Film, Queen's University, Kingston, Ontario, June 16, 1998.

Rothblatt, Martine. "An American Perspective on Transgender Health Law." In *Transsexualism, Medicine and Law* (Proceedings, XXIII Colloquy on European Law, Vrije Universitiet Amsterdam, Netherlands, April 14–16, 1993), 189–202. Strasbourg: Council of Europe, 1995.

———. *The Apartheid of Sex: A Manifesto on the Freedom of Gender.* New York: Crown, 1995.

Rubin, Gayle. "Of Catamites and Kings: Reflections on Butch, Gender, and Boundaries." In *The Persistent Desire: A Femme-Butch Reader,* ed. Joan Nestle, 466–82. Boston: Alyson, 1992.

———. "Thinking Sex: Notes towards a Radical Theory of the Politics of Sexuality." In *Pleasure and Danger: Exploring Female Sexuality,* ed. C. Vance, 267–319. Boston: Routledge and Kegan Paul, 1984.

Rubin, Gayle. "The Traffic in Women: Notes on the 'Political Economy' of Sex." In *Toward an Anthropology of Women,* ed. R. Reiter, 157–210. New York: Monthly Review Press, 1975.

Rubin, Henry. *Always-Already Men: Female to Male Transsexual Subjectivity and Embodiment.* Chicago: University of Chicago Press, forthcoming.

———. "Phenomenology as Method in Trans Studies." *GLQ: A Journal of Lesbian and Gay Studies* 4, no. 2 (1998): 263–81.

Salas, D. *Sujet de chair, sujet de droit: la justice face au transsexualisme.* Paris: Presses universitaires de France, 1994.

Salvaresi, Elisabeth. *Travelo: Enquête sur la prostitution travestie.* Paris: Presses de la Renaissance, 1982.

San Francisco Department of Public Health, AIDS Office. "HIV Prevention and Health Service Needs of the Transgender Community in San Francisco: Results from Eleven Focus Groups." San Francisco: S.F. Department of Public Health, 1997.

Savage, Jon. *England's Dreaming: Sex Pistols and Punk Rock.* London: Faber, 1991.

———. "Tainted Love: The Influence of Male Homosexuality and Sexual Divergence on Pop Music and Culture since the War." In *Consumption, Identity, Style,* ed. A. Tomlinson, 153–71. London: Comedia/Routledge, 1990.

Schecter, Stephen. *T'es beau en écoeurant.* Montréal: Nouvelle Optique, 1984.

Schwartzwald, Robert. "From Authenticity to Ambivalence: Michel Tremblay's Hosanna." *American Review of Canadian Studies* (winter 1992): 499–510.

———. "(Homo)sexualité et problématique identitaire." In *Fictions de l'identitaire au Québec,* ed. Sherry Simon et al, 117–50. Montréal: XYZ, 1991.

———. " 'Symbolic' Homosexuality, 'False Feminine,' and the Problematics of Identity in Québec." In *Fear of a Queer Planet: Queer Politics and Social Theory,* ed. Michael Warner, 264–99. Minneapolis: University of Minnesota Press, 1993.

Sciuto, Giovanni. *Le Petit livre rouge des Travestis pas comme les autres: Le 4me sexe.* Evry: Éditions du Sénart, 1974.

Scott, Ann. "A Brief on HIV/AIDS and the Transgendered Prison Population." Presentation at the International Foundation for Gender Education conference, Toronto, March 27, 1998.

Scott, Ann, and Rick Lines. "HIV/AIDS in the Male-to-Female Transsexual and Transgendered Prison Population: A Comprehensive Strategy. A Brief from PASAN [Prisoners HIV/AIDS Support Action Network]." Toronto, PASAN, 1999. (Available from PASAN, 489 College Street, Suite 405, Toronto, Ontario, M6G 1A5 [416-920-9567].)

Scott, Joan. *Gender and the Politics of History.* New York: Columbia, 1988.

Scott, Valerie. "C-49: A New Wave of Oppression." In *Good Girls/Bad Girls: Sex Trade Workers and Feminists Face to Face,* ed. Laurie Bell, 100–3. Toronto: Women's Press, 1987.

Seidman, Steven. "The End of Sociological Theory: The Postmodern Hope." *Sociological Theory* 9, no. 2 (fall 1991): 131–46.

———. "Identity and Politics in a 'Postmodern' Gay Culture: Some Historical and Conceptual Notes." In *Fear of a Queer Planet: Queer Politics and Social Theory,* ed. Michael Warner, 105–42. Minneapolis: University of Minnesota Press, 1993.

———, ed. *Queer Theory/Sociology.* Cambridge, Mass.: Blackwell, 1996.

———. "Symposium: Queer Theory/Sociology: A Dialogue." *Sociological Theory* 12, no. 2 (July 1994): 166–77.

Shaver, Fran. "The Regulation of Prostitution: Avoiding the Morality Trap." *Canadian Journal of Law and Society* 9 (spring 1994): 123–45.

Siegal, Lloyd, and Arthur Zitrin. "Transsexuals in the New York City Welfare Population: The Function and Illusion in Transsexuality." *Archives of Sexual Behavior* 7, no. 4 (July 1978): 285–90.

Silverman, D. *Interpreting Qualitative Data: Methods for Analyzing Text, Talk, and Interaction.* Newbury Park, Calif.: Sage, 1993.

Simard, Carolle. *La Place de l'autre: Fonctionnaires et immigrés au Québec.* Montréal: Fides, 1998.

Simoneau, Guy. *Plusieurs tombent en amour.* Montréal: Crépuscule, 1980.

Slamah, Khartini. "Developing Effective HIV/AIDS Programs for Transsexuals Working as Sex Workers." Presentation at the XI International Conference on AIDS, Vancouver, July 1996.

Smith, Dorothy. *The Everyday World as Problematic: A Feminist Sociology.* Toronto: University of Toronto Press, 1987.

Smith, George. "Accessing Treatment: Managing the AIDS Epidemic in Ontario." In *Knowledge, Experience, and Ruling Relations: Studies in the Social Organization of Knowledge,* ed. Marie L. Campbell and Ann Manicom, 18–34. Toronto: University of Toronto Press, 1995.

———. "Political Activist as Ethnographer." *Social Problems* 37, no. 4 (November 1990): 629–48.

Sorin, Corinne. "Quand les punks fréquentent les aînés." *Nouvelles Centre-Sud* 3, no. 19 (13 juillet 1992): 1.

SPCUM [Service de police de la communauté urbaine de Montréal]. "Mémoire sur la discrimination et la violence envers les gais et les lesbiennes." Brief presented to the Québec Human Rights Commission, November 1993. (Copy available for consultation at the Commission des droits de la personne et de la jeunesse, 360 Saint-Jacques, Montréal, Québec, H2Y 1P5.)

Spivak, Gayatri. "Can the Subaltern Speak?" In *Marxism and the Interpretation of Culture,* ed. Cary Nelson and Lawrence Grossberg, 271–313. Chicago: University of Illinois Press, 1988.

———. "Displacement and the Discourse of Women." In *Displacement: Derrida and After,* ed. Mark Krupnick, 169–95 Bloomington: Indiana University Press, 1983.

———. *In Other Worlds: Essays in Cultural Politics.* New York: Routledge, 1988.

———. "Scattered Speculations on the Question of Culture Studies." In *Outside in the Teaching Machine,* 255–84. New York: Routledge, 1993.

Spizzichino, Laura, P. Gattari, P. Casella, S. Venezia, M. Zaccareli, and G. Deeza "Immigrants and HIV Infection: The Role of Counselling." Presentation at the XI International Conference on AIDS, Vancouver, July 1996.

Spradley, James. *The Ethnographic Interview.* New York: Holt, Rinehart and Winston, 1979.

Stilz, Jay. "Transsexuals and Substance Abuse." Master's thesis, California State University, Dominguez Hills, 1986.

Stone, Sandy. "The *Empire* Strikes Back: A Posttranssexual Manifesto." In *Body Guards: The Cultural Politics of Gender Ambiguity,* ed. Julia Epstein and Kristina Straub, 281–304. New York: Routledge, 1991.

*Stratégie québécoise de lutte contre le sida Phase 4: Orientations 1997–2002.* Québec: Ministère de la Santé et des Services Sociaux, Direction générale de la santé publique, 1997.

Stryker, Susan. "Renaissance and Apocalypse: Notes on the Bay Area's Transsexual Arts Scene." *Transsexual News Telegraph* 3 (summer 1994): 14–17.

———. "A Taste of Our Own Medicine: The Health Law Project." *Transsexual News Telegraph* 2 (winter 1994): 14–15.

Sydie, R. *Natural Women, Cultured Men: A Feminist Perspective on Sociological Theory.* Toronto: Methuen, 1987.

Tayleur, Christine. "Racism and Poverty in the Transgender Community." *Gendertrash* 5 (1995): 17–20.

Taylor, Kathryn, and Merrijoy Kelner. "Informed Consent: The Physician's Perspective." *Social Science and Medicine* 24, no. 2 (1987): 135–43.

Tee, James. "Health Issues of the HIV+ MTF Transgendered Prison Population." Brief prepared for PASAN (Prisoners' HIV/AIDS Support Action Network), May 9, 1997.

Texier, Catherine, and Marie-Odile Vézina. *Profession, Prostituée: Rapport sur la prostitution au Québec.* Montréal: Libre Expression, 1978.

Thibault, Paul. *Social Semiotics as Praxis: Text, Meaning-Making, and Nabokov's Ada.* Minneapolis: University of Minnesota Press, 1991.

Tremblay, Michel. *Hosanna.* Ottawa: Leméac, 1973. Translated by John van Burek and Bill Glassco under the title *Hosanna* (Vancouver: Talonbooks, 1974).

"TS Women Enter MWMF." *Gendertrash* 3 (winter 1995): 13–14.

Tully, Brian. *Accounting for Transsexuality and Transhomosexuality.* London: Whiting and Birch, 1992.

Turmel, André. "Le retour du concept d'institution." In *Culture, institution, et savoir,* ed. André Turmel, 1–24. Québec: Presses de l'université Laval, 1997.

Turner, Bryan. *Max Weber: From History to Modernity.* New York, London: Routledge, 1992.

Tyler, Carole-Anne. "Boys Will Be Girls: The Politics of Gay Drag." In *Inside/Out: Lesbian Theories, Gay Theories,* ed. Diana Fuss, 32–70. New York: Routledge, 1991.

Valentine, G. "(Hetero)Sexing Space: Lesbian Perceptions and Experiences of Everyday Spaces." *Environment and Planning D: Society and Space* 11 (1993): 395–413.

Valerio, Max. "Speaking Truth—Sade, Leslie Feinberg and David Harrison." *Transsexual News Telegraph* 7 (summer 1997): 40–43.

Valverde, Mariana. "As If Subjects Existed: Analyzing Social Discourses." *Canadian Review of Sociology and Anthropology* 28, no. 2 (May 1991): 173–87.

Vico, Giambattista. *The New Science of Giambattista Vico.* Trans. Thomas Goddard Begrin and Max Harond Tisch. Ithaca, N.Y.: Cornell University Press, 1948 [1744].

Viegener, Matias. "'The Only Haircut That Makes Sense Anymore': Queer Subculture and Gay Resistance." In *Queer Looks: Perspectives on Lesbian and Gay Film and Video,* ed. Martha Gever, John Greyson, and Pratibha Parmar, 116–33. New York: Routledge, 1993.

von Schultess, B. "Violence in the Streets: Anti-lesbian Assault and Harassment in San Francisco." In *Hate Crimes: Confronting Violence Against Lesbians and Gay Men,* ed. G. Herek and K. Berril, 65–75. London: Sage, 1992.

Walker, Paul, Jack Berger, Richard Green, Donald Laub, Charles Reynolds, and Leo Wollman. "Standards of Care: The Hormonal and Surgical Sex Reassignment of Gender Dysphoric Persons." In *Gender Dysphoria: A Guide to Research,* ed. Dallas Denny, 633–48. New York: Garland, 1994.

Walkowitz, Judith. *Prostitution and Victorian Society: Women, Class, and the State.* Cambridge: Cambridge University Press, 1980.

Warner, Michael. "Introduction: Fear of a Queer Planet." *Social Text* 29 (1991): 3–19.

Warren, Barbara, John Capizuca, Birgit Pols, and Barbara Otter. "AIDS Prevention for Transgender and Transsexual Persons: A Collaborative Community-Based Program." Presentation at the XI International Conference on AIDS, Vancouver, July 1996.

Watson, D. "Ethnomethodology, Conversation Analysis and Education: An Overview." *International Review of Education* 38, no. 2 (1992): 257–74.

Watters, John. "The Significance of Sampling and Understanding Hidden Populations." *Drugs and Society* 7, nos. 3–4 (1993): 13–21.

Weir, Lorna. "Preliminary Observations on the Relations between Queer Theory and Social Sciences." Presentation at Queer Sites: Bodies at Work, Bodies at Play, University of Toronto, May 13, 1993.

Weitz, Cordelia, and Suzanne Osburg. "Transsexualism in Germany: Empirical Data on Epidemiology and Application of the German Transsexuals' Act During Its First Ten Years." *Archives of Sexual Behavior* 25, no. 4 (1996): 409–25.

Welzer-Lang, Daniel, and Lilian Mathieu. "Des transgenders. Le brouillage des identités sur le marché de la prostitution." *Revue sexologique* 2, no. 2 (1996): 174–77.

Welzer-Lang, Daniel, Odette Barbosa, and Lilian Mathieu. "Prostitution et (post)-modernité: un brouillage des signes et des identités?" In *Prostitution: Les uns, les unes, les autres,* ed. Daniel Welzer-Lang and Mathieu Barbosa, 174–87. Paris: Éditions Métailié, 1994.

Wilchins, Riki Ann. *Read My Lips: Sexual Subversion and the End of Gender.* Ithaca, N.Y.: Firebrand, 1997.

Will, Michael. "Legal Conditions of Sex Reassignment by Medical Intervention— Situation in Comparative Law." *Transsexualism, Medicine and Law* (Proceedings, XXIII Colloquy on European Law, Vrije Universitiet Amsterdam, Netherlands, 14–16 April 1993), 75–95. Strasbourg: Council of Europe, 1995.

Wilson, A. Neal. "Sex Reassignment Surger in HIV Positive Transsexuals." *International Journal of Transgenderism* 3, nos. 1–2 (January–June 1999) (www.symposion.com/ijt).

Wittig, Monique. "The Straight Mind." Trans. Mary Jo Lakeland and Susan Ellis Wolf. *Feminist Issues* 1, no. 1 (1980): 103–11.

Wodak, Alex, and Peter Lurie. "A Tale of Two Countries: Attempts to Control HIV among Injecting Drug Users in Australia and the United States." *Journal of Drug Issues* 27, no. 1 (1996): 117–34.

Wolf, Marjorie. *A Thrice-Told Tale: Feminism, Postmodernism, and Ethnographic Responsibility.* Stanford, Calif.: Stanford University Press, 1992.

World Health Organization. "Preamble to the Constitution of the World Health Organization." In *Biomedical Ethics,* ed. Thomas Mappes and Jane Zembaty, 243–44. Montréal: McGraw-Hill, 1986.

Young, Charles. "From Altar Boys to the Dead Boys." *The Rolling Stone* 253 (December 1, 1977): 20.

Zimmerman, Don. "Fact as Practical Accomplishment." In *Ethnomethodology: Selected Readings,* Roy Turner, 128–143. Markham: Penguin, 1975.

## DISCOGRAPHY

Buzzcocks. *Singles Going Steady.* Scarborough, Ontario: A & M Records of Canada, 1977.

New York Dolls. *Lipstick Killers.* Lille, France: ROIR [Reach Out International Records], n.d.

Siouxie and the Banshees. *Nocturne.* London: Polydor, 1983.

Smith, Patti. *Horses.* USA: Arista, 1976.

The Sweet. "A.C.D.C." On *Desolation Boulevard.* London: Capitol Records, 1973.

———. *Glam Rock.* USA: Virgin Music Video, 1988 [1972].

T. Rex. *Electric Warrior.* Canada: Reprise Records, 1971.

Vibrators. *Pure Mania.* London: CBS Records, 1977.

# INDEX

activism: legal cases, 254–55; repeal
    of cross-dressing ordinances, 14,
    276n14; transsexual community
    organizing, 65
Adkin, David, 297n44
administration: arbitrary nature there-
    of, 4; erasure of transsexuals, 41–
    44, 50. *See also* bureaucracy
Agnes. *See* ethnomethodology
alcohol, 184–86, 301n28. *See also* drugs
American College of Legal Medicine
    Foundation, 305n59
American Educational Gender Informa-
    tion Service (AEGIS), 200–201,
    218
Androgyne bookstore collective, 67
anthropology, 25–27
Ardener, Shirley, 141
Arrington, S., 298n58, 298n60
Assalian, Pierre, 208–9
ASTT(e)Q (Action Santé: Travesti(e)s et
    Transsexuel(le)s du Québec), 235
Attali, Jacques, 287n22
autobiography, 119–23, 273n3

B., Jeanne, 31–32
Baillargeon, Paule, 103
Beacon Press, 62
Beatty, Christine, 293n74
Bell, Laurie, 286n64
Benjamin, Harry, 301n2
Bennett, Marsha, 308n12
Berger, Peter, 283n29
Bibeau, Gilles, 291n32
Billings, Dwight, 33–35, 37, 280n42,
    280n43, 280n44, 280n46,
    280n52, 281n54
bisexual theory, 283n34
Black, Max, 95
Blakk, Joan Jett, 16, 276n18
Blanchard, Ray, 303n32

Bockting, Walter, 278n10, 299n9, 307n4
Bolan, Marc, 81–82
Boles, Jacqueline, 307n2, 307n5
Bolin, Anne, 26, 203; and gender identi-
    ties, 26; and psychiatry, 26, 192
Bornstein, Kate, 65
Bourassa, André, 292n62
Bowie, David, 81
Boyd, Nan, 293n78
Brake, Mike, 79–80, 88
Brassard, André, 116
Bratton, J. S., 274n10
Bullough, Vern, and Bonnie Bullough,
    26–27, 274n10, 283n31
Burchill, Julie, 79
bureaucracy: arbitrary nature thereof,
    248–55, 261; contradictions
    among institutions, 239, 255–62;
    and metaphors, 94. *See also* ad-
    ministration; civil status; Direction
    de l'état civil; identity papers
Burnham, Christine, 281n53, 282n12
Butler, Judith, 10, 13–14, 19–20, 274n1;
    and *Paris Is Burning,* 13, 275n12;
    and race, 13, 21–22; *Bodies That
    Matter,* 13, 275n12; and poststruc-
    turalist theory, 19–22
Buzzcocks, The, 82

Café Cléopâtra, 107, 148
Califia, Pat, 147, 283n31
Callahan, Daniel, 305n58
Campbell, Marie, 50, 281n3
Canadian Organization for the Rights of
    Prostitutes, 207
cancer, 168
Carceres, Carlos, 301n28, 307n6
Carrière, Daniel, 286n57
Castro, Ines Orobio de, 279n19
Catholic Discipline, 83
Cathy, 148

DISCARD